MW00560385

Russian Society
and the
Greek Revolution

Russian Society
and the
Greek Revolution

Theophilus C. Prousis

NORTHERN

ILLINOIS

UNIVERSITY PRESS

DeKalb

1994

Library of Congress Cataloging-in-Publication Data
Prousis, Theophilus Christopher.
    Russian society and the Greek revolution /
Theophilus C. Prousis.
        p. cm.
    Includes bibliographical references and index.
    ISBN 0-87580-193-5 (alk. paper)
    1. Russia—Relations—Greece.   2. Greece—
Relations—Russia.   3. Greece—History—War of
Independence, 1821–1829—Public opinion.
4. Public opinion—Russia.   5. Philhellenism—
Russia.   6. Russia—Intellectual life—1801–1917.
I. Title.
DK67.5.G8P76   1994
303.48′2470495—dc20   94-7870
                                      CIP

Contents

Preface

THE GREEK WAR OF INDEPENDENCE captured the literary and artistic imagination of Europeans more completely than any other event of the 1820s. For a continent held too rigidly in place by the system that Metternich and his allies had devised to defend legitimate rulers against nationalist unrest, the Greek struggle against the Ottoman Empire personified humankind's eternal quest for freedom. Passion for antiquity and an admiration for the genuinely popular added new dimensions to Europeans' literary and artistic vision of the Greek revolt, making philhellenism into a literary and humanitarian movement that contributed materially and morally to Greek emancipation. Lord Byron, the greatest of Europe's Romantics, gave his life for the Greek cause. In the fragmented lands of Germany, Italy, and the Balkans, others drew lessons from the Greek struggle that focused their own nationalist strivings.

In Russia, factors that lay outside the broader European experience conditioned the response of educated men and women to the Greeks' uprising. The Orthodox faith that Greeks and Russians shared, along with a chain of historical affinities that stretched from the Middle Ages to the present, shaped the context in which Russians embraced the philhellenic movement. Orthodoxy remained an integral component of Russia's autocratic government and national consciousness, and sympathy for Greek emancipation coincided with the Russian state's interest in numerous ways. Russians, who had themselves just acquired a sharpened national consciousness in their struggle to drive the armies of Napoleon from their lands in 1812, now looked back to the days before the rise of the Ottoman Turks when Constantinople had served as the fount of Russian religious culture. For men and women of such vision, defeat of the Greeks' Ottoman oppressors promised the beginnings of a crusade to restore Orthodoxy throughout the Near and Middle East.

The 1821 Greek crisis, the quest for Greek freedom via armed insurrection, nonetheless, confronted the tsarist regime with an awkward dilemma. Intervention to support the Greeks promised to disrupt the balance of power that Russia's Emperor Alexander I had vowed to defend throughout Europe, as well as threatened to kindle debate about the fate of the declining Ottoman Empire among the diplomats of Europe. Any dismantling of the Empire along ethnic and religious lines posed a dangerous precedent for the breakup of the tsar's own multinational and multiethnic domains, and no one had any doubt that a successful war for Greek independence might encourage other assaults against the stability of Europe. Yet the Greek revolt, unlike the risings of the same year in Spain and Italy, presented the Russians with a rationale for pursuing a number of strategic goals in the Balkans and the eastern Mediterranean. So, torn between his promise to uphold the Concert of Europe and the prospects of advancing Russia's national interests, Emperor Alexander I chose the former, and in the crisis of 1821, the Russian government declared its neutrality and denounced the Greeks as insurgents.

While their tsar condemned the Greeks, the educated men and women whose views shaped public opinion in the Russian Empire spoke out loudly on the Greeks' behalf. Philhellenes championed Greek emancipation and promoted the study of Greek letters and culture. Further, the revolt stirred deep emotion in a land that had long believed in its providential role to defend Orthodox Christians under Ottoman rule. The prospect of Greek liberty thus excited upholders and critics of autocracy and generated support from nearly all sectors of the public. Amid the gradual secularization of state and society, the traditional notion that Russia had a mission to protect Orthodox Christians remained a viable concern for both educated society *(obshchestvo)* and the common people *(narod)*. As the vast majority of the population was still illiterate, educated society and public opinion consisted of the small and mainly urbanized segment that gave philhellenism its most vocal exponents. Yet Greek relief aid from the grass-roots level, from villages and parishes across the Russian Empire, suggests the appeal of the Greek cause well beyond the educated and urbanized sector.

Most of the historical literature on Russia and the Greek war deals with official policy. Russian scholars have tapped archival sources to describe the Greek crisis in the context of Russo-Ottoman relations and Great Power diplomacy, a perspective emphasized in the multivolume publication of select documents from the Russian Ministry of Foreign Affairs. Works on tsarist policy have touched on the general nature of the philhellenic movement, while more specialized studies have explored the depiction of the revolt in poetry and art, the revolt's impact on the Decembrists, and Greek relief aid.

This book, therefore, is the first comprehensive examination of Russian responses to the Greek revolution. It complements the scholarly literature on Russian historical and cultural ties to the Greek East, the lands and peoples associated with Byzantium and Eastern Orthodoxy. In this sense, my work illumines the religious and cultural dimensions of the much-debated Eastern Question, usually approached from the context of Great Power political, diplomatic, and commercial rivalry in the Near East. More specifically, this study of philhellenism underscores the durability of Russian contacts with Greek-speaking areas that formed the nucleus of modern Greece, that is, the Peloponnese, the mainland, and the Archipelago.

This work also enhances our understanding of Alexandrine Russia by examining philhellenism in the context of government philanthropy, the Decembrist movement, the classical awakening, and Romanticism. Insight into political culture is provided by using the Greek cause as a mirror to clarify divisions between foes and friends of autocracy, between critics and defenders of the Metternichean order, and between educated society and the government. Support for Greek liberty often intersected, and in some cases exacerbated, lines of ideological division. Literary and intellectual life felt the impact of philhellenism as Greek themes became symbols for political engagement and civic spirit. Grecophile motif, allusion, and subject matter were frequently used as vehicles to raise the topical concerns of enlightened reform, constitutional rule, and imperial mission in the Near East.

This study has several terms that require clarification. First, "philhellenism" includes both Russian responses to the Greek revolt as well as the responses of Greek and Balkan sympathizers who resided in the Russian Empire during the Greek revolution. Second, philhellenes called Greek Christians either *edinovertsy* (coreligionists) or *edinovertsy nam greki* (our coreligionist Greeks). "Coreligionists" is thus used as a synonym for fellow Orthodox Christians, fellow Orthodox believers, and Orthodox brethren. Third, because philhellenes broadly identified the Greek cause with *osvobozhdenie* (liberation) and *nezavisimost'* (independence), both terms are employed in this study. Greek combatants were uncertain about the desired outcome of the war, and confusion reigned about the precise form liberation would take. Political objectives ranged from a revived Byzantium to an independent nation-state to regional autonomy. Some participants even envisioned a foreign protectorate over the liberated portions of Greece. Given the ambiguity of Greek goals, the open-ended "liberation" may be more appropriate, yet the concrete goal of independence also signified liberation from Ottoman control.

Historiographical debate exists on whether, or to what extent, the Greek War of Independence constituted a revolution. The conflict did not radically transform the social structure, economy, or landholding patterns in Greece, and yet it did mark a political revolution against the Concert of Europe and the Metternichean hierarchy. The war resulted in an independent Greek state; ignited revolutionary outbreaks in Europe, Russia, and the Balkans; and confirmed the fears of reactionaries who regarded Greek insurgents as rebels against the status quo. Revolution is thus an accurate and appropriate description for the War of Independence.

As with any thorough study, this one would not have been possible without the use of published and unpublished materials in the former Soviet Union. Russian libraries, archives, and manuscript repositories hold the richest and most extensive resources detailing Greco-Slavic relations. A grant in 1980–81 from the International Research and Exchanges Board (IREX) allowed me to tap periodical literature and other printed sources of the Russian State (formerly Lenin) Library and the State Public Historical Libraries in Moscow and of the Library of the Academy of Sciences and the Saltykov-Shchedrin State Public Library in St. Petersburg. I gleaned useful information on tsarist policy from the Russian State Military History Archive, the Russian State Archive of Early Acts, and the State Archive of the Russian Federation, all in Moscow. More crucial was a brief stint at the Russian State Historical Archive (RGIA) in St. Petersburg that introduced me to the wealth of archival records on Greek relief organized by the Holy Synod. Research at these institutions facilitated the completion of my dissertation, "Russian Cultural Response to the Greek War of Independence" (University of Minnesota, 1982).

Another IREX grant in 1987–88 enabled me to examine more thoroughly the relief records at RGIA and allowed me to explore the holdings of the State Archive of Odessa *Oblast'*. I received access to previously restricted documents housed in the Manuscript Section of the Saltykov-Shchedrin State Public Library and the Manuscript Section of the Institute of Russian Literature, both in St. Petersburg. This second opportunity to delve into a new variety of resources verified and corroborated the conclusions of my earlier study, which has been recast and revised. Some of the new findings have been incorporated in my published articles on prominent Greek families in Russia. These efforts bear directly on this larger study of the philhellenic movement, a work of synthesis that integrates a substantial body of secondary and primary source material. I am thus extremely grateful for the generous support of IREX and for the cooperation of the staffs at all Russian institutions where I worked. I also acknowledge the support of a Research Scholar Grant from the American Council of Teachers of Russian (ACTR), which enabled me to spend four months in St. Petersburg and Moscow in 1993. In addition to exploring new projects in the field of Greco-Russian cultural relations, I examined recent publications by Russian scholars on tsarist Eastern policy and the Greek crisis.

From its inception, this research benefited greatly from the guidance, encouragement, and high expectations of Theofanis G. Stavrou, professor of Russian and Near Eastern history and director of Modern Greek Studies at the University of Minnesota, who has trained a number of scholars in the fields of Russian history, Eastern Orthodoxy, and modern Greek culture. My study of Russian phihellenism grew directly out of Minnesota's emphasis on Russian-Near Eastern cultural contacts and on Greek-Russian relations. Russian and Greek scholars who encouraged my investigation of this topic over the years include Grigorii L. Arsh, Boris L. Fonkich, Ol'ga A. Belobrova, Nina S. Kiniapina, Iurii D. Margolis, Konstantinos Papoulidis,

Athanasios Karathanasis, Soterios Stavrou, and Louisa Laourdas. I am especially grateful to Western Slavicists who read the manuscript either in part or in its entirety and offered helpful criticism and advice. These include Stephen Batalden, Patricia Herlihy, William Mills Todd, W. Bruce Lincoln, David MacKenzie, Barbara Jelavich, Richard Robbins, Thomas Noonan, and Leonard Polakiewicz.

On several occasions, I have had the opportunity to use the rich collection at the Slavic and East European Library of the University of Illinois, and I am indeed grateful to Dr. Robert Burger and his staff of Slavic librarians. Since research depends on the Inter-Library Loan services at one's home institution, I owe a special debt to Peggy Pruett at the University of North Florida who patiently and successfully filled my orders. A sabbatical from the Department of History and Philosophy in 1991–92 gave me the time to complete the manuscript, and I am grateful for this institutional support. I also thank the editors at Northern Illinois University Press for their assistance in producing a readable text of manageable size. While I acknowledge the help of others, I take full responsibility for errors of fact and interpretation.

I am extremely fortunate in the devotion and love of my family. Elizabeth Lane Furdell, my historian wife, read the manuscript in its various stages of preparation and offered editorial suggestions. My parents and my uncle, Costas M. Proussis, Emeritus Professor of Greek and Cypriot letters at Hellenic College, bequeathed to our family a knowledge of modern Greek and an appreciation of Greek culture and tradition. Because my parents also supported and encouraged my study of Russian history and culture, I dedicate this book to my mother and to the memory of my father.

Transliteration Note

I HAVE USED A MODIFIED VERSION of the Library of Congress system in transliterating Greek and Russian names. The Greek letters *beta* and *eta* are rendered respectively with "v" (instead of "b") and with "i" (instead of "ē"). I have not Anglicized Russian names, with the exception of tsars and well-known places such as Moscow and St. Petersburg. The Russian soft sign, represented by an apostrophe, has been dropped from geographical names, such as Mariupol, but retained in all references cited in the notes and bibliography. In the case of Greeks who became Russian citizens and entered tsarist service, I have with few exceptions used the Greek rather than the Russian transliteration of their names. All dates are given according to the Julian calendar, which, in the nineteenth century, was twelve days behind the Gregorian calendar of the West and was used in Russia until 1918. I have indicated both old and new style dates in cases where specific days are mentioned, for example, 25 May/6 June 1821. Any italics that appear in quotations are taken directly from the original source. All translations are mine unless otherwise indicated in the notes. In citing periodical literature in the notes and bibliography, I have departed from customary procedure by placing the date of publication immediately after the title of the journal.

Russian Society
and the
Greek Revolution

Chapter One

Russia and the Greek National Revival

THE GREEK WAR OF INDEPENDENCE aroused widespread sympathy in Russia. The most potent impetus for this philhellenic sentiment was the Byzantine Orthodox heritage, which established religious, cultural, and political relations between the Greek world and Russia. Religious and cultural ties, together with tsarist policy, created a convergence of Russian and Greek interests. In the past, Russia's entanglement in the Eastern Question resulted in protection for the common Orthodox faith against the common Ottoman foe and contributed to a Greek national revival that sought to liberate Ottoman-ruled Greek lands. This long-standing Greco-Russian connection provided fertile ground for philhellenic responses to the Greeks' struggle for emancipation.[1]

In his seminal work *The Byzantine Commonwealth*, Dimitri Obolensky demonstrates that Byzantium, the Balkans, and medieval Russia formed an association of Christian lands and peoples linked by Eastern Orthodoxy and Byzantine civilization. The commonwealth's most essential bond, the Orthodox faith, opened avenues of contact and interaction. Thus, Byzantine models permeated Russian religious and cultural life in church ritual, monasticism, architecture, iconography, and hagiography.[2] Obolensky's study ends with the Ottoman conquest of the Balkans, but his concept of a religiously grounded commonwealth can be extended to the post-Byzantine era.

Despite the political demise of Byzantium, the subjugation of the Greek church to Ottoman control, and Muscovy's preeminence as the sole independent Orthodox state, a mutual Byzantine Christian framework continued to cement the commonwealth. There remained the reality of *"Byzance après Byzance,"* to use the phrase of the Romanian historian Nicolae Iorga in his work on the survival of the Byzantine tradition in Moldavia and Wallachia.[3] The wider commonwealth was a viable entity until shattered by nineteenth-century Balkan rivalries that were fueled by ethnic nationalism and territorial conflict. Thus, the cohesion instilled by a kindred religious consciousness fractured into competing national states often hostile toward Russia, and ethnicity and loyalty to the nation-state gradually displaced religion as the distinctive mark of national identity in eastern Europe and the Balkans.

After 1453, the fate of Ottoman Greece was increasingly tied to western Europe and Russia. Byzantine scholars contributed their classical learning to Renaissance Humanism and were among the prominent Greeks who resided in diaspora communities in Venice, Florence, Padua, and other parts of western Europe,[4] while the Byzantine Orthodox heritage continued to link Russia and the Greek East. In the theocratic Ottoman Empire, which divided its subjects into *millets* (nations) based on religion, Orthodoxy enabled Greek Christians to preserve their cultural identity and nourished hope that Orthodox Russia would protect them. The Byzantine legacy also provided channels of contact, such as Russian alms to Ottoman-subjugated churches and Muscovy's relations with the four Eastern patriarchates.[5] Emigration by Greek aristocrats, artisans, and craftsmen paralleled the diaspora settlements in the West.[6] Merchant activity in Slavic lands set the stage for the expansion of Greco-Russian commerce in the Catherinian era. Travel by Russian religious pilgrims to Mount Athos, Palestine, and other sacred shrines in the Near East constituted yet another link in the Orthodox commonwealth.[7]

Muscovy felt the Greek impact in several ways. The transfer of icons, manuscripts, and holy relics enriched Russian religious culture. Greek educators and translators contributed to church life, none more so than the learned monk Maksim Grek (1475–1556) who corrected Church Slavonic liturgical texts and authored numerous writings. Maksim's scholarly tradition was continued by the Leichoudis brothers, founders of the first institution of higher learning in Moscow, the Slavonic-Greek-Latin Academy (1685).[8] Despite the intense xenophobia of the Old Believers after the *raskol* (schism) in the seventeenth-century Russian church, respect for the Byzantine heritage remained strong because clerics supporting Patriarch Nikon's reforms deemed Greek learning essential to their mission of purifying Church Slavonic texts and rituals in line with Byzantine originals. Greeks were also instrumental in the Orthodox brotherhoods *(bratstva)* of the Ukraine, organizing educational activity that nourished a Ukrainian

Orthodox revival and that defended Orthodoxy against Catholic and Protestant advances.[9] Muscovy thus offered a conducive place for Greek Christians to practice their faith and their trades, to engage in educational and scholarly endeavors, and to solicit Muscovite aid on behalf of Orthodox brethren under Ottoman rule.

Insight into post-Byzantine Greco-Russian ties can be gleaned from Greek prophetic and oracular texts. These writings voiced two themes emblematic of Greek aspirations: the Ottoman Turks would be driven from Constantinople, and a fair-haired nation *(xanthon genos)* from the north would deliver the Greeks from Ottoman captivity.[10] The *xanthon genos* legend became part of the eighteenth-century *Agathangelos* collection of prophecies that were compiled by the cleric Theoklitos Polyedis, who founded an Orthodox church for the Greek community in Leipzig. Echoing the *xanthon genos* myth, *Agathangelos* envisioned Russia's providential emancipation and restoration of a Byzantine kingdom in Constantinople. Circulating in manuscript and printed copies and through oral transmission, *Agathangelos* appealed to a wide cross section of Greeks, including Westernized diaspora merchants who remained steeped in religious tradition.[11] Western travelers in the Near East noted the prevalence of Greek popular belief in the tales of Russian-assisted liberation.[12]

Hopes of Russian protection were not farfetched in view of Muscovite alms, the taking of Kazan and Astrakhan from the Islamic Tatars, and the recapture of Kiev and Smolensk from Poland. Moscow beckoned as the Third Rome, the citadel of the true faith, the heir of Byzantium, and the champion of Orthodoxy. Belief in the prophecies was reinforced by involvement in the Eastern Question, the diplomatic issue triggered by Great Power rivalry, Ottoman decline, and Balkan demands for self-rule. Beginning with Peter the Great's Danubian campaign, the defense of Orthodox Christians imparted a sense of mission to tsarist policy and furnished a rationale for advancing such tangible objectives as security along the Russo-Ottoman frontier, commercial access to the Black Sea and the Mediterranean, and diplomatic leverage in the Balkans.[13] Later, Catherine the Great identified Russia with Greek hopes and manipulated Greco-Russian ties for imperial statecraft more than any other tsar. She regarded the protection of Greek Christians as a pretext for expansion, best seen in the ambitious Greek Project that called for a revived Greek kingdom to be governed from Constantinople by her grandson Konstantin, who was named appropriately after the first and the last Byzantine emperors. To honor Konstantin's birth in 1779, the tsarina ordered the minting of commemorative coins bearing the image of St. Sophia's Cathedral.[14]

Although the Greek Project went unfulfilled, Catherine the Great's success against the Porte enlarged the field of Greco-Russian cooperation. Greek and Russian interests converged to their mutual benefit. The landmark Treaty of Kutchuk-Kainardji (1774) granted Russia the right to intervene in Ottoman affairs so as to ensure orderly government in Moldavia,

Wallachia, and the Archipelago. Russian ships, often manned by Greek sailors, gained unrestricted commercial access to Ottoman waters. There was also the vaguely worded clause recognizing tsarist protection of the sultan's Orthodox subjects, a wedge for subsequent interference in Ottoman affairs. To monitor these concessions, Russia won the right to appoint consuls in the Ottoman Near East. In a petition (1774) for asylum addressed to Catherine II, Archimandrite Varlaam expressed the prevalent Greek perception that Russian military might would advance their cause. The empress's military and diplomatic triumph, wrote Varlaam, "will undoubtedly serve to accelerate the much desired moment of our complete liberation."[15]

Russia did not, however, allow the plight of Ottoman Greek Christians to determine Eastern policy to the detriment of more concrete strategic interests. Tsarist expansion, nevertheless, contributed to a Greek awakening in the Ottoman Empire and the diaspora. To be sure, this revival was greatly stimulated by the Enlightenment, the French Revolution, and the Napoleonic Wars.[16] Yet the Russian impact was equally crucial as an external catalyst. Arsh and Dostian, as well as Soviet historiography in general, have emphasized Russia's support of Balkan national liberation struggles that were led by a nascent middle class composed mostly of traders and military captains. Given the social complexity of Greek society to be examined below, this Marxist-Leninist approach is difficult to endorse, and yet Arsh's basic contention is accurate because Russia identified with the cause of Greek liberation primarily through the common Orthodox faith. The religious nexus and Eastern policy facilitated concrete aspects of the Greek resurgence—military resistance, political organization, trade, and education.[17]

Frequent Russo-Turkish wars (1711, 1737–39, 1768–74, 1787–92, 1806–12) accelerated Ottoman decline and generated Greek military opposition. The Greek classical scholar and educator Adamantios Korais (1748–1833) accurately described in his *Mémoire sur l'état actuel de la civilisation dans la Grèce* (Paris, 1803) the impact of Russo-Turkish conflict on Greek resistance: "Convinced now that their oppressors were men who could be defeated, that in fact they [the Greeks] had defeated them by the side of the Russians, and that it would not prove impossible for them to defeat the Ottomans on their own provided they had able men to lead them, they felt in themselves for the first time a spark of pride." Korais had in mind the *klephts*, *armatoloi*, and sea pirates who had responded to tsarist proclamations urging them to stage local risings in support of advancing Russian armies.[18] *Klephts* were bandits or brigands in the mountainous enclaves of Greece who resisted Ottoman authority, while *armatoloi* were irregular militia hired by the sultan to maintain order and to guard mountain passes. Both groups became the backbone of Greek military forces during the 1820s. The exploits of fabled warriors, such as Daskalogiannis (1770) and

Lambros Katsonis (1790–92), assumed mythical proportion in Greek folk culture and nourished a tradition of armed resistance to Ottoman rule. More often than not, however, Greek auxiliaries were abandoned to their fate and suffered Ottoman reprisals as evinced in the aftermath of the 1770 Orlov expedition to the Morea.[19]

Still, warfare gave rise to Greco-Russian military collaboration and enabled Greek forces to train under professional officers. Stanislavskaia accurately notes that the short-lived Ionian Republic (1800–07), established and protected by Russia, was the hearth *(ochag)* of Greek independence because it constituted the first experiment in modern Greek self-rule. Tsarist officials organized a Greek corps known as the Legion of Light Shooters that drew volunteers from the Ionians, Epirus, and the Morea, including the *klephts* Markos Botsaris and Theodoros Kolokotronis, who attained military fame in the War of Independence.[20] Another Russian-sponsored Greek corps, formed in Moldavia, participated in the 1806–12 Russo-Turkish War. When Russo-Turkish warfare ended, volunteers, fearing Ottoman retribution, often requested asylum and were enrolled in units stationed in southern Russia.[21] Thus, Greek insurgents during the liberation struggle had a cadre of experienced veterans who had fought under Russian auspices. Service in foreign-directed regiments also brought together Greek forces from various regions, a development that fostered a broader sense of national, as opposed to locally rooted, Greek patriotism.

Eastern policy provided an opportunity for at least some Greeks to acquire political and diplomatic experience. Russo-Turkish hostility directly affected the fate of the Phanariots, cosmopolitan Greek and Hellenized families of noble descent named after the Phanar, or Lighthouse, quarter of Istanbul where many of them resided. They were part of the Ottoman ruling elite, serving the sultan as bankers, diplomats, interpreters, and physicians. Their power, wealth, and favorable position gave them control over ecclesiastical selections and the property of the Greek church. The sultan appointed Phanariot Greeks to replace native princes as *hospodars* (governors) of Moldavia and Wallachia in the aftermath of Peter the Great's 1711 Danubian campaign. Phanariot rule in the Principalities, an area of increasing significance as an Ottoman bulwark against Habsburg and Russian expansion, lasted until 1821 when the rising in Moldavia understandably heightened the Porte's suspicion of all Greeks in Ottoman service.

The Phanariot reign in the Danubian Principalities remains a subject of historiographical debate. The traditional view holds that this era witnessed unbridled corruption, the imposition of alien Greek culture, and the exploitation of Romanian resources so as to make tribute and grain payments to the sultan's coffers. Phanariot rule was a period of chronic instability reflecting the general breakdown of Ottoman governing institutions. From 1749 to 1821, *hospodarships* changed hands twenty-five times in Wallachia and twenty-three times in Moldavia, with the average tenure in office lasting about two and one-half years. Another approach to Phanariot rule, however, has been to focus on the positive endeavors of certain *hospodars* who tried to enact legal and social reform within the constraints of the Ottoman administrative structure.[22] One point hard to refute is Phanariot Greek patronage of learning and education, clearly seen in the founding of the Academies of Bucharest and Jassy. These institutions transmitted Western thought to the Balkans, educated Balkan intellectuals who contributed to the national awakening of their respective peoples, and in time stimulated the growth of a distinctly Romanian national consciousness in the Principalities.[23]

Several links connected the Phanariots to Russia. Along with exposure to Western secular culture, the Phanariots clung to Byzantine Christian tradition and regarded themselves as heirs of the Byzantine imperial legacy. They sought Russian military and diplomatic assistance to fulfill their vision of a restored Byzantium that would replace the Ottoman Empire and that would maintain Greek dominance of the Balkans.[24] Russia looked upon this russophile "party" as another means of penetration in the Balkans, especially after Kutchuk-Kainardji established Russian consulates. Consular officials often backed Phanariot Greek interests in return for Phanariot allegiance to the tsarist strategy of using the Principalities as a supply depot in future Russo-Turkish wars. Treaties with the Porte buttressed the Russian-Phanariot connection by giving Russia a large degree of control over the selection, tenure, and security of *hospodars*. Ottoman violation of these arrangements became a pretext for diplomatic and military intervention, which was generally supported by Phanariot partisans.[25]

Personal and social attachments strengthened the Russian-Phanariot political relationship. Fear of Ottoman reprisals for their pro-Russian activity drove Phanariot families and Phanariot sympathizers among the *boyars* (nobility) to seek haven in Russia. Here these refugees received state land grants and pensions and promoted an expansionist Eastern policy.[26] The flight of the Phanariot-*boyar* family of Skarlatos D. Sturdza after the 1787–92 Russo-Turkish War offers a case in point.[27] Leaving Jassy for St. Petersburg, the Sturdzas were awarded estates in Kherson and Tambov provinces, as well as a substantial state pension. Skarlatos continued his allegiance to tsarist Danubian strategy, serving as civilian governor (1812–13) in the newly annexed province of Bessarabia.[28] The flight of the Ypsilantis family during the 1806–12 Russo-Turkish War further exemplifies this patronage network. Deposed illegally as Wallachian *hospodar* and charged with treason for aiding the Serbian revolt, Konstantinos Ypsilantis settled in Kiev and advocated a Russian protectorate in the Phanariot-ruled Principalities.[29]

Both families produced offspring who were assimilated by Russian society but who yet were attached to their Danubian roots. Active in government service, these children espoused an aggressive Eastern policy that would realize both tsarist strategic goals and Balkan liberation hopes. Ypsilantis's four sons enrolled in the elite Household Cavalry of the Imperial Guard, and the oldest son, Alexandros (1792–1828), was awarded for distinguished service in the Napoleonic Wars and became an aide-de-camp to Alexander I. Alexandros later acquired notoriety as the romantic adventurer who led the 1821 uprising in Moldavia which triggered the War of Independence.[30] Of greater stature in the Greco-Russian relationship was Alexandros's cousin, the son of Skarlatos Sturdza, Aleksandr S. Sturdza (1791–1854), who became a prominent state official, writer, and publicist. Aleksandr served in the Ministries of Foreign Affairs and Public Education; participated in religious, educational, and philosophical debates; and upheld the principle of unfettered autocracy. His strong opposition to liberal and constitutional movements, with the exception of his call for Russian-assisted Greek liberation, made the younger Sturdza's name a byword for political reaction. He ardently advocated the defense of Greek Christians as partial fulfillment of Russia's imperial mission in the Near East. Sturdza's published and unpublished writings, scattered in numerous periodicals and archival repositories, display an acute interest in the historical and religious bonds of the Orthodox commonwealth.[31]

Sturdza's life was inextricably associated with the most illustrious Greek in tsarist service, the Corfiot aristocrat Ioannis Kapodistrias (1776–1831). Sturdza and Kapodistrias headed an unofficial Greek lobby in St. Petersburg, following the tradition of the enlightened cleric Eugenios Voulgaris who championed Greek and wider Orthodox concerns in the context of Catherinian expansion.[32] Kapodistrias began his political career in the Russian-sponsored Ionian Republic, firmly committed to the notion that Greek national hopes hinged on Russian support. When the Treaty of Tilsit placed the Ionians under French control, he emigrated and entered the Russian diplomatic corps. He soon won the tsar's confidence, rising to become joint foreign secretary with Karl V. Nessel'rode from 1815 to 1822.[33]

Sturdza also served in the Foreign Ministry, using his family background and his linguistic expertise in Moldavian, Greek, Latin, French, German, and Russian to become the Asiatic Department's specialist in Danubian matters. Sturdza and Kapodistrias were close friends and colleagues, serving together in St. Petersburg, Bucharest, Vienna, and Paris. Sturdza attended the Congress of Vienna as Kapodistrias's adviser on Danubian affairs and was the latter's chief source of information on Moldavia, Wallachia, and Bessarabia. In cogent reports on these areas, Sturdza often recommended military and diplomatic pressure to enforce Ottoman compliance with Russo-Turkish agreements. This stance, he maintained, would reinforce the conviction of Phanariots and other influential families who regarded Russia as their protector.[34]

Sturdza and Kapodistrias were prominent figures in St. Petersburg's

Greek community, along with the Cephalonian noble Spyridon Iu. Destunis (1782–1848). Destunis's uncle, the trader Ivan P. Destunis, had settled in Odessa as part of the initial wave of Greek emigrés who contributed to the newly founded port's commercial and urban growth. Ivan was burgomaster on the Odessan town council from 1797 to 1800, earning praise from Tsar Paul I for his diligent execution of official duties. Like Sturdza, Spyridon Destunis had a dual career as a Foreign Ministry official and as a publicist and translator. His writings underscored the Greco-Russian connection and Russia's role as the Greeks' protector.[35] Destunis, Sturdza, and Kapodistrias were bound by their friendship and careers, their Greek cultural patriotism, and their belief that Greek liberation was best served by Greco-Russian religious and historical ties. All three emphasized the compatibility of Russian and Greek interests, endorsed Greek educational and philanthropic endeavors, and called for tsarist defense of Greek coreligionists during the 1820s.

Kapodistrias and his two associates in the Foreign Ministry also worked to broaden the support networks for fellow Greek emigrants. Here, too, the Greek lobby built on the tradition of Voulgaris, who had helped to found the St. Petersburg Greek Gymnasium (1775) that trained youths for the army, navy, and diplomatic service.[36] Destunis, educated in Moscow and appointed consul general in Smyrna (1818–21), was one of the many Greeks selected for consular posts in the Near East. Such Greeks' linguistic skill and their familiarity with the Greek world made them good conduits of information for the Foreign Ministry. Their training and background qualified them to defend Russian interests and to protect Greek Christians from Ottoman violation of Kutchuk-Kainardji's freedom-of-worship clause. On these and related matters, they filed regular reports with the Russian embassy in Constantinople and with the Foreign Ministry in St. Petersburg.[37] The prospect of tsarist patronage encouraged Greek elites to build successful careers in government and diplomatic service. For the Phanariots and Ionian aristocrats, these positions offered political experience and an opportunity to promote an ambitious Eastern policy in accord with their hopes for Russian-assisted Greek emancipation.

The St. Petersburg lobby was the most visible manifestation of the Hellenic presence in Russia, a community that included all classes from simple sailors and soldiers to merchants and clergymen. Russia beckoned as a haven where emigrés could practice their faith, develop their skills, or simply find shelter from rapacious local authorities. The communities that sprouted were another concrete link between the Russian regime and the Greek revival, and they were also part of an extensive network of diaspora centers in London, Amsterdam, Paris, Leipzig, Vienna, Budapest, Venice, and Trieste.[38] The settlements in Russia were unique, however, in view of the tradition of Greek migration extending back to classical and Byzantine times. The post-Byzantine influx included traders who formed companies in Kiev, Lvov, and Kharkov and who became middlemen in Russian trade with central Europe and the Balkans. Nezhin in particular rose to prominence as a leading commercial center, with tsarist-granted autonomy to handle its administrative affairs and to fund its schools and churches. Greek became the lingua franca of Balkan trade, enabling Russian-based Greek merchants to expand their operations.[39]

New settlements also emerged in the Crimea and along the northern Black Sea coast after the conquests by Catherine the Great. European Russia's southern frontier formed part of the vast area known as Novorossiia, or New Russia, encompassing the provinces of Kherson, Tavrida, Ekaterinoslav, and later the territory of Bessarabia. Appropriately named for its natural resources, warm-water ports, and strategic location, New Russia was a springboard for broader involvement in the Eastern Question and a rich source of economic development. Its successful integration necessitated military and naval outposts, an administrative structure, and an effective scheme to tap the potential of this sparsely populated borderland.[40] Mindful of these imperatives, Catherine II and her favorite Grigorii A. Potemkin, governor-general of New Russia, launched an ambitious colonization program. Various incentives—cheap land, fishing concessions, favorable loan rates, tax and state service exemptions, religious tolerance—attracted native Russians, Germans, Dutch, Swiss, Poles, Italians, Armenians, Jews, Romanians, and Bulgars to populate the newly founded towns.[41] Greeks also emigrated, establishing communties in Taganrog, Mariupol, Sevastopol, Kherson, Azov, Simferopol, Nikolaev, Odessa, and other places. These new centers of Hellenism, along with older communities in Kiev, Nezhin, Moscow, and St. Petersburg, gave Russia a sizable Greek presence.[42]

Greco-Russian ties now facilitated commercial expansion. In the absence of its own southern merchant fleet, Russia relied on Greek traders, shippers, and sailors. Russo-Ottoman trade agreements, such as the 1783 Treaty of Commerce, permitted the sultan's Greek subjects to use the Russian flag on their vessels. The opening of the Black Sea and the right to fly the Russian flag created opportunities for enterprising Aegean Greeks who already held a large share of the Ottoman Empire's Mediterranean commerce. Shippers from Hydra, Spetsae, and Psara expanded their operations and became leading carriers in Russian Black Sea trade. They also reaped benefits from their adept blockade-running in the Napoleonic Wars. In addition to their importance in Russia's emerging Black Sea navy, the Aegean merchant marine spearheaded resistance to the Ottoman fleet during the War of Independence.[43]

Greek merchants established companies in Moscow, St. Petersburg, and above all, Odessa, where they participated in the burgeoning grain trade. Greek firms took advantage of Odessa's location as a commercial nexus linking the Black Sea to the Mediterranean and thus profited from contacts with business partners and compatriots. The Rallis firm, one of the largest in Odessa, had branches in Constantinople, London, Marseilles, and Manchester. Influential Odessan companies were also set up by Theodoros Seraphinos, Alexandros Mavros, Grigorios Maraslis, and Alexandros Koumbaris. Greek wealth stimulated insurance companies, banks, and other merchant institutions. Commercial capital, along with effective government by enlightened city chiefs and governor generals, transformed Odessa from a provincial backwater into one of Europe's major grain emporiums, a cosmopolitan city of ethnic diversity and cultural vitality.[44] The Ionian native Dimitrios S. Inglezis (1773–1844) typified the successful Greek merchant. His firm prospered, and he engaged in a range of municipal activity that enhanced Odessa's formative growth (including a brief stint as mayor from 1818 to 1821). Although he was assimilated by his adopted land, Inglezis retained his cultural heritage and funded Greek education with his capital.[45]

The Greek diaspora in Russia, like its counterpart in the West, contributed to the intellectual and cultural awakening known as the Neohellenic Enlightenment.[46] Several factors enabled Greeks in foreign lands to preserve their sense of national identity and to participate in the revival of Greek learning. Emigrés often formed compact neighborhoods near the center of town, evinced in Odessa's Greek street and bazaar, that became the focal point of Greek community life. Economic realities also kept emigrants together. For example, sailors, sea captains, and traders found employment in the traditionally Greek occupations of navigation and shipping. Regular traffic in the Mediterranean allowed them to maintain contact with relatives and compatriots, thereby nurturing their Greek consciousness and their abiding concern in the fate of Ottoman-ruled ancestral lands. The Greeks of Russia also cultivated their faith, language, and heritage by establishing their own schools and churches. In an era when religious faith largely defined national identity, churches were not only places of worship and prayer but vessels of cultural tradition, social community, and national feeling as seen in the Holy Trinity Greek Orthodox Church and its vital role in Odessa's Greek community.[47]

The Greek Commercial Gymnasium in Odessa was the best-known center of Greek education in Russia. Eminent local merchants, such as Dimitrios Inglezis, Theodoros Seraphinos, Ilias Manesis, and Dimitrios Palaiologos, founded the school in 1817 and organized its administration. The gymnasium taught courses in commerce, shipping, navigation, geography, history, religion, natural sciences, ancient and modern Greek, Russian, Italian, and German. Along with merchant patronage, the school's success was due to such dedicated teachers as Konstantinos Vardalachos, Giorgios Gennadios, Giorgios Lassanis, and Ioannis Makris, who instilled in their students a strong sense of cultural patriotism.[48] The historian Konstantinos Koumas, present at the school's opening ceremonies, described the new institution in a letter to the educator Konstantinos Oikonomos, who taught with Koumas at the Smyrna Philological Gymnasium. Koumas praised the Odessan school's administrators and teachers, who had tried unsuccessfully to recruit him, and indicated its significance as a center of Greek learning.[49] Within two years, nearly three hundred students were enrolled in the Commercial Gymnasium.

Odessa's Greek theater (1814) complemented the school as a vehicle for preserving national identity. The theater staged classical and Western dramas, along with original works by Giorgios Lassanis and Nikolaos Pikkolos. Performed principally by Greeks before predominantly Greek audiences, plays evoked the greatness of both ancient and Byzantine Greece and promoted patriotic sentiment. Lassanis's *Greece and the Foreigner* (*I Ellas kai o Xenos,* 1818) laments Ottoman rule and urges the Greek nation to end social and regional rivalries for the sake of national unity.[50] The play recalls the spirit of another contemporary Greek text, the anonymous pamphlet *Greek Nomarchy* (*Elliniki nomarchia,* 1806), which encouraged Greeks to rely on themselves and not on outside help for national liberation.[51] That numerous Odessan Greek youths volunteered for the 1821 Moldavian revolt suggests the success of both the theater and the school in promoting Hellenic patriotism.

The Odessan Greeks were not alone in organizing education and language study. The Commercial Gymnasium of Taganrog (1807) offered instruction in mathematics, physics, geography, commerce, bookkeeping, navigation, French, German, Italian, Latin, and both ancient and modern Greek. Its students were drawn from Taganrog merchant and noble families of Greek and Russian descent. In Nezhin, a still sizable Greek community existed, despite the town's commercial decline after 1774 when numerous inhabitants resettled in Taganrog and Odessa. Greek merchant capital from Nezhin and Moscow funded the Nezhin Aleksandrovskii School that opened in 1817. Mariupol also had its own Greek school, established in 1818 with assistance from Foreign Secretary Kapodistrias. Many Orthodox Greeks from the former Crimean Khanate who settled in Mariupol spoke Tatar, and their liturgical texts were written in Tatar but with a Greek alphabet. They were gradually assimilated to Greek language through the local Greek school and through contact with Greek-speaking settlers near Mariupol.[52] Archival material in the Ministry of Public Education reveals further Greek-language instruction given in merchant-funded schools in Taganrog and Izmail during the first half of the nineteenth century.[53]

Greek merchants in Russia financed Greek learning in the diaspora and in the Ottoman Empire. The list of trustees who contributed to the Athonite Academy's revival included traders from St. Petersburg, Moscow, Taganrog, Odessa, and Astrakhan.[54] Merchants often displayed a spirit of regional patriotism by donating large sums for schools, churches, hospitals, and orphanages in their Ottoman-controlled homeland. In addition to his philanthropic endeavors in Astrakhan and later in Taganrog, the Psara-born Ioannis Varvakis, one of the wealthiest Greeks in Russia, funded the education of Psariot students at the Gymnasium of Chios. Traders from Epirus who settled in Nezhin, Moscow, St. Petersburg, and Odessa acquired legendary fame for munificence to their native region. Zois Kaplanis, the wealthy Epirot who resided in Moscow, donated his entire fortune of 183,000 rubles for educational and charitable work in Epirus, including the Kaplanis School in his native Ioannina.[55]

The most eminent merchant patrons were the Zosimas brothers, who settled in Nezhin and Moscow. The Zosimades subsidized diaspora Greek students and founded schools, orphanages, and hospitals in their native Ioannina. They were perhaps best known for their sponsorship of *Hellenic Library (Elliniki vivliothiki)*, the multivolume edition of Greek classical texts by Adamantios Korais, the leading figure in the Neohellenic Enlightenment. In scholarly prologues to his landmark work, Korais described the Greek intellectual awakening and urged compatriots to seek political liberation through cultural enlightenment. He affirmed that the classical heritage was a stimulus for education, civic virtue, and patriotism, all of which would prepare the nation for self-rule.[56]

The Zosimades were equally generous as patrons of learning in Russia. They financed the publication of many educational texts, including a Greek-Russian dictionary, a Russian-language handbook on Greek grammar, and two Greek translations by Spyridon Destunis. Destunis's preface hailed Zosimas patronage, "known to all the *genos* [nation]" as indispensable not just for his own work but also for the broader Greek Enlightenment.[57] As members of the Russian Bible Society, the brothers subsidized the printing of five thousand copies of a modern Greek New Testament for Orthodox clergy in Chios, Smyrna, Athens, Kydonies, and Zante. They also founded a chair of Greek philology at the Medical-Surgical Academy in Moscow (1819) and donated one hundred Greek-language books to Moscow University, most of which had been published at their own expense.[58] In 1841, the last Zosimas brother in Russia willed much of the family inheritance to educational, religious, and charitable institutions in the kingdom of Greece.[59] The zeal of the Zosimades was an impetus for other diaspora merchants to promote Greek education.

The Greek lobby in the Foreign Ministry, like the Zosimades, contributed to both Greek enlightenment and Russian learning. Sturdza and Destunis participated in Russia's classical awakening by promoting the study of the ancient Greek legacy. In a noteworthy essay written in 1810 and published in 1817, Sturdza emphasized the value of teaching ancient Greek to Russian youth. His preface affirmed that classical languages were the foundation of enlightenment for all nations and that Greek had special significance for Russians in view of Greco-Russian historical ties. While Latin was useful, ancient Greek constituted "the focal point and the basis upon which the splendid edifice of learning will be raised."[60] Selections from Greek poetry and oratory would thus enliven language study and introduce students to masterpieces of the ancient heritage.

Destunis contributed to Russian classical learning with his thirteen-part translation of Plutarch's *Lives of Great Men* (1814–21), revered by Destunis as the single best source to instill in youth a love of truth and virtue.[61] He worked long and hard on this project, compiling historical and critical notes that clarified difficult passages and discussed previous renditions of Plutarch. References to Latin, French, and German scholarship demonstrated his broad knowledge of ancient history and literature. The translation might have gone unpublished had it not been for the intercession of Sturdza and other officials who grasped its value for Russian classical studies. Destunis also received help from Foreign Secretary Kapodistrias, who petitioned the tsar on behalf of his Ionian compatriot. An imperial *ukaz* (decree) (1817) awarded Destunis a state land grant and announced that his publication would be funded by the government with proceeds helping Russian invalids from the 1812 War.[62] In the 1830s and 1840s, Destunis continued to promote Greek history and culture with his Russian translations of Byzantine legal and historical texts. These contributions to Byzantine scholarship were acknowledged by Russian Byzantinists, whose ranks included Spyridon's son Gavriil Destunis (1818–95), professor of Greek philology at St. Petersburg University.[63]

The Greek lobby combined with merchant capital to play a vital role in the *Philomousos Etaireia* (Society of Friends of the Muses), an educational and philanthropic organization founded in Vienna in 1814. The *Etaireia* solicited financial patronage from European, Russian, and Greek sources to establish Greek schools in Thessaly and Athens, to fund Greek students in Europe, and to preserve Greek antiquities. Kapodistrias, who had promoted Greek education during the Russian-protected Ionian Republic, helped to organize the *Etaireia*'s Russian branch. Throughout his career in the tsarist service, Kapodistrias endeavored to advance Greek national hopes through both education and Russian Eastern policy. He believed that Russian-sponsored education was the safest means to improve Greek social and political conditions in the Ottoman Empire. In accord with this stance, he subsidized visiting Greek scholars and educators, encouraged Greek-language study in Russia's Greek communities, and exerted his influence to expedite governmental approval of Greek schools, such as Odessa's Commercial Gymnasium. His role in collecting donations for the *Philomousos Etaireia* was thus a natural extension of his Greek cultural patriotism.[64]

Kapodistrias's stature as foreign secretary and the tsar's confidence in him were instrumental in gaining Russian support for the *Etaireia*'s philanthropy. Aware of the need to counter British-sponsored educational initiatives in Athens and the Ionian Islands, Alexander I regarded Russian patronage of Greek education as a way to retain influence among Ottoman Greeks and to reinforce his image as their traditional protector. The tsar's deepened piety and religiosity after what he perceived as his divinely ordained triumph over Napoleon also explained his favorable attitude toward the charitable mission of the *Philomousos Etaireia*. Alexander I was further encouraged by Kapodistrias's espousal of a religiously grounded enlightenment that emphasized moral education rather than political activism. The tsar and his foreign secretary feared the explosiveness of Balkan, in particular Greek and Serbian, national aspirations. Additionally, endorsement of revolutionary unrest after the Congress of Vienna would have run directly counter to the Russian stance of upholding the status quo in Europe and of maintaining cordial relations with the Porte. Alexander I and Kapodistrias thus hoped that education, directed by learned Orthodox clergy and sponsored by Russia, would deflect the Greek revival from the specter of insurrection. Alexander I approved of the Greek educational society all the more because its leading proponents in Russia, such as Aleksandr Sturdza, adhered to official policy and opposed liberal and national movements that threatened to incite revolution.[65]

Kapodistrias, Sturdza, and Destunis organized the collection of donations for the *Philomousos Etaireia*. Financial patrons included the tsar and members of the imperial family; high-ranking officials, such as Minister of Public Education Aleksandr N. Golitsyn; such Phanariot Greeks as Sturdza, Alexandros Mavrokordatos Phiraris, and Alexandros Ypsilantis; and merchant-philanthropists, such as the Zosimades, Ioannis Varvakis of Taganrog, and Ioannis Dombolis of St. Petersburg. Sturdza's sister Roksandra Sturdza-Edling, known for her devout faith and Christian charity, was particularly generous in her patronage.[66] As lady-in-waiting to Tsarina Elizaveta Alekseevna, Sturdza-Edling accompanied the imperial couple to the Congress of Vienna and was one of several court figures who encouraged the tsar's religiosity and his self-portrayal as Europe's Christian savior. She was also an intimate friend of Kapodistrias and probably would have married him had it not been for the imperial family's politically motivated desire to have her marry Count Edling of Weimar. She wrote a valuable firsthand account of the *Philomousos Etaireia*'s founding in Vienna. Her memoirs and letters also described Kapodistrias's efforts to gain tsarist aid for Greek education and to improve the status of Greek compatriots under Ottoman rule.[67] The donations received from these and other Russian and Greek sources enabled the society to fund Greek students at German and Italian universities and to build schools in Ottoman-controlled Greece.

Kapodistrias and Aleksandr Sturdza, along with assisting the *Philomousos*

Etaireia, collaborated to set up a Greek-language press at the Odessan Commercial Gymnasium. Sturdza served briefly in the Dual Ministry of Religious Affairs and Public Education, which, under the direction of Aleksandr N. Golitsyn, attempted to make Christian piety the basis of education. As a member of the Academic Committee of the Central School Board in 1818–19, Sturdza drafted the "Instruction" outlining measures to propagate Christian faith and piety in the classroom. One means recommended was rigorous censorship of the content and spirit of textbooks to remove influences considered "contrary and alien" to the Dual Ministry's mission.[68] Sturdza himself supervised the inspection of texts in classical Greek and Latin philology.[69] Authorized by the Committee of Ministers and supported by Kapodistrias, Sturdza also proposed guidelines for a Greek-language press in Odessa and for a local censorship committee to oversee its operation.

The 1820 document, echoing his "Instruction" prepared for the Academic Committee, presented Sturdza's conservative educational views and his concern for church-directed Greek enlightenment in Russia.[70] Sturdza underscored that Orthodox Christianity was the main force shaping education as it instilled respect for authority and cemented the social order. He thus encouraged the printing of religious texts—sermons, catechisms, works by the Holy Fathers, church histories—all of which had to be approved by the Russian Holy Synod before their publication in Greek. Sturdza proposed that the local censorship committee regulate additional educational materials, including the classics and translations of Russian and Western writings. Thus philological and historical texts should in no way subvert Christian faith and public order, and works in logic, philosophy, and jurisprudence had to preserve the inviolability of revealed truth as the basis of civil law. According to the guidelines, any writings that advocated liberal and constitutional ideas were to be banned on the premise that political authority emanated from divine providence rather than from constitutions and charters. The censorship committee, in short, had to make sure that Greek-language publications fostered respect for established authority and upheld the sanctity of Christian belief and church dogma.

Odessa's location on a merchant nexus linking Russia, Europe, and the Greek East made it a natural point for the exchange and circulation of Greek books published in Moscow, Venice, and Vienna. The Odessan Greek school and theater also stimulated a Greek book culture. The Greek-language press and the censorship board proposed by Sturdza and attached to the Commercial Gymnasium began operations in 1827. Most of the press's early publications were language texts, translations from classical literature, and other instructional materials used at the local school.[71] The conservative regulations laid down by Sturdza changed in the course of the nineteenth century, reflecting the shifts in tsarist educational and censorship policy. By the early twentieth century, the local Greek press had produced an eclectic collection of works in literature, history, geography, science, and other subjects, making Odessa a prominent center of Greek-language publications in Russia.[72]

Sturdza's advocacy of church-led education and religiously grounded enlightenment, however, did not suit the more activist wing of the Greek national movement. The activists focused their desire for radical change on the *Philiki Etaireia* (Society of Friends), a political society founded in Odessa in 1814 for the liberation of Greece via armed insurrection. Greek nationalist historiography has traditionally described the *Philiki Etaireia* as a national organization that drew members from all Greek-speaking areas of the Ottoman Empire and from nearly all social groups. Class interests and regional attachments were secondary to the unifying patriotic goal of liberation from Turkish rule. Greek Marxist approaches have generally underlined the progressive role of a prosperous merchant bourgeoisie who galvanized the liberation struggle and forged an independent nation-state that would protect and enhance their capitalist endeavors.[73] Nationalist and Marxist interpretations of the *Philiki Etaireia* have been substantially revised by scholarship highlighting the complexities of Greek society. The *Etaireia,* and the ensuing War of Independence, reflected and indeed exacerbated deep-seated fissures that provoked factionalism and civil strife in the 1820s.

In his careful examination of the *Philiki Etaireia*'s social composition and regional diversity, George Frangos convincingly argues that it was "a premature national coalition." Although the *Etaireia* aspired to become a national organization, it failed to bridge the regional, social, and political differences of its diversified membership that was recruited from an increasingly complex and stratified society on the eve of 1821. Rather than a unified national organization, the conspiracy was a product of economic anxiety, social dislocation, and embryonic national identity. The *Philiki Etaireia* attracted recruits from a broad social spectrum of diaspora and Ottoman Greeks: peasants, *klephts,* clergy, professionals, Phanariots, and landed primates, the most dominant and influential landholders in the Morea and the Archipelago. Diaspora and Ottoman Greek merchants, making up 53.7 percent of the total membership, were the single largest group in the secret society. Most of them, typified by the *Etaireia*'s three founders, were small-time traders struggling to eke out a living.[74] Recent emigrés from rural Ottoman lands, the traders were adversely affected by falling grain prices that were caused partly by the return of Western ships to the Levant after the Napoleonic Wars. The ranks of this merchant element consisted of peddlers, clerks, and others who had failed to make the grade in the sharply competitive world of the merchant diaspora. The *Etaireia* did not appeal to affluent, established merchants whose wealth set them apart from traders enduring economic reverses. The well-to-do were understandably reluctant to join a conspiracy that might trigger Ottoman reprisals against their successful business ventures.

Frangos's work is a useful reminder that distinctions need to be made within broad social categories like the commercial bourgeoisie. Amorphous groups did not act as homogeneous units, nor did individuals who joined the *Etaireia* represent the interests of their particular social class. The variegated social and regional complexion of *Etaireia* membership explains the leadership's inability to articulate a coherent social vision or political ideology. John Petropulos has correctly noted that Greek political objectives were vague and contradictory. There was no consensus on the desired political form or content of liberation, with alternatives ranging from a restored multiethnic but Greek-dominated Byzantium; to a primarily Greek-inhabited nation-state encompassing the Morea, Attica, and adjacent islands; to local autonomy for areas controlled by powerful landed primates, Phanariots, and other provincial elites. Social and political diversity was compounded by family and kinship ties that cut across the class structure and political orientation. The Greek revolution aggravated these cleavages and added new ones as politics in the new kingdom featured divison between pro-British, pro-French, and pro-Russian factions.[75]

The *Philiki Etaireia* recruited supporters primarily in the Danubian Principalities, the Ionian Islands, Constantinople, and the Peloponnese. Because it was founded in Odessa, the *Etaireia* was also active in Russia, sending agents to Greek communities in Moscow, St. Petersburg, Taganrog, Kherson, Izmail, and other towns in New Russia. It drew members from a cross section of Greeks, including military veterans who had fought in Russian wars against the Ottoman Empire, teachers at Odessa's Commercial Gymnasium, and prominent Phanariots, such as the Ypsilantis brothers and Alexandros Mavrokordatos Phiraris. The vast majority of *etairists* who resided in Russia (85.5 percent) were petty traders and clerks struggling to make ends meet.[76] Many were hurt by the 1817–18 slump in Black Sea exports, caused in part by Western tariffs against cheap and abundant Russian grain. A locust attack and an outbreak of smallpox disrupted the harvest of Ukrainian wheat in 1820–21, compounding the economic difficulties of small-time traders.[77] They had little to lose in supporting an uprising against Ottoman rule.

The few established merchants who joined the *Philiki Etaireia,* such as Moscow's Nikolaos Patsimadis, were the exception to the rule. When Alexandros Ypsilantis accepted the leadership of the conspiracy in 1820, the prestige of his Phanariot name and his aristocratic wealth attracted several merchant patrons in Moscow and Odessa. Yet he hardly received the donations he might have expected from Greek commercial capital. Sparse donations collected from rich Odessan traders, such as Dimitrios Inglezis, Theodoros Seraphinos, and Alexandros Mavros, prompted his scorn. Ypsilantis's letter to Emmanouil Xanthos, a founder of the society, noted that affluent merchants may have sympathized with his plans but did not open their purse strings. Indeed, they were misers who "could donate five hundred thousand if they had convictions. This good cause will happen even without them."[78] The prosperous merchants in Odessa feared, prophetically, that a premature revolt would provoke an Eastern crisis disrupting their commerce in the Mediterranean.

The *Philiki Etaireia* was connected to Russia not only by its organization and recruitment on Russian soil but also by the prevalent misperception that the tsarist regime endorsed its revolutionary designs. Leaders of the *Etaireia* often misused the tsar's name, fostering the illusion that he supported the society as a natural consequence of traditional protection of Orthodox Christians. Because Russia had promoted past resistance to Ottoman rule by inciting Balkan Christian rebellion, the *Etaireia*'s link with Russia seemed historically plausible. This illusion of support had greater credence in view of the widespread rumors that Foreign Secretary Kapodistrias was a member, if not the secret leader, of the society. An Ionian noble with social prestige, diplomatic experience, and direct access to the tsar, Kapodistrias was esteemed by many Greeks, who interpreted the tsar's trust in him as a clear sign that Russia supported the liberation movement. So, the foreign secretary's presumed leadership of the *Etaireia* only strengthened Greek conviction that the tsarist government backed the revolutionary society.

The myth of Kapodistrias's direct involvement with the conspiratorial organization was sustained by the foreign secretary's record in the diplomatic corps. Kapodistrias championed independence for the Ionian Islands at the Congress of Vienna, solicited tsarist aid for Ionian war veterans who had served during the Ionian Republic, and urged diplomatic protection of the sultan's Orthodox Christians. Furthermore, numerous Kapodistrias-appointed consular officials of Greek descent in the Near East either supported or joined the *Philiki Etaireia*. They included Spyridon Destunis, consul in Smyrna; Ioannis Vlasopulos, consul in Patras; Nikolaos Mylonas, vice-consul in Chios; Grigorios Levendis, translator and secretary in Jassy and later in Bucharest; and Gavriil Katakazi, secretary at the embassy in Constantinople.[79] These areas were not only major centers of *etairist* recruitment, but such consular connections to the society substantiated rumors that Russia sponsored Greek liberation. Although diplomatic officials joined the *Etaireia* as individuals and not as representatives of official policy, their membership reinforced the notion that Kapodistrias, and behind him the Russian government, endorsed the revolutionary society.

Kapodistrias's supposed connection with the conspiratorial *Etaireia* also stemmed from his close association with the *Philomousos Etaireia*. Both societies, despite their different goals and social composition, were confused in the minds of contemporaries. Such confusion is readily understandable because of their similar names, their shared sense of patriotism, and their ultimate hope of liberation, albeit by the very different paths of enlightenment and insurrection. Confusion was further spawned because several members of the *Philiki Etaireia* contributed to Greek learning and education. Odessa's Commercial Gymnasium and Greek theater disseminated political activism through the nationalistic efforts of the teacher and writer Giorgios Lassanis, who also joined the secret political organization. Several merchant patrons of the *Philomousos Etaireia,* such as Zois Zosimas, Ilias Manesis, and Grigorios Maraslis, deemed revolt premature and unlikely to succeed, and yet they donated monies to agents of the *Philiki Etaireia,* incorrectly assuming that their funds would be used for books and schools rather than for arms and supplies.[80] Some members of the *Philiki Etaireia* further implicated Kapodistrias by deliberately using the educational society as a cover for insurgency in Greek lands. Kapodistrias was unaware that in the *Philiki Etaireia*'s secret code "to found a school" often meant "to prepare the revolt."[81] Despite the misperceptions fostered by these fabrications, Kapodistrias continued to support Greek education even after discovering in 1820 that the *Philomousos Etaireia* had frequently been used as a screen for insurgent activity.

Although the tsar knew of the *Philiki Etaireia*'s existence, his regime neither supported nor encouraged its political designs. The society never became an instrument in Balkan strategy, especially since the idea of insurrection ran counter to the current policy of seeking cordial relations with the Porte. Kapodistrias certainly knew more than the tsar about the *Etaireia* because it tried to draw the foreign secretary into its conspiratorial plans. In 1817 and again in 1820, he rebuffed approaches to secure his leadership of the secret society, on both occasions asserting that the *Etaireia* could expect no help from him or the Russian government. He steadfastly refuted the rumors and misinformation about his alleged participation in the society.[82] During a visit to his native Corfu in 1819, he deflated the hopes of compatriots by denouncing the *Etaireia* and its rumors of his involvement and support. In a speech that became the basis for his memorandum "Observations sur les moyens d'améliorer le sort des Grecs," he cautioned fellow Greeks that only time, patience, providence, and church-directed enlightenment would improve the status of the Greek nation under Ottoman rule.[83]

Kapodistrias forwarded copies of the memorandum and strongly worded dispatches to Russia's ambassador in Constantinople, Grigorii A. Stroganov, and to consuls Aleksandr A. Pini (Bucharest), S. Destunis (Smyrna), and I. Vlasopulos (Patras). These documents deny his association with the secret society, condemn its revolutionary intent, and request an end to conspiratorial intrigue that misrepresented his name and damaged Greek interests. Destunis and Vlasopulos were especially appropriate targets for Kapodistrias. They belonged to the *Philiki Etaireia* and thus had to be informed of the foreign secretary's actual relationship with the society. They also had consular jurisdiction over broad areas, Destunis over the Archipelago and Vlasopulos over mainland Greece, and presumably they could convey Kapodistrias's message to *etairists* in these regions. Kapodistrias wrote a similar letter to Konstantinos Vardalachos, his longtime friend from his student years at the University of Padua, exhorting the influential teacher at the Odessan Commercial Gymnasium to warn Greek youths of the folly and danger of the *Etaireia*'s revolutionary plans.[84]

Kapodistrias opposed the *Philiki Etaireia* on ideological and pragmatic grounds. He clung to the belief that moral awakening and education, not armed revolt, constituted the safest means to enact social and national change. A premature uprising would have dire consequences for the Greeks, whom he deemed unprepared for political independence. His caution and moderation further stemmed from his delicate position as a Greek patriot serving as the Russian foreign secretary. Kapodistrias was well aware of Alexander I's commitment to the Concert of Europe, condemnation of the 1820–21 revolts in Spain and Italy, and fear of underground societies in Europe and Russia, and the foreign secretary was not about to jeopardize his official status by joining or aiding a secret organization bent on disturbing the political status quo. By retaining the tsar's confidence, Kapodistrias could endeavor to remain useful to the Greek cause. He could seek continued patronage of Greek education and lobby for an aggressive Eastern policy to protect Orthodox Christians. Further, he recognized that Russo-Ottoman hostility, in particular chronic disputes over the Danubian Principalities, made another Russo-Turkish war virtually unavoidable. In the aftermath of such a conflict, by Kapodistrias's calculation, the Greeks might achieve autonomy as a first step toward political independence. Finally, the foreign secretary's disavowal of the *Etaireia* was bolstered by his conservative friend and colleague, Aleksandr Sturdza, Kapodistrias's adviser on Danubian and Russo-Turkish affairs. Both preferred prudence and patience to revolt, and both desired the fulfillment of Greek hopes in the context of Eastern policy.

Kapodistrias's firm opposition to the designs of the *Philiki Etaireia* and his effort to dispel rumors of his involvement failed to have the desired result because dispatches to Russian officials and appeals to influential Greeks did not dampen revolutionary ferment. Kapodistrias alone could not have stemmed the tide because *etairists* believed what they wanted to believe, regardless of the foreign secretary's attempt to clarify his position. Expectation of support from Kapodistrias and Russia reinforced insurgent preparation, but this anticipation was hardly the main catalyst for a liberation movement shaped essentially by social, economic, and political realities in the Ottoman Empire. The Greeks most likely would have staged a revolt regardless of Kapodistrias's stature in the tsarist government and regardless of intrigues fabricating his sponsorship of the *Philiki Etaireia*.[85]

After Kapodistrias refused to head their political society, *etairist* activists turned to Alexandros Ypsilantis, a likely choice given his prestigious Phanariot name, his general's rank in the tsarist army, and his position as aide-de-camp to the tsar. Kapodistrias warned Ypsilantis to shun the *Etaireia's* designs and to expect no help from the tsarist regime, but these warnings were to no avail as the Phanariot general accepted the invitation. While some controversy exists on the matter of Kapodistrias's relationship with the *Philiki Etaireia,* the foreign secretary did implicitly aid the society when he neither divulged to Alexander I all that he knew nor prevented Ypsilantis's departure from Russia in 1821.[86] Kapodistrias reasoned that silence was the prudent course given the tsar's fear of revolt in Europe and the Russian ruler's desire to maintain the status quo with the Porte. The foreign secretary realized that, even if the tsar adopted the cause of Greek liberation, Alexander I would consider the *Philiki Etaireia,* with its Masonic-like ritual and secrecy, yet another manifestation of a Europeanwide conspiracy against the social and political order. The tsar might then respond by restricting Greek nationalist activity in Russia, including education. Kapodistrias also feared that, if the sultan discovered the *Etaireia's* existence and the extent of its network in Ottoman lands, the ensuing reprisals would greatly damage Greek national interests.

When Ypsilantis assumed direction of the *Philiki Etaireia,* the focus of insurgent preparation shifted from Constantinople and the Danubian Principalities to Bessarabia. Ypsilantis, who ardently desired Greek emancipation, accelerated the drive to recruit new members and to procure supplies and arms. From his headquarters in Kishinev, he solicited aid from Greek communities in Moscow, Kiev, Odessa, Izmail, and other towns in Novorossiia. He corresponded with Greek, Serbian, and Romanian activists in the Balkans, hoping to incite a Balkanwide conflagration. He set up a clandestine press in Kishinev that printed proclamations exhorting Greek support for the upcoming struggle.[87]

The *Etaireia* decided to stage the rising in Moldavia rather than in the Morea because of Moldavia's proximity to Ypsilantis's Kishinev supply base. The society expected cooperation from Phanariot Greeks, such as the Moldavian *hospodar* and *etairist* Michail Soutsos, and from other influential Greeks in the Principalities. It also had proponents in the Russian consulates of Jassy and Bucharest. Ypsilantis was convinced that once the rebellion began, the tsar would be compelled to act because insurrection would trigger Ottoman retaliation that would violate Russo-Turkish treaties, thereby prompting Russian intervention to protect Orthodox Christians and to enforce compliance with the Russo-Turkish accords.[88] To others, Ypsilantis's distinguished service in the Russian army lent added substance to rumors that Russia endorsed the *Philiki Etaireia.* Meanwhile, this stepped-up insurgent activity in Russia and the Balkans made the position of Kapodistrias all the more tenuous. His archnemesis, Metternich, missed no opportunity to discredit him, implicating the foreign secretary in the disorders brewing in Europe and the Balkans.[89]

By 1821 the Greeks had benefited from the dichotomy of tsarist policy. Although opposed to revolt, Russia helped to foster a revolutionary situation in Ottoman-controlled Greek lands. Russian expansion rendered protection to Greek Christians, some of whom entered the Russian army, navy, state bureaucracy, and diplomatic corps. Many other Greeks emigrated in quest of shelter to practice their trades and to develop their skills. These Greek emigrants formed centers that embodied the mutually rewarding bonds linking Russia and the Greek East. More concretely, Eastern policy facilitated such key aspects of the Greek awakening as resistance, commerce, and learning. Ironically, the Russian regime, a bulwark of both political reaction and the Concert of Europe, promoted Greek enlightenment that in time inspired Greek insurgency. Russian-sponsored education, whether it was in Europe, Russia, or the Ottoman Empire, instilled a critical spirit among politically conscious Greeks. It prepared them for political action and their country for national regeneration. Imperial Russia had thus nurtured a liberation movement that represented the ideological antithesis of the Old Regime—the modern ideas of liberalism and nationalism that were ushered in by the French Revolution and the Napoleonic Wars.

Assistance to the Hellenic revival clearly indicates that philhellenism antedated the 1821 revolution. The Russian impetus to the Greek awakening, growing out of Russo-Greek religious and historical ties, prompted the widespread perception that Russia stood squarely behind the cause of Greek emancipation. Shortly after Ypsilantis launched the *etairist* uprising, Kapodistrias accurately wrote to Grigorii A. Stroganov, the Russian envoy at Constantinople: "All Greeks who are in a position to think and to act are born with the *idée fixe* that Russia protects them for the sole purpose of driving the Turks from Europe."[90] This idée fixe resounded in Greek appeals to tsarist benevolence voiced by insurgent leaders in the Morea and Principalities who requested intervention on the Greeks' behalf.[91] The conviction in Russian religious protection both reinforced Greek opposition to Ottoman rule and aroused philhellenic feeling in Russia after 1821.

Centers of Greek Settlement and Russian Philhellenism.
Reprinted from John Klier's *Russia Gathers Her Jews.*

Chapter Two

The War Party

THE YPSILANTIS RISING posed a fundamental dilemma for Alexander I. On the one hand, historical tradition and Orthodoxy justified intervention to aid fellow Orthodox Christians, and protection of religious brethren, stipulated in treaties with the Porte, even offered a pretext to pursue strategic designs in the Balkans. On the other hand, the Concert of Europe and monarchical solidarity dictated nonintervention, particularly since the revolt struck a blow against the Metternichean order and threatened to incite uprisings in Europe and to renew Great Power tension in the Near East. The 1821 crisis thus tested the tsar's balancing act between legitimacy and Orthodoxy, between the Concert of Europe and Russian national interest, and between the currents of absolutism and enlightened reform.

Unlike the tsar, Russian educated society had few reservations about the Greek cause, and as in the West, the prospect of Greek liberation aroused sympathy within nearly all sectors of the Russian public.[1] Church hierarchs were indignant over Turkish reprisals against the Greek church. The press featured regular reports on the struggle, almost always with a strident pro-Greek slant. Hellenists and Romantic writers celebrated the Greek revolution in rousing verses.

Even within ruling circles, an amorphous war party took shape and clamored for intervention. This eclectic assortment of officials, diplomats, army officers, and future Decembrists that made up the war party included both proponents and opponents of autocracy. Despite ideological differences, the informal coalition of hawks found common ground with the Greek issue because Russian-assisted Hellenic emancipation appealed to their sense of Russian nationalism, state interest, and historical tradition. For the

Decembrists, Russia's liberals who staged an unsuccessful revolt for constitutional government in December 1825, there was the added dimension
that Greek rebels were kindred spirits opposed to the political status quo.
The war party was not only an important manifestation of philhellenism,
but its emphasis on the religious aspect of the struggle resonated in the
wider philhellenic movement.

The Ypsilantis insurrection galvanized Russia's war party. When Ypsilantis crossed the Pruth River on 22 February/6 March 1821 to launch the
uprising in Moldavia, he appealed for Russian military help. His proclamation summoning Greeks to participate in "the fight for faith and motherland" had already alluded to the prospect of such tsarist aid: "Move, O
friends, and you will see a Mighty Empire defend our rights."[2] In his letter
of resignation from the Russian army, the Phanariot general implored the
tsar to protect Ypsilantis's family and relatives still in Russia, to allow Greeks
in Russian service to take part in the uprising, and above all to assume the
prestigious title "liberator of the Greeks" by driving the Turks from Europe. Ypsilantis's letter of resignation also pledged personal loyalty to the
tsar yet emphasized the former general's patriotic duty "to join my compatriots in the just cause of delivering my motherland." For Ypsilantis, this
revolt was not just a religious and nationalist endeavor but the fulfillment
of a vow to his dying father (1816) to emancipate their ancestral land.[3]

News of the Ypsilantis-led insurrection reached the tsar at the Laibach
Congress, where the European Concert was meeting to discuss the revolts
in Spain and Italy. Alexander I immediately condemned the outbreak in
Moldavia, convinced that it was inspired by a Paris-based conspiracy responsible for the disorders in Spain, Piedmont, and Naples. The tsar dismissed
Ypsilantis from Russian service, banned the latter's reentry into the country, and unequivocally rejected the call for help.[4] The Russian ruler also
condoned the sultan's military expedition to restore order in the Principalities.

The Ypsilantis venture was further doomed by the looting of the revolt's
irregular forces and by the absence of support from the predominantly
Romanian population, who resented Phanariot Greek rule as much as they
detested Ottoman imperial authority (Tudor Vladimirescu's social rebellion against Greek and Hellenized landholders, which occurred at the
same time as the Ypsilantis uprising, underscored the tension between Romanian and Greek aspirations). Defeated decisively by Ottoman troops in
June 1821, Ypsilantis fled to Transylvania, was arrested by Habsburg authorities, and remained in prison until his death in 1828. His ill-conceived and
ill-fated venture, however, ignited successful revolts in the Morea, the Archipelago, and mainland Greece, outbreaks collectively known as the
Greek War of Independence.[5]

Despite the Russian regime's disavowal of the Moldavian rising, the
Porte suspected Russian involvement because the uprising was launched

from southern Russia, Ypsilantis was a general in the Russian army, and Russian agents had traditionally incited Balkan Christians to rebel in conjunction with advancing tsarist forces. Additionally, Russia refused to extradite rebels who fled to Bessarabia, particularly the Moldavian *hospodar* and *etairist* Michail Soutsos. Thus, in response to Russia's perceived role in the crisis, the Porte breached treaties and created tensions that almost led to war. For example, despite Russian insistence that they leave, Ottoman forces occupied the Principalities after restoring order. More serious were the restrictions affecting Black Sea commerce. All ships in the Straits, in particular Greek vessels flying the Russian flag, were inspected by Ottoman officials to prevent arms and supply shipments to rebels. Because Greek piracy and defections from the Ottoman merchant fleet disrupted food deliveries to Constantinople and other Ottoman ports, the Porte closed the Sea of Marmora to all grain traffic, and Russian grain ships had to sell their cargoes to Ottoman warehouses. Black Sea grain exports plummeted by nearly 50 percent, shipping insurance rates soared, and Odessan trade firms lost a large share of their revenues.[6] The commercial slump jeopardized the continued development of Odessa and New Russia, thereby providing some members of the war party with an economic rationale for tsarist intervention.

Reprisals against the Orthodox church, in violation of the freedom-of-worship clause in Kutchuk-Kainardji, also aggravated Russo-Turkish relations. These reprisals occurred despite the encyclical of Ecumenical Patriarch Grigorios V that excommunicated Ypsilantis for his "wretched enterprise" transgressing Ottoman and divine law and for hastening "to bring common and general ruin on the whole nation." The encyclical further exhorted Orthodox Christians to remain loyal to the sultan and to sever ties with conspirators. To the Ottomans, however, the patriarch was still guilty of treason because he had failed to perform his basic duty as head of the Orthodox *millet,* namely, to ensure that his flock obeyed and submitted to Ottoman rule, and he was therefore executed. The patriarch's public hanging on Easter Sunday (10/22 April 1821), together with the execution of several other bishops, priests, and influential Phanariot Greeks, provoked random outrages against Greek life and property.[7] Armed Turkish crowds and janissaries, retaliating for the Greeks' harsh treatment of Turks in Moldavia and the Morea, roamed the streets of Constantinople and pillaged churches, shrines, shops, and homes. Similar outbreaks of sectarian violence erupted in Smyrna, Thessaloniki, Crete, and Cyprus, transforming the 1821 rebellion into a holy war between Eastern Orthodoxy and Islam.

Russia requested Ottoman rectification of these various treaty infractions. Diplomatic notes to the sultan continued to denounce the insurrection and yet urged restraint and moderation in restoring order. Russian pressure mounted, culminating in the ultimatum of 6/18 July 1821 that

demanded the Porte evacuate the Principalities, restore damaged Orthodox churches and property, distinguish between rebels and innocent subjects, and acknowledge Russian protection of Orthodox Christians in the
Ottoman Empire. If these terms were not accepted, Russia would be
obliged to offer asylum and assistance to all Christians subjected to "blind
fanaticism."[8] The sultan's failure to comply within the prescribed eight-day
period and the Russian embassy staff's return to St. Petersburg severed
diplomatic ties between the two realms. This step, however, was not followed by Russian military action to enforce compliance with treaty rights
as the tsar was reluctant to act unilaterally without the sanction of his European allies. Such sanction did not come because Austria and Britain were
intent on preserving the Ottoman Empire as a bulwark against Russian
expansion and on preventing a war that would further weaken Turkey.[9]
Although the tsar remonstrated for Orthodox brethren, he was firmly committed to the Concert of Europe and suspected that a Paris-Jacobin committee had instigated the revolt, and thus, Alexander I departed from traditional Eastern policy and Russian national interest in order to uphold his
vision of European order and Great Power harmony.

The tsar's dilemma over the Greek rising reflected broader counter currents in Alexandrine political culture, attributable in part to the tsar. Biog-
raphers and scholars of the reign have shown that Alexander I tried to
balance enlightened reform and militarism, a duality rooted in his up-
bringing. A liberal education in the humanitarian precepts of the Enlightenment, gained from the Swiss tutor F. C. La Harpe, clashed with the tsar's
rigid militaristic training under Count Aleksei A. Arakcheev, the Russian
ruler's future minister of war. While reform proposals competed with the
conservative status quo throughout the reign, Alexander I's fear of revolution proved stronger than his commitment to reform.

These contradictory strains of reform and reaction were embodied respectively in Kapodistrias and Karl V. Nessel'rode (1780–1862). Alexander
I retained ultimate say over foreign policy, yet he consulted advisers with
divergent perspectives in order to keep his options open. While Kapodistrias and Nessel'rode had a cordial working relationship and respected
each other as capable professional diplomats, they had deep-seated political differences. Kapodistrias favored constitutional government, gradual
reform, and national self-rule, while Nessel'rode regarded liberalism and
nationalism as disruptive forces against the European Concert. Nessel'rode
backed Austrian domination in the Italian peninsula and Russian control
in Poland as key aspects of the geopolitical balance in the Restoration era.
Throughout his long diplomatic career under Alexander I and Nicholas I,
he worked diligently to maintain the conservative alliance of Russia, Austria, and Prussia as a buttress against revolution. Toward the 1821 rebellion,
Nessel'rode echoed the Metternichean line that a Russo-Turkish clash

would disrupt the balance of power and provoke liberal aspirations in Europe. Although he distanced himself from Metternich's intrigues to embroil Kapodistrias in the Ypsilantis affair and to discredit the latter before the tsar, Nessel'rode opposed Russian intervention in the Greek War of Independence and sought Great Power mediation.[10]

Nessel'rode was not the only opponent to Russian action. The Greek crisis touched off debate and division in official circles about the proper tsarist response. For reasons relating to domestic and foreign affairs, an antiwar lobby emphasized the risks of intervention. This lobby argued against an aggressive policy, pointing to the state debt, lingering economic damage from the Napoleonic Wars, and the army's inadequate preparation and provisioning for war in 1821. Further, unrest among peasants and military colonists, as well as the mutiny in the elite Semenovskii Regiment, exacerbated fears of revolution at home and abroad. Intervention also promised to reopen the Eastern Question at a time when Alexander I sought to preserve the status quo in Europe and the Near East. As with Nessel'rode, many in the antiwar lobby believed that Greek emancipation would signify a victory for the national idea against the conservative hierarchy and would intensify the aspirations of Poles, Ukrainians, and other subject nations in eastern Europe. Any dismantling of the Ottoman Empire along ethnic lines thus posed a dangerous precedent for the fragmentation of the multinational Russian and Austrian Empires. These reasons for nonintervention were all the more compelling because they were shared by Alexander I. Under the growing impact of Metternich in 1820 and 1821, the tsar feared revolution more than Turkey as the chief menace to European order.

Russian scholars have identified a number of advisers besides Nessel'rode who counseled restraint and were thus part of the antiwar lobby.[11] One such was Minister of Finance Dmitrii A. Gur'ev. The precarious state of the imperial treasury would explain why Gur'ev belonged to this group. Another opponent of military intervention was the tsar's loyal servant and main domestic adviser General Arakcheev, the epitome of conservative reaction who defended the dreaded military colonies. Arakcheev had little impact on foreign affairs and had no strong allegiance to either Kapodistrias or Nessel'rode. His unwavering obedience to the tsar in virtually all matters and his rigid adherence to unreformed absolutism, however, explain his opposition to the Greek cause.

While the noninterventionists had the backing of the tsar, it was the war party that more faithfully reflected Russian public reaction. The Greek rising struck deep chords within the imperial court and the government. Drawn by religion, nationalism, and historical tradition, a disparate but vocal war lobby took shape among high officials, diplomats, and army officers. Some linked Greek deliverance to Russia's mission as protector of Balkan Christians and to the compatibility of Russian and Greek interests.

Others urged military action to uphold Russian prestige as a Great Power, to restore treaty rights, and to ensure the economic development of New Russia. To still others, the crisis beckoned as an opportunity to realize imperialist dreams, such as the Greek Project. Seen in this latter light, the war party represented an extension of the Potemkin-led expansionist group in Catherinian Russia. Above all, however, the appeals of the war lobby underscored the religious dimension of the struggle: persecuted Orthodox Christians must be defended in accord with traditional policy.

The war party's existence and clamor in St. Petersburg during the spring and summer of 1821 caught the attention of Western envoys. Their diplomatic correspondence, especially that of the French ambassador Pierre-Louis Laferronays, noted the divergent views of Kapodistrias and Nessel'-rode, the strident prowar mood in ruling circles and the public, and the apprehension felt by Western diplomats that an imminent Russo-Turkish clash would reignite the Eastern Question. War fever was no doubt kindled by Russian press reports of the Ypsilantis affair and of the ensuing revolts in the Morea, Archipelago, and Greek mainland. In line with Russia's awakening interest in classical antiquity, Greek victories at legendary battle sites, such as Salamis and Thermopylae, were compared to the feats of ancient heroes in the Persian War. More importantly for the proponents and opponents of tsarist action, reports on the crisis raised expectations and fears that Russia might intercede on the Greeks' behalf.[12]

The war lobby included a range of philhellenic attitudes that, while different in tone and motivation, agreed on the common goal of Russian-aided Greek emancipation. An extreme view was the apocalyptic message of Baroness Julie von Krüdener, the religious mystic who encouraged the tsar's belief that he was God's chosen instrument to redeem mankind. She envisioned a Christian crusade organized by Alexander I against the infidel that would lead to Greek liberation and to the broader objective of delivering the Christian East. The tsar would triumphantly raise the cross in Constantinople and Jerusalem, thus regenerating Christianity and paving the way for the reunification of Eastern and Western Christendom. Krüdener's messianic prophecy implied criticism of tsarist inaction and conjured up ambitious designs certain to fuel Great Power rivalry in the Near East. Her supplications to the tsar thus fell on deaf ears, and she was ordered to leave the capital.[13]

Krüdener's close friend and fellow pietist Prince Aleksandr N. Golitsyn did not share her religious enthusiasm for Russia's providential mission. Golitsyn, Minister of Religious Affairs and Public Education, concurred with the tsarist condemnation of Ypsilantis for violating his oath of allegiance to the Russian government. Yet Golitsyn acknowledged that Russian neutrality was inconsistent with traditional policy, stating, "For more than a century, Greeks received help and protection inspiring them with the hope of liberation from the Ottoman yoke, and even in the difficult position they now find themselves, this hope still inspires them." Another view emblematic of the war party was that of the military veteran and state patriot Count Mikhail A. Miloradovich, the military governor-general of St. Petersburg who was fatally shot in Senate Square during the Decembrist uprising. Miloradovich noted that Ypsilantis's incendiary proclamation might have appealed to the tsar had it emphasized religion, in particular the Greeks' justifiable expectation of protection from their *edinovertsy* (coreligionists).[14] A popular sentiment was also held by Grand Duchess Aleksandra Fedorovna, wife of Grand Duke and future tsar Nicholas I. Writing to her father King William III of Prussia in December 1821, the grand duchess objected to the European Concert's identification of Greek unrest with Spanish and Italian insurgency: "The cause of the Greeks cannot be compared to that of other revolts. It seems fine and just to me, and of a kind to fill the minds of all youth with enthusiasm."[15]

Foreign Secretary Kapodistrias's close relations with the tsar made him the most visible and influential spokesman of the war lobby. A Greek patriot who sought Greco-Russian cooperation, he was understandably torn between his sympathy for compatriots and his loyalty to Alexander I. The Moldavian revolt sharpened his already divided allegiances as a Greek nationalist serving autocracy in an age of conservative reaction.[16] His letter to Ypsilantis on 14/26 March 1821 from the Laibach Congress clearly conveyed official policy as he censured the uprising and warned that no military aid would be forthcoming. Revolution and war, Kapodistrias stated, were ineffective ways to advance Greek interests and would have dire repercussions. His private letter of the same day to Roksandra Sturdza-Edling echoed this tone, adding that only Ottoman reprisals would necessitate Russia's benevolent interference to protect coreligionists. Kapodistrias reiterated this stance in a private letter of 18/30 March to his friend and Foreign Ministry colleague Aleksandr Sturdza. There was also a sense of despair that Greek leaders had not heeded the foreign secretary's pre-1821 counsel of patience, providence, and moral enlightenment as the correct avenues of national regeneration. In the event of harsh retaliation and repression by the Ottoman government, Kapodistrias feared that all might be lost for the "unfortunate Greeks" and that only divine providence could save them.[17]

Ottoman persecution of Orthodox Christians and violations of treaty agreements, however, transformed Kapodistrias into an ardent hawk. The foreign secretary attempted to steer Alexandrine policy toward the war that he felt was imminent, convinced now that the sultan would interpret moderation and restraint as weakness. Kapodistrias drafted the ultimatum that led to the break in diplomatic relations, and his reports to the tsar and his private letters adamantly called for Ottoman observance of treaties and for guarantees safeguarding Greek Christians.[18] He forewarned that Russia's bid for a Great Power mandate to intervene would harden Turkish intransigence and do further damage to Russian interests. Rather, Russia had to act by occupying the Principalities, declaring war, and creating a protectorate over an autonomous Greece. Yet his various proposals did not shake the tsar from his allegiance to the Concert of Europe, and Alexander I continued to suspect a radical conspiracy in Europe, remarking to Kapodistrias in August 1821 that, "if we answer the Turks with war, the Paris directing committee will triumph and no government will remain standing. I do not intend to leave the field free for the enemies of order."[19]

Caught between his Greek patriotism and his personal loyalty to the tsar, Kapodistrias resigned in August 1822 and departed for western Europe. The import of his resignation was not lost on the conservative nationalist and court historian Nikolai M. Karamzin, who had known and corresponded with Kapodistrias. In letters of August and September 1822 to his archivist friend Aleksei F. Malinovskii, Karamzin lamented the political fate of "the amiable, intelligent Kapodistrias" and wrote that "Europe has buried the Greeks; God grant resurrection to the dead." Karamzin esteemed not only Kapodistrias but the Greek cause, praising Byron's philhellenism and disparaging the Turks in subsequent correspondence.[20]

Upon settling in Geneva, Kapodistrias worked with the Swiss banker-philanthropist Jean-Gabriel Eynard to galvanize European philhellenic committees. Both men were instrumental in raising humanitarian aid for insurgent Greece and for refugee Greek children who had arrived in western and central Europe in 1821. Kapodistrias also appealed to the diplomatic community, including Russia's former envoy to the Porte Grigorii A. Stroganov, to intercede on behalf of Greeks exiled to the remote parts of Asia Minor where, according to Kapodistrias, elders would probably perish and children would have to apostatize.[21]

Some years later, Kapodistrias made one last journey to St. Petersburg, shortly after his selection by the Troezene National Assembly as the first president of Greece. His brief stay (May–July 1827) to receive official confirmation of his resignation from tsarist service gave him an opportunity to solicit diplomatic and financial aid for embattled Greece still waging its liberation struggle. He corresponded with wealthy Odessan merchants, exhorting them to raise funds for compatriots enduring hunger and hardship. He made a special religious and patriotic appeal to Zois Zosimas and other Epirot traders in Moscow, who had sponsored Greek education in their native Ioannina. Their educational donations had earned two hundred thousand rubles in interest since 1821 when war forced the closure of Ioannina's schools. Kapodistrias wanted to use this amount for what he described as the primary task at hand, saving the nation and completing its liberation. The fate of these and all schools in Ottoman-ruled Greece, he asserted, depended on victory and national self-rule. The tsar and the merchant patrons endorsed Kapodistrias's petition, and the interest was transferred to his newly formed government through the Russian embassy in Paris.[22]

Another prominent member of the war party who strongly advocated intervention was Aleksandr Sturdza. As Foreign Secretary Kapodistrias's adviser on Danubian and Near Eastern affairs, Sturdza drafted reports that reinforced his compatriot's vocal stance in the spring and summer of 1821. A proponent of autocracy and a devout Orthodox Christian, Sturdza had a deserved reputation as a staunch conservative whose writings made him a respectable figure to reactionaries and a target of scorn for liberals. His social and political attitudes reflected the main tenets of European conservative philosophy, in particular a fear of revolution, a quest for order, and an emphasis on Christianity as the moral basis and cement of society.

A member of the Russian delegation at the Congress of Vienna, Sturdza revised and endorsed the tsar's proposal for the Holy Alliance. In several unpublished writings, Sturdza defended this effort to apply Christian precepts to Great Power diplomacy. Christian paternalism and fraternity, he stated, were the best means for Christian monarchs to reconcile their divergent interests and to wage war against impiety, radicalism, and liberalism.[23] Sturdza's very name symbolized reaction after his notorious essay on student unrest at German universities, *Mémoire sur l'état actual de l'Allemagne* (1818), prepared for the tsarist delegation to the Aachen Congress. In this essay, Sturdza denounces German universities as hotbeds of atheism and revolution that should be stripped of their traditional autonomy and placed under police control. He also presses tsarist authorities to restrict the autonomy of Russian universities, to limit the numbers of German professors, and to regulate the latters' courses.[24] When revolts broke out in Spain and Italy in 1820–21, Sturdza urged the Concert of Europe to restore legitimate monarchs through armed intervention. His reports to Kapodistrias vilified representative government, even constitutional monarchy, and disparaged Freemasons and *carbonari* (Italian liberal nationalists who instigated revolt in Naples and Piedmont) as conspirators against the established order. These latter two groups belonged to "corrosive associations," secret societies beyond state and church control that subverted social and political stability.[25]

The major exception to Sturdza's advocacy of Metternichean order was his espousal of Greek liberation, rooted in his Moldavian-Greek descent and his devout Orthodox faith. Like Kapodistrias, Sturdza believed that church-directed education and moral enlightenment were the safest means to effect national regeneration. As noted, Sturdza supported the educational goals of the *Philomousos Etaireia* and drafted the conservative proposal for a Greek-language press in Odessa. With the onset of revolt and Ottoman reprisals, Sturdza, however, sought to arouse the tsar's religious conscience by underscoring the plight of coreligionists facing annihilation. He also wanted unilateral action to rectify treaty abuses. Sturdza lobbied the tsar through Kapodistrias to defend Russian and Greek interests.

Sturdza's personal letter of 2/14 April 1821 to Kapodistrias vehemently disapproved of the tsarist declaration of neutrality. For the former, the Greek cause was a struggle between Islam and Christianity, and Turkish retaliation against innocent civilians called for immediate intervention to protect Orthodox Christians. Sturdza rejected the tsar's belief that the Ypsilantis affair was part of a Europeanwide revolutionary conspiracy directed from Paris. Further, for Sturdza, to equate the Greek issue with revolts in Spain and Italy was the same as placing Christian governments on an equal footing with the Porte. Whereas insurgents in Europe rebelled against their lawful rulers, seeking a multitude of liberties that would undermine the social and political order, the Greeks, in contrast, were tributaries rather than legal subjects of the sultan, connected to him by bondage and servitude instead of by religion or nationality. During four centuries of Ottoman rule, Greeks had the choice of slavery or apostasy. They revolted against an illegitimate monarch for "life, property, honor, and faith, which is more dear to them than all the rest." Sturdza protested that to associate their rising with rebellions in Europe was to dishonor the Greeks and compared their situation to the persecution and eventual triumph of early Christians, as well as to Russia's liberation from the Mongols.[26]

Sturdza amplified his views in a dispatch of 25 May/6 June 1821 to Foreign Secretary Nessel'rode. He again refuted the assumption that the Greeks rebelled against a legitimate monarch. Greek resistance, he claimed, was justifiable because the Greeks had never taken an oath of allegiance to their conquerors. Ottoman authorities had never guaranteed Greek life, faith, or property and had placed the Greeks under the direct jurisdiction not of Ottoman law courts but of Greek church leaders. Thus, since Orthodox Christians were not the legal subjects of the sultan, intervention on their behalf could not be interpreted as an action that encouraged sedition against legitimacy. Sturdza was on firmer ground arguing that Russia was obliged to interfere on the basis of historical tradition, common faith, and treaty infractions. Retaliation against the Greek church voided the declaration of neutrality, and Russia's continued adherence to this declaration made Russia "an accomplice in the fall of the church and in the extermination of an entire people." Sturdza warned that, if Russia neglected its duty to safeguard fellow Orthodox believers, the crisis would deepen, reprisals would escalate, more innocent civilians would be victimized, the Principalities would be ravaged by a lengthy occupation, and the Greek church would be "debased and submerged in blood." Russian neutrality would also strengthen Britain's naval position in the eastern Mediterranean, and British diplomatic support would embolden the sultan to crush the Greek resurgence. Sturdza maintained that action on behalf of

Orthodox brethren not only would be a victory for the common religion but also would deliver Russia from its traditional enemy to the South.[27]

An undated memorandum by Sturdza identified the mainsprings of the uprising, beginning with the general sense of indignation felt by most Greeks after four centuries of military occupation and political oppression. Educational advances channeled this anger toward the liberation of faith and fatherland, and only a spark was needed to ignite the surging tide of hostility. Although the ill-fated Ypsilantis uprising accelerated the emancipation drive, it was secondary to the essential reality that a revolt of some sort was bound to occur because of growing opposition to Ottoman rule. Sturdza thus emphasized that the Greek revival was engendered not by a conspiratorial Jacobin committee but by the Greeks' own national awakening.

The same memorandum also related Greek strengths in the war, accurately citing the leadership of military chieftains, the steadfast faith of the clergy, the rugged terrain of the Morea and mainland, and the naval prowess of sailors whose ships controlled the sea lanes. These assets, insufficient by themselves to ensure Greek victory, were supplemented by disarray in the Ottoman government. Sturdza wrote that "the cowardice and the apathy of sultans and *vizirs* are only matched by their ignorance and incompetence." Poor leadership explained the Empire's military, institutional, and economic decline and the consequent failure to defend its far-flung frontiers. If the Great Powers united to end Ottoman rule in the Balkans, the sultan would be unable to stem the challenge.[28]

Sturdza's thoughts in this particular report were echoed by the Russianized Pole Faddei V. Bulgarin (1789–1859), the writer and journalist who associated with future Decembrists before gaining notoriety as a reactionary publicist in the reign of Nicholas I. In a memorandum presented to Alexander I on 6/18 July 1821, Bulgarin, like Sturdza, argued for the popular, as opposed to the conspiratorial, nature of the Greek rising. Bulgarin called it a *narodnaia voina,* or popular war, an upsurge of the entire nation comparable to Dmitrii Donskoi's defeat of the Golden Horde and to Ivan IV's conquests of Kazan and Astrakhan. He presented in greater detail than Sturdza the Greek advantages in the current war. While superior in numbers and training, the Ottoman army was unable to attack Greek forces in mountain passes. The Greek fleet numbered over five hundred vessels of various sizes and shapes, patrolling the coastline and cutting off enemy troops from supplies and reinforcements via the sea. Greek merchant capital purchased arms and provisions, while numerous European officers volunteered their services "to liberate classical lands, the cradle of enlightenment, the fatherland of Homer, Socrates, Leonidas, and like men who have honored humanity." The Greeks' most precious asset, Bulgarin asserted, was their "heroic spirit" in this "just and humanitarian cause." Whereas the *carbonari* had dispersed after their initial setback, the Greeks were enduring torture and death, drawing strength from their religious fervor, their sense of honor, and their patriotism: "The destruction and the outrage of churches, bishops, and the patriarch in Constantinople have inflamed the spirit of revenge in Greek hearts, which are already kindled by love for the fatherland."[29]

When Sturdza traveled to western Europe, accompanying his wife who sought treatment at the waters, he remained a tribune of the Greek cause. His essay *La Grèce en 1821 et 1822*, published in Leipzig in 1822, consists of a dialogue between an advocate and an opponent of Greek liberation. The latter vilifies the Greeks from the perspective of the Metternichean order, linking their endeavor to outbreaks against legitimacy. The advocate, voicing Sturdza's own views, defends the Greeks as Christians fighting to deliver their faith and fatherland. The dialogue mentions the significant military and political events in Greece during the first two years of the war, as well as the nonintervention of the Great Powers. Sturdza again stated that the struggle was religiously inspired, distinguishing it from European rebellions rooted in the secular principles of the French Revolution. The Christian world, he argued, had a moral and religious duty to assist the Greeks who had retained their faith despite centuries of Islamic rule.[30]

In correspondence from Paris and Ems with his sister Roksandra Sturdza-Edling, Sturdza often referred to the Greek war and to the efforts of Western philhellenic committees to raise humanitarian aid.[31] He was particularly moved by the tragic fate of Missolonghi, the stronghold guarding the Gulf of Corinth that was besieged by Ibrahim Pasha's French-trained Egyptian army. Before the town's fall in April 1826, Sturdza and the Swiss philanthropist Jean-Gabriel Eynard collected money and supplies for its heroic defenders who were on the verge of starvation. Sturdza's appeal, written in Paris in March 1826, exhorted "generous souls" to contribute to the relief aid campaign: "This handful of Christians stood firm in their fortress, never fearing the enemy and enduring all the perils of the siege. But they fear the onset of famine, which has already begun taking its toll. Charitable souls, we implore you to contribute to the well-being of your brothers. Help them to defend their homes, graves, and altars." Sturdza and his wife donated three thousand francs, and several anonymous contributors gave fifteen hundred francs.[32] Sturdza and Kapodistrias, the two prominent spokesmen of the war party, turned increasingly to humanitarian work for their compatriots when their efforts to alter tsarist official policy did not succeed in 1821–22. As will be seen, both were instrumental in organizing and supporting Greek relief projects in Russia.

Sturdza and Kapodistrias were not the only representatives of the Foreign Ministry who advocated war. The envoy to the Porte Grigorii A. Stroganov (1770–1857) conveyed the official reaction to the Ypsilantis affair and reaffirmed existing agreements. In line with neutrality, Stroganov instructed Near Eastern consuls to check the documents of vessels flying the Russian flag and to stop the transport of arms, supplies, and food to rebels. At the same time, he remonstrated on behalf of persecuted Christians. The execution of the ecumenical patriarch and Ottoman restrictions against commerce prompted Stroganov's defense of Orthodox Christians and Russian treaty rights. The envoy urged the Porte to treat innocent subjects with justice and mercy, he protested reprisals in Moldavia and Wallachia, and he sent Nessel'rode strongly worded dispatches on Turkish abuses of diplomatic agreements. When Stroganov received Kapodistrias's ultimatum for delivery to the Porte, he was cautioned by Nessel'rode to soften its terms if he saw fit. Instead, the Russian envoy insisted on full compliance within the prescribed eight-day time period, and his departure in late July 1821 formalized the break in diplomatic relations.[33] Stroganov then joined the hawks in St. Petersburg who called for strong measures to counter Ottoman policy. When the new tsar, Nicholas I, sought Stroganov's advice on the Eastern Question, the latter recommended European action to aid the Greeks, a fellow Christian nation. Stroganov's letter of 18/30 January 1826 counseled Nicholas I that, if a collective European effort did not materialize, Russia must pursue "a national and religious policy" consonant with its own concerns. Thus, declaring war and sending troops to the Principalities would "emancipate from Ottoman oppression Christian peoples who would then become Russia's natural allies."[34]

Stroganov's grecophile views were shared by his secretary at the embassy, Sergei I. Turgenev (1790–1827). After returning to St. Petersburg in 1821, Turgenev wrote a personal memoir about the rebellion and its ramifications for Russian policy. Based on personal observations and recollections, as well as on official documents, Turgenev's account described the deterioration in Russo-Ottoman relations and the growing hostility between Greek and Turkish communities. Sympathetic to the Greek cause, Turgenev anticipated a conflict that would protect Russian and Greek interests, with tsarist defense of Orthodox Christians and treaty rights resulting in a Russian protectorate over an autonomous or independent Greece. Turgenev justified the rebellion, claiming that education and learning were insufficient by themselves to regenerate the Greek nation. Political liberation from Turkish rule was necessary. Critical of Ypsilantis's inept leadership, Turgenev accurately attributed Greek success in the Morea and Archipelago to Greek command of the sea, Ali Pasha's resistance to Ottoman troops in Epirus, and Greek outrage provoked by Turkish persecution. The public execution of the patriarch on Easter Sunday, Turgenev affirmed, sanctified the uprising and reinforced Greek religious and patriotic zeal.[35]

Consular officials in the Near East, some of them agents or actual members of the *Philiki Etaireia,* felt the direct impact of Russo-Ottoman tension. Ioannis Vlasopulos, consul general in Patras, reported to Stroganov on the unrest in the Peloponnese. One of the consul general's dispatches contained a petition for Russian protection drafted by Greek Orthodox clerics in the Morea, exemplifying the numerous Greek entreaties for Russian aid in 1821.[36] Another consul general, Spyridon Destunis in Smyrna, found himself in an extremely volatile situation. His personal diary vividly chronicled the alarm, panic, and fear which gripped Smyrna's sizable Greek community in the spring and summer of 1821. Destunis's concrete images captured the breakdown of law and order, the retribution against unarmed Christians, and the Greek flight to find shelter on ships anchored in the harbor. Dislocation of trade and chronic food shortages exacerbated communal tension and sectarian violence, triggering reciprocal outrages that for contemporary observers transformed the Greek struggle into a religious war.[37]

Destunis vented his anger toward European diplomatic officials in Smyrna and Constantinople. He claimed that these officials were largely indifferent to the plight of fellow Christians, supportive of the Porte, and suspicious of Russian machination in the Greek affair. He was particularly incensed with the British for spreading "absurd rumors" that Russia instigated the revolt, describing these fabrications as part of Britain's scheme to damage Russo-Ottoman relations and to make the Porte more dependent on British naval and diplomatic support. The consul general's diary entry on 20 July/1 August 1821 expressed bitterness and scorn, reviling the Franks for their hatred "of the Orthodox faith, powerful Russia, and defenseless Greeks." Envy consumed Westerners "who wish that Russia would perish and that the Greek people would be eliminated from the face of the earth. But God will not permit that, and the unfortunate Greeks, after centuries of political death, will arise and be loyal to Russia. And you, Franks, whether you be French, English, German, or Italian . . . , you must and will come to see that God is with us."[38]

Destunis closely followed the Greek war from Venice, where he and his family lived for five years after they fled Smyrna in late July 1821. Several of his manuscripts concurred with the views of the war party. A writing entitled "Defense of the Contemporary Greeks" (1823) evoked Sturdza's conservative philhellenism by sharply distinguishing the Hellenic rising from liberal and nationalist unrest in Europe. The Greeks were Christians fighting slavery and despotism imposed upon them by infidels, in contrast to the Jacobin-inspired *carbonari* who revolted against Christian monarchs. Destunis cast doubt on the legitimacy of the Ottoman government, noting its "degenerate and barbaric" control of European Christian territories. The Greeks, he argued, rebelled not against the order of legitimacy but with the goal of joining the European Christian family of states. Monarchical rule in liberated Greece would facilitate this political integration as absolutism represented the most stable and enlightened form of government since the age of Louis XIV.[39] Destunis's diaries from Venice also made frequent reference to the Greek issue. An undated entry from early 1826 observed that Russian caution would pave the way for British influence in the Balkans, while tsarist pressure would strengthen Russian interests and prevent British control of any Greek state that might emerge from the war. Destunis also envisioned that a future Greek kingdom would seek to extend its frontiers in order to liberate compatriots still ruled by the sultan.[40]

Staying abreast of naval and military campaigns, Destunis was moved by the fall of Missolonghi (April 1826). The defenders of the town, according to his diary entry of 5/17 May 1826, were martyrs whose fate touched all Christian believers. Yet the demise of the fortress had occurred "before the eyes of civilized Europe, at a time when a holy alliance [set up by Great Powers in 1815]" promised peace and brotherhood to most Christian nations, except Greece. Greece's "sacred soil" was instead shrouded in "a funeral veil," and visitors to Missolonghi would only hear "the silence of the tombs." Destunis's reflections on Missolonghi's fate prompted antipathy toward the Turks, and he disparaged Turkish "fanaticism, ignorance, and fatalism." He portrayed a declining Ottoman Empire with despotic central government, unruly local governors, and an absence of guarantees for subjects' life, faith, and property. Destunis highlighted this last point by mentioning reprisals against Christians in Cyprus, Asia Minor, and other areas not directly involved in the Greek rebellion.[41]

Additional Russian officials pressed for action in 1821. Envoys in London (Khristofor A. Lieven), Vienna (Iurii A. Golovkin), and Paris (Karl O. Pozzo di Borgo) adhered faithfully to tsarist policy in their dealings with European diplomats, yet their correspondence with Nessel'rode and Kapodistrias advocated measures to counter treaty violations. Pozzo di Borgo drafted a memorandum in July 1821 reminiscent of the Greek Project, proposing that Russia drive the Turks from Europe, transform Constantinople into a Russian-protected free city, and restructure the Balkans into a Macedonian Kingdom governed by a member of the imperial family. Dynastic, religious, and trade ties would connect this new configuration to its Russian ally.[42]

The correspondence between the St. Petersburg postal director Konstantin Ia. Bulgakov and his brother Aleksandr Ia. Bulgakov, an official in the Moscow College of Foreign Affairs, often mentioned the Greek crisis and rumors of Russian action. Aleksandr's letter of 15/27 March 1821 noted that local Greeks gathered in Moscow's coffee houses and heatedly discussed news of the Danubian unrest. Aleksandr called the revolt "a sacred cause, an outburst by an entire oppressed nation," and captured the mood of many philhellenes when he wrote, "It is shameful that in our enlightened century, barbarians in Europe and oppressors of our coreligionists and friends have been tolerated." Both brothers had been born in Constantinople, the illegitimate offspring of Catherine II's envoy Iakov I. Bulgakov, thus explaining Aleksandr's expressed desire "to serve and to free my native land, Tsargrad." The letter closed by speculating on tsarist policy: "What will our court say of this? Is it possible we will allow the unfortunate Greeks to be sacrificed . . . ? I am eager to see how this affair will end, but I pray to God for the Greeks."[43]

Along with advocates from the Foreign Ministry and the state bureaucracy, the war party drew support from the army. When Alexander I condemned the Ypsilantis rising, he ordered General Petr Kh. Wittgenstein, chief commander of the Second Army based in the Ukraine, to observe strict neutrality, to monitor the situation in the Principalities, and to safeguard the border of Russian Bessarabia. The general, however, was further instructed to permit safe passage to refugees fleeing danger and disorder. Wittgenstein fulfilled these orders, as evinced in the detailed reports on Danubian events located in the Second Army's archival files. Some of the information came from letters and memoranda sent by consuls in Jassy (Andrei N. Pizani) and Bucharest (Aleksandr A. Pini).[44] The correspondence of numerous Second Army officers shows that they questioned official policy and sympathized with the Greeks. The officers' proximity to the unrest and their expectation of war made them hopeful that Russia would intervene in the Greek struggle.

General Ivan V. Sabaneev (1772–1829) of the Tiraspol-based Sixth Corps shared the mood of the war lobby. His letter of 22 February/6 March 1821 to General Pavel D. Kiselev (1788–1872), chief of Second Army Staff Headquarters in Tulchin, praised Ypsilantis for endeavoring to emancipate the latter's fatherland. The uprising signified that "the Greeks, until now scorned, appear to be worthy descendants of Aristides, Themistocles . . . and others." As for Russian policy, Sabaneev wrote that "it is impossible to think we can remain spectators. . . . One move from our side would suffice for their salvation." This attitude was shared by Aleksandr Ia. Rudzevich (1776–1829), commander of the Kherson-based Seventh Corps. His letter of 2/14 March 1821 to General Kiselev remarked that, since the Greeks revolted against "a barbarous yoke which they have borne for so long, this era will be the most noteworthy in our life." A subsequent letter of 13/25 March to Kiselev raised the religious aspect, asking "Will we help our coreligionists? It is time, indeed high time, that we take to arms to participate in the restoration of a Greek kingdom." Rudzevich reacted sharply to news of Ottoman reprisals, stating in his 12/24 May letter to Kiselev: "The cruelty and barbarism of the Turks, extending to our coreligionists, remains without any impact on the European Powers. It is time to crush these barbarians and to drive them from Europe, thus delivering the Greeks from the yoke they have endured for more than three hundred and fifty years."[45]

General Kiselev, Nicholas I's future Minister of State Domains who introduced measures to help the state peasantry, also criticized Alexandrine policy. He feared that restraint would damage Russian influence in the

Balkans, the Black Sea trade, and the economic development of Novoros-siia. His reports to the government conveyed merchant and gentry complaints about slumping trade revenues and falling grain prices, due largely to Ottoman commercial restrictions.[46] Kiselev contended that religion alone necessitated a vigorous response as the Greek war was a struggle between Islam and Christianity in which Russia was obliged to defend Orthodox coreligionists.

Kiselev expressed his initial reaction to the Ypsilantis outbreak in his letter of 14/26 March 1821 to General Arsenii A. Zakrevskii (1783–1865), the state patriot and reactionary who headed the General Staff, pointing out that this affair "is no joke, much blood has been shed. . . . Ypsilantis, in crossing the border, has left his name to posterity. Greeks reading his proclamation have rushed with joy to his banner. God help him in this sacred cause, and Russia, too, I might add." Another letter (4/16 April) to Zakrevskii relayed news of atrocities against Greek Christians. Eight days later, on 12/24 April, Kiselev again wrote to Zakrevskii and underlined the religious aspect of the conflict: "It is necessary to live here to realize how the Turkish government humiliates its subjects and how legal this so-called revolt of the Greeks actually is. We judge events as private persons, while governments judge them otherwise and perhaps more in line with government interests. Yet all the same, the lot of our coreligionists is worthy of pity, and as a human being I sincerely pity them."[47] Further insight can be gleaned from a letter Kiselev received from General Aleksei P. Ermolov, commander-in-chief in the Caucasus and an 1812 war hero. Writing on 30 March/11 April 1821, Ermolov showed that he shared Kiselev's philhellenic attitude: "Resurrected Greece gives you a worthy preoccupation. I saw from the letter to Zakrevskii that events inflame the heart of a hero who desires to rush to the aid of a renowned land. I will be sorry, together with you, if the flame of the Greeks is extinguished by their own blood. God grant them success."[48]

Escalating Russo-Turkish tension over treaty infractions stirred war fever among the generals in New Russia. Kiselev, Ermolov, and Zakrevskii expected a declaration of war, and their correspondence expressed impatience with the tsar's reluctance to uphold Russian prestige as a Great Power. Kiselev wrote to Zakrevskii on 5/17 June 1821 that "without bayonets nothing will be settled. The Turks commit many improprieties against us." Another letter (18/30 June 1821) to Zakrevskii vilified the Turks: "The Turks act toward us as though we are subject Tatars. . . . [I]t would be shameful to permit barbarians to disturb the boundaries of a great, powerful government. By all accounts, the barbarians are ready for anything, especially for pillage." Subsequent correspondence with Zakrevskii and Ermolov reinforced Kiselev's anticipation of war in the summer of 1821, and Kiselev and Zakrevskii actively prepared for the conflict after the break in Russo-Turkish diplomatic ties, both being concerned that Russian troops in the Principalities would have difficulty finding enough provisions after the pillaging by the Ottoman army.[49]

Government authorities and the Greek communities in southern Russia fully shared the expectations of Second Army officers. By virtue of their indirect aid to the Greek national movement before and after the Ypsilantis uprising, the two highest officials in New Russia must be considered part of the war party. The French emigré Count Aleksandr F. Langeron (1763–1831), governor-general of Novorossiia and city chief of Odessa, contributed to that port's urban and commercial growth with his enlightened administration. General Ivan N. Inzov (1768–1845), *Namestnik* (vicegerent) of Bessarabia, stimulated agrarian development and supervised foreign settlement in the region.[50] When insurrection erupted in the Principalities, both were ordered by the central government to explain what they knew about the *Philiki Etaireia* that had hatched the unrest and why they had not suspected Ypsilantis. Their benign neglect of insurgent activity reinforced Greek illusions, not to mention Ottoman suspicions, that the tsarist regime endorsed the secret society and the revolt.

In his dispatch of 24 April/6 May 1821 to Foreign Secretary Nessel'rode, Langeron disclosed his awareness of the *Etaireia* and its goal to emancipate Greece. The governor-general maintained, however, that he had never thought the society posed a danger to Russia because, to his knowledge, it had no contact with revolutionary organizations in the West. Most of the Odessan *etairists,* he asserted, were loyal subjects of the tsar and respected members of the Greek community. Langeron acknowledged that Ypsilantis had often mentioned his hope of liberating ancient Greece, but the governor-general had not suspected the Phanariot general of conspiratorial designs during the latter's 1820 visit to Odessa. Langeron affirmed that he had issued passports to Greeks who were Ottoman subjects, largely because they claimed that they had commerce-related business in Moldavia and he had not wanted to disrupt Russo-Ottoman trade.[51] Inzov followed Langeron's lead in his dispatch of 28 April/10 May to Kapodistrias, stating that Ypsilantis had led a quiet life while visiting his mother in Kishinev and had given no indication of revolutionary intrigue. Inzov had approved Ypsilantis's request for a passport to visit the waters near Laibach, with transit through Moldavia where the Phanariot general claimed that he had family business. With many Greeks in Bessarabia seeking to join insurgents across the border, however, Inzov had already notified Langeron on 9/21 April to prevent Greek travel from Odessa.[52]

It is implausible that Langeron and Inzov, two capable state servants, did not know more about the *Philiki Etaireia* than they publicly revealed, particularly in light of the organization's preparations during the months before the uprising. The secret society recruited members in Odessa, Kishinev, Izmail, and other Greek centers; solicited merchant donations; stockpiled arms and supplies in Bessarabia; and distributed Greek and Russian circulars announcing the upcoming struggle. Despite Langeron's observation that the society was not linked to revolutionary groups in western Europe and thus posed no threat to Russia, he and Inzov were aware that Greek insurgency ran counter to Alexander I's defense of legitimacy. Their tolerance or neglect of the *Etaireia* may have resulted from their supposition that Russia supported Greek liberation, in line with its traditional protection of Orthodox Christians. Ypsilantis's generalship in the Russian army and his position as aide-de-camp may also have persuaded Inzov and Langeron that the regime endorsed the secret society's plans.[53] That both officials probably expected war in the wake of the Ypsilantis venture is suggested by their responses to Greek nationalist ferment.

News of the Moldavian uprising galvanized Greeks in Moscow, St. Petersburg, Odessa, Taganrog, Kishinev, and other towns. These Russian-based Greeks organized volunteer units, sent arms and supplies to insurgents, and echoed the call of Russian hawks for intervention.[54] The Taganrog merchant Ioannis Varvakis donated one hundred thousand rubles to purchase weapons and to hire Western philhellenic officers. Another Taganrog trader, Iakov Vulgaris, sold his family diamonds and raised forty thousand rubles for arms, provisions, and volunteers. The Odessan merchant Dimitrios Inglezis collected donations from Greek compatriots, aid that Ypsilantis acknowledged in his letter of 11/23 March 1821 that praised Inglezis as "a benefactor of the fatherland and the *genos* [nation]."[55] Kiselev, in his letter of 14/26 March to Zakrevskii, noted the ardent patriotism of Odessan Greeks: "They are captivated by the hope of freedom and salvation. Old and young, rich and poor, healthy and ill, all depart for abroad and make sacrifices for the fatherland." The recollections of the poet and writer Aleksandr F. Vel'tman (1800–1870), who served as a military topographer in Bessarabia, captured the mood of Greek excitement: "In Kishinev, at every step there was animated discussion about the Greek affair. News spread like an electric current through the Greek community."[56] Other eyewitness accounts, including that of the exiled Pushkin, commented on the upsurge in Hellenic national feeling.

While the Greek communities in Russia mobilized, Langeron and Inzov had explicit instructions to comply with neutrality. The two officials were ordered to tighten border controls, to stop issuing passports, and to prevent shipments of arms and provisions. These measures, however, did not dampen Greek patriotism or war fever. Langeron noted in his dispatch of 24 April/6 May 1821 to Nessel'rode that local Greeks were surprised by Russian policy yet still anticipated intervention. The governor-general subsequently reported on 14/26 May that Greeks continued to mobilize support for the liberation struggle, despite his compliance with government orders.[57] The Greeks were agitated by the fate of their compatriots and by their own commercial reverses, and Greek participation in Odessa's municipal government, in particular the city council, the port authority, and the quarantine board, diluted attempts to tighten customs and quarantine controls. Merchant vessels sailed with arms and volunteers, which violated tsarist policy, confirmed Ottoman suspicion, and kindled expectation of a Russo-Turkish conflict. That Langeron believed war was likely is evinced by his August 1821 proposal to the Main Staff of the military administration in which he urged Greek auxiliaries to cooperate with Russian forces.[58] A special battalion of Odessan Greeks would join the Russian army in the Balkans, while Hydriot ships would help the tsarist fleet in the Mediterranean. The project, although not approved by the central government, evoked the traditional partnership of Greek national hopes and Russian imperial strategy in the Near East.

Langeron continued to permit Greek patriotic activity in Odessa. In September 1821, he endorsed the newly formed Greek Philanthropic Society, administered by former members of the *Philiki Etaireia*'s Odessan branch.[59] The new society's ostensible purpose was humanitarian aid for rebels and noncombatants who fled to Russia. While it did indeed collect and distribute relief, the Philanthropic Society also used some donations to buy arms and supplies. It even planned to send emissaries to Western capitals to solicit philhellenic support. The Philanthropic Society was banned by the tsar in December 1821. As Nessel'rode indicated to Langeron in his note of 16/28 December, Alexander I rejected the organization because the tsar feared that its stated humanitarian mission was only a screen for conspiratorial designs. Chided for approving the society after his failure to suspect the radical intent of the *Philiki Etaireia*, Langeron was ordered to dissolve the Philanthropic Society. Henceforth the society's humanitarian aim would be fulfilled by the Greek relief drives established by the Russian regime. Langeron complied with his instructions, but his return dispatch (31 December/12 January) to Nessel'rode defended his previous position. He again stated his opposition to underground political networks and his genuine belief that the Philanthropic Society was a charitable endeavor. The governor-general specifically noted the society's help to several hundred Greek sailors and needy families during its short existence.[60]

As noted, the Greek cause won the sympathy of such diverse proponents of autocracy as the religious mystic Krüdener, the conservative nationalist Karamzin, the political reactionary Sturdza, and numerous officials and officers in high places. The variegated war lobby found additional support among liberals, as philhellenism intersected with the main political and ideological cleavages in Alexandrine society. The liberal intelligentsia consisted primarily of well-educated and reform-spirited aristocratic officers imbued with patriotism, liberalism, and constitutionalism. Expecting political and social reform after the victory over Napoleon, they deeply resented the regime's reactionary turn, in particular the military colonies, the obscurantism in educational policy, the tsar's growing mysticism, and the Russian ruler's cooperation with Austria and Prussia in crushing liberal stirrings.

Disillusionment prompted the formation of underground societies—the Union of Salvation (1816–18), the Union of Welfare (1818–25), and the Northern and Southern Societies (1821–25)—that discussed constitutional government, rule of law, and abolition of serfdom. Political and social ferment culminated in the unsuccessful revolt against the government in St. Petersburg in December 1825.[61]

The Decembrist-Greek connection had social and political disparities. Russian liberals were educated according to the precepts of the French and German Enlightenment, and many were officers in elite guards regiments. Although the Northern Society espoused a constitutional monarchy and the more radical Southern Society a democratic republic, this fissure did not detract from the members' common vision of a transformed constitutional Russia. Greek *etairists* and rebels represented a broader cross section of Greek society, encompassing a majority with less prestigious social roots and educational credentials than the Decembrists. The divergent Greek political goals ranged from a restored Byzantium, an independent nation-state, to local autonomy for select regions. These divisions, as noted, led to civil strife and factionalism in Greek politics during the 1820s and after. Despite the social and political differences between Greek insurgents and Russian constitutionalists, however, Decembrist activists and their sympathizers strongly advocated Greek liberation.[62]

Decembrist secret societies were part of the general liberal ferment in Europe and were partially modeled on conspiratorial groups like the *Philiki Etaireia*. The Hellenic resurgence contributed to the Russian liberal awakening, as did the revolts in Spain and Italy. Future Decembrists regarded Greek fighters as fellow rebels against the status quo and the Greek struggle as another link in the chain of European protests against the Metternichean order. Philhellenism thus became an extension of the Decembrists' constitutionalism and liberalism. The Greek revolution symbolized the liberals' own battle against arbitrary despotism and for representative government and national regeneration. Russian neutrality exacerbated the ideological polarization between proponents and opponents of change, specifically those opponents, such as Nessel'rode and Arakcheev, who rejected intervention. The tsar's reaction to the Eastern crisis was another reason for criticizing government policy. Liberals hoped that successful Greek emancipation would strengthen their cause everywhere, thus accelerating Russia's social and political transformation. Some Decembrists also played upon the regime's worst fear. They wanted the crisis to provoke a Russo-Turkish clash that would fuel Great Power rivalry and disturb the balance of power. The demise of the Concert of Europe would then facilitate the success of liberal and national movements. While the tsar dreaded the Greek affair as a strike against the ruling order, Decembrists backed the Greek cause precisely because they hoped it would upset the status quo and incite rebellion elsewhere.

The Decembrists' philhellenism was also rooted in their state patriotism and national consciousness. Like many nineteenth-century liberal nationalists, especially in eastern and central Europe, the Decembrist liberals were ardent nationalists for whom liberal political ideology and national expansion were the chief means to build a viable nation-state. Many Decembrists zealously studied the Russian historical past, seeking inspiration in the free republics of Pskov and Novgorod and in Moscow's deliverance from the Mongols. Along with liberalism, their mission to renew Russia was grounded in their perception of historical tradition, including religious and cultural ties to the Orthodox East. The Greeks were not just rebels but fellow Orthodox Christians who were traditional allies against the Turk and whose liberation under Russian auspices would benefit state interest. Liberal philhellenes thus found common cause with their archnemesis Sturdza and with other opponents of reform who were sympathetic to the Greek struggle. Liberal and conservative voices of the war party advocated intervention that would fulfill Greek hopes, uphold the religious protectorship of Russia, and extend its strategic position in the Balkans. The philhellenism of the Decembrists represented an extension of both their liberal ideology and their sense of nationalism.

The liberals echoed the war lobby view that neutrality was inconsistent with Russian national interest. Aleksandr V. Podzhio (1798–1873), a member of the Northern and Southern Societies, favored war to halt the decline in Black Sea commerce and to maintain Russian influence among Balkan Christians, whose hopes for liberation had traditionally hinged on Russian aid. The religious theme was underlined by Vladimir I. Shteingel' (1783–1862), a member of the Northern Society. Shteingel' recollected that "events in Spain, Piedmont, and Greece inflamed minds about freedom in Russia. Yet the Greeks were left to their fate, and the bond of common religion, which had existed inviolably for eight centuries and was always feared by the Porte . . . , was suddenly destroyed." A similar note was struck by Aleksandr M. Murav'ev, the Decembrist sympathizer whose brother Nikolai headed the Northern Society: the tsar, "in contrast to the sentiments of Russians, remained deaf to the wails and misfortunes of the Eastern church and was an indifferent spectator to the cruelties inflicted by Muslim fanaticism against our coreligionists."[63]

Liberals were incensed by the Great Power decision at the Verona Congress (September 1822) to sanction French intervention in Spain and to ignore fellow Christians fighting Muslim Turks. Mikhail A. Fonvizin (1788–1854), commander of the Thirty-Seventh Hussar Regiment and a founding member of the Northern Society, was dismayed by the Concert's "incomprehensible and humiliating logic" that classified the Greeks with Spanish and Italian insurgents. He contended that the Greek struggle was part of the broader historical process of nation-state building in Europe:

Russia freed itself from Tatar enslavement. At the same time, the Swedes delivered themselves from the Danish yoke, and the Spanish freed themselves from the Moors and recently from the French. All this, without dispute and with rejoicing, was accepted in Europe, but the Greeks are not allowed to deliver themselves from the Turkish yoke, under which they have suffered for several centuries. I say "not allowed" because the right of Greeks to emancipation is rejected by the Verona Congress, which recognizes them as insurgents and rebels.

If war broke out over the Greek issue, Fonvizin continued, "the Holy Alliance would swiftly recognize the legality of the Greeks' right to fight for the independence of their fatherland [nezavisimost' svoego otechestva]." For now, "the Holy Christian Alliance abandons Christians perishing under the sword of barbarians, is unconcerned with their misfortune, and will assist them only when favorable political circumstances permit. This is not the time, while later may well be too late to save the Greeks."[64] Fonvizin used "Holy Christian Alliance" in a pejorative sense, as did most European liberals. The Holy Alliance symbolized the revival of divine right absolutism so as to stifle reform and the diplomatic and military alliance of the three conservative east European monarchies of Austria, Russia, and Prussia.

Another piece of Fonvizin writing accurately depicted the divergent stances of the European Concert and philhellenes: "Many friends of humanity impatiently awaited the Greek revolt. Catherine II had ardently desired it, and today many noble-minded Europeans help the unfortunate Greeks by word and deed. . . . Yet the alliance has rendered them to the arbitrary will of fate." Fonvizin's essay on Russian public opinion noted that educated society was generally indignant with the government's reactionary policy in foreign affairs, citing as an example the tsar's "inhumane indifference to suffering coreligionists and Hellenes who had the right to expect from him not only sympathy but active help, all the more because from time past Russia has aroused the Greeks against their oppressors and has promised them independence."[65]

The Decembrist conspirator Petr G. Kakhovskii (1796–1826), executed for fatally shooting Governor-General Miloradovich in Senate Square, defended the Greek cause in his letter to Nicholas I written from prison. Like Fonvizin, he disparaged the Concert of European Christian states for its indifference to the plight of Greek Christians, noting that "Our coreligionist Greeks [edinovernye nam greki], several times rising against Muslim tyranny, drown in blood. An entire nation is being exterminated," while the Great Powers seemed indifferent "to the destruction of mankind." Kakhovskii compared Greek national hopes to the aspirations of other oppressed nations and predicted the eventual triumph of liberty over despotism: "A single feeling enlivens all peoples in Europe and however much it is persecuted, it is impossible to destroy it: compressed gunpowder acts all the more powerfully! As long as there are people, there will also be the desire for freedom."[66] Kakhovskii's testimony to the Commission of Inquiry that investigated the Decembrist conspiracy shed light on the formative factors stimulating liberal activism, especially the dual inspiration of classical civilization and contemporary rebellion: "Ideas develop with age. I cannot say precisely when my ideas were formed. Having studied Greek and Roman history from childhood, I was inflamed by ancient heroes. The recent revolutions in the political structure of Europe also influenced me profoundly."[67] Classical antiquity for many Decembrists symbolized moral idealism, civic liberty, and representative government, the very goals they sought to achieve in Russia.

Greek liberation loomed large in the thoughts and plans of another executed Decembrist, Pavel I. Pestel' (1793–1826), founder of the radical Southern Society.[68] He espoused the overthrow of autocracy and the formation of a temporary dictatorship that would lay the groundwork for a republic. A lieutenant-colonel in the Second Army and an aide-de-camp to its chief commander, General Wittgenstein, Pestel' was one of several Kishinev-based reformist officers who had met Ypsilantis and who had knowledge of the *Philiki Etaireia*. When the rising occurred, Pestel' was assigned to report on the Danubian unrest. His dispatches and letters to General Kiselev from February to June 1821, although they frequently exaggerated or misread the Ypsilantis affair, registered support for the Greek endeavor. His letter of 3/15 March affirmed that the Ypsilantis outbreak had no connection with the *carbonari* and was "worthy of the highest respect." The movement was "united in brotherhood with a common political goal," which Pestel' identified in a report of 15/27 April as the creation of "a federal republic resembling the United States of America."[69]

Ottoman persecution of rebellious and innocent subjects alike convinced Pestel' that Russia had to intervene to help the Greeks and to guard state interests. His letter to Kiselev on 25 May/6 June asserted that "the eyes and the expectations" of all Greeks were focused on Russia, "which in previous times always acted as their firm defender." He stressed the religious dimension and the violated treaty agreements: "The Greeks . . . hope to see the arrival of the Russian army not to help insurgents or *etairists* but to avenge their profaned religion. Altars are desecrated, treaties are held in contempt, and the most sacred and legitimate interests of the state are not recognized." Pestel' warned that tsarist inaction would force the sultan's Balkan Christians to look elsewhere for support because these subjects "no longer know what to think, and it is thus very possible their devotion to and love of Russia will dampen and they will turn to another Power."[70] The information provided by Pestel' reinforced Kiselev's own attitude that military measures against Ottoman policy were necessary.

Russian intervention and Greek emancipation were addressed in an

1821 memorandum, the "Greek Kingdom," which is associated with Pestel'. Although scholars have debated whether the conspirator drafted the plan on his own, they concur that Pestel' and the Southern Society advocated the projected "Greek Kingdom."[71] This memorandum proposed that a Russo-Turkish war would liberate the Balkans, which would then be politically restructured as a confederation of Greek, Slavic, Romanian, and Albanian lands, with each region enjoying autonomy. Influenced by the *Philiki Etaireia*'s vision of a Greek-dominated Balkan state, the "Greek Kingdom" gave Greeks the key role in administrative, commercial, and ecclesiastical affairs. Consistent with Russian strategic designs, the plan called for Russia's annexation of Moldavia and its protectorship over the Balkan confederation. Pestel' endorsed intervention in the Greek crisis both as a nationalist who championed Catherinian expansion and also as a revolutionary. War would disrupt the Concert of Europe, thereby ensuring the triumph of Greek liberty and triggering revolt in Europe and Russia. Pestel' incorporated the "Greek Kingdom" plan into the foreign affairs program of the Southern Society, which employed some of the structural and organizational aspects of the *Philiki Etaireia*. Despite Ypsilantis's failure, Pestel' remained convinced that armed revolt by an underground conspiracy was the best means to seize power and to enact political and social change.

Major-General Mikhail F. Orlov (1788–1842) was another prominent liberal officer in the Second Army who linked the Greek revolution with reform in Russia. Commander of the Sixteenth Infantry Division and a founder of the Union of Welfare, Orlov personally knew Ypsilantis and hoped to coordinate the latter's outbreak with an armed rising against autocracy. The Orlov estate in Kishinev became a center of political debate and discussion, where Ypsilantis and his brothers met the exiled poet Pushkin and such liberal officers as Pestel' and Vladimir F. Raevskii. Orlov sought to use the *Philiki Etaireia* as a model to improve the organizational structure of the Union of Welfare, but his proposal was rejected at the Union's Moscow meeting in January 1821. Orlov's plan, the first attempt by future Decembrists to stage an armed revolt against the tsar, evinced the ideological and organizational ties between the Greek conspiratorial society and the Bessarabia-based liberal officers who participated in the Decembrist movement.[72]

After the Danubian uprising erupted, Orlov praised the boldness of Ypsilantis and anticipated war. Writing to his fiancée on 21 March/2 April 1821, the major general romanticized the Phanariot general: "Do not laugh at Ypsilantis. He who lays down his head for his fatherland is always worthy of respect no matter how successful his undertaking. Anyway, he is not alone and his attempt . . . should not be scorned."[73] With Russo-Turkish tension escalating, Orlov readied his troops for conflict. Like Pestel', he firmly believed that military aid to Greek rebels would promote Balkan liberation and spark Russia's own transformation. The Southern Decembrist officer Sergei G. Volkonskii (1788–1865) also envisioned war, noting that several units in Bessarabia "were captivated by the hope of crossing the Danube and delivering the Greeks from the cruelties of Muslim rule." Some officers acted on their own, purchasing arms and supplies for Greek insurgents in Kishinev and Akkerman.[74]

The Greek issue prompted debate not just in the ruling establishment but also among Russia's liberal thinkers. Not all liberals linked the revolt to reform in Russia, nor did they seek intervention to liberate Greece. Nikolai I. Turgenev (1789–1872), convicted *in absentia* for his part in the Decembrist conspiracy, avidly followed the crisis because he feared for the safety of his brother Sergei Turgenev at the diplomatic mission in Constantinople. While Nikolai wished the Greeks well, he believed that tsarist action on their behalf would hardly advance the prospect of Russian reform. His diary entry of 26 August/7 September 1821 emphasized what he considered the task at hand, namely, the plight of the peasantry:

> It is necessary to stand up for the Greeks, but if recruits are necessary for this then I would never agree to war. . . . It is strange that everyone—diplomats, ministers, and the public—more or less display concern for the Greeks, vilify the Turks, and collect donations for helping Greeks [refugees] in Odessa. All this is fine. But who is concerned about the fate of our peasants? Let us assume that people are unable to speak or to think about the military colonies, but they can speak out without danger about the *muzhiks* [peasants], about the yoke that burdens them. This responsibility is more sacred than speaking out on behalf of the Greeks. Is it better to live as many of our peasants under their landowners or as Greeks under the Turks? Are there not peasants who are martyrs and victims of barbarism . . . ? How many exhausted sufferers! How many fathers bemoaning the honor of their wives and children . . . ! Righteous God, God of Russia, when will your Justice finally descend upon this unfortunate land?[75]

N. Turgenev returned to this theme, writing in his diary on 24 January/ 5 February 1822 that "I do not speak my mind on the affairs of the Greeks. For all their importance, they are secondary for us." For Turgenev, then, war would divert attention from pressing social issues and require more sacrifice from the masses. After resolving domestic concerns, in particular the serf problem, Russia might then help Balkan Orthodox Christians. Yet even Turgenev expressed outrage at Ottoman reprisals, calling them "the triumph of barbarism over right." On another occasion (14/26 September 1822), he suggested that the governments of Europe were obliged to help the Greeks because Ottoman control of European territory constituted "an eternal shame to enlightened governments."[76]

While the war lobby espoused Greek deliverance and expected war, bolder philhellenes from Russia actually joined Western officers and soldiers of fortune in the War of Independence. When remnants of Ypsilantis's forces fled to Bessarabia after their defeat, quarantine authorities compiled a list of names that included nearly thirty Russians and Ukrainians. A celebrated case of a would-be volunteer was the unsuccessful attempt to flee his family estate by the seventeen-year old Aleksei S. Khomiakov (1804–60), the future religious thinker and architect of Slavophilism.[77] Other volunteers succeeded in their mission. One such volunteer was Vasilii I. Sultanov, a retired lieutenant who led a small detachment in Moldavia and who returned to Kishinev to raise additional military help before being placed under house arrest.[78] Greek archives have unearthed material on twenty-one other Russian philhellenes who engaged in combat in the Morea, Crete, and the Archipelago. Ivan Afanas'ev commanded ships from Hydra and Psara, while the retired artillery captain Iosif Berezinskii volunteered with his two brothers "as coreligionists and as philhellenes" to fight in Crete and the Peloponnese.[79] Russian published sources relate the exploits of Nikolai A. Raiko (1794–1854), a Decembrist sympathizer and artillery commander who participated in several Greek campaigns. President Kapodistrias appointed Raiko military governor of Patras so as to consolidate Greek control of the region. Upon Raiko's return to St. Petersburg in 1832, he testified to the Third Section that his philhellenism had been aroused by "news of the military feats of coreligionists" and by "a sense of national honor to aid the Greeks."[80]

The war party's continued call for military action, however, did not alter official policy, nor did the break in diplomatic relations with the Porte lead to the anticipated conflict as Alexander I firmly adhered to the Concert of Europe. Yet the Eastern Question remained unsettled. The Greek revolt intensified, Great Power mediation failed to defuse the crisis, and Russo-Turkish tension over broken treaties continued. There is some evidence that, near the end of his reign, Alexander I seriously considered an independent stance toward the Greek issue, a position reinforced by the success of Ibrahim Pasha's forces in the Morea and by the Egyptian commander's intent to repopulate the area with Muslims after Greek Christians were massacred or enslaved. The tsar instructed General Ivan I. Dibich, the chief of staff who accompanied the Russian ruler to Taganrog in September 1825, to ready the Russian army for seizing the Principalities in 1826 if the Porte still abrogated treaty agreements. Thus, before his death, Alexander I appeared to be placing national concerns above his commitment to the Metternichean system.[81]

The Eastern policy of Nicholas I, Alexander I's successor, emphasized unilateral action to safeguard Russian interests. Sultan Mahmud II, in need of a respite in order to organize a new army after eliminating the unruly janissary corps, consented in the Akkerman Convention (1826) to evacuate Ottoman troops from the Principalities and to abide by treaty obligations.

Nicholas I maintained that the Greek issue was not a factor in the Akkerman accord since that issue was a separate matter requiring collective mediation by the Great Powers. The gendarme-tsar loathed the Greeks as rebels, remarking to the Austrian envoy in St. Petersburg that "I abhor the Greeks, although they are my coreligionists. They have behaved in a shocking, blamable, even criminal manner. I look upon them as subjects in open revolt against their legitimate sovereign. I do not desire their enfranchisement. . . . [I]t would be a very bad example for all other countries if they succeed in establishing it."[82] Try as he might to isolate Europe's Greek affair from Russia's relationship with Turkey, Nicholas I found that the two issues interlocked. The Greek rising had precipitated Russo-Ottoman tensions, and the Akkerman Convention became a casualty of the Greek war. Furthermore, as the Eastern crisis of the late 1820s indicates, Nicholas I's disdain for Greek rebels did not prevent him from using their struggle to advance Russian designs.

Russia, Britain, and France agreed at the London Convention in 1827 to an autonomous Greece under Ottoman suzerainty. When the Porte rejected these countries' mediation, their combined fleets destroyed the Turco-Egyptian navy at the battle of Navarino, a turning point in the Greek revolution.[83] With French troops in the Morea forcing the evacuation of Ibrahim Pasha's army, the sultan repudiated the Akkerman Convention, closed the Straits, and declared holy war against Russia. During the Russo-Turkish War of 1828–29, the fledgling government of Kapodistrias received military, naval, and financial help from the Allies. Turkish troops were diverted to confront Russian forces in Ottoman Bulgaria, enabling the Greeks to extend their liberated border slightly in the north. The Adrianople Treaty (1829), ending the war, granted autonomy to Moldavia and Wallachia under Russian protection, restored commercial navigation in the Straits, and rectified other violations. It also contained a clause by which the Porte recognized Greek autonomy. The status of Greece was finally settled at the 1830 London Conference that established an independent Greek kingdom guaranteed by Russia, Britain, and France.[84] Russian aid to the Greeks during the Turkish war was prompted not by the tsar's philhellenism but by the exigencies of Great Power politics. Thus, British and French influence in the new state had to be countered, while Russian prestige among Balkan Christians had to be preserved.

In the end, the war lobby's call for Russian-assisted Greek liberation had been realized, albeit in a roundabout fashion. Yet the Russo-Turkish War did not strike the responsive chord in Russian society that it would have had it occurred in 1821 or 1822 when interest in the Greek cause was extremely high. Letters between the former hawks Generals Kiselev and Zakrevskii conveyed the fears of officials who were increasingly alarmed by the country's economic and industrial backwardness. Kiselev noted that war with Turkey would strain the treasury and other resources, thereby threatening to make the state "a colossus with feet of clay."[85] Such fears were justifiable in view of Russia's performance in the war. Military losses and supply problems validated the noninterventionists' argument that the army was insufficiently prepared for war.

The public remained largely indifferent to the Russian regime's proclamation of war, mainly because the announcement failed to address Russian defense of Orthodox Christians, the tsar's antipathy for rebels explaining this deliberate omission. The declaration of war, according to a secret police report, did not stir deep emotion in the public because it contained "incomprehensible political pronouncements" about trade, the Principalities, and treaty violations. The proclamation "said nothing that went to the heart. There was no mention of Greece, the Orthodox faith, or Mother Russia," references rich in historical symbolism that would have elicited public interest and enthusiasm.[86] Public indifference toward the war may also have reflected the general sense of gloom and despair that pervaded educated society, especially the liberal intelligentsia, in the wake of Nicholas I's harsh reaction to the Decembrist uprising.

The Greeks of Russia, however, grasped the import of the Russo-Turkish conflict for Greek national aspirations. A. Sturdza, assigned to the Foreign Ministry chancellery in Bucharest that administered the Russian-occupied Principalities, stated in a dispatch that war should have come sooner, preferably at the outset of the Greek crisis, because Orthodox Christians directly benefited from restored treaty clauses on religious protection and Levantine commerce.[87] For this reason, as well as for the broader goal of aiding Ottoman Greek compatriots, many Odessan Greeks contributed to the war effort. They shipped grain and supplies to Russian troops in the Balkans, raised money for the wounded, and served as translators who recruited Ottoman Greeks and Bulgars to resettle in New Russia.[88]

The Odessan Greek participants in the Russo-Turkish conflict were also members of Russia's war party, an informal coalition of supporters and critics of tsarist absolutism that endorsed the Greek struggle. Although the war party had minimal impact on official policy—given the nature of autocracy and the tsar's agreement with Nessel'rode and the noninterventionists—it both reflected and helped to shape philhellenic feeling in Russia. More specifically, its emphasis on the religious dimension generated humanitarian aid from the government and the public, and while tsarist arms did not intervene to protect persecuted Orthodox Christians in 1821, officialdom and society did cooperate in Greek relief drives strongly encouraged by the war party.

Chapter Three

Greek Relief Aid

HUMANITARIAN AID FOR GREEK REFUGEES and captives provides a most illuminating index with which to measure the extent and depth of Russian philhellenism. The regime's neutrality necessitated some form of help as an alternative to military intervention, and the relief projects became that alternative. These projects, which were organized by the Holy Synod, upheld Russia's traditional protection of Orthodox coreligionists and demonstrated continued patronage of Greek settlement in New Russia. Fund-raising drives, however, underscored the religious rather than the political aspect of the Greek war, which most Russian philhellenes perceived as a conflict between Islam and Orthodoxy and not as a revolution for national liberation and constitutional rule. Since the Greeks were thus regarded as persecuted fellow believers and not as insurgents against the order of legitimacy, historical memory, national interest, and religion compelled Russia to lend a charitable hand, and the enthusiastic response of state and society indicated the strength of the many Greco-Russian ties.[1] The appeal of Greek relief cut across diverse regions and social groups, as well as personal, political, and religious antagonisms within the Alexandrine government.

Although Ottoman reprisals aroused the war party and provoked public outrage, it was the fate of the ecumenical patriarch that transformed Russian support for the Greek cause into a religious and national crusade. Despite the patriarchal encyclical excommunicating Ypsilantis and denouncing the revolt, Turkish guards seized Grigorios V and officiating bishops during the Easter Eve (10/22 April 1821) service in the patriarchal church. The immediate public hanging of the patriarch and the bishops,

together with the execution of numerous hierarchs and eminent Phanariots, such as Konstantinos Mourouzis, *dragoman* (interpreter) to the Porte,
prompted random Turkish attacks against Greek churches, shrines, and
property. Further insult was given by the Ottomans when the patriarch was
left hanging for three days at the Phanar gate near the Greek quarter, a
vivid reminder of the penalty for rebellion. Ottoman authorities then ordered members of the Jewish community to remove the corpse and to drag
it by the neck to the Golden Horn. According to Reverend Robert Walsh,
chaplain at the British embassy, "the distance was not far but the way was
through a very dirty market where offals of all kinds were lying about in
foul masses. Through these they drew it [the patriarch's corpse] with gratu-
itous insult, exulting, as it were, in the detestable employment in which
they were engaged; and after defiling the body in every way, it was cast into
the harbor, where the waters closed over it."[2]

An Ionian merchant ship named St. Spyridon, skippered by Nikolaos
Sklavos and flying the English flag, retrieved the defiled corpse and sailed
to Odessa, where the body was received with respect and dignity by Orthodox Christians. The quarantine report of 8/20 May 1821 recounted the
hanging and the aftermath and noted that corpses were generally buried
upon arrival in the port but that, as Grigorios V posed a special case because of his stature, the quarantine board awaited further instructions from
city officials.[3] At the behest of the tsar and the Holy Synod, the patriarch
received a ceremonial funeral in Odessa on 19 June/1 July. His remains in
the Holy Trinity Greek Orthodox Church were venerated by religious pilgrims until their removal to Athens in 1871.[4]

Educator and church scholar Konstantinos Oikonomos (1780–1857) delivered the eulogy at the funeral. A former deacon and steward, Oikonomos taught philology, rhetoric, history, and geography at the Smyrna
Greek Gymnasium from 1809 to 1819. He then served for two years in
Constantinople and was closely associated with the patriarch before fleeing
to Odessa. Oikonomos remained in Russia until 1831, becoming a member
of the St. Petersburg Theological Academy and the Academy of Sciences
and advocating Russian-aided Greek liberation.[5] His funeral oration, published in Greek and Russian, eulogized the patriarch as a religious and
national martyr whose fate renewed the inviolable bond between the Russian and the Greek churches. Just as Byzantine Christianity had enriched
Kievan Russia, the remains of the patriarch sanctified Odessa. The Greek
church and nation, Oikonomos exclaimed, now placed their hope in "Emperor Alexander I, the successor of Saint Vladimir and the august defender
of Orthodoxy," to ensure victory against the infidel. He beseeched the
tsar's compassion for the many refugees seeking sanctuary "under the
wings of the great double-eagle" and summoned Russia's Greek communities to help their compatriots.[6]

Oikonomos was only one of a large contingent of Orthodox Christians

who fled Constantinople and the Danubian Principalities in fear of reprisals. Odessa and Bessarabia, to which many of these refugees went, were
logical havens for defeated insurgents and uprooted noncombatants by
virtue of their proximity, their Greek centers, and the patterns of Balkan
migration. Many Ottoman Greeks had found work in Black Sea trade and
shipping companies, while Phanariots and Hellenized nobles had sought
asylum for their support of tsarist policy against the Porte. Within days of
the Ypsilantis outbreak, inhabitants from the Principalities began crossing
the Moldavian border with the permission of General Ivan N. Inzov, vicegerent of Bessarabia and subsequently governor-general of New Russia. Their
numbers reached seven thousand by late April 1821 and more than forty
thousand by September, after which the influx abated as Ottoman patrols
sealed the border to prevent migration to Russia and Austria. Inzov received regular reports from customs and police officials about the arrivals
quarantined in Kishinev, Izmail, Reni, Orgeevo, and other towns. These
quarantine files, useful for a collective portrait of the refugees, recorded
basic information, that is, name, age, religion, nationality, birthplace, occupation, and number of accompanying family members. Odessa under Aleksandr F. Langeron, governor-general of New Russia, was likewise inundated
with Greek refugees, and by mid-1822 more than twelve thousand were
registered in Odessan quarantine and customs reports.[7] Later, flight from
the Balkans resumed during the 1828–29 Russo-Turkish War when several
hundred Greek and Bulgarian families made their way to Odessa, the Crimea, and Bessarabia.[8]

The Russian government authorized regional officials to grant asylum
to Ottoman Christians. Foreign Secretary Nessel'rode reported to Stroganov on 1/13 May 1821 that religious and humanitarian concerns obliged
Russia to protect all refugees whether or not they had participated in the
revolt.[9] The subsequent July ultimatum to the Porte pledged that Russia
would accept and assist Greek coreligionists, most of whom had left homes,
property, and livelihoods. Local officials, including the Decembrist officers
Pavel I. Pestel' and Mikhail F. Orlov, offered immediate help in the form
of food, shelter, and medical care. This emergency aid, funded by state
monies in the Odessan treasury and by Greek donations, did not, however,
satisfy the needs of all the refugees.[10] So, the refugees' presence and plight
prompted a fund-raising drive endorsed by the regime and supported by
Russian society.

Prince Aleksandr N. Golitsyn (1773–1844), head of the Dual Ministry of
Religious Affairs and Public Education, played by far the most vital role
in mobilizing and coordinating the relief effort. His correspondence with
church hierarchs throughout the Empire stated that "several persons,
moved by sympathy for inhabitants of Greece who have abandoned their
country, homes, property . . . , have raised the idea of opening a subscription on behalf of unfortunate refugees who by the thousands stream into

Odessa and Bessarabia."[11] Golitsyn did not identify who originated the proposal, but several likely candidates emerge. One is Oikonomos, whose eulogy called attention to the plight of coreligionists and urged mercy and compassion for the refugees. Kapodistrias is another candidate because he had championed Greek concerns during his service in the Foreign Ministry, interceding for Greek centers in Novorossiia and raising money for Greek learning. Still another is Sturdza, who was a personal friend of Golitsyn and who briefly served in the Dual Ministry, promoted Greek education, and participated in numerous charities during the Alexandrine era.[12] For Kapodistrias and Sturdza, assisting refugees was a natural extension of their Greek identity and patriotism. While they may not have actually initiated the project, they greatly contributed to its success by supporting its mission and by interceding personally for families who needed aid.

The relief effort, however, most likely originated with Golitsyn, descendant of an old and prominent aristocratic family and longtime confidante of the tsar. As chief procurator of the Holy Synod and as Minister of Public Education, Golitsyn served with distinction, acquiring a deserved reputation as a resourceful and able administrator. He sought to create an ecclesiastical ministry in line with the ministerial administrative order introduced in 1802, and he tried in particular to regulate Synodal supervision of diocesan affairs by, among other things, requiring regular reports from diocesan leaders. The pinnacle of his government career came as head of the Dual Ministry from 1817 to 1824 when he had authority over all religious groups, as well as the entire educational structure of the Russian Empire. This position afforded him the opportunity to propagate his fervent brand of religious piety based on mysticism, ecumenical tolerance, and Christian benevolence. Along with his extensive private charity, Golitsyn sponsored many humanitarian endeavors, most notably the Imperial Philanthropic, the Bible, and the Prison Reform Societies.[13] Greek relief exemplified his Christian philanthropy and his sympathy for Greek coreligionists. As Sturdza and Oikonomos affirmed in their tributes to Golitsyn, the dual minister's charitable impulse, his close relations with the tsar, and his zeal for this particular cause were indispensable for the success of the Greek relief project. Sturdza's praise is especially significant because he criticized Golitsyn's Western-inspired mysticism, claiming that Eastern Orthodoxy was the only true and correct faith.[14]

If Golitsyn was the driving force behind Greek relief, its context was provided by Alexandrine government-endorsed and public-supported philanthropy. Charity toward the poor, an imperial virtue for Byzantine rulers, became an integral part of Russia's Byzantine inheritance, with compassion being a moral duty rooted in Christianity and autocracy. Thus, politics and religion intertwined, elevating the tsar to God's annointed earthly representative obliged to exemplify piety and benevolence. The church, through

Orthodox saints and princes, such as St. Vladimir, fostered charity by promoting the belief that mercy toward the needy held the promise of personal salvation. Additionally, the humanitarianism and service ethic instilled by the Russian Enlightenment emphasized the individual's moral and social obligation to help the less fortunate as a way to improve society. Charity also felt the impact of the general religious revival in post-Napoleonic Europe, and the quest for a meaningful spiritual life found expression in Freemasonry, mysticism, and pietism, all of which helped to inspire the Holy Alliance, the Russian Bible Society, and the Dual Ministry. Sources of Alexandrine philanthropy were the royal family, state institutions, churches and monasteries, and civic-spirited individuals, many of whom saw charity as one of the few legal channels for socially useful work. With the growth of an educated society, the tradition of imperial charity elicited greater public involvement, best seen in the benevolent projects sponsored by the Imperial Philanthropic Society during the reigns of Alexander I and Nicholas I.[15]

Greek relief was rooted more specifically in the tradition of alms-giving to Orthodox patriarchates, monasteries, and shrines in the Greek East. Muscovite patronage, reinforced by the Treaty of Kutchuk-Kainardji, solidified Russia's status as protector of Orthodox Christians. With Golitsyn's impetus, the regime called on church and state officials to collect public donations for Greek refugees. Golitsyn officially launched the subscription in a written circular of 24 July/5 August 1821 that underscored the project's religious and humanitarian intent:

> The terrible events in Constantinople are known to all Russians. Many of our coreligionists, in order to escape death, have fled to the borders of Russia. Thousands of unfortunate victims of persecution, as of March 1821, continue to seek haven in Odessa and Bessarabia. The refugees are received hospitably, thanks to the mercy of the tsar and the compassion of local inhabitants. But the assistance rendered is insufficient to care for such a large number of families, increasing from day to day. In just one day in Odessa, they numbered almost four thousand. Salvaging only their life and the honor of their women and children, they abandoned property and possessions. This calamitous lot of our brothers calls for help. Pious Christians, in faith and love, will certainly lend a helping hand and will not refuse to take part in the newly opened subscription for Greek and Moldavian refugees in Odessa and Bessarabia.[16]

The announcement went on to state that donations should be forwarded to Governor-General Langeron and to Vicegerent Inzov for distribution to needy individuals and families.

Along with copies of the circular, Golitsyn sent cover letters requesting church hierarchs and governors to organize the collection of relief in their respective dioceses and provinces. He instructed church and state authorities "to call on persons . . . , known to you by their love and compassion, to take part in this benevolent enterprise." In fulfilling the tsar's will, officials were to use their position and influence to facilitate the drive. Golitsyn's letter emphasized the religious aspect of the campaign, evoking Russia's debt to Byzantium for the Christian faith: "When it pleased providence to bring them [the refugees] to Russia and to preserve their life amid horrors of death, they were without doubt not deceived by the hope that they would find hospitality and help within the blessed borders of the fatherland of those who at one time borrowed from them the sacred learning of the Gospel, the teaching of mercy, love, and mutual aid."[17]

A different cover letter went to the military governors of Moscow (Prince Dmitrii S. Golitsyn), St. Petersburg (Count Mikhail A. Miloradovich), and the Ukraine (Prince Nikolai G. Repnin-Volkonskii). The military governors were encouraged to seek donations from inhabitants of their respective regions, in particular from the numerous Greeks "obliged by a sacred duty not to abandon their suffering compatriots." In accord with this special request, copies of Golitsyn's announcement in Greek, Russian, and French circulated in the Greek communities of Moscow, St. Petersburg, and Odessa. His accompanying letter, urging Greeks to assist refugees out of charitable impulse and patriotism, concluded by citing Greece's classical and Christian legacy: "Without a doubt the success of this benevolent endeavor will justify the hopes of friends of humanity desiring to help the sons of that country which fostered enlightenment in Europe and to which Russia is even more obliged having borrowed from it the enlightenment of faith, which firmly established the saving banner of the Gospels on the ruins of paganism."[18]

In addition to church hierarchs, provincial governors, and Greek communities, Golitsyn addressed his announcement to various potential contributors. He petitioned members of the nobility known for their philanthropy, such as Countess Anna A. Orlova-Chesmenskaia, to demonstrate renewed humanitarian zeal by helping indigent Greeks. Municipal officials in St. Petersburg were summoned to solicit donations from merchants, artisans, and craftsmen in order to alleviate the plight of Greek arrivals. "I am sure," Golitsyn wrote, "that Russian merchants are eager to show once again their virtue in philanthropic work, which alone can bring eternal treasure and before which all the riches of the world are nothing." Aleksandr L. Naryshkin, marshal of the St. Petersburg nobility, and Aleksei P. Ermolov, commander of forces in the Caucasus, were called upon to support the relief effort. In his note to the *hetman* of the Don Cossacks, Golitsyn stated that "the brave and courageous residents of the Don have never been alien to compassion and humanity." He encouraged the participation of Catholic, Uniate, and Armenian Orthodox hierarchs, emphasizing that "you, as guardians of Christian life, will no doubt alleviate their lot."[19] That Golitsyn succeeded in mobilizing support for the refugee project can be seen in the published one-year report *(otchet)* announcing that 973,500 rubles from various sources had been collected by mid-August 1822.[20]

Along with the martyrdom of the patriarch and the influx of refugees, other events prompted religiously inspired humanitarian aid. As had been the case in Turkey's wars against Christian Europe since the fifteenth century, Ottoman troops often took prisoners of war as booty. Christian captives, forced to convert to Islam, were sold in the Crimean and Mediterranean slave markets of Kaffa, Azov, Kerch, Taman, Constantinople, Smyrna, Aleppo, and Alexandria.[21] Enduring this ordeal were thousands of Greeks from three particular places devastated during the War of Independence— Kassandra, a peninsula in the Chalkidiki area of Macedonia; Kydonies, a coastal town of Asia Minor; and Chios, an island located five miles from the Turkish mainland. Nearly all the inhabitants of these regions were massacred, enslaved, or displaced in three separate Ottoman attacks from June 1821 to April 1822. Of the three episodes, the Chios massacre galvanized public sympathy in Europe and Russia.

After its conquest by the Turks (1566), Chios enjoyed autonomy, flourished economically, and was known for its scenic beauty, pleasant climate, productive soil, and industrious people. It was also acclaimed as the supposed birthplace of Homer. With the expansion of Greek trade, Chios became a commercial and educational center, featuring a merchant-funded school, a large library, and a printing press that published, among other things, new editions of the Greek classics. When a band of zealous adventurers from the nearby island of Samos landed in February 1822 and raised the flag of liberation, most Chiots remained skeptical. They understandably feared that Samiot boldness might jeopardize their autonomy and prosperity. Cautious Chiots questioned the prospect of successful rebellion on their island, given its proximity to Turkey and its distance from the main Greek naval base at Hydra. Fears became reality when an Ottoman fleet approached. The Samiot defenders, the would-be liberators, fled and left Chios to its bitter fate.[22]

Turkish regular and irregular forces exacted a high price in retribution, plundering the island and treating the unarmed inhabitants as rebels. While some of the wealthy managed to buy protection or escape to Psara, most Chiots were massacred or enslaved. According to Robert Walsh, who visited Chios a few months after its destruction, roughly twenty thousand houses and buildings were looted and burned. Of the island's approximate population of seventy thousand, twenty thousand were dead or wounded and thirty thousand, mostly women and children, were in captivity. Walsh recorded his impressions of the gutted island:

> I cannot convey to you an adequate conception of these atrocities. You have yourself seen towns attacked, houses destroyed, and lives wasted, but still you

cannot understand it. If you think the ruins of Chios like any other effects of modern war, you are entirely deceived. . . . The ruins are as complete and desolate as those of Teos on the opposite coast, and would appear almost as ancient, if it was not that the numerous bodies lying about the streets and houses indicated that they had been within a few months full of life and inhabitants. . . . In fact, we met nothing that had life, in the country no more than in the city; the very birds seemed to have been scared away by the carnage—we neither saw nor heard them or any other sound than the dismal yell of a solitary dog, which seemed to be howling over the remains of his master.[23]

European travel and diplomatic reports noted the public sale, the brutal treatment, and the forced apostasy of Chiot slaves in Constantinople. Walsh compared terrified young girls in the city's slave mart to young cattle roughed up by butchers. The British consul in Constantinople wrote that "females and children are doomed to slavery from which there will be little chance of redemption, as all possible means are taken to prevent the sale of them to Christians."[24]

The Chios tragedy indelibly etched itself in the European and Russian conscience. The episode gave renewed impetus to the philhellenic movement and was immortalized in Eugène Delacroix's compelling memorial, "Scenes from the Massacres of Chios" (1824).[25] The Russian response took shape in a new subscription to raise ransom money for enslaved Greeks from Chios, Kydonies, and Kassandra. The drive was initiated by three Greek clergymen in Bessarabia, identified in Russian sources as Metropolitan Grigorii of Irinopol, Bishop Konstantin of Buzev, and Archimandrite Parfenii of Galatz. They petitioned the tsar (3/15 July 1822) to allow ransom donations from the Greek communities, emphasizing their religious and charitable intent by focusing on the plight of captive Christians forced to become Muslims: "We hope that your Imperial Majesty, in considering the nature of such a charitable endeavor, will deign in your mercy and extreme piety to grant us your high permission to save from the abyss of perdition as many Christians as providence will allow."[26] The three churchmen did not send their supplication directly to Alexander I but channeled it through Vicegerent Inzov, the highest-ranking official in Bessarabia. They assumed correctly that this approach would lend greater credence to their appeal and would expedite a favorable response.

Brought to the tsar's attention by Inzov or by a close adviser, possibly Golitsyn or Kapodistrias, both of whom corresponded with Inzov about the refugees, Alexander I accepted the ransom petition on 3/15 August 1822 in Tsarskoe Selo. Minister of Interior Viktor P. Kochubei notified Inzov of the tsar's decision and requested him to ascertain the approximate number of captives and the amount needed for their redemption. Kochubei also instructed the governors of Moscow, St. Petersburg, and the Ukraine to open a ransom subscription among their Greek communities. Inzov replied on 7/19 October 1822 that, according to estimates by Archbishop Dmitrii of Kishinev and Khotin, about one hundred thousand individuals were in captivity and at least five hundred thousand rubles had to be raised to meet the ransom cost of five rubles per person. These figures broadened the scope of the original proposal. Kochubei informed Golitsyn that the tsar now felt obliged to enlist contributions from Greek and non-Greek subjects who were "willing to participate actively in this humanitarian deed." Calling on Golitsyn's compassion and charity to support the new campaign, Kochubei concluded:

> With regret, we must realize that we cannot flatter ourselves with the hope of redeeming all our coreligionists cast into captivity by the recent disastrous events. Yet the eager benevolence of your Highness without a doubt will not grow cool. It is equally comforting to know that out of a sense of humanity and Christian duty, we can save at least a few from terrible slavery and dangerous temptation [a reference to voluntary conversion to Islam which sometimes alleviated the plight of captives].[27]

Golitsyn's announcement of the ransom subscription, approved by the Holy Synod in November 1822, recalled the Christian appeal of his earlier circular on refugee aid. The dual minister emphasized that the plight of enslaved Greeks offered another opportunity for pious Russians inspired by faith and humanity "to extend help to coreligionists burdened by all the woes of captivity and confronted with the threat of being torn from the Church of Christ." Golitsyn exhorted devout believers that "now is the time to show that fortune and wealth have value only when used for the salvation of our neighbors. To return to the fold of the church its sons . . . , to disconsolate fathers their children, and to hopeless children their fathers—this is a feat worthy of the charitable zeal of all friends of humanity."[28] Golitsyn sent copies of the Synodal circular to diocesan leaders, such as Metropolitan Serafim of St. Petersburg and Novgorod, Metropolitan Evgenii of Kiev, Archbishop Filaret of Moscow, Archbishop Avraam of Astrakhan, and Archbishop Amvrosii of Kazan. He solicited contributions from prominent nobles, such as Dmitrii N. Sheremetev, and from Greek merchants influential in their communities, including Moscow's Zois Zosimas and Nikolaos Patsimadis, Taganrog's Ioannis Varvakis, and Odessa's Dimitrios Inglezis, Alexandros Mavros, and Theodoros Seraphinos. Upon Golitsyn's request, Minister of Interior Kochubei instructed the governors of Moscow, St. Petersburg, and provinces throughout the Empire to collect ransom donations with the help of regional and district officials. Kochubei's dispatches to the governors maintained that "faith and humanity must arouse zeal to alleviate the suffering of coreligionists."[29]

Both relief drives met with broad support from Russian officialdom and the imperial family. The latter's contributions were fully expected in view of tsarist munificence for such Eastern Orthodox shrines as Mount Athos, St. Catherine's Monastery on Mount Sinai, and the Holy Places. Charity for coreligionist institutions and individuals was also part of the tsarist creed to protect the Orthodox faith and to render help to the needy. Alexander I personally donated one hundred thousand rubles in October 1821, and he subsequently instructed Minister of Finance Dmitrii A. Gur'ev to transfer thirteen thousand rubles monthly from the imperial treasury to local authorities in New Russia and Bessarabia in order to assist refugees. Nicholas I continued these monthly allotments and maintained the relief campaigns until an independent Greek kingdom was established in 1830.[30] Renowned for her charity, the Dowager Empress Mariia Fedorovna was another generous patron, contributing fifteen thousand rubles as well as helping refugee Cypriot clergy in Marseilles.[31] Empress Elizaveta Alekseevna responded to the appeal of her lady-in-waiting Roksandra Sturdza-Edling, calling the refugee subscription a worthy cause and thanking the latter for "showing me the way to alleviate the lot of unfortunate victims." Among the beneficiaries of the empress's charitable spirit were Athonite monks who petitioned the empress for support in 1825 after Turkish forces had attacked and looted Vatopedi Monastery.[32]

Government agencies participating in Greek relief included the Committee of Ministers, the Ministries of Foreign Affairs and Justice, and the Departments of Foreign Trade, Engineering, and Religious Affairs. Heads of departments and ministries, such as the noninterventionist Nessel'rode, organized collections from their civil servants. Numerous high-ranking officials, such as Minister of Finance Gur'ev and Government-Comptroller Baltazar B. Kampengauzen, made personal donations. Minister of Interior Kochubei not only instructed governors to coordinate drives in their regions but donated three thousand rubles.[33] The Empire's educational and postal districts provided another source of help. Prince Adam Czartoryski, rector of Vilna University and curator of the Vilna Educational District, contributed two thousand rubles and raised additional funds from administrators, faculty, and school supervisors under his jurisdiction. Other educational donors were the Academy of Sciences, the Imperial Lycée in Tsarskoe Selo, Kazan University, and the Holy Synod's Commission of Ecclesiastical Schools.[34] The Postal Department mobilized its administrative network, largely due to Golitsyn's direction of that state agency from 1819 to 1842. Control over the postal system was vital to the success of the relief effort, with Golitsyn and key officials, such as the St. Petersburg postmaster Konstantin Ia. Bulgakov, distributing circulars, organizing collections, and expediting the transfer of donations from the entire Empire to the Holy Synod.[35]

Army officers and soldiers also contributed to the relief endeavor. Donations were made by the elite Imperial Guards units—Semenovskii, Izmailovskii, Preobrazhenskii—as well as by the Hussar Regiments and the Don

Cossacks. Commander Petr Kh. Wittgenstein collected nearly four thousand rubles from the Second Army stationed in Bessarabia and the Ukraine.[36] In their pledges to Golitsyn, officers often elaborated on the reasons for their support. Thus General Iakov A. Potemkin of Voronezh wrote that his fund-raising among staff officers was prompted by a desire to take part in "this humanitarian deed of saving coreligionists," and Colonel Arkadii V. Kochubei voiced his willingness to participate in an endeavor "that accords so well with my faith and with my own personal feelings." Kochubei went on to say that his collection came from officers "who empathized with the calamitous condition of Greeks perishing under the burden of barbarians for the Orthodox church and for the freedom of their fatherland." All Russians, he concluded, "will not be indifferent to the sufferings of coreligionists and will hasten, each according to his means, to take part in this campaign for our unfortunate brothers."[37] While Golitsyn and the regime emphasized the religious bond, many philhellenes grasped the political as well as the religious dimension of the War of Independence. At stake for the Greeks were both religion and national liberty.

Russian society in general cooperated with officialdom to make Greek relief the most widespread manifestation of Russian philhellenism. Golitsyn received donations from provinces and dioceses spanning the Empire, from the Kingdom of Poland to Siberia, from the Duchy of Finland to Odessa and the Crimea. Synodal records document that substantial funds came from the densely populated regions of European Russia, such as Moscow, St. Petersburg, Pskov, Tver, Iaroslavl, Kostroma, Tula, Riazan, Penza, Kazan, Simbirsk, Viatka, Astrakhan, Kursk, Voronezh, Smolensk, Minsk, Mogilev, Kiev, Kharkov, Kishinev, and Ekaterinoslav.[38] Files from the relatively remote areas of Olonets, Arkhangelsk, Perm, Orenburg, Tomsk, Tobolsk, and Irkutsk indicate that fund-raising extended beyond the main urban and administrative centers.[39] Archbishop Amvrosii of Tobolsk notified Golitsyn in December 1821 that his diocese had contributed 1,833 rubles for "unfortunate Greeks seeking salvation in Russia." In January 1824, he informed Golitsyn that he had collected 11,685 rubles to deliver Greek captives. Similarly, the diocese of Irkutsk under Bishop Mikhail raised nearly four thousand rubles in ransom money by April 1824.[40]

Synodal records shed light on the general procedure for organizing aid in provinces and dioceses. For provinces, Minister of Interior Kochubei requested civilian and military governors to solicit the participation of regional and district officials, especially marshals of the nobility and police superintendents *(ispravniki)*. For dioceses, church leaders answered Golitsyn's summons by vowing to open subscriptions for these "God-pleasing endeavors" that fulfilled "our sacred duty to help coreligionists." Their pledges to Golitsyn expressed their intent to call upon the administrative apparatus of the church to raise funds. As in other diocesan matters, Synodal instructions reached individual parishes through an ecclesiastical network of consistories *(konsistorii)*, district boards *(dukhovnie pravleniia)*, and ecclesiastical superintendents *(blagochinnye)*.⁴¹ Parish priests, overburdened with multiple liturgical and sacramental duties, now had the additional task of announcing the drives to parishioners and urging their assistance "to save coreligionists suffering in Odessa and Kishinev" and "to redeem Greeks from Chios, Kassandra, and Kydonies in Turkish captivity."

Governors and church hierarchs, after collecting donations, sent them to Golitsyn with a cover letter affirming their continued promotion of the subscriptions. The Holy Synod then transferred refugee monies to regional authorities in New Russia, using as an intermediary the Ministry of Finance that deposited the funds in the Odessan State Commercial Bank. Some diocesan leaders, such as Bishop Evgenii of Kursk, Bishop Amvrosii of Viatka, and Archbishop Iova of Ekaterinoslav, sent refugee collections directly to Odessa.⁴² The ransom monies remained in the St. Petersburg State Commercial Bank until a viable method was devised to rescue Greek captives.⁴³

In addition to the geographical scope and the organization of relief subscriptions, Synodal files illumine the concrete support from all major social estates *(sosloviia)*, nobility, church hierarchs and clergy, merchants and townsmen, state peasants and serfs. Records often identified donors, their social status and occupation, and the amount of their offerings.

The list of aristocratic subscribers reads like a who's who of Russian counts and princes. The following families made generous contributions ranging from five hundred rubles to eight thousand rubles: Sheremetev, Orlova-Chesmenskaia, Kurakin, Rumiantsev, Lobanov-Rostovskii, Razumovskii, Buturlin, Naryshkin, Tolstoi, Stroganov, Kochubei, Czartoryski, Bariatynskii, Bezborodko, Lopukhin, Liven, Iusupov, Belosel'skii, Golitsyn, Saltykov, Gagarin, Shcherbatov, and Musin-Pushkin.⁴⁴ Based on their pledges to Golitsyn, these families were prompted by religious and humanitarian sentiment. Countess Anna A. Orlova-Chesmenskaia expressed gratitude for the opportunity to participate in "this God-pleasing cause" of helping "our brothers in faith." In like fashion, Count Dmitrii N. Sheremetev gave "with an open heart to alleviate the burdensome lot of our coreligionists seeking salvation from Turkish barbarism."⁴⁵

The church hierarchy—metropolitans, archbishops, bishops—both organized collections in their dioceses and made large personal donations. For example, Archbishop Filaret of Moscow gave one thousand rubles. Charity was forthcoming from many well-known monasteries, such as Aleksandr Nevskii in St. Petersburg; Pechera Lavra in Kiev; and Donskoi, Novospasskii, Simonovskii, Troitskii, Novodevichyi, Rozhdestvenskii, and Predtechenskii in Moscow.⁴⁶ Archimandrites and hierarchs sometimes donated liturgical vessels, gold and silver, and other sacred valuables from their treasuries, as did Metropolitan Evgenii of Kiev who raised ransom money from the sale of gold and silver medals.⁴⁷ Diocesan registers, like those from Kazan and Kursk, disclose that many subscribers belonged to the secular (white) clergy consisting of archpriests, priests, deacons, and sacristans. The secular clergy's harsh lot reflected their economically deprived parishes, and although legally part of the clerical social estate, they eked out a meager existence not far removed from that of the peasantry because they had insufficient income from holiday collections, emoluments, and cultivation of parish land. The small personal offerings from parish priests testified to the appeal of the Greek cause at the grass-roots level of society.[48]

The same pattern holds true in relief help from merchants, townspeople, and peasants. Traders in Novgorod and Smolensk and Old Believer merchants in Moscow contributed, as did the St. Petersburg merchant community that raised twenty-five thousand rubles by 1823.[49] Given the strong grecophobia of the seventeenth-century *raskolniki* (schismatics), the philhellenic response of their Old Believer descendants indicates the broad Christian appeal of the Greek issue for Orthodox and non-Orthodox alike. Russian and German craft guilds in St. Petersburg, including tailors, bakers, bootmakers, blacksmiths, and makers of surgical and medical instruments, donated a total of five thousand rubles in ransom aid, with individual contributions ranging from five to one thousand rubles. Funds were also collected from masters, craftsmen, apprentices, and workers at the St. Petersburg Aleksandrovskii textile factory.[50] Registers from many provinces, broken down by district, town, and village, recorded donations not only from traders and townspeople but also from peasants. Peasant offerings were generally quite small, usually ranging between ten kopeks and several rubles, although in the exceptional case of Vladimir province, state peasants and serfs from the towns of Vladimir and Suzdal and from the village of Matsheva gave larger sums that ranged from one to one hundred rubles.[51]

Non-Russian ethnic and religious groups were also among the subscribers to the relief campaigns. Roman Catholic hierarchs in Mogilev and Vilna translated Golitsyn's circulars into Polish and urged Catholic believers to help "fellow Christians." Catholic churches, monasteries, and schools in Poland, Lithuania, and the Ukraine made donations, as did members of the Uniate and the Evangelical religious communities.[52] Tsarist officials collected funds in the Duchy of Finland and from Baltic German pastors, traders, and civil servants in Riga, Dorpat, and Vyborg. A pastor (identified simply as Dunkel) of the Dutch Reformed Church in Stockholm called on "all German friends of Greece and humanity in Swedish and Russian lands to help on behalf of Christianity." Among the more generous non-Russian donors in the first year of Greek relief was banker James Rothschild, who donated one thousand rubles. Records from Georgia document offerings from Exarch Iona and fellow Georgian Orthodox clergy and monks, from army officers and townsmen in Tiflis, and from local Muslims.[53]

Armenian sympathy for the Greeks stemmed from a common faith, a shared historical experience of Ottoman rule, and a joint migration to New Russia. The Greek revival also helped to kindle Armenian national consciousness. Archbishop Ioann of Astrakhan's Armenian enclave notified Golitsyn that he had raised 2,235 rubles from "people of the Armenian nation for the Greeks' plight." For some Armenian donors, such as the Moscow civil servant Iakim Lazarev who gave five hundred rubles, the fate of refugees and captives evoked the misery of compatriots under Ottoman subjugation. Lazarev noted in his pledge that "The poor condition of the Greeks truly merits compassion. Yet it is not superfluous to add that similar to their ill-treatment, thousands of my countrymen, residing in Turkish lands and deprived of property, wander from place to place receiving little help, as the Armenian nation, with limited means, is unable to offer sufficient assistance to alleviate the lot of oppressed subjects."[54]

The Greeks of Russia understandably promoted both relief and ransom drives. Their participation was a natural extension of their contribution to the Greek awakening, particularly their patronage of Greek learning. They responded with enthusiasm to the Ypsilantis insurrection, organizing volunteer units, shipping supplies to insurgents, and adding their voices to the war lobby clamoring for intervention. Meanwhile, funds originally collected for education were used to help refugees, while the Odessan branch of the *Philiki Etaireia* was transformed into the Philanthropic Society to aid rebels and noncombatants seeking haven in Russia. Though tolerated by regional authorities, the society was banned by tsarist decree because Alexander I feared that its stated charitable intent harbored conspiratorial designs like its predecessor. The Greeks' support of Synodal subscriptions stemmed not just from their sense of national identity and patriotism but from their civic activism. Emigrés in Moscow, St. Petersburg, Taganrog, Nezhin, Odessa, and Kishinev were important local figures and had carved out respectable niches in municipal affairs, commerce, education, and philanthropy.

A case in point is Dimitrios S. Inglezis of Odessa, active in a range of humanitarian projects, such as plague and cholera prevention, famine relief, and street-paving. Inglezis also founded a city hospital and church. During the 1812 War, he collected one hundred thousand rubles from local Greeks, more than any other ethnic group in Odessa.[55] His distinguished public service made Inglezis one of the influential Greeks targeted by Golitsyn to open subscriptions in their communities. Golitsyn described the ransom drive as another opportunity for Inglezis to demonstrate his civic and charitable impulse: "Where faith summons and humanity calls, your heart will inspire you to continue assisting your compatriots and thus to gain an eternal reward." The refugee orator and scholar Konstantinos Oikonomos reinforced Golitsyn's appeal, writing to Inglezis that "faith and fatherland" were at stake and calling him "a friend and fellow countryman."[56] Along with his personal donation of one thousand rubles, Inglezis

collected ransom funds with the help of fellow traders Alexandros Koumbaris and Alexandros Mavros. They also organized financial aid for the
Greek government of Kapodistrias. For their philhellenic contributions,
the Greek kingdom awarded Gold Crosses of the Order of the Savior to
Inglezis and other Odessan benefactors in 1844.

Greek communities elsewhere in Russia also heeded Golitsyn's call.
Greek-language circulars solicited help for individuals and families victim-
ized by reprisals. Merchant-philanthropists who donated and collected
funds were Zois Zosimas, Nikolaos Patsimadis, and Athanasios Notaras in
Moscow; Ioannis Dombolis in St. Petersburg; and Matvei Rizaros in Nezhin.
Offerings included money, provisions, and clothing (Moscow trader A.
Mimis gave fifty furs to make winter hats for refugees in Bessarabia and
Odessa). The pledge of Moscow's Anastasios Gorgolis, who raised a combined six thousand rubles for both projects, echoed the sentiment of many
Greeks in Russia. He wrote to Golitsyn that he was moved "by humanitarian
love, patriotism, and an obligation to help impoverished and unfortunate
. . . compatriots who suffer and are without food, shelter, and clothing."[57]

Greek contributions were insignificant compared to the generous and
sustained help from Russian state and society. Personal donations by Zosimas (2,000 r.), Patsimadis (2,000 r.), Inglezis (1,000 r.), Notaras (1,000
r.), and Rizaros (1,000 r.) were far surpassed by pledges from such eminent
Russian nobles as Anna A. Orlova-Chesmenskaia (8,000 r.), Dmitrii N. Sheremetev (7,000 r.), and Aleksei B. Kurakin (6,000 r.). This imbalance was
partly attributed to Greek aid for relatives and countrymen who fled to the
western diaspora. Reversals in Mediterranean and Black Sea commerce
also reduced Greek offerings. Ottoman authorities confiscated Russian
grain cargoes and closed the Straits to Greek merchant ships flying the
Russian flag. Michail Psalidas of Moscow, after raising 185 rubles in 1822,
lamented his scant five-ruble donation, saying that "Because of sad events
in our fatherland that caused a decline in my commerce, I am in extreme
straits and thus unable to be more helpful in alleviating the plight of compatriots." The merchant N. Patsimadis, also of Moscow, attributed his relatively small collection (1,620 r.) of ransom support to falling trade revenues, which compelled many acquaintances "known for their compassion"
to restrict relief aid.[58] Even in Odessa, the wealthiest Greek center in Russia, the refugee subscription had pledges for only nine thousand rubles by
August 1822, with most personal offerings ranging from ten to one hundred rubles.[59]

Prominent Greeks often did intercede with Russian officials on behalf
of refugee families. Before departing for Switzerland in August 1822, Kapodistrias successfully petitioned Golitsyn to give one thousand rubles from
the refugee fund to the family of Antonios Isaii, who had fled from Smyrna
to Odessa. Oikonomos and Aleksandr Sturdza endorsed the entreaties of
Greek clergymen seeking pensions and placement in Russian monasteries

and educational institutions. Sturdza solicited help for such Phanariots as Anastasios Kalliardjis who lost property in Bucharest and Constantinople and whose brother, the archbishop of Ephesus, was executed along with the ecumenical patriarch. Golitsyn notified Vicegerent Inzov to grant the Kalliardjis family three thousand rubles in aid and an annual pension of four hundred rubles.[60] Sturdza's effort was matched by the generosity and compassion of his sister Roksandra Sturdza-Edling as Greek relief was one of her humanitarian efforts during a lifetime of Christian charity and piety.[61] When her brother retired to Odessa in 1830, he organized a new subscription for the families of Greek sailors and fishermen who had recently emigrated from the Ottoman Empire. He followed this benevolent project with many other charitable endeavors that accorded well with the tradition of Greek philanthropy and civic activism in Russia.[62]

Aid from Russian state, society, and the imperial family; from provinces and dioceses; and from Russian and non-Russian communities reached several million rubles. More telling than the estimated total, however, is the longevity of the relief effort. The lion's share of donations came in the early 1820s when the lot of Greek Christians aroused immediate attention and widespread zeal. Response to charities often slackens after the initial crisis is passed, and in the case of Greek relief, contributions diminished when the urgent needs of most refugees were addressed. Such new issues as the crop failure in White Russia and the St. Petersburg flood elicited public and government aid. Yet the refugee and ransom projects were maintained, and sizable donations were forthcoming until 1830.[63] Nicholas I continued the annual donation of thirteen thousand rubles from the imperial treasury, while diocesan and provincial leaders continued to send collections from their regions. The Synodal treasury in 1827 gained twenty-five hundred rubles from Metropolitan Evgenii of Kiev, twenty-nine hundred rubles from Archimandrite Polykarp of Novospasskii Monastery in Moscow, and thirty-five hundred rubles from Metropolitan Serafim of St. Petersburg and Novgorod. In 1829, offerings from the dioceses of Kostroma, Kaluga, and Pskov totalled almost twenty thousand rubles, while the St. Petersburg Ecclesiastical Consistory collected forty-three hundred rubles. Also in 1829, Metropolitan Filaret of Moscow received eighty-eight hundred rubles from the sale of liturgical vessels and other sacred treasures offered by diocesan churches for the release of captives.[64]

The longevity of Greek relief demonstrates that Golitsyn's philhellenism was not a factor in the personal, political, and religious pressures that prompted Alexander I to remove the former from the Dual Ministry in 1824. Several accounts have described the anti-Golitsyn conspiracy organized primarily by Arakcheev and an ultraconservative Orthodox faction within the Russian church.[65] Arakcheev resented Golitsyn's close relationship with the tsar, regarding the dual minister's dismissal from high office as a way to become supreme as Alexander I's most trusted domestic adviser.

Archimandrite Fotii and Metropolitan Serafim of St. Petersburg galvanized clerical opposition to Golitsyn's control over church affairs. They especially disliked the minister's brand of religious pietism and Christian universalism that placed Russian Orthodoxy on an equal footing with other Christian denominations in the Empire. Golitsyn's notion of a religious brotherhood to be achieved through ecumenical harmony and tolerance struck the religious nationalists as heretical, Protestant-influenced, and dangerous to Orthodoxy's primacy. Fotii and the clerics also opposed the Golitsyn-led Bible Society, viewing it as a threat to church authority over dogma, canon law, and Biblical interpretation. In his letters and speeches and in his personal audience with Alexander I, the fanatical Fotii exerted sufficient spiritual force to convince the tsar of the looming threat that Golitsyn posed to Russian religious tradition. Fotii provoked the tsar's fear of liberal and radical unrest by implicating Western-inspired religious trends with secret societies and with other forms of antigovernment activity.

Alexander I may have removed Golitsyn and abolished the Dual Ministry, but the Christian-spirited Greek projects were immune to the conflicts that caused the minister's downfall. The evidence suggests that Arakcheev's opposition did not extend to the relief effort. Indeed, Arakcheev was a key member of the Committee of Ministers that authorized and organized the drives, and a case can be made that Arakcheev, like Nessel'rode and other noninterventionists, saw humanitarian aid as an acceptable alternative to military intervention. Additionally, church hierarchs who opposed Golitsyn, such as Metropolitan Serafim, continued to collect donations.

Even more telling was that the philhellenism of Anna Orlova-Chesmenskaia did not prevent her from joining the anti-Golitsyn conspiracy. Orlova-Chesmenskaia was the daughter of Aleksei Orlov, whose 1770 naval expedition had rallied Morean Greeks to the Russian cause and whose triumph at Chesme endeared him to Russians and Greeks alike. She inherited a vast fortune and was one of the wealthiest, most influential women in Russian society. A pious believer, she was renowned for her unwavering Christian charity and donated millions of rubles to monasteries, churches, and shrines. Drawn to Fotii by his asceticism and apparent holiness, she became his patroness, and he became her spiritual father. She introduced Fotii to members of high society and interceded for him with important church officials, such as Metropolitan Serafim. Fotii's renovation of the eleventh-century Iurevskii Monastery in Novgorod was largely subsidized by Orlova-Chesmenskaia's munificence.[66]

As noted, Anna Orlova-Chesmenskaia contributed to the relief effort and pledged to Golitsyn her devout support for Greek Christians. She nevertheless sided with Fotii, her father-confessor, against the dual minister, and the cabal often met at her St. Petersburg home. Indirect evidence suggests Fotii's support for Greek aid. His spiritual impact on Orlova did not diminish her philhellenism, and this lack of effect may well mean that he condoned Greek relief or, at the very least, did not prevent her from donating, perhaps because she still had ample monies for the restoration of Iurevskii Monastery. Fotii's letter to Anna in December 1821 described one of his religious visions that portrayed the final triumph of Russia and the Great Powers over the Turkish moon and crescent.[67]

One can also speculate that Greek relief survived Golitsyn's fall because of Alexander I's continued high regard for the former minister, as evinced by the ousted Golitsyn's retaining his directorship of the Postal Department and his seat on the Committee of Ministers. The tsar's respect gave Golitsyn the chance to lobby for the relief drives. Archival records document that Golitsyn's two successors continued Greek relief. With the dismantling of the Dual Ministry, Golitsyn's twin posts were occupied by Chief Procurator Petr S. Meshcherskii and Minister of Education Admiral Aleksandr S. Shishkov. Meshcherskii had been a loyal executive officer in the Golitsyn Ministry and was active in several philanthropic endeavors, including the Bible Society. Statesman and philologist Shishkov was known for his staunch political and linguistic conservatism, opposing French-inspired enlightened reform and Karamzin's French-influenced literary prose. His defense of Orthodoxy and his opposition to Western pietism made him part of the anti-Golitsyn conspiracy. Shishkov did, however, translate into Russian two philhellenic appeals originally written in Greek and translated into German.[68] Published in the *Hamburg Gazette,* these appeals urged European support of the Greek cause. Shishkov's Russian translations, combined with his view that modern literary Russian should be rooted in Old Church Slavonic and Greek, suggest his philhellenic attitude.

The sustained campaign to raise Greek aid would not have been initially possible without the administrative talent and Christian philanthropy of Golitsyn. Later, even after the dual minister's religious piety was discredited as anti-Orthodox, the relief projects flourished because they accorded well with Russian traditional policy, national identity, and Orthodox religious culture. Further, because the drives were controlled by state and church authorities, they did not pose a direct threat to autocracy's hierarchical order. In addition, as Zacek's research on the Imperial Philanthropic Society indicates, some of Golitsyn's other Christian-inspired charitable ventures were continued after his downfall.

The Russian regime, both before and after Golitsyn's fall, did more than organize and solicit relief help from diverse sources. It also ensured that funds were properly administered because the ultimate success of the drives depended on their concrete results. Based on archival information, one can readily conclude that the refugee subscription achieved more than the ransom project. The Holy Synod authorized the formation of the Odessa Relief Committee (ORC) and the Kishinev Relief Committee (KRC) to administer the donations and to apportion the monies to refugees. The committees worked closely with regional officials, in particular

Langeron, Inzov, and their successor as governor-general, Mikhail S. Vorontsov (1782–1856), a major architect of Novorossiia's urban and commercial growth. The committees obtained relief monies either from the Holy Synod, channeled through the Ministry of Finance, or directly from provincial and diocesan leaders. Funds were kept in the Odessan State Commercial Bank and in the Bessarabian regional treasury in Kishinev until withdrawn upon request by the ORC and KRC.[69] Local authorities corresponded regularly with Golitsyn, describing the committees' activity and proposing ways to augment their sums. On one occasion, Vorontsov recommended that a captured supply of weapons for Greek rebels should be sold to Don Cossacks and the resulting monies used to help refugees. Approved by Golitsyn, the scheme raised 875 rubles.[70]

Of the two committees, a clearer picture emerges of the ORC based upon its elaborate records in the Synodal collection and in Odessan regional archives.[71] Langeron selected as ORC president Matvei Ia. Minchaki, a Russian diplomat of Greek descent who had served as consul in the Morea before heading the embassy's commercial office in Constantinople. Familiar with Greek and Balkan life, Minchaki personally knew many of the arrivals from Constantinople and could attest to their property losses. Also on the committee were the merchants D. Inglezis, A. Mavros, D. Schinas, and S. Kosmandas, all having business and familial ties with compatriots in Greek-inhabited lands. Langeron hoped that a Greek-directed committee would be able to assess accurately the losses and the needs of fellow Greeks, thus expediting the distribution of aid commensurate with the actual condition of individual refugees.

Inglezis was treasurer, preparing detailed reports *(otchety)* documenting ORC revenues, expenditures, credits, and debits. These records, along with the less elaborate but still valuable inventories kept by the KRC, indicate the concrete help rendered to refugees. The reports usually identified the names of donors and recipients, the sums collected and distributed, as well as the various types of assistance, whether they were money, medical care, shelter, or educational support for youths. Twice a year, in June and December, New Russia's governor-general sent the *otchety* to Golitsyn.[72] Inglezis's reports were models of organization and clarity, earning him high praise from government officials. Golitsyn notified the merchant in June 1822 that Alexander I expressed gratitude for the ORC's "diligence, righteousness, and good sense" in dispensing funds. Later Vorontsov wrote to Inglezis in July 1826, conveying Nicholas I's approval of the ORC's continued good work on behalf of the refugees and the well-being of Odessa.[73] Letters of appreciation from Golitsyn to key participants in the subscriptions were more or less pro forma, but the efforts of Inglezis and the ORC were especially crucial given the arrival of so many refugees in southern Russia.

The primary task of the Odessa Relief Committee was to help the roughly twelve thousand persons who flocked to the Black Sea port in 1821. Nearly forty thousand crossed the border into Bessarabia, necessitating a separate relief organization in Kishinev. Quarantine records, detailing the emigrants' names, occupations, and family status, gave the ORC an excellent social profile of the newcomers. The main social groups were identified as merchants and traders; boatmen and sailors; and craftsmen, artisans, and shopkeepers, whose ranks included tailors, bakers, cobblers, butchers, silversmiths, furriers, gardeners, and weavers. Widows and orphans were classified separately. The ORC then grouped the refugees into three broad categories. First class was comprised of merchants, traders, and others of "significant wealth"; second class included craftsmen, artisans, and shopkeepers; and third class consisted of manual workers, servants, and sailors. Aid allotments were arranged on a graded scale, with the first class receiving more than the second and the second class more than the third. In addition to social classification, relief sums were based on marital status and the number of accompanying family members. Married couples received more aid than single persons, larger families more than smaller ones. For example, with relief tabulated on a daily basis, a family of three from the first, second, and third classes was assigned respectively four, three, and two rubles. By October 1821, the ORC had issued 55,560 rubles to 1,251 persons, both married and single. By December 1821, the corresponding figures were 117,054 rubles and 2,020 persons, with the bulk of support going to members of the second and third classes.[74] Depending upon available resources, the committee dispensed aid every few months.

To qualify for help, arrivals had to petition the relief committees or Governors Langeron and Inzov. These entreaties, written in Greek, Russian, and French, highlight the human drama and magnitude of the refugee problem.[75] After identifying their place of birth, homeland, and occupation, supplicants recollected in poignant terms the ordeal of flight and the loss of property, home, and family. The majority emigrated from Constantinople, Smyrna, the Principalities, the Morea, Crete, and the Ionian Islands. In relating their current plight, the refugees invariably mentioned the religious bond between Russians and Greeks and appealed to the compassion of the tsar, calling him the guardian of the faith. Petitions often had multiple signatures of family members, many were submitted by widows, and those written in French and Greek had a Russian summary on the bottom of the page. The committees tried, with various degrees of success, to verify the information provided by the supplicants before issuing aid. The former envoy Grigorii A. Stroganov and Greeks in Russian service interceded for families they personally knew, attesting to the refugees' previous status and to the losses these families had sustained.

It was not uncommon for petitioners to address their appeals directly to Golitsyn, especially if they needed money to return home, to locate missing relatives, or to assist recently arrived family members. Spyros Panagiotis, a wine merchant from Ithaka who received a twelve-ruble allotment from the ORC, traveled to St. Petersburg and successfully lobbied Golitsyn for three hundred more rubles to return home.[76] Not all such requests, however, were fulfilled, as evinced in the case of Dimitrios Gobdelas, a doctor of philosophy and medicine who had benefited from Russian patronage before 1821. After issuing him three hundred rubles in emergency aid, the ORC refused Gobdelas's subsequent appeals on the basis that a person of his intellect and credentials could readily find his own means of support.[77]

For understandable reasons, Greeks who were not refugees tried to solicit funds from Golitsyn and the committees. They had served in the Russian army, navy, or diplomatic corps and regarded the relief effort as an opportunity to seek help for various endeavors, such as returning to their native lands, augmenting their meager pensions, or ascending the Petrine Table of Ranks. In one case, a naval colonel who had served in the Russian-protected Ionian Republic claimed that he had never received his promised grant of state land in Saratov province. His appeal for compensation from the relief fund, like most petitions from Greek servitors who had entered Russia before 1821, was rejected.[78] To prevent misappropriation of subscription monies, the committees and local authorities tried to enhance the credibility of supplications with vouchers from influential Greeks or government officials.

In line with the traditional patterns of Greek migration and tsarist patronage of Balkan elites, clergymen and aristocrats were generously treated. Greek and Moldavian clerics received substantial monthly stipends: forty-five to seventy-five rubles for deacons, monks, and priests; one hundred fifty rubles for archimandrites, bishops, and archbishops; and one hundred seventy rubles for metropolitans. The relief committees, at the behest of Golitsyn and often with the intercession of Sturdza and Oikonomos, tried to place Greek clergy in monastic and religious institutions in Taganrog, Kiev, Kharkov, St. Petersburg, and Moscow. Some accepted positions in seminaries to teach Greek, while others intended to return to their homelands.[79]

Eminent Phanariot Greeks and Moldavian nobles from Istanbul and the Principalities found haven in southern Russia. Their ranks included members of the Soutsos, Ghikas, Manos, Mourouzis, Mavrokordatos, Handjeri, and Schinas families. The tsar authorized the Minister of Finance to deposit thirteen thousand rubles monthly in a special pension fund exclusively for aristocratic families. These sums were distributed by the Odessa and Kishinev Relief Committees under the supervision of Langeron, Inzov, and later Vorontsov. The governors of New Russia sent regular reports to Golitsyn and Foreign Secretary Nessel'rode, identifying the aristocratic recipients and the amounts of their pensions. From 1822 to 1830, forty-seven families in Odessa were granted monthly stipends ranging from seventy-five to twelve hundred rubles, while twenty-four families in Kishinev were issued monthly allotments from two hundred forty to twenty-five hundred rubles.[80] Phanariots and Moldavian nobles comprised about five percent of the 1821 arrivals, yet they were apportioned the lion's share of relief. The ORC distributed 1,421,247.66 rubles to aristocrats and 1,469,200.97 rubles to widows, orphans, sailors, the indigent, and other emigrants grouped in the first, second, and third classes.[81] Preferential treatment for nobles included tsarist-funded and ORC-sponsored educational support for aristocratic children in Odessa's Richelieu Lycée and Institute for Noble Girls. Nonaristocratic youths were placed in the Greek Commercial Gymnasium and in a temporary school established for the refugees.[82] Although reduced, pensions for families of the nobility extended into the 1860s, well after the Greek war had ended.[83]

State sponsorship of Greek relief was motivated by pragmatic, as well as humanitarian, concerns. Confronted with the refugee influx, officials hoped to provide not only emergency help but productive work that would enhance the settlement and economic development of Novorossiia. Foreign Secretary Nessel'rode proposed one such scheme in June 1822, instructing Langeron and Inzov to cooperate with the ORC to implement the plan. While Nessel'rode expressed gratitude for the ORC's "justice, mercy, and good sense" in dispensing aid, he cautioned that steps must be taken to offer permanent assistance. Such steps were all the more crucial since the relief fund would dwindle and future donations might not keep pace with demand. Without support and unable to return home, the arrivals had to stay in Russia for at least the duration of the war, and although they had obtained temporary "shelter and care rendered from the heart of the Russian tsar," they should become self-reliant. Nessel'rode also feared that the tsar's continued generosity and compassion would accustom the Greeks to a life of idleness, "corrupting their morals and destroying the spirit of charity."[84]

The Nessel'rode plan called for the ORC to classify indigent Greeks by craft and occupation as a first step in finding them suitable employment. It would then contact regional officials in the Crimea, Bessarabia, Podolia, Georgia, the Ukraine, and adjacent southern lands in order to settle refugees where their various skills were most needed. For instance, sailors who did not enroll in the Russian navy would be stationed in Nikolaev and other naval bases. The committee was instructed to use relief monies to make the necessary arrangements and to defray the travel expenses of those who relocated. In the event of scarce funds, it could tap the state treasury, although only as a last resort and with discretion. Nessel'rode urged the ORC, however, not to announce the tsar's readiness to subsidize the scheme as this would foster continued reliance on government patronage. Above all, the committee had to exhort emigrants to become self-supporting by finding permanent work. If carried out successfully, the proposal would aid impoverished Greeks, hasten regional development, and save state monies.

The Odessa Relief Committee expressed reservations about the plan in a memorandum to Langeron that was subsequently sent to Nessel'rode.[85] The main obstacle was that most arrivals expected to return to abandoned families, livelihoods, and homes at the earliest opportunity. Those with skills in demand in southern Russia—fishermen, viticulturists, tailors, cobblers—"worked in an Asiatic manner" more suited to the ethnically diverse Odessa. Instead of relocating Greeks to areas where they did not know the language or the customs, it made more sense to let them stay in Odessa, the rapidly growing port in which newcomers might find work with relatives and compatriots in the Greek community. Further, some of the refugees did not want to leave Odessa because they had family members too sick or elderly to travel. As for the many boatmen and sailors, these mariners hoped to follow the path of three hundred fellow seamen who, with partial ORC support, had recently embarked for home via Brody and Trieste. Despite these impediments, the ORC pledged to abide by the Nessel'-rode proposal and to contact authorities in southern provinces about the available labor pool. It would also compile a list of applicants who desired to relocate and furnish them with travel expenses and documents. At the same time, the committee underscored its basic mission to continue assisting widows and orphans, the sick and the poor, and those seeking to return home.

According to a January 1823 Committee of Ministers report, only seventeen persons opted for settlement in Podolia province in response to the Nessel'rode initiative. Because more than one thousand refugees still needed help and because ORC funds had dwindled to twenty-six hundred rubles, the Committee of Ministers authorized a transfusion of state monies amounting to fifty thousand rubles.[86] It instructed the ORC to continue aiding the elderly, the indigent, and the orphaned. Help should also be rendered to returnees now that the Austrian government permitted transit through Habsburg territory to those with sufficient money to sustain themselves during their travels. To protect against misuse of funds, the ORC was warned to reject petitions submitted by permanent Greek residents of Bessarabia, the Crimea, and Taganrog who solicited support from the refugee relief fund.

A more specific settlement plan came from Major-General Count Vasilii V. Orlov-Denisov in November 1822. He proposed to relocate one hundred Greeks to his estate near the Sea of Azov, promising them food, shelter, medical care, and employment in fishing-related enterprises. Other landowners, he noted, also needed labor on their sparsely populated Crimean estates. The ORC printed and circulated a Greek copy of the invitation but questioned its feasibility in a memorandum to Golitsyn and Langeron. The committee stated that the refugees, consisting mostly of seamen, shopkeepers, artisans, and small-time traders, did not wish to remain permanently in Russia and were thus reluctant to settle in areas where their skills were needed. The committee further asserted that the predominantly maritime Greeks were not accustomed to the sedentary life offered in the Orlov-Denisov proposal. When sixty-three persons, mostly sailors, accepted the invitation, the committee complied with Golitsyn's instruction to cover their expenses for travel, clothing, and shoes.[87]

Numerous emigrants, particularly the Greeks, Bulgars, and Moldavians who arrived during the 1828–29 Russo-Turkish War, did seek and obtain Russian citizenship, settling primarily in Bessarabia and Odessa.[88] Yet the ORC was on target when it raised doubts about the relocation schemes of Nessel'rode and Orlov-Denisov because the vast majority of refugees who arrived in 1821 eventually returned to their homelands at the conclusion of the Greek war. The ORC had to respond to aid requests by many returnees, the above-cited Committee of Ministers report instructing the committee to help such returnees, and before ceasing operation, both the Odessa and Kishinev committees aided returnees from the remainder of their relief funds.[89] Regional authorities provided travel documents, while the ORC and KRC issued small grants of aid. Travelers sometimes encountered difficulty, such as one group whose weapons were confiscated by customs officials in Bessarabia and another that was imprisoned in Izmailov and Kinburn by Don Cossacks, despite having proper travel papers.[90]

The ransom drive was not as successful as the refugee project in its ultimate mission. By July 1823, five hundred thousand rubles had been collected for the approximately one hundred thousand captives. This sum and subsequent offerings sent to the Synodal treasury by provincial and diocesan officials were deposited in the St. Petersburg State Commercial Bank until the government authorized a viable means to redeem the prisoners. To mobilize additional support, Golitsyn established a committee in Kishinev comprised of the three Greek clerics who originated the ransom subscription. Prominent Greeks volunteered to solicit donations in Bessarabia, the Crimea, Odessa, Nezhin, Moscow, and St. Petersburg.[91] Both the ransom committee and Golitsyn received appeals from refugees who sought help in liberating enslaved relatives. The petitions, written mostly by natives of Constantinople, Thessaly, and Chios, poignantly described the loss of property and homes and the fate of loved ones who "faced the abyss of perdition and apostasy."[92] Supplications to Golitsyn praised his Christian zeal and charity toward Greek coreligionists. As Sturdza and Oikonomos did for refugee aid recipients, the two men interceded for some petitioners by vouching for credibility and by verifying personal stories. Golitsyn recommended that the Kishinev committee honor requests for ransom support, even when the supplicants did not elaborate as to how they intended to extricate their relatives from captivity.

The appeal of the Chiot native Dimitrios Kostandulakis sheds light on the inherent obstacles in devising an effective plan to free captives.[93] Kostandulakis settled in Nezhin after escaping the Chios massacre and, with Sturdza's backing, requested thirteen thousand rubles from the Kishinev committte to rescue four family members. When the committee offered two thousand rubles, Kostandulakis appealed for additional aid to Golitsyn, who urged the committee to fulfill the original request. The ransom organization questioned this recommendation, reporting to Golitsyn in February 1824 that giving so much money to one individual was imprudent. If Kostandulakis used thirteen thousand rubles to deliver only four souls, the captors would raise their price and enslave more Christians for greater profit. More importantly, the report underscored the need to establish a clear mechanism to arrange ransoms. Honoring individual appeals was commendable in view of the compelling accounts of personal tragedy, but it depleted the redemption fund and did not achieve the objective of the drive, namely, to retrieve as many souls as possible from slavery.

Several schemes were advanced to redeem captive Greeks. Oikonomos suggested that Odessan traders use their business ties in the Levant to discover the location and price of Greek slaves. The merchants would then become conduits, transferring ransom monies to their business partners who would negotiate the purchase of captives. The Kishinev committee had reservations, arguing that the revolt and the ensuing disruption of commerce reduced regular contact between Odessan traders and their agents. The committee instead recommended that Greek merchants from the Ionian Islands and the Mediterranean diaspora, including Trieste, Livorno, Ancona, Venice, and Marseilles, serve as intermediaries to transmit sums to the Greek provisional government. Oikonomos concurred with this modification, proposing that half the funds be sent to the Karitsiotis merchant firm in Trieste that had frequent contact with representatives of the Greek government. The ransom monies could then be used by the government to arrange redemption transactions. The Kishinev committee would report to Golitsyn about the rescue operation, including the names of former prisoners and their ransom prices.

Another approach was suggested by Dmitrii V. Dashkov, a high-ranking member of the Constantinople mission who directed embassy affairs after the departure of Grigorii A. Stroganov. In a memorandum to Golitsyn, Dashkov maintained that contact of any sort between the Kishinev organization and the Greek government would escalate Russo-Turkish tension and violate Russia's neutrality. Funneling Russian funds to the new government via diaspora merchants would also be interpreted by the sultan as covert aid to rebels. Dashkov instead proposed that churchmen on the Kishinev committee initiate private correspondence with select hierarchs in liberated Greek lands about ransoming captives. Appropriate choices to organize ransoms were the patriarch of Alexandria, then residing on

Hydra, and the archbishops of Patras and Corinth. Dashkov knew these clerics personally and thus could guarantee that they would use the funds properly. He cautioned Golitsyn and the ransom committee not to implicate church hierarchs in Constantinople, Smyrna, and other Turkish-ruled lands. They were closely watched by Ottoman officials, who would confiscate the monies and punish the hierarchs.

Foreign Secretary Nessel'rode rejected these schemes to rescue Greek slaves. He agreed with Dashkov that any contact on this matter with Greek hierarchs in Constantinople posed a grave risk. He also warned against channeling ransom funds to the Greek government via a third party as this would violate Russian neutrality and signify recognition of an insurgent-established government. In line with his noninterventionist stance, Nessel'-rode concluded that the best strategy was to keep ransom donations in a state bank until more conducive circumstances allowed their transfer to the Greek government. Russian-sponsored efforts to negotiate the release of captives would further embroil Russia in the Greek crisis, heighten Ottoman suspicion of tsarist machination, and raise ransom prices. It was imperative to preserve the monies until they could be safely used for their original charitable intent.[94]

Governor-General Vorontsov, who played an instrumental role in both subscription drives, supervising the refugee committees in Odessa and Kishinev, corresponding regularly with Golitsyn and Nessel'rode about the distribution of relief, and directing the ransom committee after the death of its initial head, Archbishop Dmitrii of Kishinev, echoed Nessel'rode's caution. The governor-general was sensitive to the obstacles entailed in arranging the purchase of slaves. His November 1824 report to Nessel'rode stated that at the current ransom fee of fifteen hundred rubles per person, only four hundred souls could be delivered. He feared that even this figure was high because the captors kept raising their prices. Vorontsov further noted that, if the Kishinev committee tried to honor all the individual appeals for ransom help, funds would soon be squandered without an authorized means or channel to supervise the process. In view of these risks, Vorontsov suggested that some ransom donations be set aside for the more concrete charitable endeavor of refugee assistance. These supplemental monies, at no cost to the state treasury, would allow the Odessa and Kishinev relief committees to continue their important work. With winter approaching in southern Russia and with both organizations short on resources, Vorontsov requested Nessel'rode's approval.

The tsar endorsed Vorontsov's plan, and the two refugee committees received 256,000 rubles from the ransom subscription. Vorontsov urged the ORC and KRC to continue its distribution of monthly pensions to aristocratic families and smaller allotments to nonnobles, in particular the elderly, the sick, the indigent, widows, and returnees.[95] The fate of the remaining ransom monies indicated that Vorontsov and Nessel'rode carried the day. When Kapodistrias visited St. Petersburg in 1827, he petitioned Nessel'rode to transfer this collection (388,740 r.) to the Greek government in order to combat hunger and poverty in liberated Greece.[96] Nicholas I granted the request, and the funds were transferred, except for sixty thousand rubles used by Vorontsov to assist refugees embarking for their homelands after the 1828–29 Russo-Turkish War.[97]

While it remains unclear if Russian ransom donations were ever used for their original intent, the release of captives did indeed occur. British and French diplomatic reports mentioned efforts to achieve this goal. Francis Werry, Britain's consul in Smyrna, wrote to the Levant Company in May 1822 that, although Ottoman officials banned the sale of slaves to Christians, "many are redeemed by general subscription." Werry commented in a subsequent report that "in these severe moments, everyone is called on to assist in redeeming the poor children who are continuously paraded through . . . the streets for that purpose." Many females and orphans, he noted, were "exposed to sale—or redemption." The French envoy to the Porte tried to deliver Greek Catholics through French consular and church officials in the Near East.[98] Like their Western counterparts, Russian diplomats participated in the ransom process. While no details were cited about its operation, Nessel'rode reported to Nicholas I in June 1826 that a special committee in Constantinople had arranged the release of an undisclosed number of captives. This committee was directed by the Russian chargé d'affaires Matvei Ia. Minchaki, who had previously served in the Morea, Livorno, and Bucharest.[99] Russia's consuls and vice-consuls most likely played a key role in Russian-sponsored efforts to redeem slaves. Most of these officials were of Greek and Balkan descent and thus sought to improve the status of their compatriots, as well as worked to extend Russian protectorship over Greek-inhabited lands.

An 1823 anonymous account in the journal *Kazan Messenger (Kazanskii vestnik)* reveals that, along with diplomatic mediation, private initiative succeeded in saving souls. A Turkish-speaking Greek, Konstantinos Vostanoglou, was in Constantinople when Chiot slaves were sold in the local mart. Moved by the misery of two orphans owned by an Arab from Aleppo, the Greek rescued them. The Arab, who had tried unsuccessfully to convert the boys to Islam, agreed to the transaction arranged by Vostanoglou's acquaintance, an Orthodox believer who outwardly professed Islam. When Vostanoglou found out that the Arab owned another Chiot boy, the Greek purchased all three—Michail and Pandelis Antonis and Stamatis Pouladas—for sixty-five hundred Turkish piastres and placed them in a Greek school. The prevailing mood of anti-Greek and anti-Orthodox fervor in the Ottoman capital compelled Vostanoglou to transport the youths to Odessa, where he hoped "compassionate souls" would fund their education since he had exhausted his resources on their ransom and travel expenses.

Odessa's relief committee, as it had done for six other refugee youths

placed in the Bezborodko Historico-Philological Institute in Nezhin, interceded for the Chiot orphans. With the help of Golitsyn and Vorontsov,
the three were sent to Kazan Gymnasium, whose director was Mikhail L.
Magnitskii (as curator of the Kazan Educational District, Magnitskii became notorious for his obscurantism and was a key participant in the anti-
Golitsyn conspiracy). The ORC provided the necessary monies (1,353 r.)
for the orphans' travel expenses and clothing. The report in *Kazan Messenger* comments that the unexpected arrival of the three youths, whose parents had perished in the massacre, was a fitting reward for the Christian
charity and generosity exhibited by Kazan during the relief drives.[100] While
generalizations based on this one case are necessarily thin, the episode
suggests that individual enterprise and compassion were instrumental in
rescuing Greek Christians.

Aid for refugees and captives, one of the many charitable projects sponsored by the regime, accorded well with the strains of Christian pietism
and mysticism that helped to shape the ethos of the Alexandrine era. Even
when these ideals were discredited by the downfall of the Golitsyn Ministry
and the Bible Society, support for Greek relief remained an act of simple
Christian benevolence. More concretely, the subscription drives manifested tsarist sympathy for the plight of fellow Orthodox Christians, while
humanitarian help reinforced the protectorship of Orthodox subjects in
Ottoman lands, promoted Greek settlement in southern Russia, and enhanced the prospect of Russia's influence in liberated Greece. This was
neither the first nor the last time that tsarist philanthropy in the Balkans
carried potential political capital. State-endorsed relief was also less costly
in financial and human resources and more acceptable politically than direct military intervention in the Greek crisis.

Along with offering moral and material aid to insurgent Greece, the
subscriptions kept the Greek issue in the public eye. Donations represented a case of state and society working in common cause, with the government creating a framework for philhellenism and mobilizing broad support for the drives. All sectors of society contributed, indicating that public
sympathy rather than compulsion from state and church officials was the
mainspring for donating. That the Russian church played such a key part
in organizing the relief collection illumines its traditional status as the
guardian of the poor and the needy. Its role further suggests the enduring
impact of Russian Orthodoxy in society, culture, and national identity, in
particular its presence as a cohesive force bridging different social groups.
Offerings from a cross section of urban and rural society symbolized Russia's continued affinity with Orthodox believers of the Greek East, and especially at the district and the parish level, the Greek cause was regarded
as a religious struggle between Orthodoxy and Islam.

The groundswell of Russian support for the relief effort substantiates
the statement by the nineteenth-century historian Dmitrii Bukharov that,

"Up until that time, not one revolt of the people [*narodnoe*], no matter where it took place, aroused as much general attention and intense sympathy as the revolt of the Greeks."[101] Attention and sympathy were prompted both by the historical bonds of faith and religious culture between Russia and Greece and by an awakening Russian fascination with antiquity. For the literary community in particular, the insurgent Hellenes evoked the deeds and legacies of their renowned classical forebears.

Chapter Four

Russia's Classical Awakening

THE GREEK REVOLUTION INSPIRED THE IMAGINATION of European writers and artists as did no other contemporary event. In Russia, the bonds of Eastern Orthodoxy and Byzantine civilization created fertile soil for the Greek struggle's warm reception in the domestic literary community. This favorable response was also stimulated by Hellenism, the enthusiasm for Greek antiquity that Russian culture experienced in the late eighteenth and early nineteenth centuries. So for Russian writers, poets, and critics, the Greeks were fellow Orthodox Christians and descendants of the classical Hellenes. Philhellenism in Russian letters manifested itself in two closely related phenomena: classical learning made important strides, and Romantic poets penned tributes to Greek freedom. In both its classical and contemporary dimension, literary philhellenism was shaped by the growing appreciation of the ancient Greek heritage.

European thought in the Age of Reason renewed its admiration for Greek and Latin antiquity, and thinkers and reformers sought to emulate various aspects of classical culture, society, and government. Humanistic Athens and militaristic Sparta competed for ascendancy in the blueprints for a perfect society designed by the *philosophes,* underlying whose approach to antiquity was the concept of universality, the notion of a changeless human nature immune to the impact of time, place, and national culture. Idealized portraits of the ancient world continued during the French Revolution as delegates to French national assemblies frequently discussed France's social and political reorganization from their perspectives of the classical era. Ancient Greece and Rome were generally exalted by these delegates as the embodiment of liberty, civic virtue, and patriotism.[1]

European art and culture also experienced a renewed fascination with the ancient world that became a cult of antiquity often called the Classic Revival or Neoclassicism. Archaeological discovery stimulated the Classic Revival as excavations in Herculaneum, Pompeii, Athens, and other sites unearthed new treasures of ancient and, especially, Hellenic civilization. The monumental publications in the middle of the eighteenth century by the German art critic and historian Johann Winckelmann (1717–68) eloquently described the hallmarks of ancient art. According to the eminent German Hellenist, the qualities of harmony, proportion, restraint, and balance produced the very essence of the Greek achievement in art, its "noble simplicity and serene grandeur."[2] Winckelmann's aesthetic sensibility profoundly influenced European perceptions of antiquity, and a visit to Rome, or preferably to Greece, became indispensable for artists, architects, and archaeologists, whose professional training encouraged them to seek inspiration directly from classical masterpieces rather than from copies or imitations.

Neoclassicism prompted a spate of published travel and archaeological literature on ancient sites. There appeared translations of Greek and Latin works, many designed to render the spirit and letter of the originals more faithfully than previous versions. Scholarly studies on Homer and other ancients enriched Western classical learning. Original works by prominent poets, such as Goethe, Schiller, Holderlin, Keats, and Shelley, were inspired by classical motifs, with each poet seeking to capture in his work the features Winckelmann had attributed to ancient Greece. Painting, decorative art, furniture, and costume design exuded Grecian style and taste, while Greek Revival architecture created many national landmarks in Britain and the United States.[3]

The Classic Revival, like most Western literary and artistic trends, found fertile ground in Russian secular culture. While the West was developing an appreciation for the ancient heritage in the late medieval and Renaissance era, Russian literature remained steeped in the Byzantine Greek religious tradition. Russian Orthodox priests did not need to learn Greek or Latin to celebrate the divine liturgy, and Church Slavonic translations of Greek writings consisted mainly of Byzantine theological, hagiographical, and other religiously inspired texts. As Serge Zenkovsky has noted, classical Greek and Latin learning was relatively scarce in Muscovy until the late seventeenth century.[4] The growing relationship with the West during the Petrine period and after imparted to Russian secular culture an aroused interest in classical letters.

This classical awakening was initially manifested in the literary trend of Classicism, exemplified by the writings of Antiokh D. Kantemir (1708–44), Mikhail V. Lomonosov (1711–65), Vasilii K. Trediakovskii (1703–69), and Aleksandr P. Sumarokov (1718–77). The epics, odes, tragedies, and verse satires of these writers were heavily based on French interpretations of and derivations from Latin authors. This influence was part of the general pattern of Gallomania, the hegemony of French style and taste in Russian secular culture. When Russian Classicists sought direct inspiration from the ancients, they usually turned to Latin writers because published Russian translations of classical Greek works were relatively rare in the first half of the eighteenth century.[5] Drawing from French models of antiquity, Russian Classicism promoted the qualities of clarity, balance, and good form in creative writing. Eventually Russia's classical awakening felt the impact of the Winckelmann-inspired cult of antiquity and the revived enthusiasm for Greek civilization. His emphasis on the Hellenic achievement caused Greek authors gradually to displace French and Latin writers as wellsprings of Russian creativity and as sources for understanding the ancient world.

That classical influence existed also at the state level is seen in the reign of Catherine the Great, during which classical allusions and associations permeated many of her governmental policies and actions. Medals commemorating Catherine II's accession portrayed the empress as a crowned Minerva, the bearer of wisdom and justice. Catherine II praised ancient Greece in her correspondence with Voltaire and other *philosophes,* convincing them that she intended to introduce reform based on classical and Enlightenment ideals. Her self-styled image as an enlightened empress, however, was part of an orchestrated public relations campaign to win the support of European educated opinion and to enhance her legitimacy in Russia.[6]

Catherine II's ambitious Eastern policy highlighted Russian connections with both classical and Byzantine Greece. The naval triumph of Aleksei Orlov-Chesmenskii was commemorated in odes and medallions. The storied Greek Project evoked the glory of Hellas and Byzantium. As ruler of this Constantinople-centered Greek kingdom, Catherine II designated her grandson Konstantin Pavlovich, appropriately named after the first and the last of the Byzantine emperors. As a means to attract Greek settlers, many new towns in southern Russia were given Greek names: Olviopol, Tiraspol, Melitopol, Nikopol, Grigoriopol, Aleksopol, and Mariupol. Kherson, after the Greek *chersonisos* for peninsula, conjured up memories of ancient Hellenic colonies in the Crimea. Odessa was named after Odysseus and after the ancient settlement Odessos that supposedly existed near the site of the new town. Catherine II and her court favorite Grigorii A. Potemkin hoped to develop New Russia by transforming Ekaterinoslav into a new Athens, making the former an intellectual and cultural center symbolizing the empress's enlightened statecraft and grecophilia. The numerous writings of the scholar Eugenios Voulgaris, archbishop of the new diocese of Slaviansk and Kherson, echoed Catherine II's effort to underscore Russian identification with classical and Byzantine Greece.[7]

The cult of antiquity extended beyond the imperial court and Eastern policy, and developments in Russian culture indicate that Hellenism became a guide to artistic perfection. The aesthetics of Winckelmann, in particular his idealization of ancient art, nurtured Russian cultivation of the classical Greek heritage. Russian treatises on art summarized his views and discussed the qualities and achievements of Hellenic culture. No doubt the most enduring landmarks of the classical awakening in Russia were the masterpieces of Neoclassical architecture in St. Petersburg and Moscow. Most of them were commissioned and constructed during the reigns of Catherine II and Alexander I. Classical forms and motifs also prevailed in Russian decorative art, painting, and monumental sculpture, as evinced in Ivan P. Martos's statues of Minin and Pozharskii in Red Square.[8]

Travel literature on the recently annexed Crimea reflected the lively interest in pre-Christian Slavic history that characterized Russia's emerging national consciousness. The study of contacts between the Slavic world and ancient Greece understandably focused on the Crimea because of its geographical location, its Mediterranean climate, and its classical sites dating to the sixth and fifth centuries B.C. Greek colonies had dotted the shores of the Black Sea, while Greek mythology included legends associated with the Crimea (Iphigenia) and the Caucasus (Prometheus). Travel and archaeological descriptions of the northern Black Sea region, commissioned by the Imperial Academy of Sciences, unearthed new evidence about classical civilization in the Russian South. The accounts of Pavel I. Sumarokov contained valuable historical and topographical information on such ancient towns as Panticapaeum (Kerch), as well as material on contemporary Greek settlements that sprouted after tsarist wars against the Ottoman Empire.[9]

The 1823 travelogue by Ivan M. Murav'ev-Apostol, *A Journey through Tavrida in 1820 (Puteshestvie po Tavride v 1820)*, was praised in several Russian journals for its scholarly content and literary style.[10] The author, who had served briefly as tutor in classical languages to Grand Dukes Aleksandr and Konstantin Pavlovich, prepared for his eight-week tour by reading accounts of the Crimea by Homer, Herodotus, Strabo, and Pliny. The work of Murav'ev-Apostol fascinated the exiled Pushkin, who had visited the Crimea in 1820. Pushkin's letter of 1823 to the writer Petr A. Viazemskii, written just after Pushkin had completed the verse narrative "Fountain of Bakhchisaray," commented favorably on Murav'ev-Apostol's description of Bakhchisaray. In an 1824 letter to the poet Anton A. Del'vig, Pushkin remarked that he had read *A Journey through Tavrida* "with extreme pleasure" because he had toured the area at the very time of Murav'ev-Apostol's journey. Pushkin did not evaluate the author's scholarly citations and explanations, noting only that "to check them one would need the wide knowledge of the author himself." The letter went on to recount Pushkin's own impressions of Tavrida's exotic landscape and natural beauty. His vibrant recollections were published in Del'vig's literary almanac *Northern Flowers (Severnye tsvety)* in 1826. They were subsequently printed as an appendix to "Fountain of Bakhchisaray," along with relevant excerpts from the work of Murav'ev-Apostol.[11]

Published travel literature prompted Western and Russian researchers to investigate the numismatics, the inscriptions, the palaeography, and the archaeology of the Black Sea region.[12] This scholarship was significantly facilitated and enhanced by the Odessan Society of History and Antiquities, founded in 1839 for the explicit purpose of studying the topography, ethnography, history, and archaeology of southern Russia. The Odessan Society conducted extensive excavations of ancient sites; established its own museum of artifacts, coins, and antiquities; and published over thirty volumes of *Notes (Zapiski)* with rich materials on Greco-Russian relations during the classical, Byzantine, and post-Byzantine eras.[13]

Translations were another key aspect of the classical revival. Catherine II's Commission for Translating Foreign Books published numerous items about the ancient world.[14] Works by Greek poets, historians, philosophers, and tragedians appeared, many for the first time in Russia, in separate editions or in literary journals. Some of these periodicals had Greek-inspired names, such as *Muse* (*Muza*, 1796), *Hippocrene* (*Ippokrena*, 1799), *Aurora* (*Avrora*, 1805–6), *Minerva* (1806–7), and *Amphion* (*Amfion*, 1815).[15] Journals excerpted ancient texts and offered additional material about classical philosophy, letters, drama, art, and archaeology. There were also translations of Western writings on antiquity, most notably Jean-Jacques Barthélemy's *Voyage du jeune Anacharsis* (1788), the popular novel about a fictional journey to Greece during the Athenian Golden Age. The Barthélemy novel's idyllic picture of the ancient world captures the essence of European idealized perceptions of antiquity.[16] The prose writer and future historian Nikolai M. Karamzin (1766–1826), who praised *Anacharsis* as an outstanding work of the eighteenth century, published excerpts in several of his journals. *Anacharsis* also inspired Karamzin's short story "Athenian Life" ("Afinskaia zhizn'," 1795), which portrayed classical Athens as the epitome of harmony, intelligence, and enlightenment.[17]

Russian writers exploited classical allusion, setting, and motif to comment on current events. The epic poet Mikhail M. Kheraskov (1733–1807) celebrated Russia's naval victory in his narrative poem "Battle of Chesme" ("Chesmenskii boi," 1771), which is rich in imagery evoking Greek hopes in Russian-assisted liberation. The dramatist Vasilii T. Narezhnyi (1780–1825) criticized despotism in his *Bloody Night, or the Final Fall of the House of Cadmus* (*Krovavaia noch', ili konechnoe padenie domu Kadmova*, 1800), based on Aeschylus's *Seven against Thebes* and Sophocles's *Antigone*. The message of Narezhnyi's play had topical relevance during the harsh reign of Paul I. The historical dramatist Vladislav A. Ozerov (1769–1816) drew inspiration from antiquity for his *Oedipus in Athens* (*Edip v Afinakh*, 1804) and *Polyxena*

(*Poliksena*, 1809).[18] *Oedipus* implicitly extolls the liberal initiatives of Alexander I by idealizing the Athenian king Theseus. Ozerov's sympathetic portrayal of an Oedipus who expiated his unwitting crime suggests the tsar's moral atonement for complicity in patricide. Literary works based on Greek mythology and tragedy not only commented on current events but also popularized ancient myth, legend, and historical information. This, too, was an integral part of the classical awakening in Russian literary culture.

Alexandrine literature cultivated the classical legacy in a more profound manner than simply using antiquity as a treasure trove of allusion, imagery, and subject matter. The classical florescence occurred simultaneously with a quest for national self-definition, and Hellenism interacted with a growing sense of national consciousness, fueled by the sharp reaction against Gallomania and by the victory over Napoleon. One of the prominent debates in this age of intellectual ferment raised questions about the national identity of Russian culture, with writers and poets hoping to forge a distinctly Russian literature unencumbered by excessive foreign influence. In Russia, as in the West, Hellenism also felt the impact of early Romanticism, in particular the Romantic nationalism articulated by the German thinker Johann Herder. His concept of *Volksgeist* maintained that each nation expressed its creative genius in language, art, literature, and folklore. Each national culture, springing from its own people, embodied that nation's soul or spirit. National consciousness and *Volksgeist* prompted the Russian literary community to tap domestic historical and cultural tradition as a source for an authentically national modern culture.[19] Thus the intersection of Hellenism and Romanticism, as well as other cross-currents, imparted a diversity to Alexandrine letters that stimulated creative work.

This diversity was seen in the various Alexandrine literary societies—Colloquium of Lovers of the Russian Word, Arzamas, and Free Society of Lovers of Russian Literature—that espoused different styles, tastes, even literary languages. Shishkov's proponents, for example, favored a language rooted in Old Church Slavonic, while Karamzin's supporters advocated the spoken language of the aristocracy. Yet all of these societies shared a deep concern for *narodnost'* (national identity) and *samobytnost'* (uniqueness) in literature. They sought to adapt foreign models, without imitating them, to national tradition. The quest for *narodnost'* makes the Alexandrine period a transitional era that led to the more fully developed Romantic nationalism of the Slavophiles in the 1840s.

Paradoxically, emphasis on the unique in national culture deepened Russian understanding of the ancient heritage. Romanticism in the West is generally associated with a revived interest in the mystery and religion of the Middle Ages in contrast to classical reason and logic. The telescoping of the Classic Revival and early Romanticism explains the Russian anomaly of linking the classical and the national in a manner reminiscent of Renaissance Humanism. Classical letters had inspired the development of Western vernacular literatures with distinct national identities. Herder himself suggested this linkage by reinforcing Winckelmann's idealization of ancient Greece. Herder lauded Homer as the most authentic poetic expression of the Greek spirit and praised Greek art as the embodiment of natural beauty, grace, and vitality. Russian Hellenists shared Herder's view and were convinced that knowledge of classical civilization would both enrich Russian national culture and stimulate the composition of uniquely Russian works.

For a Russian generation in search of a national voice, Greek works rooted in native myth, legend, and history were spontaneous and organic manifestations of Hellenic civilization and were esteemed as models, more so than the French interpretations of antiquity, suitable to shape a national culture grounded in Russian history and tradition. Familiarity with the ancient heritage provided direct access to such qualities as *narodnost'* and *samobytnost'* deemed essential for original composition. With their enthusiasm for Greek antiquity, Russian writers and artists hoped to rediscover their own literary and historical roots in Slavic myths, Cossack tales, and Russian folklore, songs, and chronicles, just as classical writers had turned to ancient myths and legends as wellsprings of creativity. The classical heritage thus became a guide and an inspiration to develop a Russian vernacular literature that was both classical in form and national in spirit. An appreciation of the ancient legacy and the spirit of Romantic nationalism combined with other elements to produce masterpieces in the Alexandrine Golden Age of Russian poetry.[20] Numerous Hellenists paved the way by seeking to blend the classical with the Russian national specific. In the process, they enhanced classical studies and generated scholarly interest in modern Greek language and culture.

Aleksei N. Olenin (1763–1843) did more than any other individual of his generation to advance ancient learning in Russia. As Mary Stuart has demonstrated in her fine biography, Olenin occupied a significant place in Russian culture by virtue of his patronage of art, letters, and scholarship; his ties with gifted writers and artists such as Pushkin and Zhukovskii; and his administrative skill as founding director of the Imperial Public Library (1808–43) and as president of the Imperial Academy of Fine Arts (1817–43).[21] Olenin imbued his scholarly and artistic activity with the zeal to create a national culture by seeking inspiration from the ancients and by adapting classical standards to Russian art and letters. Olenin's aesthetic sensibility was decisively shaped by Winckelmann during the former's education in Dresden in 1780–85, and throughout his life, "the Russian Winckelmann" maintained that the Greeks had attained superiority in the arts and should thus be emulated. Russia's foremost Hellenist also championed the synthesis of the classical legacy with national tradition.

Olenin's multifaceted endeavors enriched many aspects of Russian Hellenism. As an art historian, he specialized in archaeology, epigraphy, palaeography, and vase-painting, and his series of well-illustrated publications are still useful for the study of ancient art.[22] As president of the Academy of Fine Arts, Olenin promoted the ideals of proportion, harmony, and perfection of form in sculpture and architecture. Under his guidance, antiquity in the visual arts reached its apogee. He was also responsible for Russia's first journal devoted entirely to the fine arts. Appearing in 1823–25, the *Journal of the Fine Arts (Zhurnal iziashchnykh iskusstv)* had a wealth of information on art history and theory, including excerpts and summaries of Winckelmann's writings; sketches and illustrations of ancient monuments; a description of the Elgin Marbles; and news on contemporary Russian sculpture, such as the classically inspired statue of Duc de Richelieu in Odessa.[23] Olenin also worked diligently to enlarge the antiquities' collections of the Public Library and the Academy of Arts. His 1818 instructions to Spyridon Destunis urged the newly appointed Russian consul general in Smyrna to acquire bas-reliefs, coins, inscriptions, and pottery during the latter's stay in antiquity-rich Asia Minor, and Destunis subsequently donated his artifacts to the archaeological museum founded by the Odessan Society of History and Antiquities.[24] The letters of Olenin to Mikhail S. Vorontsov, governor-general of New Russia, registered his understandable interest in the recently excavated antiquities of the Black Sea region.[25]

Olenin's home in St. Petersburg and his country estate at Priiutno attracted a diverse group of artists, writers, scholars, and intellectuals, all of whom were key figures who profoundly shaped Alexandrine culture and who shared their host's esteem for the ancient heritage. Olenin encouraged writers and poets not only to study the classics but to use them as models for original work that was classical in form and national in content and that had themes and subject matter drawn from Russian history. Olenin played an important role in the success of Vladislav A. Ozerov's tragedy *Oedipus in Athens,* first rehearsed at Priiutno before its 1804 premiere in St. Petersburg. Olenin's set and costume designs, based on ancient models, enhanced the play's historical veracity and authenticity. Olenin also designed sets, costumes, and illustrations for Ozerov's *Polyxena* in 1809.[26]

The Imperial Public Library became another magnet for Olenin's protégés. The writers and scholars employed under his direction lent this institution an aura of literary excellence, and many of their contributions to Russian culture and to ancient learning were launched with Olenin's encouragement and financial support. The preeminent fabulist Ivan A. Krylov (1769–1844) was assistant librarian in the Russian Division while he perfected the fable as a Russian literary genre. Adapted from La Fontaine and Aesop, his widely read and still venerated *Fables* satirized the human foibles of vanity, greed, and incompetence and instilled the virtues of common sense, honesty, and moderation. His settings were authentically and distinctly Russian, and the colloquial language of his characters often corresponded with their social status or government rank. The admired qualities of *narodnost'* and *samobytnost'* are reinforced because many of Krylov's moral truths became Russian proverbs. Olenin worked closely with Krylov, suggesting some of the themes incorporated in the fabulist's work. Late in life and with Olenin's prompting, Krylov even learned enough ancient Greek to read Homer in the original and to translate passages from the *Odyssey*.[27]

Konstantin N. Batiushkov (1787–1855), assistant curator of the Manuscript Division of the Imperial Public Library, was a lyric poet who influenced the poetic style of Pushkin. Although Batiushkov did not know ancient Greek, he intuitively grasped the essence of the classical era. He portrayed with striking clarity a world of beauty, perfection, and passion before insanity cut short his literary activity at the age of thirty-four. His essay "A Stroll to the Academy of Arts" ("Progulka v akademii khudozhestv," 1814) extolled the ancients for their faithful depiction of nature and human emotion. As a Hellenist, he was best known for such evocative poems as "Bacchante" ("Vakkhanka," 1815), which visually captures the joyous festival of Bacchus's priestesses; "Hesiod and Homer—Rivals" ("Gesiod i Omer—Soperniki," 1817), which presents the tragic fate of a talented artist isolated from, and unappreciated by, the public; and "Imitations of the Ancients" ("Podrazhaniia drevnim," 1821), which is a series of concise word-pictures mainly on the theme of death.[28] The classical site of Olbia aroused Batiushkov's poetic sensibility during his travel in the Russian South en route to a diplomatic post with the Russian embassy in Naples (1818–21). In correspondence with Olenin, Batiushkov sketched and described the ruins near Olbia.[29]

Another illustrious member of the Olenin circle was Sergei S. Uvarov (1786–1855), president of the Imperial Academy of Sciences from 1818 to his death and Olenin's personal assistant in the Public Library. Best remembered as the formulator of Tsar Nicholas I's conservative ideology of Official Nationality, Uvarov was a recognized scholar of classical and oriental civilizations and published erudite essays on ancient Greek ritual, legend, and tragedy.[30] Like his mentor Olenin, Uvarov tried to integrate the classical tradition with Russian culture. Praising Hellenic culture as "the most perfect product of the human mind," Uvarov believed that Greek literature should become the basis for Russian literature. "The thorough study of Greek," he wrote in a publication of 1810, "will open an inexhaustible source of new ideas, of fecund images for Russia. It will give to history, to philosophy, to poetry, the purest forms and those closest to true models." He also noted that the Greek language was inextricably tied to Church Slavonic, the Russian Orthodox faith, and medieval Russian literature. Convinced that ancient learning enhanced the life of the mind and instilled the virtues of wisdom and love of knowledge, Uvarov advocated a classical curriculum in public schools during his supervision of the St. Petersburg Educational District (1810–21) and during his subsequent headship of the Ministry of Public Education (1833–49).[31]

Uvarov and Batiushkov undertook the joint publication of selections from the *Greek Anthology,* the compendium of Greek epigrams from the seventh century B.C. to the tenth century A.D. Uvarov translated some of the short poems from the Greek original into French prose, and Batiushkov rendered Uvarov's prose into Russian verse. Their collaborative effort included mostly love epigrams from the Hellenistic era. Batiushkov's concrete and precise imagery evokes the beauty of antiquity, thus explaining the literary success of this 1820 publication.[32] The Russian epigrams were preceded by Uvarov's incisive introduction that describes them as "gems of the ancient world." Familiarity with the epigrams allowed readers "to become contemporaries of the Greeks, to share their passions and ideals, and to participate in their games, festivals, and domestic life." According to Uvarov, the most learned classicist could hardly compile a more accurate depiction of "the mores, the customs, and the national spirit of the ancient Greeks, a people occupying first place in the civilized world."[33] Acquaintance with this valuable Greek collection, Uvarov hoped, would establish high standards for Russian poetry and would inspire original compositions.

After his education at the Tsarskoe Selo Lycée, Anton A. Del'vig (1798–1831) joined the distinguished writers, poets, and scholars working under Olenin at the Imperial Public Library. Del'vig's duties at the library were not onerous, leaving him ample opportunity for endeavors that contributed to Russian Hellenism. He became a prominent critic and publisher, editing the successful literary almanac *Northern Flowers* (1825–31), which featured prose, poetry, and criticism by Golden Age talents.[34] Del'vig experimented with the genres of elegy, epistle, epigram, and sonnet and attained near perfection and mastery of form in the idyll. His classically inspired idylls, with mythological allusion and a lucid style, depicted the joys of pastoral life in Arcadia. "Bathing Women" ("Kupal'nitsy," 1824), considered Del'vig's masterpiece, vividly captures his perception of the beauty, harmony, and tranquility of antiquity. Published in the first issue of *Northern Flowers* (1825), "Bathing Women" has been called by the literary historian Mirsky "unquestionably the highest achievement in Russian poetry in the more purely sensuous vision of classical antiquity."[35]

The Hellenists patronized and employed by Olenin also contributed significantly to Russian ancient learning. Their diverse activities planted seeds reaped by Ivan I. Martynov (1771–1833) and Nikolai I. Gnedich (1784–1833), classical scholars who cultivated the ancient heritage and who developed a strong interest in modern Greek letters. This classical-modern connection was readily understandable as the classical awakening prompted curiosity in the contemporary Hellenes. Various publications indulged in the fashionable trend of viewing Greece's current inhabitants through the prism of their celebrated classical past. The land of Hellas might have become a wasteland under Turkish oppression, but the Greeks retained traces of their ancient heritage. References to antiquity were frequently used to portray the moderns and their future regeneration as a nation.

The Romantic poet Vasilii A. Zhukovskii (1783–1852) expressed hope for a revived Hellas in an article published in *Messenger of Europe (Vestnik Evropy)* during his editorship of that prominent biweekly: "Piraeus and Phaleron, arising from ruin, will be filled with countless ships, and travelers will no longer compare the ruins of the Temple of Zeus to the sorry plight of the current inhabitants. . . . Greece, like a Phoenix, will rise from ashes . . . and its rebirth will glorify our century."[36] Observers compared the fighting spirit of the Maniots, inhabitants of Mani in the southern Morea who successfully defended their land from Ottoman rule, to the Spartans' martial prowess. The Sparta parallel was also used in an historical drama inspired by the valor and courage of the Suliots, who resisted Albanian and Turkish attack of their mountainous enclave Suli in Epirus.[37] Two accounts of Russia's naval expedition in the Mediterranean (1805–10) described the Archipelago and other Greek lands from the perspective of the classical past. One of the authors of these accounts, Pavel N. Svin'in, echoed a common sentiment in Russian and Western travel writing on Greece. He lamented the transformation of "this beautiful land, the home of the muses, art, and fine taste," into "a wasteland, with fertile soil uncultivated, forests despoiled, once glorious cities abandoned, and remnants of Greek architecture destroyed. . . . How can one reconcile oneself to the thought that barbarous mosques have replaced magnificent shrines, that where Solon and Lycurgus once drafted laws, the Turks have built harems filled with eunuchs."[38] Advances in learning and education, however, made Svin'in hopeful about the Greeks' future.

In building on the work of Russian Hellenists, Martynov and Gnedich were deeply influenced by the prevalent juxtaposing of classical and modern Hellenes. Familiarity with the ancient tradition aroused interest in the fate of the current Greeks. The philhellenism of Martynov and Gnedich thus encompassed the ancient and the modern dimension of Greek culture, and their literary endeavors enhanced Hellenism and established a firm foundation for modern Greek studies in Russian scholarship.

Martynov's most significant work was his multivolume publication of Greek classics during the 1820s. He learned ancient and modern Greek at Poltava Seminary from Nikiphoros Theotokis, archbishop of Slaviansk and Kherson. Martynov then pursued Greek philological study in St. Petersburg, where he came into contact with the Greek prelate Eugenios Voulgaris, perhaps the most respected classicist in late eighteenth-century Russia. Among Voulgaris's publications were a three-volume Greek translation of the *Aeneid* (1791–92) and a Russian translation of verses by the ancient poet Anacreon (1794). The latter was a joint endeavor with the poet and scholar Nikolai A. L'vov (1751–1803), who rendered the prose translation of Voulgaris into poetry. Martynov's classical training and literary activity benefited greatly from his association with Voulgaris, who reinforced his student's interest in the ancient tradition and tutored him in modern Greek. After a brief teaching stint at the Aleksandr Nevskii Theological Seminary, Martynov served as director of the Department of Public Education from 1803 to 1817. His most noteworthy accomplishment as an educational official, drafting the 1804 liberalized censorship edict, stimulated growth in the publishing and book-trade industries.[39]

Martynov participated in the intellectual ferment of the early Alexandrine era, spreading Western and classical learning as a publicist, translator, and journalist. He published a translation of Catherine II's correspondence with Voltaire and contributed to several periodicals. Two journals that he edited, *Northern Messenger* (*Severnyi vestnik*, 1804–5) and *Lycée* (*Litsei*, 1806), carried translations of Gibbon, Montesquieu, Holbach, and such ancient writers as Pindar and Polybius. In a commemorative piece for *Lycée* upon the death of his mentor Voulgaris in 1806, Martynov detailed the prelate's productive scholarship and eulogized the Greek churchman as an educator and author who combined the rare talents of Homer and Demosthenes.[40]

Martynov's commitment to the classical heritage shaped his creative work as a publicist and translator. Because he knew ancient and modern Greek, Martynov sincerely believed that he had a special obligation to publicize the treasures of Greek antiquity. Like Uvarov and several other educators of the time, Martynov regarded the classics as an indispensable source not just for a classical education but for the advancement of enlightenment and culture in Russia. He specifically linked ancient learning to the broader issue of creating a national literature liberated from French hegemony in style, genre, and subject matter. He believed that knowledge of Greek civilization, including the Greek language, would quicken the development of an authentically Russian vernacular literature. This was in line with what had occurred during the Renaissance when the Latin classical tradition enriched Western culture and stimulated vernacular literatures with distinct identities.[41]

Martynov certainly did his part in publicizing the Greek heritage, undertaking the monumental project known as the *Greek Classics*. From 1823 to 1829, he published a twenty-six volume bilingual edition of Homer, Sophocles, Pindar, Anacreon, Callimachus, Aesop, Herodotus, Plutarch, and other classical authors. Martynov prefaced each volume with useful information on the life, work, and times of the featured writer. All the writings, except Anacreon's, were rendered into Russian prose and appeared alongside the original Greek. The introduction to *Aesop's Fables* (*Basni Ezopovy*) succinctly states the aims of the project. Martynov hoped to acquaint readers with classical texts in ancient Greek and Russian translation, to deepen Russian appreciation of the Hellenic legacy, and to augment Russian historical and literary knowledge of the ancient world. These goals were emphasized in the frequent announcements Martynov submitted to Russian periodicals. The press notices summarized his progress, projected publication dates, and identified the bookshops in St. Petersburg and Moscow that carried the volumes.[42] This self-promotion campaign to arouse public interest and to improve book sales was encouraged by Minister of Public Education Aleksandr N. Golitsyn, Metropolitan Evgenii (Evfimii Bolkhovitinov) of Kiev, and Nikolai P. Rumiantsev, the patron of Russian historical scholarship.

Martynov's endeavor was hardly a great success with the reading public, especially as such respected writers as Zhukovskii and Pushkin sharply criticized the project's clumsy style and awkward language. Martynov also had to contend with the disastrous St. Petersburg flood of 1824, which destroyed many works at the press and in his apartment. Metropolitan Evgenii offered consolation in his correspondence with Martynov, suggesting that future generations would recognize the value of the *Greek Classics*.[43] Although its objectives were laudable, the translation project was simply too ambitious for one person to implement successfully, even someone like Martynov who was trained in the classics. The undertaking demanded the talents of numerous classical scholars, as well as writers capable of rendering the various genres and styles into literary Russian. Despite the lack of poetic grace and the small public readership, the multivolume bilingual *Greek Classics* was the first systematic attempt to introduce the Russian public to the ancient Greek heritage. The efforts of Martynov provided a foundation for subsequent Russian classicists, just as Metropolitan Evgenii had envisioned in his correspondence.

In addition to Greek antiquity, Martynov's philhellenism embraced the contemporary inhabitants of ancient Hellas. He published an essay in 1822 on the correct pronunciation of various Greek letters often mispronounced by foreigners studying the language. Addressed primarily to Russian students of Greek philology, Martynov's essay matched Greek letters and sounds with their Russian equivalents. His preface stated that, at a time when the fate of the Greeks preoccupied many people, he felt inspired "to present this brief work on the pronunciation of several letters of their beautiful language. No less than others I too am moved by the condition of this classical nation and wish them good fortune."[44]

This publication was only one of several Russian handbooks for modern Greek language instruction.[45] By far the most detailed of these texts was Greek educator and scholar Konstantinos Oikonomos's three-volume bilingual study of the relationship between Greek and Russian. His work, published in St. Petersburg in 1828 after five years of research, compared the sounds and the derivations of many Russian and Greek words. Oikonomos sought to demonstrate that linguistic affinities complemented the bond of a common faith. His dedication to Nicholas I summoned the tsar to advocate the liberation of "oppressed Hellas" in accordance with Russia's traditional protection of Orthodoxy. Martynov acknowledged the impressive philological scholarship of Oikonomos in his revised essay on Greek pronunciation, published in 1831 and heavily dependent upon the findings of the Greek scholar.[46]

Like other Russian writers, the poet Nikolai I. Gnedich also cultivated classical and modern Greek culture. He labored over twenty years on the first complete Russian rendition of the *Iliad,* which is still considered the standard Russian verse translation of the Homeric epic, and he translated selections from modern Greek folk poetry. Gnedich came from an impoverished Ukrainian family of Cossack descent and studied Greek at Poltava Seminary. Like Martynov, he benefited from the school's Greek philological curriculum established by Voulgaris and Theotokis. Gnedich continued his studies at Moscow University, after which he served in the Ministry of Public Education and became another protégé of Olenin. Joining the circle of Hellenists, Gnedich formed a close friendship with Batiushkov and worked in the Imperial Public Library. He began in 1811 as an assistant librarian in charge of the Greek Manuscript Collection and was promoted in 1826 to full librarian. The Public Library offered a congenial environment for a stimulating and mutually rewarding relationship between Olenin and Gnedich, the two foremost Hellenists in Alexandrine Russia. Olenin encouraged and supported Gnedich's classical pursuits, above all his *Iliad* translation.[47]

Gnedich devoted much of his creative work to synthesizing the ancient heritage with Russian culture. He viewed the Hellenic legacy as the epitome of intellect and beauty and as the wellspring of moral development and literary inspiration. The study of antiquity would, he believed, also enhance the quality of learning and culture in Russia. In a speech delivered at the opening ceremony of the Public Library, Gnedich applauded Greek poetry for accurately reflecting the relationship between man and society and between art and reality. He urged Russian writers to emulate the classics, praised by Gnedich as "models of truth, power, and simplicity, especially in poetry, for no one can surpass the Greeks in poetry."[48] In a speech occasioned by his active membership in the Free Society of Lovers of Russian Literature, Gnedich stated that familiarity with ancient literature would allow writers to integrate the classical legacy with native Russian tradition and subject matter. He thus reiterated the views of fellow Hellenists that Greek antiquity constituted a rich source for creating an authentic and uniquely Russian literature.[49]

Blind in one eye from a childhood bout with smallpox, Gnedich had a particular fondness for the blind bards Milton, Ossian, and Homer. He began the *Iliad* translation in 1807, hoping to introduce readers to what he deemed the first and greatest masterpiece in world literature. Before the publication of Gnedich's two-volume *Iliad* in 1829, the only Russian version of this work was the partial translation by the poet Ermil I. Kostrov (1755–96), whose first six books, dedicated to the grecophile Catherine the Great, were published in 1787, with excerpts from books seven, eight, and nine appearing posthumously in 1811. When Gnedich launched his project, he initially intended to complete Kostrov's work by employing the same French-derived alexandrine verse commonly used in epics and dramas of eighteenth-century Classicism.[50] He later came to change his mind.

Gnedich's preoccupation with the Homeric epic had topical significance for Russians in light of the national triumph over Napoleon. To Gnedich and to many familiar with the *Iliad,* the glowing account of the exploits of Achilles and other protagonists of the epic evoked the heroism, courage, and patriotism of Russian soldiers and civilians in the 1812 War. The Gnedich endeavor was also an aspect of Russian culture's rejection of Gallomania. Encouraged by Olenin, Uvarov, and Zhukovskii, Gnedich abandoned the French-based alexandrine in favor of the hexameter used in the Greek original. In an 1813 letter to Gnedich, Uvarov voiced a preference for the classical meter: "When instead of the flowing, majestic hexameter, I hear the meager, dry alexandrine, adorned with rhyme, I seem to be seeing the divine Achilles in French costume." Zhukovskii followed suit in an 1814 letter, noting that Russia would be grateful to Gnedich for his hexameter *Iliad.*[51] Disenchanted with his initial alexandrine verses, Gnedich experimented with a Russian version of the ancient hexameter that would capture the beauty and power of the Greek original. His use of this medium reflected his desire to seek guidance directly from classical sources rather than from French models of antiquity. He and his supporters hoped that a viable Russian hexameter would allow lyric and epic poets to create original works based on national tradition.[52]

Gnedich's manuscripts in the Saltykov-Shchedrin State Public Library indicate his diligent working and reworking of the *Iliad.*[53] Beginning in 1813, he redid his previous alexandrine translation, and over the next sixteen years, he tapped the expertise of numerous classical scholars to complete his magnum opus. The Olenin-Gnedich correspondence clearly reveals that Olenin's knowledge of art, archaeology, and vase-painting provided invaluable insight into Hellenic civilization. Olenin's command of ancient Greek further helped Gnedich to understand and to translate particularly difficult passages.[54] Published in two volumes in 1829 and dedicated to Nicholas I, the Gnedich *Iliad* appeared in an extremely attractive edition featuring a map of Troy; illustrations of Agamemnon, Achilles, Nestor, Odysseus, Paris, and Menelaus; summaries of the twenty-four books; explanatory notes; and an introduction on Gnedich's views of Greek antiquity.

After acknowledging Olenin's assistance, Gnedich described Homeric Greece as a unique civilization with distinct religious, moral, and artistic principles. To fathom this era, students and scholars had to place themselves in the world of Homer. They had to live and breathe the atmosphere of Homer's heroes, gods, and myths. Gnedich claimed that his *Iliad* would facilitate this cultural transfer, allowing readers to understand Homeric Greece on its own terms. He called the *Iliad* an excellent encyclopedia of antiquity, "a marvelous portrait aflame with life and movement." The epic illumined the classical world "with its gods, religion, philosophy, history, geography, morality, customs—everything, in a word, that was ancient Greece."[55] Gnedich's introduction conveyed the spirit of Herder's historicism by affirming that masterpieces of any one nation were rooted in its unique historical experience and could not be imitated by another nation. Writers could hardly copy the ancients because of the historical and cultural differences between their respective eras and peoples. Homer captured the creative genius of his time and place. His works embodied authenticity, originality, and *narodnost'*, the key qualities in any national literature. While the Homeric epic could not be imitated, it could indeed guide and inspire writers to create Russian works with national spirit and identity.

Eagerly awaited before its appearance, the Gnedich *Iliad* was a major cultural event of the time. Critics acknowledged the high quality of the translation and its significance for Russian letters and classical learning. Laudatory reviews of Gnedich's 1821 recitation of Homeric passages at the Imperial Russian Academy set the tone for the wide acclaim aroused by the publication of the complete epic in 1829.[56] The exiled Pushkin, in a letter of March 1821 to Gnedich, alluded to the *Iliad* in progress when he addressed the translator as "You, given by fate a bold mind and a lofty soul and doomed to solemn songs, to comforting the solitary life, O you, who resurrected the majestic ghost of Achilles, who manifested Homer's Muse to us and liberated the bold singer of glory from clanking bonds. Your voice has reached me in isolation."[57] Pushkin heralded the publication of the epic as a landmark event in Russian literature and dedicated several poetic tributes to the Russian Homer for evoking the spirit of Homeric Greece. One such Pushkin accolade declared that "Sacred, sonorous, is heard the long-muted speech of the Hellenes. Shaken, my soul knows thee near, shade of the mighty old man."[58]

Pushkin elaborated on Gnedich's dedication and effort in a critique of the translation published in 1830 in *Literary Gazette* (*Literaturnaia gazeta*):

> The translation of the *Iliad*, so long and so impatiently awaited, has at last appeared! When writers spoiled by fleeting success have for the most part concentrated on brilliant trifles, when talent shuns work and fashion sets at nought the lofty models of the ancient world, when poetry is no longer a

form of dedicated service but only a frivolous pastime, we regard with feelings of the deepest respect and gratitude a poet who proudly gave the best years of his life to something which claimed his entire attention, to disinterested inspiration, to the completion of a single, sublime task. The Russian *Iliad* is before us. We turn to studying it so that in time we can give an account to our readers of the book which is bound to exercise such an important influence in our native literature.[59]

The literary critic Vissarion G. Belinskii (1811–48), the founder of Russian critical realism, shared the sentiments of Pushkin. He called the Gnedich *Iliad* an eternal gift to Russian culture for which there was no sufficient reward. The *Iliad* "constituted an epoch in our literature, and the time will come when it will be a reference work for every educated person."[60] The Romantic writer Zhukovskii paid Gnedich perhaps the supreme compliment by rendering Homer's companion epic, the *Odyssey*, into Russian hexameter. Since Zhukovskii did not know enough ancient Greek, he thus worked from the German *Odyssey*. Zhukovskii labored for seven years (1842–49), finally producing a Russian *Odyssey* that was inspired and greatly facilitated by Gnedich's achievement.[61]

Gnedich clearly succeeded in his major literary creation. His poetic accomplishment fashioned the Russian hexameter into an effective instrument for translating classical poetry. It also enriched Russian letters, offering poets a viable medium for original work because appreciation of the Homeric world, with its charm and grandeur, intensified artistic interest in Russian folk tales and legends, a mainspring for creativity in Russian art, music, and literature during the nineteenth century. That the Gnedich *Iliad* remains the standard Russian translation is telling evidence that he fulfilled his basic objective of introducing readers to what he considered the first and best masterpiece in world literature.

Gnedich's esteem for Homer and the Greek classics inspired him to undertake related endeavors. He translated Homeric hymns to Minerva, Diana, and Venus (1809–11). Classical motif and allusion animated his original verse, such as "Lament of Thetis over the Grave of Achilles" ("Setovanie Fetidy na grobe Akhillesa," 1813), "To Morpheus" ("K Morfeiu," 1816), and "Birth of Homer" ("Rozhdenie Gomera," 1816), which he dedicated to Uvarov for encouraging use of the hexameter. In addition to the epic, Gnedich admired the classical idyll as a genre worthy of emulation. He thus adapted Theocritus's "Cyclops" ("Tsiklop," 1813) to Russian life by making Polyphemus an inhabitant of St. Petersburg and translated another Theocritus idyll, "Syracusan Women" ("Sirakuzianki," 1820–21). Gnedich's most important effort in this genre was his national idyll "Fishermen" ("Rybaki," 1822), set in St. Petersburg and depicting Russian reality with concrete imagery. His Neva fishermen, despite their stylized language, evoke the simplicity and charm of Theocritus's shepherds.[62]

The philhellenism of Gnedich encompassed the modern as well as the ancient Hellenes, and he pioneered the study of modern Greek poetry in Russia. Immersion in Homer and the classical legacy also prompted his interest in the fate and the poetry of the modern Hellenes. Gnedich's sympathy for Greek liberation stemmed as well from his support of liberal causes, being in line with many writers in Russia and the West whose philhellenism was rooted in their political liberalism. Although Gnedich did not participate in the Decembrist uprising, he advocated the ideals of liberty and reform that shaped the Decembrist movement. His contacts and friendships with Decembrist poets who championed Greek freedom reinforced his philhellenic zeal.[63] Gnedich translated the incendiary "War Hymn" ("Thourios") of Rigas Pheraios (1757–98), the Greek poet-martyr executed by Ottoman authorities for his political radicalism. "War Hymn" was Rigas's most popular writing and had a wide circulation among Greek subjects of the Porte. The poem's ardent patriotism and Rigas's martyrdom incited national feeling that fueled the Greek resurgence.

The Gnedich translation, "War Hymn of the Greeks" ("Voennyi gimn grekov"), was published in 1821 in *Messenger of Europe*. The translator faithfully conveyed the martial tone and spirit of the original: "Take heart, people of Greece! The day of glory has arrived. We will show that the Greek has not forgotten freedom and honor. We will overturn centuries of slavery and tear the fetters from our neck. We will avenge the sacred fatherland, covered with shame. Let's be off. God sides with the just! Let the blood of tyrants seethe like a river beneath our feet." Gnedich further captured Rigas's appeal to the ancients to rise up and embolden their enslaved descendants: "O slumbering shadows of heroes and wisemen! O Hellenes of times long past! Rise up from the graves! . . . The road to glory is known to you. Lead your offspring to the seven-hilled city!" The contemporary Hellenes, in turn, were summoned to emulate their heroic ancestors:

> O Sparta, Sparta, mother of heroes! What, you sleep the sleep of a slave? Heed Athens, your ally. To the call of its vindictive warriors! To ranks! In song we will call on the heroic Leonidas before whom the mighty Persian forces fell to the dust. We remember, brothers, Thermopylae, the battle for freedom! With three hundred brave fighters, one man held back the Persians and became an eternal exemplar of love for the fatherland, fighting like a proud lion amid waves of blood.[64]

That Russian authorities grasped the revolutionary message of "War Hymn" is evinced in the attempt by the censorship committee to exclude the poem from the 1832 edition of Gnedich's collected works.[65]

Gnedich deepened and broadened his knowledge of modern Greek poetry, publishing a collection of *klephtic* ballads entitled *Folk Songs of the Modern Greeks* (*Prostonarodnye pesni nyneshnikh grekov*, 1825). The collection was

largely based on the two-volume work *Les chants populaires de la Grèce moderne*
(Paris, 1824–25) by the French poet, folklorist, and Neohellenist Claude
Fauriel (1772–1844).[66] The ballads, part of the demotic tradition in Greek
folk culture, depict the bravery and tenacity of freedom fighters *(klephts)*
who inhabited the mountainous enclaves of the Peloponnese and Greek
mainland. The Greek fighters' four-century opposition to Ottoman rule
made the *klephts* heroic symbols of Greek resistance. Ballads narrated concrete episodes of battle, death, and valor, celebrating the *klephtic* code of
honor and commitment to liberty. Songs composed in the early nineteenth
century voiced a growing national awareness that reflected the upsurge in
Greek patriotism. Gnedich thus rendered into Russian not just verse tales
about the daring deeds of individual warriors but also Greek national
hopes for liberty from alien rule.[67]

The Gnedich collection of Greek ballads represented a natural extension of his preoccupation with the Homeric epic. Both types of poems were
intimately connected and mutually inspired by his philhellenic muse.
Along with publicizing the cause of Greek freedom, the *klephtic* songs were
a useful guide for understanding Homeric Greece, and the Greeks fighting
for emancipation must have struck Gnedich as the living embodiment of
the warriors depicted by Homer. Studying the image and lifestyle of the
klepht thus allowed Gnedich to grasp and to delineate more firmly the features of Homer's protagonists. The *Folk Songs* should therefore be considered a companion piece to the *Iliad* translation.

The impact of Romanticism also kindled Gnedich's interest in the ballads. Herder's concept of Romantic nationalism, which appealed to Russian thinkers and writers, spawned a renewed appreciation of folk cultures.
While each nation had a unique historical and cultural heritage, folk traditions were regarded as similar because of their shared general qualities
of directness, spontaneity, and authenticity. Familiarity with Greek songs
enhanced Gnedich's awareness that Russian folklore and legend were a
potential source for a distinctly national literature. Gnedich may also have
been influenced by the Romantic cult of the brigand. Romantic writers
and artists portrayed the bandit in various guises: as folk hero and legend,
as revolutionary and freedom fighter, as guerrilla warrior and partisan
against Napoleonic armies, as instigator of the 1821 revolts in southern
Europe, and more generally as rebel against authority and society. The
klephtic ballads of Gnedich thus manifested the Romantic fascination with
both folk culture and the image of the brigand.[68]

Folk Songs was dedicated to the Hellenist Olenin and included twelve
ballads from Fauriel's collection of thirty-five. Gnedich selected those songs
that he felt best exemplified *klephtic* bravery and love of freedom. His translation benefited from the philological expertise of Konstantinos Oikonomos, who urged Gnedich to modify Fauriel's version by omitting, replacing, or adding certain verses in order to render more faithfully the demotic

originals. Each song appeared in modern Greek/Russian parallel text, prefaced by a description of its content and accompanied by explanatory notes on personal and geographical names. In a lengthy introduction drawn partly from Fauriel, Gnedich discussed the historical context of the ballads and their place in Greek folk culture. Relying on the writings of Herodotus, Thucydides, and other ancients to explore the classical ante-cedents of the songs, Gnedich departed from Fauriel's emphasis on the similarities between ancient and modern Greek poetry. Gnedich instead underscored their differences and suggested affinities between Slavic and Greek folk poetry. In approaching the ballads from the perspective of Greco-Slavic literary and linguistic ties, he was influenced by the research of Oikonomos on the relationship between the Greek and Russian lan-guages. Citing works by Byzantine historians and by contemporary Euro-pean travelers in Greece, Gnedich identified parallels in Greek and Slavic songs, folk customs, and place names. With tenuous evidence, he traced Slavic elements in Greek folk culture to the settlement of Slavs in Thrace, Illyria, and the Morea in the sixth century A.D. and to the Slavic presence in the Crimea during the Byzantine era.[69]

Gnedich's *Folk Songs* received laudatory press reviews and wide acclaim in the Russian literary community.[70] In a letter of February 1825 to Gned-ich, Pushkin incisively summed up his legacy for both Russian Hellenism and Russian poetry:

> Your Greek songs are charming and are a *tour de force*. . . . My brother has told me of the early completion of your Homer. This will be the first classical European feat in our fatherland. . . . But when you have rested after your *Iliad*, what will you take up in the full flower of your genius, after you have matured in the temple of Homer, like Achilles in the Centaur's den? I am expecting an epic poem from you. "The shade of Svyatoslav is wandering, unsung," you once wrote me. And Vladimir? and Mstislav? and Donskoy? and Ermak? and Pozharsky? The history of a people belongs to the poet. When your ship, laden down with the treasures of Greece is entering the haven while the crowd awaits expectantly, I am ashamed to speak to you of my small-wares shop No. 1. I have much that is begun; nothing is finished.[71]

Pushkin emphatically hoped that Gnedich, after honing his poetic skills on the *Iliad*, would compose an original epic celebrating the heroic deeds of prominent historical figures in Kievan and Muscovite Russia. Pushkin's description of the *Folk Songs* as "a *tour de force*" can indeed be extended to Gnedich's lifelong zeal for the Greek heritage. His achievement with the Homeric epic and his experimentation with the classical idyll influenced subsequent generations of Russian writers.

Because of the popularity of Rigas's "War Hymn" and the *klephtic* bal-lads, rich sources for Greek prose and poetry, Gnedich also kindled Rus-sian interest in modern Greek letters. After the publication of his transla-tion of "War Hymn," a review in *Messenger of Europe* (1824) praised the collection of *Odes* by the national poet Andreas Kalvos and quoted passages from Kalvos's tribute to his native Zakynthos. The poetic genius of Kalvos, heralded as "the patriotic lyre of Greece," was compared to the creative talent of Pindar. In 1825, the same journal carried the words and music of demotic folk songs from Macedonia, Thessaly, Aetolia, Chios, and Crete. One of the first publications by the folklorist and future Slavophile Petr V. Kireevskii was a lengthy review (1827) of Iakovos Rizos-Neroulos's *Cours de littérature grecque moderne* (Paris, 1827), an important early survey of Greek writing.[72] In the decades after Gnedich's *Folk Songs,* several translations and descriptions of Greek poetry carried forth his tradition of modern Greek studies in Russia.[73]

The philhellenism of Gnedich illumined the inextricable relationship between Russia's classical florescence and Russian poetry of the Greek cause. The cult of antiquity, deemed a vital source with which to forge a uniquely Russian national literature, prompted writers to express solidarity and sympathy with the Greek War of Independence. This reaction was especially true for poets who championed the ideals of political liberalism, and in an age of liberal uprisings, no revolt attracted as much attention and support as the Greek rising. Russian philhellenic poetry commemorated the Greek revolution, and the prevailing sentiment of this verse echoed Russian Hellenism's portrayal of ancient Greece as the embodiment of liberty, beauty, harmony, and creative inspiration.

Chapter Five

Russian Writers

THE GREEK WAR OF INDEPENDENCE profoundly moved the Romantic imagination, including the Russian, and many Russian poets of the Golden Age penned tributes to Greek liberty. Writers were indeed faithful barometers of the widespread philhellenic sentiment in the literary community and in society at large, with poetry of the Greek cause being directly inspired by the classical awakening, the stirring events of the Greek revolution, and the participation and death of Lord Byron. Russian writers enthusiastically supported the Greek struggle and lionized the insurgents, and their poems portrayed the Greeks as heirs of the classical legacy, as martyrs for the Orthodox religion, as freedom fighters against despotism, and as supplicants for European and Russian help. Philhellenic themes in these works also commented indirectly on Russian domestic and foreign policy. Writers thus conveyed prevalent attitudes both toward the Greek rising and toward Russian social and political reality.

The Greek revolt occurred during a period of Russian intellectual transition that led from the Decembrist movement to the Romantic nationalism of the Marvelous Decade. Instrumental to this transition were the abortive uprising of 1825, Nicholas I's harsh repression, and the growing appeal of German idealistic philosophy, emblematic of the Romantic reaction against the Enlightenment's emphasis on reason. The Decembrist generation imbibed the liberal and radical ideologies of the Age of Reason and sought to adapt them to Russia—by revolution if necessary. The early 1820s witnessed the zenith of Decembrist ferment for progressive reform. As patriots and nationalists, the Decembrists also felt the impact of *Volksgeist* and cultivated the Russian national past.[1]

In an age of cross-fertilizing literary and intellectual currents, philhellenism received impetus from Decembrist activism and the Romantic quest for national spirit. Poems dedicated to Greece thus alluded to Russian issues and affairs, with philhellenic images suggesting comparisons between Ottoman and tsarist despotism, provoking reflection on the liberation of Russian society under an enlightened government, and serving as a reminder of the clash between Metternichean legitimacy and Russian national tradition as the protector of Orthodoxy. The educated public's keen interest in Russian foreign policy attested to its abiding concern for Russia's international role in an age of growing nationalism. The Greek crisis in particular conjured up Russia's Byzantine roots and its imperial mission in the Near East. Philhellenism in Russian intellectual and literary circles was thus fueled by liberalism and nationalism, in addition to the classical awakening and Romanticism. In a sense, Greece-inspired poetry bridges the Decembrist radicalism and the Romantic nationalism that later stirred the Slavophile-Westernizer debate.

Philhellenic poetry provides a concrete example of the social and political trend within Russian Romanticism. This trend was variously called literary Decembrism, civicism, or Decembrist civicism. Debate exists on the terminology and the content of civic literature during the Alexandrine era. Soviet scholarship has traditionally identified civicism as the most dynamic and progressive current in Russian Romanticism. Although Soviet specialists recognize the presence of metaphysical and other nonpolitical elements in Russian Romanticism, they emphasize the political ideals that infused Decembrist writing and revolutionary activity.[2] The Western scholar of Russian Romanticism William E. Brown takes a much different approach, arguing that literary Decembrism as a distinctive trend was nonexistent, and he disparages and shuns the politically charged label Decembrist for civic-spirited writing. Brown contends that the stylistic heterogeneity of Alexandrine poets, in particular their divergent tastes, techniques, rhyme schemes, and even literary languages, precludes lumping them together on the basis of content.

Another difficulty, according to Brown and the Western scholar Lauren Leighton, is the elastic definition of "Decembrist writer."[3] The term can refer to conspirators, participants, and all others arrested and punished for complicity in the uprising. The political ideals of these Decembrists, as seen in the cases of Ryleev and Kiukhel'beker, were embodied concretely in both writing and revolution. The phrase "Decembrist writer" also stretches to embrace sympathizers and fellow travelers, such as Gnedich, Viazemskii, Somov, Griboedov, and others who were closely tied to the rebels and who echoed their zeal for liberal reform. Taken even more broadly, the term "Decembrist" encompasses every writer of the era who at one time or another expressed civic ideals in poetry, prose, or criticism. This latter catchall description would include members of the *liubomudry,* the Society of Lovers of Wisdom, who were primarily interested in German philosophical idealism and who subsequently developed intellectual views in sharp contrast to Decembrism. Yet some metaphysical poets, such as Venevitinov, were personally associated with conspirators and sympathizers and composed civic-inspired verses. Decembrist is thus often an extremely broad category embracing virtually every writer of the period who at one point or another articulated criticism of the regime. If one, however, restricts the label to the first two groups of writers—revolutionaries and fellow travelers—one can then identify literary Decembrism as a specific current within the broader stream of Russian Romanticism.

While the variegated ranks of Decembrist writers may have featured artistic and stylistic diversity, as well as different degrees of political engagement in both literature and life, these writers still shared certain themes and qualities that lent cohesion to their creative work. These traits reinforce the notion that a distinct, albeit brief, Decembrist trend existed in Russian literature. Decembrist writers espoused a core of social and political ideals: liberty, patriotism, rule of law, peasant emancipation, and constitutional government. Since free discussion was not possible under autocracy, especially during the *Arakcheevshchina* (the era of harsh repression associated with Arakcheev, Alexander I's chief domestic adviser after 1815), civic-minded authors used literature as a medium to raise social, political, and ethical questions. This practice largely explains the didactic, moralistic, and agitational tone of much Decembrist literature and criticism. Decembrist writing exemplified the Romantic concept of the poet-prophet, whose sacred and divinely entrusted task is to expose injustice and to voice the truth. Decembrist work also manifested the related notion of the poet-citizen, whose public duty is to combine art with social conscience and to promote enlightenment values. Decembrist hopes were conveyed by allusion and imagery drawn from antiquity, the Russian past, and contemporary events. Themes of patriotism and rebellion against tyranny were depicted in such historical settings as republican Novgorod and Pskov and against such historical actions as Muscovite resistance to the Mongols, Russia's triumph over Napoleon, and liberal ferment in southern Europe. Literary icons of freedom included Prometheus, Leonidas, Brutus, Socrates, Dmitrii Donskoi, General Kutuzov, George Washington, and Lord Byron.

The poetry of the Greek cause naturally occupied a prominent place in Decembrist civicism, and Decembrist philhellenic verse often carried implicit criticism of the Russian regime's official declaration of neutrality. Both the Russian revolutionaries and their sympathizers deeply admired classical Greece as the wellspring of liberty, rule of law, and representative government, which were the very goals the Decembrists hoped to attain in Russia. Decembrists believed that Greek and Latin classics instilled the virtues of civic duty, patriotism, and public service, as evinced in testimony to the Commission of Inquiry that investigated the 1825 revolt.[4] These Russian revolutionaries regarded Greek insurgents not just as heirs of classical Greece but as kindred spirits animated by the political ideology of the French Revolution. Praise for Greek liberation thus evoked opposition to autocracy, serfdom, military colonies, and educational obscurantism, realities of post–1812 Russia that exacerbated the liberals' disillusionment with Alexander I's reform intentions and that gave rise to the Decembrist conspiracy. Zeal for Greek rebels, therefore, symbolized aspirations for liberty and reform in Russia. Romanticism also imparted a special urgency to the Greek issue for writers who championed the rights of underdogs against despotic rulers, in this case Greek Christian Davids against infidel Goliaths. The quest for *narodnost'* in Russian letters and the renewed fascination with the Russian historical past prompted further enthusiasm for the Greek struggle, which served as a reminder of the religious and cultural ties between Russia and the Greek East, a unique feature of Russian civilization.

The philhellenism of Russian writers captured more than simply their personal attitude and political ideology. Tributes to Greece, in diverse meter, style, and literary language, mirrored the grecophile sentiment broadly shared in educated society and officialdom. The philhellenic poets were hardly isolated or peripheral figures. They were among the elite of their generation and were well-educated and gifted, with most of them being from aristocratic backgrounds. They generated the intellectual and literary electricity of the Golden Age, evoked the era's hopes and ideals, and served as prominent public officials in the bureaucracy, army, and government departments. They enlivened the social circles of both capitals, belonged to the main literary societies, and contributed to the leading periodicals. That so many and such diverse writers, from the firebrand Ryleev to the contemplative Venevitinov, praised Greek emancipation highlights the wide appeal of the Greek cause in the literary community.

Press coverage of the Greek struggle was the main channel of information for philhellenic writers. Before 1821 journals had published considerable material on the Greek intellectual and cultural revival,[5] but after the War of Independence began, grecophile sentiment was amplified by regular reports on Greek military, naval, and political events. Drawn mainly from Western periodicals, these descriptions were supplemented by topographical and historical information on such key battle sites as Patras, Corinth, Missolonghi, Navarino, and Nafplion. Readers were exposed to the human dimension of the struggle through biographical portraits of prominent leaders, such as admirals Andreas Miaoulis and Konstantinos Kanaris, military captains Odysseas Androutsos and Theodoros Kolokotronis, and the legendary heroine Bouboulina.[6] Periodical literature resonated with a marked Greek bias that reflected Russia's classical awakening and Byzantine Orthodox heritage. Press reports, together with the classical translation projects of Gnedich and Martynov, focused the attention of the literary community on the Greek quest for liberty.

Press coverage, however, was not the only influence on Russian writers. Philhellenic verse clearly indicates that Russian writers kept abreast of European Romantic trends. Such major Western poets as Byron, Shelley, and Hugo composed works on civic themes and glorified the Hellenic rising, and reviews, translations, and news reports in Russian periodicals disseminated information about the Western philhellenic movement, including the writings dedicated to insurgent Greece. This material further inspired Russian writers to commemorate the Greek struggle. Like its Western counterpart, Russia's philhellenic literary community articulated various themes, such as admiration for the classical legacy, compassion for the modern Hellenes whose plight contrasted with their storied ancestors, hatred for the Turk who symbolized oppression and persecution, moral exhortation for Great Power aid to fellow Christians, historical retribution and divine redemption for the ordeal of Turkish rule, faith in the ultimate victory of liberty, and heroic praise for Lord Byron.[7]

The officer and poet Fedor N. Glinka (1786–1880), cousin of the famous nationalist composer Mikhail Glinka, fought at Borodino and authored a thematically and stylistically diverse collection of writings during his long life. He participated in conspiratorial political activity until 1821 and espoused the ideals of justice, reform, and rule of law. As president of the Free Society of Lovers of Russian Literature from 1819 to 1825, Glinka had ties with liberal and radical writers and was deeply influenced by their civic verse. While Glinka upheld Decembrist political values and wrote patriotic hymns, he also experimented with metaphysical and religious themes, especially in his later writing. Glinka sympathized with the Greek struggle and was particularly struck by its concurrence with Napoleon's death in exile. His "Fate of Napoleon" ("Sud'ba Napoleona," 1821) juxtaposes the mortality of one man, even someone of Napoleon's stature, who had moved men and nations, with the immortality of an entire nation reviving itself after centuries of oblivion:

> But Greece will arise from the grave and break forcefully from its fetters! Whose blood flows in Aegean waters? Attention, all nations! There, in a whirlwind, they build a new world! There, the ships of courageous Achaeans rush to death as to a feast! There, oaths and prayers are raised to heaven, and in Istanbul the proud Ottoman flies into rage upon hearing the roar of battle. The cross crowns Thermopylae, and on Olympus a military camp appears.[8]

During his brief imprisonment in the Peter and Paul Fortress for suspected complicity in the Decembrist rebellion, Glinka dedicated another poem to the Greek war. His "To Greeks Seeking Alms" ("Grekam, prosiashchim podaianiia," 1826) recalls the plight of refugees and captives:

> As Europe celebrates general peace and grows accustomed to the bliss of tranquil life, the persecuted Greek, orphaned and poverty-stricken, flees

> from his sweet fatherland, from the land of Ionia, from dear shores, where the battle is for life and death, where Hellas stands up to fight! The *yataghan* [Turkish saber with double-curved blade] of enraged enemies shines there! The words salvation and mercy are not to be found there! Women in captivity, homes cast adrift, infants killed, and destitute emigrants of Athens and Sparta in a foreign land!

In contrasting the surface calm of the Metternichean order to the tremors of war-ravaged Greece, Glinka implies criticism of European and Russian nonintervention. Although disappointed by Alexandrine neutrality, he applauded Russian and Western humanitarian aid for refugee Greeks, "torn by calamity from their native lands" and seeking food, clothing, and shelter "among brother Christians."[9]

Another politically active philhellenic writer was Vladimir F. Raevskii (1795–1872), who fought in the 1812 War and gained legendary status among Russian liberals and radicals for his fifty-year ordeal of imprisonment and Siberian exile. Raevskii served in the Bessarabia-based Second Army in the early 1820s, debating constitutional and republican ideas with fellow reform-spirited officers. Kishinev, the main town in Bessarabia, became a center for political discussion and Masonic groups, whose participants included the exiled Pushkin and the liberal officers Pavel I. Pestel' and Mikhail F. Orlov. Raevskii founded a local organization of future Decembrists and subsequently joined the radical Southern Society of Pestel'. Arrested in 1822 for sedition and propaganda among his troops, Raevskii was imprisoned and interrogated for six years. When he refused to divulge information about the activities of his Kishinev associates, he was sentenced to Siberian exile in 1828.

While incarcerated in Tiraspol, Raevskii wrote several poems that were smuggled out to fellow officers and conspirators. His "To Friends in Kishinev" ("K druz'iam v Kishineve," 1822) urges liberals to act in accord with their civic duty and describes his own steadfastness despite confinement and threats. The poem's last ten lines allude to the Greek revolt as a symbol of rebellion against despotism:

> The morning star shines in the East, and dawn's light is reflected in the whirling stream of blood. Under the sacred protection of the banner, on battlefields of glory, duty summons you to a holy and worthy cause. Hurry! Vulcanian thunder shook the subterranean vaults there, arousing the people's sleep and the hydra of slumbering freedom![10]

The cataclysm of the Greek uprising, likened in the poem to an eruption from the underground forge of the Greek god of fire Hephaestus (Vulcan), shook the Metternichean order and emboldened European liberals. While Metternich and Alexander I feared the Greek outbreak as yet another manifestation of the European hydra of revolution directed by a mythical Paris Committee, liberals and radicals alike greeted the insurrection as a sign of hope and renewal. Raevskii's poem suggests the Decembrists' conviction that the Greek revolt was a decisive event not just for Greece but for Russia's own reform aspirations.

Of all the Decembrist poet-citizens, the foremost was Kondratii F. Ryleev (1795–1826), who was executed for his leadership of the revolt in Senate Square. A major activist in the Northern Society that favored a constitutional monarchy, Ryleev also organized a radical wing advocating republicanism and regicide. His ardent civic poetry enjoyed popularity among the Decembrists, as well as in the wider literary community. His best known work, *Meditations* (*Dumy*, 1822–23), consists of short historical poems about eminent national figures, such as Dmitrii Donskoi, Boris Godunov, Ermak, and Peter the Great, all of whom symbolized patriotism, bravery, and dedication to a noble cause. Ryleev's "Civic Heroism" ("Grazhdanskoe muzhestvo," 1823) and "Citizen" ("Grazhdanin," 1824) proclaim his commitment to freedom and rebellion against tyranny. Along with the Russian historical past, Ryleev relied on classical antiquity for imagery and allusion resonant with contemporary political significance. His ode "Love of the Fatherland" ("Liubov' k otchizne," 1813), dedicated to the recently deceased General Kutuzov, exhorts compatriots to emulate the heroic stand of Leonidas at Thermopylae. Ryleev also promoted literary civicism in the Decembrist almanac *Polar Star* (*Poliarnaia zvezda*, 1823–25), which he edited along with the writer and translator Aleksandr A. Bestuzhev-Marlinskii (1797–1837). The three issues of *Polar Star* were the main vehicle for the civic-inspired prose, poetry, and criticism of Russian Romantic writers.[11]

Ryleev's philhellenism manifested itself in several poems. His "To A. P. Ermolov" ("A. P. Ermolovu," 1821) summons General Aleksei P. Ermolov (1777–1861) to order his troops to fight for Greece. Ermolov, decorated for service in the Napoleonic Wars and commander-in-chief of Russian forces in Georgia, was popular in Decembrist circles. Not only did he advocate military aid to insurgent Greece but he detested Arakcheev, the hated symbol of political reaction, and protected Decembrists banished to the Caucasus. In his rousing address to Ermolov, Ryleev hoped to incite the general to participate in the Greek war:

> Confidant of Mars and Pallas Athena, hope of citizens, faithful son of Russia, Ermolov! Rush to save the sons of Hellas, you, the genius of northern troops! Behold, glory's favorite, by moving your hand formidable regiments will rush like a whirlwind to wage bloody battle with fierce enemies. Like a young Phoenix, casting aside the shackle of involuntary fear, Greece will arise from the ashes and, taking after you, will attack with its valor of old! Already in the fatherland of Themistocles's descendants the banners of freedom are raised everywhere. The earth is soaked with the blood of heroes and saturated with enemy corpses. Slumbering thunderbolts have awakened, and brave warriors stream forth everywhere![12]

Ryleev's closing appeal, "Move, O young knight, warriors and victories await you," went unheeded. Despite Ermolov's call for tsarist intervention against the Turks, he did not lead his forces to Greece. The general was preoccupied with pacifying the turbulent Caucasus, an operation that provoked the enmity of the region's non-Russian inhabitants and diminished Decembrist admiration of Ermolov as a liberal opponent of the regime.

Ryleev's "Desert" ("Pustynia," 1821), another call for political activism, expresses the poet's desire to join Greek rebels: "War seethes! In the Morea a flame blazes! Raising the banner of freedom, the Greek seeks revenge against the Ottoman. But I have not the power to fly as an arrow where my soul aspires." His epistle "To Alexander I" ("Aleksandru," 1821) refers to "a holy war" in "the land of Themistocles's descendants, fertilized with the bones of its sons and soaked with Greek blood." The poet summons the tsar, "a knight of truth and freedom," to "the heroic, sacred, and glorious feat" of Greek emancipation.[13] The Greek-inspired writings of Ryleev capture the enthusiasm of Russian philhellenes and complement the Decembrist literature of political engagement.

The Greek resurgence also had a profound impact on the poet and critic Vil'gel'm K. Kiukhel'beker (1797–1846). A classmate of Pushkin at the Imperial Lycée in Tsarskoe Selo, Kiukhel'beker became a fervent Russian patriot despite his German extraction, serving as an official in the Moscow Archive of the Foreign Office and traveling to western Europe as a diplomatic secretary. The Russian embassy in Paris ordered him to return to Russia in 1821 because he gave public lectures on Russian literature that criticized serfdom and autocracy. Kiukhel'beker then contributed to the underground ferment in St. Petersburg, wrote civic poetry, and coedited the literary and philosophical almanac *Mnemosyne* (*Mnemozina*, 1824–25) with the writer and critic Vladimir F. Odoevskii (1804–69). Named after the Greek goddess of memory and the mother of the muses, *Mnemosyne* bridged the gap between the political and metaphysical concerns of Russian Romanticism. Along with civic literature, the almanac featured philosophical writings by the *liubomudry*, the Society of Lovers of Wisdom (1823–25), whose president was Odoevskii and which immersed itself in German idealistic philosophy.[14] Kiukhel'beker, who belonged to the Northern Society, took part in the 1825 rebellion and was sentenced for life to penal labor in Siberia. The Greek revolt coincided with the Decembrist phase of his literary work, and philhellenism became an integral part of his political liberalism.

Well-versed in the classics from his education at the Lycée and from independent reading, Kiukhel'beker exhibited a firm grasp of Greek antiquity in many original works and translations. Some of his finest poems, such as "Cassandra" ("Kassandra," 1822–23), which depicts the Trojan prophetess blessed and then cursed by Apollo, are infused with classical subject and motif.[15] Kiukhel'beker was fascinated by Aeschylus's *Agamemnon* and by ancient tragedy in general. His appreciation of the classical heritage and his commitment to political liberty found expression in the five-act historical tragedy *Argives (Argiviane)*, written between 1822 and 1823. The play exemplifies Russian Neoclassicism, bypassing French interpretations of antiquity and seeking guidance directly from ancient tragedy.[16] Kiukhel'beker adapted *Argives* from Plutarch's account of the conflict between Timophanes, the despot of Corinth, and his republican-minded older brother Timoleon. The play focuses on the inner struggle of Timoleon, who, after agonizing hesitation, kills his brother out of a patriotic duty to free Corinth from tyranny. Unpublished and unperformed in Kiukhel'beker's lifetime, the drama circulated among the Decembrists. It had obvious appeal for conspirators and sympathizers who recognized Timoleon as the embodiment of moral courage, civic virtue, and devotion to liberty and fatherland. *Argives* had additional political importance in the context of the Greek revolt as Kiukhel'beker regarded Timoleon as a precursor of contemporary Greek insurgents against despotism.[17]

Similar to *Argives* in tone and message is the tragedy *Andromache (Andromakha)* by the Decembrist officer and poet Pavel A. Katenin (1792–1853). Only his banishment from St. Petersburg in 1822 for political activism prevented his participation in the 1825 rebellion. Katenin's *Andromache*, begun in 1809 and finished in 1818, was published and performed in St. Petersburg in 1827. Based on the *Aeneid* and *Trojan Women*, the play evokes the valor and civic spirit esteemed by the ancients and the Decembrists. Like Kiukhel'beker, Katenin also followed the Greek war, to which he referred in correspondence as "the sacred Greek cause against the new Scythians." He compared the defense of Orthodoxy to "the ancients' defense of the honor of their gods."[18] His poem "Genius and the Poet" ("Genii i poet," 1830) alludes to the July Revolution in Paris and to Greek liberation as stimuli for poetic creativity. Katenin's images of Pallas Athena leading her charges and of the cross triumphant over the crescent illumine the classical and Christian sources of philhellenism.[19]

Kiukhel'beker was more radical and outspoken than Katenin in both political activism and civic verse. The philhellenic poems of Kiukhel'beker faithfully express the exuberance and enthusiasm that marked his personality, political conviction, and literary work. His ode "Greek Song" ("Grecheskaia pesen'," 1821), later entitled "To Rum" ("K Rum'iu") after the Muslim name for the fallen Byzantine Empire, presents the Greek uprising as a harbinger of radical change in Russia: "The ages march toward a glorious goal. I see them! They are moving! The statutes of authority have grown old. Peoples until now sleeping have awakened, look around, and rise up. O joy! The hour, the happy hour of freedom, has struck!" The poem captures with dramatic flair Kiukhel'beker's romantic sense of involvement in the Greek struggle:

Friends! The sons of Hellas await us! Who will give us wings? Let us fly! Mountains, rivers, cities: Hide yourselves! They await us, to them in haste! Fate, hear my prayers, send to me the moment of first battle! Let me, slain by the first arrow, shed all my blood. Happy is he who parted with his young life in fiery battle, who fled from bonds and boredom, and who was able to purchase glory after a brief instant of torment!

Kiukhel'beker voices the poet's obligation to memorialize fallen warriors whose fate will inflame subsequent generations to resist tyranny: "Nothing, nothing will drown in the river of the rolling ages. The soul of heroes flies forth from their forgotten graves, fills the strings of bards, and hurls against tyrants the thunderbolts of peoples!"[20]

Another ode by Kiukhel'beker echoes the desire of Romantic writers to seek glory, fame, and martyrdom in the Greek revolt. His "To Achates" ("K Akhatesu," 1821), addressed to the trusted friend and companion of Aeneas, was originally entitled "To Tumanskii" ("K Tumanskomu") after the lyric poet Vasilii I. Tumanskii (1800–60). Kiukhel'beker had met Tumanskii in Paris in 1820–21, and they continued their association in St. Petersburg. The bold and dramatic happenings in Hellas beckoned the two kindred spirits to experience firsthand the fight for freedom:

Achates, Achates! Do you hear the voice calling us to battle, to exploits? My ardent youth, leap up! O friend, let us fly to the sacred battlefield! Joyous blood seethes in our veins. Love for immortality, for freedom blazes. We are bold, we are young. Let us fly to the sacred banners of Marathon! No! No! I will not remain in deadly sleep, in dishonorable, mute, and deathly silence. Sweet battle awaits me, and if I fall I will fall as a hero. Like me, you love freedom and glory, you are forever linked to my soul. Let us rush together there, there, where the star of freedom rises! A fire blazes in lofty hearts. Hellas casts its fetters to the dust! Achates! Ancestors summon us, soon we will begin the divine labor! We will scorn comfort, luxury, and laziness. That triumphant day has dawned for us, when for the fatherland our sword shines for the first time among joyous battles! As the clap of thunder then resounds, the bullet whistles, the sword blazes, in that gloomy and fiery feast: the world will believe us "that we love freedom!"[21]

Instead of joining the Greek rebels, Kiukhel'beker hoped his pen would rouse others to enter the fray. Like Homer, the Russian poet felt obliged to immortalize the deeds of heroes waging war for Greek freedom or, in the Russian context, for liberal reform. The bond between poet and warrior, a common theme for Romantic writers, inspired "To Ermolov" ("K Ermolovu," 1821), composed during Kiukhel'beker's assignment to the Caucasus. The epistle was prompted by a rumor of General Ermolov's willingness to fight for Greek emancipation. Here, the poet pledges to commemorate such a deed, alluding to the patriotic odes of Gavrila R. Derzhavin (1743–1816) that celebrate the exploits of General Aleksandr V.

Suvorov and to Homer's epics that memorialize the deeds of Achilles: "From the depth of ages past, Homer's poem has captivated the universe, and the soul of the great Achilles will never die!"[22] Ermolov, preoccupied with taming the Caucasus, however, turned a deaf ear and in fact dismissed Kiukhel'beker from his service after the poet quarreled with the general's nephew.

In "To Viazemskii" ("K Viazemskomu," 1823), Kiukhel'beker reiterates the Romantic notion of the poet's task to sing feats of valor. The poem is addressed to poet and critic Petr A. Viazemskii (1792–1878), who was dismissed from state service for civic verse critical of serfdom and despotism. In the poem, Kiukhel'beker recalls the euphoria when in Paris he had first heard of the Greek rising: "From the Seine's shores I heard your cry, resurrected heroes, I heard your joyous call, your triumphant battle cry! Impatiently holding a sword, I thought: Will I find an immortal end there amid amazing battles?" The epistle closes by underscoring the power of the poet's pen, as opposed to his sword, in the fight for freedom: "But the poet will preserve the courageous voice of hope. My voice, resounding from exile, will strike proud hearts! . . . Not in vain was passion given me. Even in chains I am free. . . . The celestial temple beckons, will I be fortunate to sit in state near Pushkin and Tyrtaeus?"[23] Pushkin at the time was in exile for his "Ode to Liberty" (1817), while the ancient Spartan Tyrtaeus was popular with the Decembrists for his poems about patriotism and civic virtue.[24]

The capture of the Morean fortress Tripolitsa by Greek rebels and Kiukhel'beker's study of Old Testament prophets combined to inspire "Prophecy" ("Prorochestvo," 1822). The poem emphasizes the Romantic concept of the writer as bearer of truth and as messenger of God's "fire and power to awaken peoples." In this particular case, the poet is obliged to proclaim that God himself "has roused Hellas and broken the iron yoke. Her soul will not be given over to Hell. She will be cleansed by the sword, tried in the furnace, and will rise up before me. Deadly battle will exalt her, and she will shine in new glory." The poet substantiates his vision, portraying the siege of Tripolitsa with images that clearly suggest the active role of the Greek clergy in the liberation endeavor:

> Fires and tears fill the rivers. Joyous Greeks rushed to the terrible and sacred task! An infant draws a sword, women take up arms with men, and men are transformed into lions amid fires, tortures, and battles! . . . God shakes thrones and smites them with thunder. He's the shield of the righteous and the free! . . . Tripolitsa lies in siege, and the loyal army camp, hale and hearty, does not sleep! The holy priest lifted trembling palms to the god of war. In animated prayers and tears, the entire army gathered round on the earth. . . . The inspired *starets* [venerable spiritual elder, usually a monk or a priest] jumped up, sword in right hand, cross in left hand. In a flash, he rushed to the enemy's walls amid fire, smoke, thunder. Blood avenged the murdered

children, young girls, orphans, and widows. In the besieged town there are no besieged, a deadly ditch devours all, all! And the banner of salvation is with you, Peoples! The time is near, near . . . the sun of renewal is rising.

The poet-prophet Kiukhel'beker envisions resurgent Greece enduring trial and tribulation before achieving final victory. Fierce battle strengthens the national spirit and symbolizes Hellas's redemption through pain and sacrifice. Such is the divine message announced by the poet even from exile and prison: "Like the tempest over the plain, my voice will be carried abroad and will resound in the ears of the powerful."[25]

The idea of salvation through ordeal and repentence was echoed in Kiukhel'beker's *Izhorskii* (1835), a Romantic drama in three parts written while in Siberian exile. The turbulent main character Izhorskii, named after the Izhora River in the Russian North, resembles the Byronic portraits of Pushkin's Onegin (Onega River) and Lermontov's Pechorin (Pechora River).[26] Alienated from society and disillusioned with intellectual discourse, the demonically possessed Izhorskii murders his friend out of jealousy, abandons the woman he loves, and commits other misanthropic deeds. Yet he is granted a reprieve to save his soul. Like Goethe's *Faust*, the last part of *Izhorskii* finds the protagonist in Greece helping the rebels in their liberation endeavor. Izhorskii contributes to Greek freedom, thus atoning for his sins and gaining redemption before his death by a Turk.

The War of Independence also appealed to writers who, although they held liberal ideals, neither joined conspiratorial societies nor took part in the revolt against autocracy. The philhellenic verse of these poets, while less strident in tone than that of Ryleev or Kiukhel'beker, reflected the popularity of the Greek cause in the broader literary community. One such writer was Orest M. Somov (1793–1833), a Ukrainian who edited and contributed to numerous journals. Somov is perhaps best known for his essay "On Romantic Poetry" ("O romanticheskoi poezii," 1823), considered a landmark in Russian Romanticism because it encouraged writers to seek artistic inspiration in national legend and folkore. The result, Somov affirmed, would be a national literature with *narodnost'*, *samobytnost'*, and *mestnost'* (local color). Somov practiced what he preached, composing imaginative prose tales based on Russian and Ukrainian historical tradition. These stories anticipated Gogol's use of Ukrainian legend and folklore in his prose collection *Evenings on a Farm near Dikanka* (1831–32). Somov also wrote incisive annual reviews of contemporary prose and poetry for the almanac *Northern Flowers,* which he coedited with the poet Del'vig. These essays greatly influenced the quality and direction of Russian literature and criticism during the Romantic era.[27]

Somov was active in the philhellenic movement as editor of *Champion of Enlightenment and Beneficience* (*Sorevnovatel' prosveshcheniia i blagotvoreniia,* 1818–25), the journal of the Free Society of Lovers of Russian Literature.

This periodical published contributions by Decembrist writers and included several philhellenic poems, such as Somov's "Greece" ("Gretsiia," 1822), an adaptation from a French elegy of 1812 that had won first prize at the Toulouse Academy of Literature. "Greece" contrasts the Hellenic Golden Age with the contemporary plight of the country under Ottoman rule. The poem opens with the poet-traveler's imaginary flight to distant lands: "Where does my imagination take me? I feel rapture and emotion in my soul! Is it to your shores, O Ilis? Is it on your earth I tread, land beloved once by the heavens and inhabited by demigods? Once . . . but now silent and cold." Hellas has become a wasteland under Turkish occupation, with ignorance and persecution replacing the learning and tolerance that had previously flourished:

> Where are those heroes whose mighty hands, threatening their enemies on the field of battle, built a shrine to sacred freedom in these lands? O glorious shadows, hear my tearful voice! Look: Today the Greek, your descendant, is enchained! He is useless, languishing in miserable slavery . . . ! This country, mother of the arts, is sacrificed to barbarians, given over to ignorance! Look how she moans, bent under the burden of fetters! Look how she washes with tears the tombs of valiant sons! In this vast wasteland, falling into scorn from slavery, is it possible? . . . The timid descendants of Pericles behold with cold eyes the ruins of their sublime fatherland! For them there are no great ancestors, no glorious sanctuaries of learning, they have neither grief nor recollections. Their swords have grown rusty, only their chains are audible! Alas, all Greece is but a burial tomb! She is alive only in her ruins. And the traveler, looking around with sorrowful gaze, beholds traces of evil tyrants everywhere. He sees deserted, moss-covered graves. The monument of heroes—here stood Thermopylae! To the earth of these men the Greek bent his back, groaning under the painful blows of the whip!

The poet seeks to embolden the modern Hellenes with memories of ancient glory, but "alas, all is quiet and deserted at my summons, the throng of demigods dead for centuries! Pluto in his world does not return his victims! Here resounds only the sad moan of slavery! When my revered voice repeats the names of great heroes, ignorance with its insolent hand shamelessly destroys the shrines of antiquity!" In adapting the French original, Somov added his own final lines that convey his zeal for the rebirth of Greece:

> My prayer has been heard! The Greek stood up for freedom and sows fear in tyrants! The shadows of ancestors behold with rapture their noble spirit living in their sons! Strike, in a heat of rage, strike blow upon blow! Take heart, the terrible hour of revenge has come! With blood remove your former shame, with the sword gain a reliable peace! You are for liberty, and God is for you![28]

Somov transformed the original's melancholic nostalgia for the splendor of antiquity into a joyous vision hailing the triumph of Greek freedom, a central theme in Russian philhellenic verse.

Somov also published two prose narratives inspired by the Greek struggle. One was a two-volume translation of *Mémoires sur la guerre actuelle des Grecs* (Paris, 1823), which was written by the French volunteer Colonel Olivier Voutier. Somov's preface, based on his previously published article on the subject, dealt with the revival of Greek learning. He then memorialized the Chios tragedy in *Fall of Chios (Padenie Khiosa)* (St. Petersburg, 1824), translated from the account by F. Pouqueville, French consul in Ioannina.[29] An acute observer of Greek and Turkish life, Pouqueville wrote numerous studies of the Ottoman Near East that were excerpted in the Russian press and contributed to the popularity of travel literature on the Levant.[30]

Another liberal writer from the Ukraine was Vasilii V. Kapnist (1758–1823), who was of Greek origin, being descended from one of the numerous Ionian Greek families that settled in the Russian Empire and contributed to their adopted society and culture. Kapnist's grandfather (Kapnisos) arrived from his native island of Zante after taking part in Russian military action against the Turks during the Danubian campaign of Peter the Great. Vasilii Kapnist became a poet, satirist, and playwright. His "Ode to Slavery" (1783) criticizes Catherine II for extending serfdom to the Ukraine. Kapnist subsequently translated Anacreontic and Horatian odes, and his manuscripts contain Russian excerpts from the Homeric epics.[31]

Kapnist wrote one of the longest and most moving tributes to the Greek endeavor. "Appeal to Aid Greece" ("Vozzvanie na pomoshch' Gretsii," 1822) is an ode with vivid classical and Christian imagery. The opening stanzas allude to the tumult of revolution and war:

> What thunderbolts resound at noon, becoming confused with wails and clamors? From where arise the columns of smoke billowing to the clouds? There the cries of dreaded battle are heard, the wild voices of the cruel murderers, and the languishing cry of the murdered victims. The earth shook from blows, fire flared, and the distant horizon flushed. It is Greece, powerless to bear any longer her sorrowful oppression, powerless in sorrowful captivity to endure all the cruelty of misfortune. Against the spiteful tyrant gripping her with fierce brutality, she unveiled the sword of defense, united around the cross, and decided to emulate the glorious path of her renowned ancestors.

Kapnist graphically depicts the sad state of affairs in Ottoman-controlled Greece, equating Turkish rule with destruction, persecution, and oppression:

> But the enemy, for three centuries drinking the blood of this oppressed victim, gathering forces, bringing forth revenge, extended a villain's hand over Greece, defiled sacred shrines, killed innocent clergy, and brought to shame wives and maidens. Villages were burned, cities levelled to the ground,

corpses of citizens heaped in piles like a mountain. Alas, the blood flowing in rivers does not slake the villain's thirst. He wants to cover the entire land with heads, trampling them underfoot. From the vengeance of pride, he wants to transform the entire land into a desert and, with unrestrained rage, to bring death to the living so that all of Greece will become a conflagration. . . . O, ill-fated land, doomed to be inundated by calamities! Exhausted from cruel plagues, stained with your progeny's blood, what will you do in your sorrowful condition?

Kapnist presents the choice facing Greece as "Will you languish in mighty captivity again, or transform yourself in the grave amid your enemies' graves, gathering the remnants of strength to overthrow slavery's hated fetters?" He urges the modern Hellenes to rally behind the cross and to resurrect the deeds of classical and Christian forebears:

You firmly undertook either to fall or to wipe out the painful yoke, you called to your valiant children: "Freedom, brave ones, or death!" The brave rushed for their swords, regiments sprouted as though from the earth. Young and old all in one spirit, inflamed wives also extending courageous hands for battle, and the mortal blow was repulsed. In those lands where glorious ancestors built monasteries and shrines in the fields, where the iron staff and sword of Xerxes were plunged into the earth, where at proud Thermopylae a handful of Greeks held off the Persian forces, and where valiant warriors, saving the fatherland and not retreating a step, were laid to rest, there again a courageous force rushes to the battlefield against the fierce ruler. The tribes of Sparta will rise up again. Beating fetters into swords, all are ready to fly into heated combat without helmets, armor, and shields. Their helmet—the sacred righteousness of battle. Their armor—a strong chest and hands. Their shield—the protection of the All Highest. Be daring, brave children! Already the seas where gallant ancestors sank countless Persian ships recognize your flag. Already your sword flashes and the wind unfurls the banner in those fields where the enemy regiments were laid to rest.

The poet exhorts Europe to assist the struggle for faith and liberty being waged by a fellow Christian people: "You, mighty realms that have pledged to serve the cross! Do you want to estrange yourselves from immortal glory in this fight? Is it possible for you to behold patiently the enemy trampling with haughty foot your coreligionist land and the cross of the East thrown to the ground by the hand of a false prophet?" The Great Powers are summoned "to be daring, to give your hands to the battle. The voice of all faiths will unite and soon the fateful hour of battle against the Muslim will strike." The last two stanzas, addressed to Alexander I, urge the tsar's protection and defense of Greek Christians:

You whose thunders have long been ready to fall upon tempestuous pride, who are accustomed to breaking foreign fetters and to humbling the power of tyrants! Hurry, and from your thunderous chariot, with the stroke of your right hand . . . strike, destroy the nest of evil-doers, and shatter the Achaeans' heavy chains like fragile glass. To you it has been ordained by fate to come, to see, to conquer, and with the hand that saves thrones to restore the order of the East. God himself calls you to the righteous path. He knows that neither lure of glory nor recompense is the aim of your soul, that the peace of empires is your joy, the bliss of subjects your reward, and the victory of the cross your trophy.[32]

Kapnist was the close friend of Gavrila R. Derzhavin, Catherine II's court poet whose odes glorify Catherine's victories over the Turks and her vision of a revived Greek state. Seen against this background, the ode by Kapnist entreats Alexander I to fulfill the Eastern policy of his grandmother.

Kapnist's Greek descent explains his literary philhellenism, yet it is important to note that numerous writers from the Ukraine registered support for the Greek revolt. The Greek cultural tradition in the Ukraine, not to mention the region's Greek communities, may account for the philhellenism of such Ukraine-born writers as Martynov, Gnedich, and Somov. The Greece-inspired works of these authors exemplify the important contribution of Ukrainian writers, scholars, and publicists to Russian literary and cultural life in the Alexandrine era.[33] Another concrete example of Ukrainian impact on Russian letters is the work of Mikhail T. Kachenovskii (1775–1842), a Kharkov native of Greek descent who was Moscow University's first professor of Slavic studies. Kachenovskii acquired notoriety for his criticism of Karamzin's *History of the Russian State*, arguing that the court historian relied over heavily upon tale and legend rather than upon verifiable evidence. As editor of *Messenger of Europe* from 1815 to 1830, Kachenovskii published diverse material on ancient and modern Greece. His philhellenic treatment of Greek themes helped to shape the attitudes of the literary community and the broader educated public toward the Hellenic revolt.[34]

Still another Ukrainian writer who embraced the Greek cause was Vasilii I. Tumanskii, a minor official in the Ministry of Foreign Affairs who served in Odessa from 1823 to 1828 as a clerk and translator for Governor-General Mikhail S. Vorontsov. The Ukrainian writer was subsequently assigned to Russian diplomatic missions in the Danubian Principalities and Constantinople. A talented Romantic lyric poet, Tumanskii contributed to several periodicals and composed introspective verses on love, nature, and nostalgia for youth. While stationed in Odessa, he held a prominent place in that cosmopolitan city's literary milieu and was acquainted with Pushkin during the latter's 1823–24 exile in the Black Sea emporium. It was the poetry of Tumanskii and Pushkin that introduced the Russian South and Odessa into Russian literature. Tumanskii's "Odessa," "To Odessan Friends" ("K odesskim druz'iam"), and "A Thought on the South" ("Mysl' o iuge") evoke the natural beauty, charm, and landscape of his native Ukraine.[35] Tumanskii and Pushkin also dedicated poems to the Greek revolt, an issue avidly followed by Odessa's Greek and Russian communities.

Tumanskii's enthusiasm for the Greek cause was stimulated by his association with Kiukhel'beker. The two men had met in Paris in 1820–21, and Kiukhel'beker's philhellenic ode "To Achates" was initially addressed to Tumanskii. In return, Tumanskii, with his friend stationed in the Caucasus under General Ermolov, recited Kiukhel'beker's "Greek Song" at a meeting of the Free Society of Lovers of Russian Literature in St. Petersburg. Tumanskii later composed his own "Greek Ode" ("Grecheskaia oda," 1823), which voices the battle cry of a Greek warrior seeking revenge for the ordeals imposed by the Turkish occupation:

> Our shining, swift sword smites the enslavers of Hellas. We will fight to the death, without mercy. As *rayahs* [flock or herd, a pejorative term designating Christian subjects of sultan] we thirst for frightful battles. Our waters will be turned to blood until we redeem freedom. We witnessed the execution of friends, the frenzy of the infidel rabble [*chern*'], cities on fire, the profaning of the Lord's sacred altars. Neither sorrow nor threats will help us, blood is necessary for our tears! So, with the . . . insignia on these banners, with the beauty of the inherited shore, with the shame of betrayal and flight, with the dishonor of our children and wives, we take up the sword to wage battle and vow to revenge our enemy!

Until Greek retribution is successfully carried out "for the memory of the ages," fields will remain untilled, young maidens will stay unwed, and people will live without joy. Tumanskii ends the ode with a rousing call for vengeance against Turkish oppression: "O dreams, gratifying the heart! Hopes for the imminent, terrifying funeral feast! Descend from the mountains, sons of the fatherland, close ranks, armor, and shields! Go forward, holy army! In the name of God exact revenge, revenge!"[36]

Tumanskii's two sonnets entitled simply "Greece" ("Gretsiia," 1825) capture the dichotomy of the country's long subjugation and its Phoenix-like revival. The first sonnet laments enslaved Greece's tarnished appearance and lost glory:

> For how long was your cry, like a widow's sorrowful cry, a just reproach to your sons? O Greece, it seemed that God condemned you to the punitive sword! The rock of barrenness, darker than the walls of prison, it seemed that you perished forever, and the Greek vegetated in the glorious earth like moss on a marble tomb. Beholding you, we exclaimed: "No! The flame of great men has been extinguished there! There, in the land of slaves, the weight of fetters is not a burden, and inherited rights for them are not a sacred vow."

The second sonnet portrays the rejuvenation of Greece in a spirit of militant Christianity:

> Take heed! Whose summons shook the vaults of caves, the deep stillness of these ancient leafy groves? The heart trembles, recognizing the familiar voice. . . . The noble spirit of freedom arose, arose! Raising the cross, girding the sword like an angel of battle, it calls to you, persecuted peoples, to redeem glorious rights! The roar of battle drifted overhead as Hellas stirred like a military camp. Warriors for the holy cause closed ranks. Formidable stronghold, unshakeable rock, like divine thunder their sword trampled the enemy and their glory began to resound the world over![37]

Tumanskii's unpublished manuscripts include a short poem honoring Lord Byron and the military captains Markos Botsaris and Giorgios Karaiskakis for their devotion to Greek freedom. All three are praised as fallen heroes bound by their sacrifice for Greek emancipation. The undated manuscript was most likely written shortly after the 1827 death of Karaiskakis, which followed the deaths of Botsaris (1823) and Byron (1824).[38]

Several Russian writers, deeply moved by particular events from the revolt, depicted specific episodes of Greek patriotism. By focusing on the emotional state of one or two persons, the works of these writers dramatize the human dimension of the war and highlight the sacrifice of the entire Greek nation. For example, in 1821 and 1822 most of the Greek Christian inhabitants of Kassandra, Kydonies, and Chios were displaced, massacred, or enslaved. The agonizing experience of Turkish captivity inspired "Captive Greek in Prison" ("Plennyi grek v temnitse," 1822) by the lyric poet Ivan I. Kozlov (1779–1840). Although on friendly terms with Ryleev and Kiukhel'beker, Kozlov composed poems that neither espoused nor sympathized with Decembrist political aspirations. He was probably best known for his personal tragedy. In 1821 paralysis of the legs and total blindness terminated his twenty-year service career and confined him to bed the rest of his life, thus launching his literary career. Much of Kozlov's original and translated verse deals with his private struggle to endure his fate and to find solace in religious faith.

Kozlov's "Captive Greek in Prison," dedicated to the insurgent leader A. Ypsilantis, was one of this poet's rare tributes to the civic theme of liberty. In the poem, the Greek in captivity laments that bondage will prevent his engaging in combat in the liberation struggle:

> Sacred native land, my delightful land! Dreaming of you always, I hasten toward you in my soul. But, alas, they hold me here in bondage, and I am not able to fight on the field of battle! Day and night I am tormented by your fate. In my heart the sound of your chains has echoed. Is it possible for a compatriot to forget his brothers? Ah, either to be free or not to be at all! And boldly with friends we charged like a destructive storm into battle for

the holy cause. But, alas, they hold me here in bondage, and I am not able to fight on the field of battle! In captivity I do not know how the war rages, I await news.

The captive hears rumor of "massacres, the consequence of terrible vengeance," and desires immediate action because "Blood of the native land flows, and I am not there! Ah, amid the storm your fruit ripens, O liberty. Your bright day glows in a flaming dawn!" The captive is consoled by his closing thought: "Let me, an unknown prisoner, suffer if I know you are free, my pleasant native land!"[39] The Greek's acceptance of confinement as a burden worth bearing if Greece is delivered from enslavement perhaps suggests Kozlov's own belief that his physical suffering had to be endured to receive God's eternal salvation.

Anguish over one's native land also moved poet and translator Vasilii N. Grigor'ev (1803–76) to compose "Greek Girl" ("Grechanka," 1824), which eloquently conveys the reflections of a woman warrior after the loss of her parents and the destruction of her native Psara. Captured by Turkish forces in 1824, the island of Psara was victimized by fire and sword. Together with Chios and Missolonghi, Psara came to symbolize the enormous human sacrifice that Greeks were making for their freedom. The poem, written at a time when Grigor'ev was under the influence of Decembrist civic themes, opens with the image of a young Psariot woman in full battle attire: "Why is there a dagger in your hand, daughter of the inspired East? Why does armor grip your young breasts and a helmet crease your curls? . . . You were destined by nature to attract youths with your enchanting glance." The poet wonders why she marches to battle. Is it because of her native land's quest for vengeance, her own besmirched honor, or her betrayal in love? The woman warrior's response poignantly relates the tragic lot of her homeland and her desire for retribution:

> Love did not betray me. Ah, painful blows of fate! That with which I lived will never come again! There, over the ruins of Psara, Greek blood flows! Do not ask: Where is my father, where does my mother languish in torment . . . ? There, there, tomb of my hopes, Psara—crown of thorns! But amid disaster, my spirit did not fall, I can hear the moan of the fatherland. . . . The sound of chains does not deafen the voice of freedom awakened in the heart: Revenge to the barbarians is my firm shield! . . . Do not be despondent, for in the heaven the sun of Leonidas will not be extinguished and the earth of Hellas has not grown cold.[40]

The militant tone of the Psariot woman resounds in "Song of the Greek" ("Pesn' greka," 1825) by Dmitrii V. Venevitinov (1805–27), the gifted poet who served in the Moscow Archive of the Foreign Office. Before his premature death at the age of twenty-two, Venevitinov was a prominent writer, critic, and philosopher. He and Vladimir F. Odoevskii founded the

Society of Lovers of Wisdom *(liubomudry)* (1823–25), the first Russian philosophical circle to focus on the German idealist philosophy of Kant, Schelling, and the Schlegels. Venevitinov authored a relatively small collection of poems (less than fifty), most of them emblematic of the metaphysical current in Russian Romanticism. His verses exalt nature, the poet as philosopher, and poetry as the love of wisdom. Venevitinov was also an ardent proponent of national uniqueness and originality in Russian letters. In combining *narodnost'* and German idealism, Venevitinov and the *liubomudry,* whose ranks included Ivan and Petr Kireevskii, were forerunners of the Slavophiles. Venevitinov and other members of the Society also came together to establish the short-lived *Moscow Messenger* (*Moskovskii vestnik,* 1827–30) as a vehicle for their literary and philosophical writings.[41]

Venevitinov's "Song of the Greek" is one of his few verses animated by the civic ideals of liberty, patriotism, and protest against tyranny. Its setting, drama, and imagery make the poem a powerful tribute to the Greek struggle. Venevitinov portrays the emotional state of a Greek youth torn by despair over the destruction of his village and the death of his parents:

> Under the sky of rich Attica, a fortunate family came forth. Like my father, a simple peasant, I sang about freedom behind the plough. But the wicked forces of the Turks inundated our land. My mother perished, my father was killed, my young sister escaped with me. I hid with her, repeating "for all this my sword will avenge you!" I did not shed tears of bitter grief, but my chest felt constrained and tight. Our small boat rushed us to sea, our gutted village blazed, and the billowing smoke blackened over the rampart. My sister sobbed, her veil covering her sorrowful expression. But hearing her quiet supplication, I consoled her: "For all this my sword will avenge you!"

During the two's escape attempt, a turbaned Turkish sentry guarding a coastal fortress shoots and kills the sister. The incident intensifies the boy's desire for retribution, and he inscribes on his sister's gravestone his sacred promise to avenge her death. In the roar of battle, Muslims came to recognize him by the vow he often declares: "Destruction of my homeland, the death of my fair one, all, all I recall in the terrible hour. Every time, as my sword gleams and a turbaned head falls, I say with a bitter smile: 'For all this my sword will avenge you.' "[42] The quest for retribution, a main theme in the philhellenic poetry of Venevitinov, Grigor'ev, and Tumanskii, underlined a key aspect of the Greek revolution. Greco-Turkish ethnic, religious, and communal tension prompted reciprocal outrages and atrocities, and pervasive fear, alarm, and panic escalated the cycle of violence and transformed the conflict into a war of revenge.

Russian poetry and Russian philanthropy combined in the narrative poem "Chiot Orphan" ("Khiosskii sirota," 1828) by Platon G. Obodovskii (1803–64). A minor official in the Ministry of Foreign Affairs and a teacher in the St. Petersburg Educational District, Obodovskii published verse tales and translations of Schiller and Shakespeare. His most highly acclaimed writing, "Chiot Orphan," is a unique example of literary philhellenism converging with Greek relief aid. Dedicated to "friends of Greece and of suffering humanity," Obodovskii's lengthy work was composed for the express purpose of raising money to ransom a Greek captive in Smyrna and to support the boy's refugee mother in Odessa.

Obodovskii described the genesis of "Chiot Orphan" in a letter of December 1828 to President Ioannis Kapodistrias of Greece, the former tsarist foreign secretary. Obodovskii was touched by the plight of the Dimitrios Lambros family from Chios. During the 1822 Turkish invasion of the island, the father was killed and the mother and three children were taken captive to Constantinople. After separation from her sons and the death of her daughter, the mother was reunited with her older son Kostakis. The two escaped to Odessa, finding haven in the Russian South like thousands of refugees who fled Ottoman reprisal. Then, with the help of Greek compatriots, Kostakis Lambros traveled for medical care to St. Petersburg, where his benefactors included members of the imperial family, who also subsidized his education at the St. Petersburg Gymnasium. From Kostakis, Obodovskii heard the account of the Lambros family's ordeal and learned that the grief-stricken mother, still in Odessa, bemoaned the Smyrna captivity of her younger son Lambrini, fearing his forced conversion to Islam. Obodovskii thus decided to write a verse narrative on the Chios tragedy that focused on the plight of the Lambros family. He sent copies of the poem to President Kapodistrias and to Russian diplomatic officials in Greece, informing them that all funds from the sale of "Chiot Orphan" were to be used for ransoming Lambrini and assisting his mother.[43]

Obodovskii personalized the traumatic fate of Chios by concentrating on the specific experience of one family. He drew heavily on the recollections of Kostakis and on Russian press accounts of the island's destruction. In the poem, Kostakis, the orphaned Chiot, remembers with painful nostalgia his happy childhood, "alive, clear, unforgettable like a song," on the bright Archipelago island lapped by the Aegean's crystal waves, abundantly endowed by nature, and vibrant with commercial activity. In sharp images, amplified by Obodovskii's explanatory notes, Kostakis refers to Ottoman religious discrimination. With few exceptions, Greek Christians are forbidden to raise crosses on graves and to ring church bells, and many churches became mosques, with the crescent supplanting the cross. Kostakis then paints the stark realities of the invasion, sharing sights and sounds indelibly etched in his memory: black smoke billowing, shots ringing out, groans and cries of loved ones, the bloodied sword of the Turk, the decapitated corpse of a parent.

While confined on a ship with his family and other captives, Kostakis had caught a final anguished glimpse of his native land and remembered the sound of fetters, the flashing of swords, and the blood that flowed like a river. The poem recounts Kostakis's one-year ordeal in Constantinople, during which the young Greek loses his sister and is separated from his mother and brother. Reunited by fate with his mother, he and she escape with the aid of Constantinople Greeks to "coreligionist Russia, haven for orphans and defender of suffering Hellenes." Their Odessa-bound ship encounters stormy seas and threatening skies, arousing "holy terror" in the boy. The cry "land, land" brings relief, and "with an eager glance from the ship I [Kostakis] embraced the blessed land illumined by the sunset's ray, the peaceful fields of Russia."[44]

Obodovskii's introduction to "Chiot Orphan" relates both the current status of Kostakis in St. Petersburg and the charitable objective of the poem. The author's explanatory notes, based on published accounts of the Chios massacre, provide valuable historical information that gives readers a context for Kostakis's story. "Chiot Orphan" received laudatory press reviews for its poignant depiction of the agonies of lost homeland, exile, captivity, and forced apostasy. The enthusiastic reception of Obodovskii's work suggests its importance and popularity not so much as an artistic masterpiece but as an expression both of compassion for the Chios victims and of public support for the author's humanitarian aim.[45]

At least one other factor was of crucial importance to popularizing philhellenism: Lord Byron's association with the Greek revolt stimulated the philhellenic muse in both Russia and the West more than any other event in the War of Independence. Byron's disdain of conventional society, his poetic talent, and his political engagement in liberal causes exerted a profound effect upon the imagination of Romantic writers and artists. Byron's famed Eastern tales—"Bride of Abydos," "Giaour," "Siege of Corinth," "Childe Harold"—capture the allure and the picturesque of the Near East. His vision of Hellas embraced the classical splendor and the contemporary landscape, encompassing not just marble statuary, archaeological treasure, and natural beauty but also living people striving for freedom. Byron also created the Byronic hero, a lonely, arrogant, mysterious figure alienated from society and disenchanted with life. The Byronic hero, or antihero, personified the discontent and anguish of Byron's own complex character and turbulent life and, more importantly, evoked the disquiet and melancholy of the Romantic age. Byronism also embodied an attitude of rebellion against virtually everything: political authority, social custom, religious belief, and established canons of literary and artistic taste.[46]

The philhellenism of Byron exemplified his championship of such liberal causes as constitutional rule in Spain and Italy and abolition of the slave trade. For diverse reasons—boredom, restlessness, adventure, fame, poetic inspiration, service in a noble endeavor—Byron volunteered to fight in the Greek war. Upon arrival in Missolonghi in January 1824, he organized the Byron Brigade and publicized the Greek issue abroad by his mere presence in the embattled country. In Greece, Byron encountered fractious Greek military chieftains, whose divergent interests he could not reconcile. He also had to contend with quarrelsome philhellenes, whose misplaced idealism he could not dispel. The most notable of the latter was a disciple of Jeremy Bentham, Leicester Stanhope, whom Byron labeled "the typographical Colonel" for Stanhope's schemes to liberate Greece through Lancastrian schools and printing presses that promoted utilitarian doctrines.

Although Byron was now skeptical about the prospect for Greek freedom, he still supported the war's goal. Byron's time in Greece, however, was short. Suffering an epileptic fit from which he never fully recovered and then catching a cold while riding in a rainstorm, he endured bouts of medicinal bleeding and died of a fever during Orthodox Easter (April 1824). His death transformed him into a poignant symbol of liberty eternally linked to the Greek revolution.[47] Byron's fate enhanced his Romantic image and imparted renewed zeal to the philhellenic movement. Poetic eulogies contributed to the Byronic legend—the heroic fighter for Greek liberation—and kept the Greek issue in the public eye.

Byron, the literary icon of philhellenism, was popular in Russia. Journals carried reviews, translations, and adaptations of Byron's writings, not to mention lively reports of his activity and death in the Greek war.[48] Writers, depending on their style, aesthetics, and political conviction, reacted differently to Byron's poetry, personality, and activism. Devotees admired the turbulent Byronic hero and the exotic Eastern settings, while detractors criticized the rhetoric and bombast in both his life and writings. Yet virtually all Russian poets and critics considered Byron synonymous with literary innovation and experimentation, and he thus cast a large shadow over the Russian Romantic generation. Byron's verse tales and dramas gave rise to the Russian version of Byronism, which, like its Western counterpart, conjured up images of rebellion, alienation, isolation, demonism, and misanthropy.[49] Byronism in Russia received perhaps its most eloquent expression in Lermontov's poetry and prose, including *Hero of Our Time* (1837–40).

In mourning Byron's loss, Russian tributes celebrated his philhellenic fervor. Byron the freedom fighter and citizen of glorious Hellas overshadowed Byron the Romantic poet who was instrumental in shaping the literature and ethos of Romanticism. Shortly after Byron died, poet and critic Petr A. Viazemskii affirmed to his lifelong friend and correspondent Aleksandr I. Turgenev (1784–1845) that Byron's passing offered a rich source of poetic creativity. Turgenev was a key public figure during the Alexandrine era, and he spanned the Russian philhellenic movement by virtue of his official involvement in Greek relief and his association with writers who advocated Greek liberation.[50] Turgenev was thus an appropriate recipient of Viazemskii's letter that saw the poetic potential in the passing of Byron: "What a poetic death, the death of Byron. . . . I envy the poets who with dignity will sing of his demise. . . . Ancient Greece, Greece of our own day, and Byron's death—this is an ocean of poetry."[51] Viazemskii himself received a similar note in June 1824 from the Decembrist writer Aleksandr A. Bestuzhev-Marlinskii, whose Romantic prose tales emulated the verse narratives of Byron:

> We lost a brother, Prince, in Byron. Humanity—its own fighter. Literature— its own Homer of thoughts. . . . He died for Greece, if not for the Greeks. . . . He bequeathed to humanity great truths. In his own amazing talent and in the nobility of his soul one finds a lofty example for poets. . . . History will add him to the number of those few people who were not carried away by self-interest but who acted for the benefit of all parts of humanity.[52]

The death of Byron did unleash Viazemskii's envisioned "ocean of poetry" by major and minor Decembrist and non-Decembrist writers. These commemorative lyrics hold a prominent place in Russian philhellenic verse, in addition to enhancing the appeal of Byron and Byronism in Russian literature.[53] For Decembrist revolutionaries, Byron represented the ideal poet-warrior and poet-citizen, the engaged writer taking up the banner of liberty in literature and social action. He thus symbolized the fusion of poetry and politics, the dual role of the artist as creator and freedom fighter. The radicals' image of Byron, adapted and molded to suit their own self-image, inspired their civic verse and aroused their revolutionary action against the tsarist regime. Byron's impact on the Decembrists was all the more profound in view of their zeal for Greek emancipation, the cause for which Byron had sacrificed his life.[54]

Kiukhel'beker, exiled for his part in the 1825 insurrection, eulogized Byron as a crusader and martyr for freedom in his ode "Death of Byron" ("Smert' Bairona," 1824). In an essay on Russian lyric poetry, published in 1824 before Byron's death, Kiukhel'beker did not highly esteem Byron's literary style, arguing that Shakespeare rather than Byron should be the model for genuinely Russian works.[55] The Decembrist poet and critic now called Byron the patron saint of Greek liberation and the poetic genius whose legacy would enrich the world:

> The amazing comet has fallen, dying amid clouds of thunderbolts! The voice still quivers on the strings but there is no mighty poet! He fell, and amid bloody battles the free Greek drops the sword. Hellas, mother of bright progeny, covers its eyes. . . . Bard, painter of brave souls, thundering, joyous, immortal, forever soar, mighty one, over restored Hellas![56]

Kiukhel'beker's frontispiece depicts Byron with classical features and ancient tunic, thus providing readers with an artistic, as well as a literary, philhellenic remembrance of the British poet-warrior.

The revolutionary Mikhail P. Bestuzhev-Riumin (1803–26), executed for his leadership of the abortive revolt, idealized Byron's ardent muse and his devotion to liberty. His epitaph "Byron on His Deathbed" ("Umiraiushchii Beiron," 1826) paints a fictional deathbed scene, with the poet voicing his dreams and hopes. Greece figures prominently in this depiction of Byron's final thoughts:

> With worthy resolution you decided to dethrone the yoke of slavery, you rushed to resurrect the freedom of ancestors in a glorious feat. O Greeks, Greeks, you armed yourselves against your enemies. Glorious days came for you. You were inflamed by the feelings of your noble ancestors! Spread the word about their glory! They were not burdened by the bridle of slavery. They lived in proud freedom! They must reawaken in you! Take heed of their heroic voice! They summon you from the graves and bless your deed. Respect your ancestors and resurrect their glory!

Bestuzhev-Riumin incorporates Christian and classical imagery to convey Byron's message to Greece:

> You today, O Greeks, were ashamed to be slaves of the impious, you grew tired of bearing disgraceful tribute to Mohammed! . . . For a long time the days of slavery have dawned, for a long time you have been deprived of freedom! Sons of Christ! You have risen, putting trust in the assistance of the church. Your sacrifice glorifies the Christian faith! Do not fear death and do not die as slaves! Seek to acquire the glory of Christ like free sons! The time has come for you to overthrow the yoke of your tyrants and to dethrone Mohammed! Resolve to fall or to triumph! Take vengeance on the barbarians for their villainy, for all the families destroyed, for your brothers, wives, and children. Complete your task—it is holy! And grateful descendants, respecting your famous actions, will pronounce your glory![57]

In reality, Byron was not a practicing Christian believer nor did he couch his philhellenism in religious appeals, but through the classical and Christian allusion, Bestuzhev-Riumin evokes Hellenism and Eastern Orthodoxy as the twin sources of the Russian philhellenic movement.

The firebrand poet Ryleev, also executed for his major role in the Decembrist rising, interpreted Byron's death as martyrdom for Greek independence. This stirring event reinforced Ryleev's revolutionary activism against the regime. His ode "On the Death of Byron" ("Na smert' Beirona," 1824) captures the diametrically opposed reactions of Greek and Turk to Byron's death:

> Why, amid the horrors of war, is there anguish and funeral mourning? Where do the sons of sacred Greece run upon hearing the sorrowful cry? For a long time now Greece has been soaked with tears and blood during the holy struggle. With what new calamity do the Fates threaten the fatherland of Themistocles? Why does the tyrant of the sumptuous East, on his shaky

throne, rejoice? Why do old and young in Istanbul hurry to give thanks to the Prophet? I see: A coffin stands before the holy altar in the church of Missolonghi, the entire catafalque gleams like fire in the transparent smoke of the incense. A crowd of stirring, sobbing people surges by it, as though the freedom of resurrected Greece lies in the grave, as though age-old fetters are ready to oppress her once again.

In Ryleev's ode, Byron's fate has special significance for Great Britain: "Proud queen of the seas! Be proud not of gigantic strength but of lasting civil glory and the valor of your children. Soaring intellect, noble spirit, luminary of the century, your son, your friend, your poet, Byron died in the prime of his years in the holy struggle for Greek liberty." The poet believes that future generations of British citizens will honor Byron's tomb, proclaiming with national pride to their children that "Here sleeps the sublime poet! He lived for England and the world, he was, to the astonishment of the age, a Socrates in mind, a Cato in spirit, and the victor over Shakespeare. He divined everything under the sun. He was indifferent to persecution by fate, he was obedient only to genius, and he did not recognize other authorities." Ryleev closes his encomium with Greece's lament for the fallen Byron: "When he ended his young life in a country far from his native land, the grief-stricken Greek spoke of him to Europe: 'The friends of freedom and of Hellas are everywhere in tears, reproaching fate. Only tyrants and slaves rejoice over his sudden death.' "[58] In actuality, the death of Byron was mourned by Greeks and philhellenes and came as a relief to Metternichean statesmen who had condemned the 1821 revolt as a blow against legitimacy and who now hoped that public zeal for the Greek cause would abate. Byron's fate was also hailed by the sultan who had denounced Byron as a state enemy for assisting rebellious subjects.

Epitaphs by writers who shunned liberal activism portray Byron more faithfully than the politically charged accolades by radical civic poets. The nonpoliticized tributes, while still associating the British poet with Greek liberty, generally depict Byron as a complex, complicated personality and as a poetic master whose turbulent nature and misanthropic streak precipitated his premature death. One writer who certainly did not sing Byron's praises was Zhukovskii, Russia's premier Romantic poet until Pushkin and the future translator of the *Odyssey*. Zhukovskii wrote numerous works that introduced Russian readers to German and English Romanticism, and although he initially favored Byron's lyrics and rendered some of them into Russian, including "Prisoner of Chillon," the Russian Romantic then grew disenchanted with Byron's self-indulgence and lack of restraint. Byron's rebuke of conventional morality and his reproach of religious tradition, which appealed to Romantics rebelling against the established order, repulsed the introspective and contemplative Zhukovskii. No two spirits within the same broad literary movement could have been more unlike, with the melancholy and pensiveness of Zhukovksii clashing with Byron's iconoclasm. This dichotomy was underscored in their very different positions in society: Byron the social outcast and the champion of the politically oppressed, Zhukovskii the upholder of autocracy and the longtime Russian language tutor to the imperial family.[59]

Confined to bed by paralysis and blindness, the poet Kozlov echoed Zhukovskii's nostalgic and melancholic tone. Kozlov also rejected Byron's excesses and his rebellion against the Christian faith, and yet he deeply admired Byron's verse and learned enough English to translate "Bride of Abydos," as well as passages from "Corsair," "Childe Harold," and "Don Juan." These works, along with Kozlov's renditions of Robert Burns, Thomas Moore, and William Wordsworth, contributed to the popularity of English Romantic literature in Russia.[60] Kozlov's "Byron" ("Beiron," 1824), dedicated to Pushkin, is one of the first epitaphs to the English poet. It portrays Byron as endowed with noble blood, wealth, and property but notes that his prize possession is "a miraculous-sounding lyre." The poem also depicts Byron as having a proud soul that is restless and brooding, haunted by anguish and alienated from society:

> In the stormy outbursts of all youthful feelings, the love of freedom always breathed, and the sharp flame of fateful passions blazed in the proud soul. The young spirit was troubled, a sorrow without grief drew him afar after a secret phantom. The waves began to roar behind him! He seized the lyre with trembling hand and pressed it to his heart with sullen melancholy. The strings sounded mysteriously. He wandered for a long time in Eastern lands and celebrated magical nature. Under the joyous sky, in sweet-scented forests, he sang freedom to the oppressed. He, the ecstatic singer of love's sufferings, expressed to the heart all the secrets of hearts, all the raptures of turbulent passion. . . . Time flowed pensively in songs, wonderful songs crowned the young brow with rays of immortality, but did not drive away the gloom from his face. Despondently he looked at the world and people. Stormily he lived out life in his springtime. He feared to believe in hopes. Visible on him were traces of deep, weighty thoughts, the seething abyss of fire and dream, and his soul was on friendly terms with grief.

The poet suggests Byron's concern for humanity by emphasizing the latter's action in Greece:

> But the battle for freedom, faith, and honor in Hellas inflamed him. Glory arose from the dead, and vengeance blazed. . . . At the sound of drawn swords, he was first with his money, army, and lyre and decided to complete the deliverance. He's there, in the fateful struggle he supports with great soul the great deed, the sacred salvation of Hellas. . . . O land of poetry and valiant deeds . . . Hellas! He unites his destiny with your fate at your bloody hour, the radiant genius glows over you like a star of rebirth and glory. He is there!

> He saves! Death hovers over the singer! The young flower fades in its bril-
> liance! He will not be the creator of beautiful deeds, and the miraculous
> strings have grown silent![61]

During his final hour, according to the poem, Byron dreams of his native
land, his wife and daughter, and his reunification with them in heaven.
Kozlov's Byron thus found in Greece spiritual comfort for an anguished
soul. Kozlov and the Decembrist writers linked Byron's fate to the Greek
struggle, with Byron becoming the icon of liberty esteemed by both the
invalid poet and the revolutionaries. Kozlov added a religious dimension
to his portrayal, interpreting Byron's self-sacrifice as a manifestation of the
latter's altruism and as a vehicle for the English poet's redemption.

The metaphysical poet Venevitinov eulogized Byron in one of the former's few civic-spirited verses, "Byron's Death. Four Excerpts from an Unfinished Prologue" ("Smert' Bairona. Chetyre otryvka iz neokonchennogo
prologa," 1825), which opens with Byron's personal reflections on his
flight to Greece:

> I rushed to you, land of enchantments! I dreamed of you in your brilliance,
> and in the magical hours of dreaming your clear image flew before me on
> iridescent wings. You promised to grant me healing rapture to satiate my
> greedy spirit with the treasure of ages. The harmonious chorus of your sing-
> ers, resounding with enchanting harmony, lured me to your distant southern
> shores. Here I thought to lift the mysterious shroud from the brow of mysteri-
> ous nature, to discern up close its concealed features, and in an ocean of
> beauty to forget the deception of love and to forget the deception of
> freedom.

The ensuing dialogue between an anonymous Greek leader and Byron,
identified simply as "Son of the North," confirms the British poet's readiness to join the fray and to die if necessary in battle. The Greek then recounts with specific detail his experience of naval warfare near Chios:

> Yes! Death is sweet when you bear the flower of life in tribute to your father-
> land. I myself encountered it more than once among our valiant forces. . . .
> I recall the glorious shore of Chios, it is also in the memory of our enemies.
> Spending the night in a secure haven, the slumbering Muslims did not think
> about the roar of battles. Rest lulled them into carelessness. But we, we
> Greeks were not afraid to disturb the sleep of our enemies. We sailed in ten
> boats, fateful lightning soared overhead, and in a flash the naval ramparts
> caught fire. Heaps of ships flew about, and everything subsided in the abyss
> of the waters. What did the bright ray of morning illumine? Only the deserted
> ocean, where now and then ship debris floated to the green shores and a
> cold corpse with turban swayed gently over the waves.

The chorus announces the approach of another Ottoman fleet: "On ships
in the distance turbans gleam and crescents sparkle on white sails. The

sultan's slaves set sail, but the Koran's commandmant is no guarantee of their victory. Let courage embolden them! The sons of the Archipelago will send death after them." The final segment of the poem focuses on Byron, with the chorus mourning his death and promising to remember his sacrifice for Greece:

> Eagle! What hostile thunderbolt ceased your bold flight? Whose voice with magical force summoned you to the darkness of graves? . . . Let the distant shore of Albion, trembling, hear that he fell. Gather round, tribes of Hellas, sons of freedom and victories! Instead of laurels and rewards let our vow thunder over the grave: "To fight with ardent soul for the fortune of Greece, for revenge, and in sacrifice to the fallen hero to offer the faded moon!"[62]

Viazemskii, the poet whose letter to Aleksandr Turgenev had forecast an "ocean of poetry" commemorating Byron, paid homage in "Byron" ("Bairon," 1827). Viazemskii admired the English bard's individualism as a writer and as a man of action, calling him "a brave giant, a Columbus of modern days." Just as the explorer "foresaw a young, primitive world, so did you, consumed by insatiable anguish and disdaining boundaries," break new ground in literature. Byron expanded the frontiers of artistic expression by "fusing in his songs the poetry of the soul with the poetry of nature, the harmony of heaven with the harmony of earth." His verse was inspirational, arousing slumbering spirits with "his lightning-quick word and thought like the thundering arrow of a fire." Viazemskii lamented fate's verdict on the poetic talent whose creative work was cut short, yet he praised Byron's commitment to the Greek struggle.[63]

Russian writers who portrayed Byron as the martyr of Greek freedom would no doubt have been disappointed had they known his actual state of mind in Missolonghi. An ardent champion of Greek liberation, Byron was one of the few volunteers with firsthand knowledge and understanding of the cultural differences between Levantine and Western societies. Like many philhellenes, he also became disillusioned with chronic Greek fractiousness that hindered the national resurgence and that triggered civil war. He vented his frustration in letters from Missolonghi, describing a situation that hardly amounted to a united Hellenic crusade to resurrect the world's first and oldest democracy.[64] Byron never took part in combat and failed to reconcile warring Greek factions, yet he lost neither his zeal for Greek liberty nor his desire to serve the Greek endeavor in a useful capacity. He wrote to a friend in March 1824 shortly after his epileptic fit that "I am not unaware of the precarious state of my health, nor am I now, nor have I ever been deceived on that subject. But it is proper that I should remain in Greece; and it were better to die doing something than nothing."[65]

The Greek revolution animated the Romantic imagination and provided a rich mine of creativity. Philhellenic verse portrayed the rebels as heirs of antiquity, as Christian soldiers and martyrs, and as freedom fighters. Epitaphs to Byron reinforced these images and kept the Greek issue alive for the educated public. The Greek cause also embodied the political liberalism and the cult of antiquity that shaped the Decembrist generation. Philhellenic themes epitomized Decembrist civic ideals and thus hold a prominent place in the Romantic literary trend of civicism. The Greek crisis further evoked the Byzantine Orthodox heritage that became central to the Romantic nationalism of the Slavophile generation. The divergence between official policy and public support for Greek deliverance suggests the tension between state and educated society over a host of social, political, and foreign policy matters, and statements of solidarity with Greek liberation symbolized aspirations for progressive reform at home and for national assertiveness in a region historically and culturally tied to Russian civilization.

Chapter Six

Pushkin and Greece

THE GREEK REVOLT MADE AN INDELIBLE IMPRESSION on the poetic imagination of Aleksandr Sergeevich Pushkin (1799–1837), Russia's greatest, as well as most Russian, writer. As the premier Romantic poet in Russia, his views on literary, social, and political issues carried significant weight in the literary community. From his unique vantage point of exile in Kishinev and Odessa, Pushkin observed firsthand the preparations and consequences of the abortive 1821 uprising in Moldavia. He had direct contact with Alexandros Ypsilantis and with other activists involved in the revolt. After the uprising's failure, Pushkin encountered Greek patriots who found haven in southern Russia. While most writers composed only verses celebrating the Greek cause, Pushkin wrote about it in letters, poems, and prose tales. His attitude in these various writings ranged from romantic idealism and excitement to skepticism and disillusionment, yet he continued to support the goal of Greek liberation.[1] His fascination with Greece had an added artistic dimension, manifested in the profiles of Ypsilantis and *klepht* warriors sketched in notebooks and in the margins of rough drafts.[2] These drawings, like his many sketches of historical and contemporary figures, friends and lovers, and targets of scorn and ridicule, constitute a visual diary that provides insight into his creative process.

Several factors shaped Pushkin's keen interest in the Greek revolution. While attending the prestigious Lycée in Tsarskoe Selo from 1811–17, he received an education steeped in the classics and the ancient tradition. His early verses resonate with allusion, motif, and subject matter drawn from mythology and antiquity. Influenced by the French poet André Chénier and by the Hellenist Konstantin N. Batiushkov, Pushkin developed a classical poetic style that featured concision, clarity, restraint, and measure. Batiushkov's Russian translation of selections from the *Greek Anthology* (1820) became a source of poetic experimentation that reinforced Pushkin's epigrammatic style. His brief 1820 visit to the Crimea kindled an interest in archaeological excavation, mythological legend, and other traces of antiquity in the Black Sea littoral.[3] Like most writers of his generation, Pushkin anxiously awaited the completion of Nikolai I. Gnedich's *Iliad*. He praised the translator for "having resurrected the majestic spirit of Achilles" and hailed his masterpiece as "the first classical European feat in our fatherland."[4] Pushkin succinctly captured his classically inspired image of Greece in a September 1822 letter to his brother Lev Sergeevich. Pushkin chided Kiukhel'beker for using Church Slavonic verses in the philhellenic poem "Prophecy" that depicts the embattled land of ancient heroes: "What a strange fellow! Only into his head could come the Jewish thought of lauding Greece—magnificent, classical, poetic Greece; Greece, where everything breathes of mythology and heroism—in Slavonic-Russian verses taken completely from Jeremiah. What would Homer and Pindar have said?"[5]

Exposure to the liberal ferment that culminated in the Decembrist revolt prompted Pushkin's sympathy for Greek liberty. His friendship with Ivan I. Pushchin and Kiukhel'beker, fellow Lycée classmates and future Decembrists, nourished his love of freedom, as did the outpouring of Russian patriotism generated by the 1812 War. Pushkin's social and political views, like those of fellow liberal and Westernized aristocrats, embraced the ideals of constitutional monarchy, rule of law, and emancipation of the serfs by an enlightened tsar-liberator. His gentry liberalism found expression in epigrams and poems critical of despotism, censorship, and serfdom, most notably "Ode to Liberty" ("Vol'nost'. Oda," 1817), "To Chaadaev" ("K Chaadaevu," 1818), and "Countryside" ("Derevnia," 1819). These works circulated widely in manuscript among the Decembrists, who hailed Pushkin as their poet-warrior and poet-citizen.[6]

Although he did not join any of the secret societies that began to form in St. Petersburg, Pushkin's politically charged writing made him the key spokesman for the enlightened liberal opposition to autocracy. His reputation as the poetic voice of liberalism and the anti-authoritarian streak in his conduct heightened the regime's suspicion of him. As a result, in 1820 Pushkin was removed from his position as an archival official in the Ministry of Foreign Affairs and exiled to Kishinev. He received an administrative transfer placing him under the supervision of General Ivan N. Inzov, vicegerent of the recently annexed (1812) Ottoman province of Bessarabia.

Pushkin's actual relationship with the future Decembrists remains a subject of some controversy. His subsequent disappointment with liberalism and his association with Nicholas I, Pushkin's personal censor after 1826, raise questions about the sincerity of his liberal convictions. Walter Vickery has suggested that Pushkin was never as consistently liberal as his reputation among contemporaries or as his exile might lead one to expect.[7] The ambivalence surrounding Pushkin stems in part from the fact that he wrote a great deal of poetry with political, moral, and philosophical themes, but although each poem may ring true, as a body these poems do not cohere to a consistent political philosophy. Victor Terras is probably correct in observing that "Pushkin responded to a given idea, emotion, or insight with the instinct of an artist, perceived it as a theme, and gave it objective expression without projecting onto it any preconceived idea."[8] Although Pushkin's verse may not have satisfied the political taste of Decembrist radicals, the fact remains that, prior to exile, this work was inspired by the liberal ferment and championed the liberal cause.

Pushkin's liberal outlook, however, did radicalize in the remote outpost of Kishinev.[9] Isolated from his friends and from the literary and social excitement of St. Petersburg, Pushkin sought stimulating company. He associated with the progressive-thinking army officers Vladimir F. Raevskii, Pavel S. Pushchin, and Mikhail F. Orlov, and he befriended retired colonel and 1812 war hero Vasilii L. Davydov (1792–1855), whose estate in nearby Kamenka became a political magnet where future Decembrists discussed their ideals and reform plans. Pushkin frequented these gatherings and joined the Masonic lodge Ovid No. 25, composed of liberal officers who aspired to improve the status of their soldiers through education. Pushkin's ties with such groups were risky as the tsarist regime suspected Masons of conspiratorial designs and included them in the 1822 ban on secret societies. Pushkin also met and thought highly of the radical thinker Pavel I. Pestel', the organizer of the Southern Society who espoused regicide and republicanism in the fight against autocracy. In a diary entry of 1821, Pushkin wrote that "only a revolutionary like M. Orlov or Pestel' can love Russia, in the same way as only a writer can love language. Everything must be created in this Russia and in this Russian language." He thus linked his efforts to craft a supple literary language and versatile style with the political reform endeavors of Orlov and Pestel'.[10]

It was in Kishinev that Pushkin composed his most outspoken political poem, "Dagger" ("Knizhal," 1821), dedicated to the assassins Brutus, Charlotte Corday, and Karl Ludwig Sand, who murdered the reactionary German playwright and tsarist agent August Friedrich von Kotzebue in 1819, resulting in Metternich's repressive Karlsbad Decrees and in Sand's execution. Classical allusion and imagery highlight the theme of Fate's retribution for the injustice of tyrants, a revenge exacted by "the secret guardian of freedom, the avenging dagger, the final arbiter of shame and insult."[11] The poem's incendiary ring made it widely popular in radical Decembrist circles. A year later, Pushkin specifically addressed Russian despotic rule in "Notes on Eighteenth-Century Russian History," which criticized Catherine II for extending serfdom, persecuting the free-thinkers

Novikov and Radishchev, posing falsely as an enlightened legislator, and allowing her lovers to plunder the treasury.[12] Pushkin's radical fervor was also manifested in his initial zeal for the 1820–21 uprisings in Spain, Portugal, and Naples.

Exile in Kishinev (1820–23) and later in Odessa (1823–24) profoundly altered Pushkin's literary development. As Stephanie Sandler has noted in her recent study, Pushkin became Pushkin in exile.[13] His predicament gave him firsthand experience of the writer's precarious status in tsarist Russia's authoritarian political culture. More importantly, his poetic talent flowered and matured under the influence of new sights, sounds, and sensations gleaned from travels in the Caucasus, the Crimea, and Bessarabia. His letters and southern-inspired works captured the radiance and the ineffable charm of the Russian South, with its snow-peaked mountains, bright sea, lush vegetation, and picturesque enclaves of Tatars, Gypsies, and Circassians dotting the landscape.[14] The scenery not only captivated Pushkin but enriched his poetic genius and sharpened his perception of the diverse lands and peoples encompassed within Russia.

Along with the allure and natural beauty of the Russian South, Pushkin felt the impact of Byron and Byronism.[15] The Caucasus and the Crimea evoked the geographical and cultural atmosphere of the Near East, the setting for Byron's Eastern tales. The experience of exile induced in Pushkin a mood echoing the disquiet, the protest against authority, and the estrangement from society that characterized the Byronic outlook. Aleksandr N. Raevskii (1795–1868), who accompanied Pushkin on his trip to the Caucasus and the Crimea, reinforced this Byronic mood and the poet's fascination with Byron's works. Many who knew Raevskii considered him the epitome of Byronic skepticism and cynicism. Whether from conviction or from fashionable pose, Raevskii negated all positive values and rejected ethical, religious, and aesthetic principles. Pushkin referred to Raevskii in a letter of October 1823 as "my mentor as regards ethics," and the former's 1823 poem "Demon" portrays an evil spirit of doubt and denial that many contemporaries interpreted as a psychological profile of Raevskii.[16] So, all these various factors made Pushkin receptive to the literary influence of Byron, in particular the English poet's Eastern tales.

The three verse narratives in Pushkin's southern cycle—"Prisoner of the Caucasus" (1820–21), "Fountain of Bakhchisaray" (1821–23), and "Gypsies" (1823–24)—evince a Byronic impact in their exotic setting and their characterization. Pushkin's protagonists have distinct traits of the Byronic hero, melancholy, alienation, arrogance, individuality, and a misanthropic streak combined with noble intention. In adapting these features of Byronism to Russian literature, Pushkin, however, diverged from Byron in poetic style. Byron's verbosity and vagueness contrast sharply with Pushkin's brevity, precision, and lucidity. The Russian poet's epigrammatic, craftsmanlike style demonstrates that, even in his Byronic phase, he retained the unique attributes of his poetic genius. These qualities, cultivated in his early work under the influence of French and Greek literary tradition, helped to make Pushkin the most versatile and gifted writer of the Golden Age of Russian poetry.

Pushkin's interest in Greek liberation was thus rooted in his appreciation of the classical heritage, his political liberalism, and his experience of exile in the Russian South. His first response to the Ypsilantis-led insurrection in Moldavia came in a lengthy letter to Vasilii L. Davydov, whose estate in Kamenka had drawn fellow liberal-minded officers and Pushkin to discuss political reform. Davydov later joined the radical Southern Society led by Pestel'. The voluminous correspondence of Pushkin, in addition to casting light on contemporary Russian culture and society, provides an invaluable source for tracing his literary growth and political views. As William Mills Todd has shown, the intimate, or familiar, letter attained a high level of stylistic excellence during the Golden Age and was characterized by allusion, parody, digression, exuberance, and occasional social commentary. Correspondence for members of the literary society Arzamas resembled "written conversation, free and spontaneous."[17] Letters circulated widely among authors and critics, and many were penned with an eye to posterity and to possible publication. Letter writing enriched the literary language and helped to forge a viable instrument for Russian prose. The epistles of Pushkin exemplified these features, being especially remarkable for their clarity, wit, and perceptive reaction to current affairs, such as the Greek War of Independence.

Pushkin's March 1821 letter to Davydov, the first of several on the Greek revolt written from exile, opens with the prescient announcement that occurrences in the Danubian Principalities "will have consequences of importance not only for our land, but for all Europe." Pushkin noted that "Greece has revolted and proclaimed her freedom. . . . the Greeks can no longer endure the oppressions and plunderings of the Turkish chiefs . . . they have decided to free their native land from an illegal yoke." He then described in some detail the outbreak of unrest, in particular the various proclamations issued by Ypsilantis to incite Greek patriots:

> On February 21, General Prince Alexander Ypsilanti with two of his brothers [Giorgios and Nikolaos] and Prince George Kantakuzen arrived in Jassy from Kishinev, where he [Ypsilanti] left his mother, sisters, and two brothers. He was met by three hundred Arnauts [Albanian forces], by Prince Sutzu [Michail Soutsos, *hospodar* of Moldavia], and by the Russian consul [Andrei N. Pizani], and he immediately took over the command of the city. There he published proclamations which quickly spread everywhere—in them it is said that the Phoenix of Greece will arise from its own ashes, that the hour of Turkey's downfall has come, and that *a great power approves of the great-souled feat!* [Pushkin's italicized reference to Ypsilantis's hope of Russian support.] The Greeks have begun to throng together in crowds under three banners,

of these one is tricolored, on another streams a cross wreathed with laurels, with the text *By this sign conquer* [the phrase used by Roman Emperor Constantine the Great after his vision to convert to Christianity], on the third is depicted the Phoenix arising from its ashes. I have seen a letter by one insurgent: with ardor he describes the ceremony of consecrating Prince Ypsilanti's banners and sword, the rapture of clergy and laity, and the beautiful moments of Hope and Freedom.

Pushkin captured a sense of the hopes and fears provoked by the war. He went on to evoke the escalating cycle of communal and sectarian violence by relating the massacre of Turkish civilians in the town of Galati: "Turks, one hundred people in number, have been butchered; twelve Greeks have likewise been killed. News about the rebellion has astonished Constantinople. Horrors are expected, but there have been none so far." Pushkin also cited the prevalence of false rumor, such as the war lord Ali Pasha's alleged conversion to Christianity and his intention to join forces with the Suliots. Ali Pasha controlled part of the Greek mainland from his base in Ioannina and claimed to support the Ypsilantis campaign against Ottoman authority, yet most Ypsilantis followers feared the treachery of Ali and recalled his ruthless suppression of the Suliots. Pushkin was on firmer ground when he described the patriotic response by the Greek communities in southern Russia:

> The rapture of men's minds has reached the highest pitch; all thoughts are directed to one theme, the independence of the ancient fatherland. I missed a curious scene in Odessa: in the shops, on the streets, in the inns—everywhere crowds of Greeks had been gathering together. All had been selling their property for nothing; they had been buying sabers, rifles, pistols. Everybody was talking about Leonidas, about Themistocles. All were going into the forces of the lucky Ypsilanti. The lives, the property of the Greeks are at his disposal. At first he had two million [piastres]. One *Pauli* gave six hundred thousand piastres, to be repaid upon the restoration of *Greece*. Ten thousand Greeks have signed up in his troops.

Before the revolt, Pushkin had met Ypsilantis and other activists who belonged to the Kishinev-based *Philiki Etaireia,* the secret society that hatched the uprising.[18] In the same letter to Davydov, he conveyed his knowledge of the *Etaireia*'s existence, its goal of liberating Ottoman-ruled Greece, and its means for recruiting "freedom-loving patriots." Although many segments of Greek society endorsed the *Etaireia*'s revolutionary plans, Pushkin clearly exaggerated when he wrote that "all the merchants, all the clergy to the last monk have joined the society, which is now triumphing." In reality, the social, political, and ideological divisions of Greek society precluded such unity within the merchant and the clerical classes.

Pushkin was more accurate in his assessment that the Greeks, as a result of their rebellion, now joined the Spaniards and the Italians in challenging the Metternichean order: "What a strange picture! Two great peoples [Greeks and either Italians or Spaniards], who fell long ago into contemnable insignificance, are rising from their ashes at the same time, and rejuvenated, are appearing on the political arena of the world." As for Alexandros Ypsilantis, Pushkin sketched a romanticized portrait of the Phanariot prince who had served in the Russian Imperial Guard and had lost an arm at the 1813 battle of Dresden: "The first step of Alexander Ypsilanti is excellent and brilliant. He has begun luckily. And, dead, or a conqueror, from now on he belongs to history—twenty-eight years old, an arm torn off, a magnanimous goal! An enviable lot. The dagger of a renegade is more dangerous for him than the saber of the Turks."

Pushkin closed his letter to Davydov with the urgent question posed by philhellenes in the spring of 1821: "What is Russia going to do? Shall we seize Moldavia and Wallachia under the guise of peace-loving mediators? Shall we cross beyond the Danube as allies of the Greeks and as enemies of their enemies? In any case I shall let you know."[19] Pushkin did not intimate his view regarding tsarist policy toward the revolt, but his attitude can be surmised from the nationalistic feeling evinced in his praise of Russia's military prestige.

Pushkin, in the above-mentioned "Notes on Eighteenth-Century Russian History" (1822), while criticizing the domestic initiatives of Catherine II, lauded her expansionist policy and victories against Poland, Sweden, and Turkey. Pushkin in fact faulted the empress and Potemkin for not pursuing a more aggressive policy so as to establish the Danube River as the border between the Russian and the Ottoman Empires.[20] His support of imperial expansion was also voiced in an 1820 letter to his brother Lev. Describing a two-month visit to the Caucasus, Pushkin waxed eloquent on General Aleksei P. Ermolov's pacification of that turbulent area:

> The Caucasian region, the torrid boundary of Asia, arouses interest in all respects. Ermolov has filled it with his name and his beneficient genius. The savage Circassians have become timorous; their ancient audacity is disappearing. The roads are becoming less dangerous by the hour, and the numerous convoys are becoming superfluous. It is to be hoped that this conquered land, which until now has brought no real benefit to Russia, will soon form a bridge between us and the Persians for safe trading, that it will not be an obstacle to us in future wars, and that perhaps we shall carry out Napoleon's chimerical plan of conquering India.[21]

Pushkin continued to admire Ermolov and his exploits, even after the general had fallen from favor and had been placed under house arrest. In a letter of April 1833, reflecting the poet's sensitivity to historical memory and his investigation of the Russian national past, Pushkin exhorted Ermolov to record his recollections of the storied Transcaucasian campaign because "Your glory belongs to Russia and you do not have the right to keep it hidden."[22]

Based on his praise of tsarist military might, in particular his dismay that Catherine II had not been sufficiently aggressive against Turkey, Pushkin most likely wanted Russia to take action in the Eastern crisis. "Seizing Moldavia and Wallachia under the guise of peace-loving mediators" and "crossing beyond the Danube as allies of the Greeks and as enemies of their enemies" would fulfill the imperial vision articulated by the empress and championed by many Russian nationalists. This position was also the stance advocated by the philhellenic war party in government circles.

Pushkin's continuing philhellenic interest reappeared in an early April 1821 entry in his Kishinev diary that caught some of the drama and excitement expressed in the Davydov letter:

> Spent the evening at N. G.'s—a charming Greek lady. [Pushkin knew several Greek women in Kishinev but no record remains of who N. G. was.] We talked about A. Ypsilantis. In the company of five Greeks, I alone spoke like a Greek. They all despair over the success of the *Etaireia*'s undertaking. I firmly believe that Greece will triumph and that twenty-five million Turks [an inflated number, most likely he meant twenty-five thousand] will leave the flourishing country of Hellas to the lawful heirs of Homer and Themistocles.[23]

Philhellenism is found in several poems composed in exile that project the romanticized image of Ypsilantis first portrayed in the letter to Davydov. In "To V. L. Davydov" ("V. L. Davydovu," 1821), the poet identifies the Ypsilantis uprising as one of the catalysts for liberal reform in Russia: "When everywhere young spring with a smile has melted the snow into mud . . . on the banks of the Danube our one-armed prince incites revolt."[24] The tribute by Pushkin to the Latin poet Ovid, exiled by Augustus in 8 A.D. to a Moldavian town near the Danube, evokes biographical, historical, and contemporary events. Pushkin admired Ovid, who endured the same fate of exile in roughly the same land, and the Russian poet traveled to some of the places Ovid supposedly visited. Yet Pushkin disapproved of Ovid's paeans to Augustus pleading for mercy and an early return to Rome.[25] The last few lines of Pushkin's "To Ovid" ("K Ovidiiu," 1821) refer to the Ypsilantis rebellion: "Here, sounding the lyre of the northern wilderness, I wandered in those days, when on the banks of the Danube the magnanimous Greek called people to freedom."[26]

Pushkin also made reference to the Ypsilantis affair in the poet's greatest literary achievement, the novel in verse *Evgenii Onegin* (1823–31), which depicts with encyclopedic range current Russian society and manners, as well as the author's personal experience of exile. The work reflects the diverse thoughts, feelings, and moods, including Pushkin's aspirations for liberal reform, that comprised the poet's versatile poetic personality. The manuscript fragments of one unfinished chapter allude to the various stimuli that prompted the protagonist's involvement in the Decembrist movement. One such event was the groundswell of rebellion in southern Europe and the Balkans in 1820–21, briefly described by Pushkin in the following manner: "The Pyrenees shook ominously; Naples's volcano blazed. The one-armed prince from Kishinev gave a sign to friends in the Morea."[27] The poet clearly suggests that Ypsilantis had attempted to coordinate his endeavor with an uprising in the Peloponnese that was also organized by the *Philiki Etaireia*. Although the Ypsilantis rising failed, it did succeed in diverting Ottoman attention and troops from the far more successful revolt in the Morea, the epicenter of the Greek revolution and the subsequent nucleus of an independent Greek kingdom.[28] Pushkin acknowledged the four-year anniversary of the Moldavian venture in a February 1825 letter, which praised Gnedich for his *Folk Songs* and *Iliad,* by noting "February 23, the day of Alexander Ypsilanti's announcement of the Greek uprising."[29] The Greece-inspired writings of Gnedich no doubt reminded Pushkin of the Ypsilantis spark that had ignited the War of Independence and aroused the liberal aspirations of such Decembrist sympathizers as Evgenii Onegin.

Pushkin's philhellenism extended well beyond allusions and tributes to the instigator of rebellion. Two poems of 1821 register his zeal for the insurrection as a whole and his identification with the Greeks' heroic struggle. "War" ("Voina") voices the poet's eagerness for decisive action and his desire to join the fray:

> War! At last, the banners of military honor are hoisted and unfurled! I will see blood, I will see a feast of vengeance. The fatal bullet begins to whistle around me. How many powerful impressions for my greedy soul! The charge of impetuous armies, the anxieties of camp, the clash of swords, and in the battle's fateful fire the fall of warriors and leaders! Subjects of proud poetry will arouse my slumbering genius! All that is new will be mine: the simple canvas of the tent, the fires of the enemies, the thunder of the cannon, the screech of the cannonball, and the anticipation of dreaded death. Will you arise in me, blind passion of glory, you, thirsting for death, the fierce ardor of heroes? Will a double crown be my fate, or has the destiny of battles ordained a dark end for me? Everything will die with me: hopes of youthful days, sacred passion of the heart, aspiration for the sublime, recollection of brother and friends, vain excitement of creative thoughts, and you, love! Is it possible that neither martial din, nor military effort, nor the murmur of proud glory, that nothing will muffle my everyday thoughts? I languish, a victim of evil poison. Peace pursues me, I have no control over myself, and an oppressive idleness possesses my soul. Why is the horror of war delayed? Why is the first battle not yet in full swing?[30]

This work was published anonymously as "Dream of a Warrior" in the civic-Decembrist literary almanac *Polar Star (Poliarnaia zvezda)* in 1823.

Pushkin described the poem's autobiographical aspect in a letter to his brother: " 'The Dream of a Warrior' has reduced to pensiveness a warrior serving in the Foreign Service and now located in the Bessarabian office."[31] One can safely surmise that the boredom and monotony of Kishinev exile were additional factors that prompted Pushkin's excitement for the Greek struggle. His other well-known philhellenic verse composed in 1821, "Loyal Greek Woman" ("Grechanka vernaia"), consoles a widow whose husband had died in battle:

> Loyal Greek woman! Do not cry—he died a hero, an enemy's bullet piercing his chest. Do not cry—did not you yourself before the first battle send him down the blood-stained path of honor? Foreseeing a painful separation, your husband extended a solemn hand to you and blessed his tearful child. But the black banner of freedom stirred. Like Aristogiton [Athenian patriot of sixth century B.C. who together with Harmodius opposed tyranny], he entwined his sword with myrtle, rushed fearlessly into battle, and in falling, performed a great sacred deed.[32]

The Hellenic muse of Pushkin, in accord with the broad humanity of his poetic talent, extols Greek beauty as well as Greek courage and patriotism. His numerous poems addressed to women friends and lovers express a range of feeling from sorrow and grief to jealousy and passion. These verses also evoke the image of women as a source of artistic inspiration. For example, "Freedom" ("Elleferiia," 1821) memorializes an unknown woman named after the Greek word for liberty: "Before you all other charms are eclipsed, I am yours forever, Elleferiia. The din of society frightens you, court splendor is unpleasant for you. I love your passionate, righteous mind. Your voice is understood by the heart. In the south, in peaceful darkness, live with me, Elleferiia, for cold Russia is harmful to your beauty."[33]

One of Pushkin's numerous affairs in exile was with a Greek refugee from Constantinople, Calypso Polychroni, who joined her mother in Kishinev and boasted that she had been kissed by Byron. Her melodious voice, sensual beauty, and romantic connection with Byron prompted Pushkin's "To a Greek Girl" ("Grechanke," 1822):

> You were born to inflame, captivate, and arouse the imagination of poets, with your animated face, your Oriental voice, your brilliant visionary eyes, and your indiscreet little foot. You were born for sensuous voluptuousness, for the ecstasy of passions. Tell me: When the poet of Leila [character in Byron's "Giaour"] imagined his immutable ideal in heavenly dreams, was it not you the tormented, dear poet imagined? Was it perhaps in a distant land, under the sky of sacred Greece, that the inspired sufferer saw you in a dream and then concealed your indelible image in the depth of his heart? Perhaps the magician seduced you with his happy lyre. An involuntary quiver arouse

in your proud breast and you, leaning on his shoulder . . . No, no, my friend, I do not want to fan the flame of jealous dream. Happiness has been alien to me for a long time, I delight in it again. Yet overcome by a secret sadness, I fear that everything dear is unfaithful.[34]

Calypso inspired another verse by Pushkin, "To a Foreign Girl" ("Inostranke," 1822): "In a language unintelligible to you I write farewell verses. Yet in pleasant delusion I beg your attention: My dear, until I fade away, having lost all feeling in our separation, I shall not cease adoring you, my dear, you alone. Gazing at alien features, believe only my heart, as formerly you believed it, not understanding its passions."[35] Pushkin sketched several profiles of Calypso's slender figure and hawklike nose.[36] He also cited her as one of Kishinev's attractions in an April 1823 letter inviting his close friend and regular correspondent Petr A. Viazemskii to visit him. Pushkin wrote that he would acquaint Viazemskii with Greek heroes from the Danubian campaign and "with a Greek girl whom Byron kissed."[37]

The poet Vasilii I. Tumanskii, an acquaintance of Pushkin during the latter's exile in Odessa, commemorated Calypso in his own "To a Greek Girl" ("Grechanke," 1827). Tumanskii's version, resonant with classical allusion, depicts her charm and sensuality in images strikingly similar to Pushkin's verse.[38] The two poets also shared an attraction for Odessa and the Russian South that figures prominently in their poetry. The surviving fragments of "Onegin's Journey," one of the unfinished chapters in *Evgenii Onegin*, refers to Tumanskii's "sonorous verses" and "enchanting pen" that celebrate the gardens of Odessa. The same chapter conveys with crystalline clarity Pushkin's own impressions of the port's charms: its azure sea, southern climate, ethnic diversity, commercial vibrancy, lively theater, and Italian opera.[39] Pushkin's and Tumanskii's mutual fondness for Calypso symbolized their fascination with the allure of the Russian South and their philhellenic enthusiasm for the Greek struggle.

In addition to these lyrics applauding Greek beauty and battle, Pushkin devoted several other works to the War of Independence. His sensitivity to the historical aspects of the Danubian revolt manifested itself in two prose fragments, "Note sur la révolution d'Ipsylanti" and "Note sur Penda-Deka," and in an unfinished poem on the *Philiki Etaireia*.[40] These pieces indicate that Pushkin not only followed the course of the Moldavian insurrection but intended to describe in some detail the defeat of Ypsilantis's forces at the battles of Skulyani and Seku (July and September, 1821). This plan was an extension of the Russian writer's interest in Russian historical studies, which paralleled his experimentation with prose. The preliminary notes on the rebellion, enriched by his Kishinev recollections, ultimately found expression in the 1834 prose tale "Kirdjali." With precision and simplicity, the story depicts the exploits of the Bulgarian brigand Giorgii Kirdjali who fought with the Ypsilantis army and then sought refuge in

Bessarabia. Russian authorities later extradited him to the Turks, but the crafty bandit escaped from his guards and resumed his raids in Moldavia. Archival research in Moldavia by two Russian scholars has unearthed convincing evidence that Kirdjali was an authentic historical person who sought haven in Kishinev in 1821 and was extradited sometime in 1822–23. While the tale does not always conform to historical detail, it accurately portrays the real deeds of the hero.[41]

The image of the brigand fascinated Pushkin, as it did many Romantic artists and writers. Romantic art and literature often portrays the bandit as a folk hero and popular legend, a symbol of resistance to injustice and oppression.[42] To the era's vast brigand literature, Pushkin contributed the unfinished verse tale "Bandit Brothers" ("Brat'ia razboiniki," 1821–22). The excerpts, influenced by Byron's "Corsair," were directly inspired by an 1820 encounter with Volga bandits in Ekaterinoslav that Pushkin later recollected in a letter to Viazemskii.[43] Far more important, however, was Pushkin's vivid portrayal, in both nonfiction and fiction, of the Don Cossack rebel Pugachev: *History of Pugachev* (1834) and *Captain's Daughter* (1836).

"Kirdjali" touched on the Balkanwide phenomenon of brigandage, which while not uncommon in Bessarabia, became endemic in southeastern Europe with the decline of Ottoman authority. Greek *klephts* and Serbian *haiduks* (bandits or brigands) defied local officials and protested social and economic oppression by resorting to robbery and plunder. Folk song and popular myth memorialize their exploits and Robin-Hood-like code of honor. With the development of national consciousness, Balkan outlaws assumed the mantle of freedom fighters and participated in national liberation struggles, although their circumscribed sense of patriotism focused almost exclusively on their native districts. Amid the chaotic breakdown of Ottoman law and order, bandits were often joined in their brigandage by locally recruited Ottoman police and militia, such as Greek *armatoloi* and Bulgarian *kirdjalis*.[44] The result was a hodgepodge of legal and illegal armed bands with clashing interests.

Pushkin met some of the bandits who fled to Kishinev after their participation in the Ypsilantis revolt and heard their stories. In relating the adventures of Kirdjali, he embellished historical fact with legend and anecdote to paint a romanticized image of his hero. The humble, brave, and wily Kirdjali embodies the tradition of Balkan outlaws, whose resistance to Ottoman subjugation inspired Balkan liberation movements. Kirdjali, a name commonly used by brigands in the Balkans, is synonymous with robber and thief, and the story opens by noting that "Kirdjali was a Bulgarian by birth. In Turkish *kirdjali* means 'knight-errant' or 'daring fellow.' I do not know his real name." We read later that Kirdjali "seemed to be about thirty.

The features of his swarthy face were regular and grim. He was tall, broad-shouldered and his general appearance seemed to indicate unusual physical strength. . . . His expression was proud and calm." He also has a wife and child in a Bulgarian village not far from Kilia.[45]

By focusing on specific episodes from Kirdjali's life, the story illumines particular factors that explain the Ypsilantis defeat. "Kirdjali" also depicts in more realistic terms the Phanariot Greek leader whom Pushkin idealized in the 1821 Davydov letter and in subsequent poetic tributes. The story clearly suggests that looting and brigandage by armed bands fighting with Ypsilantis wreaked havoc and disorder, severely weakening the revolutionary potential of the Danubian rising. Many bandits like Kirdjali flock to the Ypsilantis banner with little or no understanding of the revolutionary leader's proclamations about the glorious ideal of resurrecting liberty in the land of Leonidas and Miltiades, but the brigands do recognize that the insurrection provides a splendid opportunity for plunder:

> By his acts of brigandage Kirdjali brought terror on the whole of Moldavia. To give some idea of him, I will recount one of his exploits. One night, he and the Arnout Mikhailaki together fell upon a Bulgarian village. They set it on fire at both ends and then progressed from hut to hut, Kirdjali doing the killing, Mikhailaki gathering the spoils, and both of them crying: "Kirdjali! Kirdjali!" The entire village fled.
>
> When Alexander Ypsilanti proclaimed the revolt and began to form his army, Kirdjali presented himself with several of his old comrades. The real object of the Hetairists was not very clear to them, but war was an opportunity to get rich at the expense of the Turks, or perhaps of the Moldavians—and *that* was clear to them.[46]

The reality behind "Kirdjali" was that lack of experienced and competent leadership doomed the brief Danubian campaign. The entire undertaking from the outset was ill-conceived, ill-prepared, and ill-conducted. The motley band of irregular forces lived off the land and were exceedingly difficult to command. While individual Serbs, Bulgars, and Romanians volunteered, the desired pan-Balkan uprising never materialized. Most of the native Romanians in the Principalities opposed and resented direct Phanariot rule more than they detested distant Ottoman authority. They also had their own social and national aspirations that clashed with those of the Greek-led *Philiki Etaireia*. Tsarist Russia, expected by many Greek activists to intervene on their behalf, unequivocally denounced the rebellion as a strike against the order of legitimacy. At the battle of Dragastani in June 1821, Turkish forces decisively defeated the insurgents, including the Sacred Battalion composed of Greek and non-Greek volunteers. Ypsilantis abandoned his army, fled to Transylvania, and spent the last seven years of his life in a Habsburg prison.[47]

The tale "Kirdjali" succinctly relates the leadership flaws of Ypsilantis:

> Alexander Ypsilanti was personally brave, but he did not possess those quali-
> ties essential to the role he had assumed with such ardor and imprudence.
> He had no idea how to control the people over whom he was obliged to
> exercise command; and they had neither respect for him nor confidence in
> him. After the unfortunate battle in which the flower of Greek youth per-
> ished [Dragastani], Iordaki Olimbioti [Giorgakis Olympios] advised him to
> retire and himself took his place. Ypsilanti hastily removed himself to the
> borders of Austria from where he sent his curses upon the people, describing
> them as disobedient, cowardly, and villainous. The majority of these cowards
> and villains perished within the walls of the Seku monastery or on the banks
> of the river Pruth, desperately defending themselves against an enemy ten
> times their number.[48]

The story contrasts the cowardice of Ypsilantis to the courage and bravery
of such warriors as Giorgakis Olympios, the renowned *klepht* who joined
the *Philiki Etaireia* and fought at Dragastani. Historically, after Ypsilantis
deserted his men, Olympios and fellow *klepht* Ioannis Pharmakis tena-
ciously defended the Seku monastery in Moldavia against a much larger
Turkish force. The besieged set fire to explosives and blew themselves up
rather than surrender. Pushkin's fragments and outline notes for the unfinished poem on the *Etaireia* evinced his desire to commemorate the heroic stand by Olympios at the Seku monastery.[49]

Another band of Ypsilantis's dispersed forces fought with valor at Skulyani on the Pruth River, a skirmish cited in "Kirdjali": "Kirdjali found himself in the detachment of Georgi Kantakuzin, of whom the same could be
said as of Ypsilanti. On the eve of the battle of Skulyani, Kantakuzin asked
leave of the Russian authorities to enter our lines. And so his detachment
was left without a leader; but Kirdjali, Safyanos, Kantagoni, and the others
had no need whatever of a leader." Pushkin parodied the ensuing battle,
gently urging the reader to "imagine seven hundred men—Arnouts, Alba-
nians, Greeks, Bulgars, and rabble of every sort—without the least idea of
the arts of war, retreating in the face of fifteen thousand Turkish calvary."
The wounded Kirdjali crosses the Pruth and finds shelter within Russian
lines, while Safyanos and Kantagoni continue fighting:

> Kantagoni and Safyanos were the last to remain on the Turkish bank. Kirdjali,
> wounded the previous evening, already lay within our lines. Safyanos was
> killed. Kantagoni, an extremely fat man, was wounded in the belly by a lance.
> With one hand he raised his sword, with the other he seized the enemy lance
> and thrust it further into himself; and in this way he was able to reach his
> murderer with his sword. They fell together.[50]

Pushkin fabricated Kirdjali's presence at this battle because the brigand's participation in Skulyani is not corroborated by the historical evidence brought to light by the Russian scholars Trubetskoi and Oganian. Pushkin also transformed Safyanos (G. Sophianos) and Kantagoni (I. Kontogonis) into Homeric legends. They indeed took part in the skirmish but did not die in the heroic manner suggested in the tale. The poet exaggerated the two's roles and invented Kirdjali's, most likely to underscore his sympathy for the bandit-warriors. These men fought to the end, in contrast to their cowardly leaders who instigated the uprising and then fled.

The value of "Kirdjali" as an historical source on the Danubian campaign, while questionable on the Skulyani episode, has more credence in its depiction of the aftermath. The story concisely notes that "It was all over. The Turks remained victorious. Moldavia was cleansed." Among the refugees who escape to Bessarabia in fear of reprisals by the Turkish army are "about six hundred Arnouts [brigands]" who had served in the Ypsilantis army and who are now "scattered throughout Bessarabia." The tale's lively picture of their presence in the Russian South, a scene enriched by Pushkin's personal impressions and observations, evokes their contribution to Kishinev's local color and ethnographic diversity:

> Although they had no means of supporting themselves, they were nevertheless grateful to Russia for her protection. They led lives of idleness, but were not licentious. They could always be seen in the coffee-houses of half-Turkish Bessarabia, long *chibouks* [tobacco pipe with long stem] in their mouth, sipping coffee-grounds from small cups. Their figured jackets and red-pointed slippers began to wear out; but they continued to wear their crested skull-caps on the side of their heads, and *yataghans* [Turkish saber with double-curved blade] and pistols still stuck out from behind their broad sashes. Nobody complained of them. It was impossible to conceive that these poor and peaceful men were the notorious rebels of Moldavia, comrades of the redoubtable Kirdjali who was himself among them.

Kirdjali prides himself on living a quiet life in his new home but pleads in vain to the local police who arrest him before his extradition: " 'Since I crossed the Pruth, I have not touched so much as a hair of another person's property, nor given offence to the lowliest of gypsies. To the Turks, the Moldavians, and the Wallachians I am of course a brigand, but to the Russians I am a guest.' "[51] Kirdjali's escape from his Turkish guards, who sympathize with his lot, and his resumption of banditry reaffirm his image as a folk hero and legend.

Pushkin referred to the Moldavian rising, in particular the battle of Skulyani, on two additional occasions. His October 1824 letter to Zhukovskii described "a matter which touches me to the quick."

> Eight-year-old Rodoes Sophianos, the daughter of a Greek who fell a hero in the battle of Skulyani, is being brought up in Kishinev at Katerina Kh. Krupenskaia's, the wife of the former vice-governor of Bessarabia. Can't the orphan be given refuge? She is the niece of a Russian colonel, and consequently can be considered of noble rank. Move Mariia's heart, O poet, and we shall justify the ways of providence.[52]

Pushkin hoped that Zhukovskii, a tutor to the imperial family, would assist the orphan by presenting her case to the Dowager Empress Mariia Fedorovna, widely known for her benevolent works and Christian charity. Several weeks after the first letter, Pushkin again wrote to Zhukovskii about this matter: "What about it, dear fellow? Will there be something for my little Greek girl? She's in a pitiful plight and her future is even more pitiful. The daughter of a hero, Zhukovskii! Heroes are akin to poets through poetry."[53] Pushkin's intercession on the girl's behalf, the outcome of which is not known, suggested his empathy for human suffering and his continued identification of Sophianos as a hero.

Skulyani also figured prominently in "The Shot" ("Vystrel"), one of the *Tales of Belkin* (1830). The sullen, enigmatic Silvio is Pushkin's parody of the Byronic hero obsessed by a secretive, self-destructive passion. After serving in the hussars, Silvio resigns his commission and with single-minded dedication perfects his marksmanship to conclude the duel he had interrupted with his hated rival Count B. Driven by jealousy and revenge for six years, the brooding Silvio settles the score by humiliating the Count in front of his new wife. The tale closes with the rumor that Silvio had commanded a detachment of *etairists* during the Ypsilantis affair and had been killed at Skulyani.[54] Why would Pushkin send Silvio to his death at this battle, where some fifteen thousand Turkish troops defeated seven hundred insurgents in a debacle that J. Thomas Shaw has compared to "that of Davy Crockett and his comrades at the Alamo"?[55] A case can be made that Silvio's is a valiant death under fire for a noble cause. By volunteering for the Greek struggle, he has found a constructive outlet for his personal attributes of courage, honor, and strength of will. Yet as Paul Debreczeny has convincingly noted, the futility of Silvio's death mirrors the aimlessness of the protagonist's life, above all his misdirected energy and skill. In this sense, Silvio's end foreshadows the demise of Turgenev's Rudin on the Paris barricades in 1848.

The outcome of the Danubian phase of the Greek revolution dampened Pushkin's enthusiasm for the prospects of an early Greek victory. Sober reflection, skepticism, even a note of cynicism supplanted the romantic idealism of his 1821 letter to Davydov. Pushkin, like many philhellenes including Byron, became acutely aware of the disparity between the actual liberation struggle and the imagined ideal of a united Hellenic crusade for freedom and statehood. Defeats, compounded by military dissension, political infighting, and civil strife, prolonged the war and necessitated Great Power intervention to resolve the Eastern crisis.[56] The harsh realities of the revolt altered the perceptions of Pushkin about the likely attainment of Greek liberty.

Skepticism about the Greeks reflected the psychological disquiet Pushkin felt during his exile in Odessa from July 1823 to July 1824. This was a period when his poetic genius continued to mature, as he completed "Fountain of Bakhchisaray" and began *Evgenii Onegin* and "Gypsies." While he enjoyed the theater and the opera that enlivened the cosmopolitan ambience of the vibrant Black Sea emporium, his Odessan correspondence described a much different aspect of his life. To his brother and friends, Pushkin voiced a litany of complaints about boredom and melancholy, the dust and mud of the city's unpaved roads, and his precarious health.[57] He bemoaned "living in the Asiatic manner" and "in stifling Asiatic imprisonment" when he vents his frustration over repeated delays in receiving Russian-language publications from Moscow and St. Petersburg.[58] He protested the unpredictable nature of censorship, writing to Viazemskii in November 1823 that "there is no use even to think of publishing. . . . Our censorship is so arbitrary that it is impossible to determine the sphere of one's acting with it. It is better not even to think of it." In a letter of April 1824 to Viazemskii, Pushkin disclosed his fear that censorship would hold up publication of *Evgenii Onegin,* an apprehension that was "no joking matter because what is involved is my future fate, the independence which I must have."[59]

Numerous letters agonized over his financial straits and underscored his chronic need of money, despite a civil service salary of seven hundred rubles. His family had lost much of its wealth, and no doubt his aristocratic lineage exacerbated his anxiety over the shortage of money. Pushkin expressed dismay that Gnedich had paid him only five hundred rubles for publishing the first edition of "Prisoner of the Caucasus." In a letter of August 1823, he pleaded with his brother Lev to exhort their father to send more money, as "it is impossible for me to live by the pen under the present censorship."[60] Writing again to his brother in February 1824, Pushkin stated: "If only there were money, but where am I to get it? As for fame, it is hard to be satisfied with that alone in Russia. . . . 'But why did you sing?' To this question of Lamartine's I answer: I have sung as a baker bakes, as a tailor sews . . . for money, for money, for money. This is what I am like in the nakedness of my cynicism."[61]

Another source of discontent for Pushkin was his resentment of his administrative superior, Mikhail S. Vorontsov, governor-general of New Russia. General Inzov had treated the Kishinev-exiled Pushkin with indulgence, kindness, and tolerance, all of which was fondly recalled by the poet in his recollection of "Old Inzov" as the Freemason with whom he discussed the Spanish revolt. Considering himself a writer rather than an exiled civil servant, Pushkin was insulted and humiliated when Vorontsov assigned him to inspect districts infested with locusts, a cause of periodic plague in southern Russia. Pushkin came to loathe Vorontsov, denouncing him in a July 1824 letter to his longtime friend and fellow Arzamasian Aleksandr I. Turgenev as "a Vandal, a courtier boor, and a petty egotist." Doggerel written after his departure from Odessa scorned Vorontsov as "half-hero, half-ignoramus, and, to boot, half-scoundrel."[62]

Pushkin's indiscreet courtship of Vorontsov's wife fanned the flames of mutual antipathy between the poet and the governor. So, too, did Pushkin's bold assertion that he had fathered Elizaveta Vorontsova's daughter Sophia, born nine months after he had left Odessa.[63] In addition to Vorontsov's personal animosity toward the philandering poet, there was the serious matter of the latter's letter to Kiukhel'beker in May 1824 saying that he was "taking lessons in pure atheism." This "philosophic system is not so consoling as it is usually thought to be, but unfortunately it is the most plausible."[64] Intercepted by the police, the letter gave Vorontsov the pretext to arrange Pushkin's discharge from the civil service and his official exile to Mikhailovskoe, the estate of the poet's mother near Pskov.

Pushkin's reassessment of his social and political views reinforced his sense of disquiet in Odessa. Walter Vickery has suggested that 1823 marked a crucial year in Pushkin's intellectual development.[65] The poet scrutinized his liberal aspirations and became skeptical about their feasibility. The failure of liberal revolt in Spain, Portugal, and Naples and the triumph of Metternichean reaction eroded his ardor for revolution. Pushkin doubted the genuine determination of oppressed peoples to attain liberty and independence, and he seriously questioned the efficacy of armed revolt as a means to implement social and political change. He also speculated whether liberal political institutions could actually promote and enhance the general welfare of society. In a letter of December 1823 to his friend A. I. Turgenev, Pushkin bid adieu to what he called his "liberal delirium" and enclosed his verse adaptation from Luke 8:5, "Sower of Freedom in the Desert" ("Svobody seiatel' pustynnyi"). The poem's contempt for the masses voices Pushkin's frustration over the thwarted uprisings in southern Europe. The poem likens the gifted artist to a sower of freedom who casts life-giving seed to enslaved peoples but who wastes his time and effort. The slumbering masses are content to graze in peace: "What use have herds for freedom's gifts? The butcher's or the shearer's knife were better and from age to age the yoke, the harness bells, and the whip."[66]

Pushkin's disappointment with liberalism altered his attitude toward liberal reform in Russia. The recent failures in southern Europe demonstrated that a revolt by an enlightened aristocratic elite would not succeed without mass support, but in Russia the revolutionary potential of the masses raised the danger of widespread peasant violence against state and nobility. Pushkin was increasingly aware that reform stirrings in Russia might not go far enough to satisfy the masses. Reform might indeed unleash another *Pugachevshchina,* the large-scale social revolt against autocracy and serfdom in the 1770s that was organized by the Don Cossack Pugachev. Fear of peasant violence, with the very real threat to the writer's own aristocratic landowning class, tempered his radical fervor. Further, Pushkin's immersion in Karamzin's multivolume *History of the Russian State* sharpened his criticism of armed insurrection as the path to enlightened reform. His reflection on Russian history eventually produced prose and verse masterpieces with historical themes, such as *Boris Godunov,* "Poltava," "Bronze Horseman," "Moor of Peter the Great," and *Captain's Daughter,* an historical novel drawn from his research for *History of Pugachev.* Pushkin also came to believe, like the official state historian Karamzin, that enlightened monarchy was Russia's best source and guarantee for stability, progress, and moderate reform.

The abortive Decembrist revolt reinforced Pushkin's political skepticism. To avoid charges of complicity and to protect friends and acquaintances mentioned in his notes, Pushkin burned his memoirs shortly after the rebellion.[67] The tragic fate of many conspirators aroused poetic tributes by Pushkin, not necessarily memorializing their liberal convictions and political activism but commemorating their friendship with Pushkin. His "Message to Siberia" (1827) urges exiled Decembrists to remain patient, steadfast, and hopeful until they are free.[68] In "Arion" (1827), based on the legend of the ancient Greek poet who invented the dithyramb, the poet recalls his warm association with the Decembrists. He has been their bard, accompanying them on their journey and composing lyrics while they manned the sails and steered the boat. Their arrest and punishment oblige the poet to memorialize their work and to perpetuate their legacy: "I alone, the mysterious singer, swept ashore by the storm, I sing the former hymns."[69] Pushkin still had strong feelings of loyalty for his exiled friends, and he was still concerned about serfdom, injustice, and despotism. He now, however, regarded social and political problems with a broadened understanding of the complex process of historical change and with a deepened sense of human nature's basic immutability.[70]

Pushkin's skeptical attitude toward political liberalism and romantic idealism manifested itself in his Odessan correspondence about the Greek struggle. In a letter written sometime between July and November 1823 and addressed to his friend A. N. Raevskii in Kiev, Pushkin harshly criticized the refugee Greek patriots whom he had come across in Odessa and Kishinev. Raevskii, the Russian personification of Byronic cynicism and irreverence, was an appropriate target for this spiteful and scornful letter. The heroic freedom fighters of Pushkin's philhellenic imagination had now become vagabonds and beggars, stripped of their romantic allure by defeat and flight and depicted with biting sarcasm. From Constantinople there arrived

> a crowd of cowardly beggars, thieves, and vagabonds who were not even able to sustain the first fire of the worthless Turkish musketry. . . . As for the officers, they are worse than the soldiers. We have seen these new Leonidases in the streets of Odessa and Kishinev. We are personally acquainted with a number of them, we attest to their complete worthlessness. They have found the art of being dull even at the moment when conversation with them ought to interest every European—not the slightest idea of the art of war, no concept of honor, no enthusiasm. The French and the Russians who are here show them disdain of which they are only too worthy; they will endure anything, even blows of a cane, with composure worthy of Themistocles. I am neither a barbarian nor an apostle of the Koran, the cause of Greece interests me acutely; this is just why I become indignant when I see these poor wretches invested with the sacred office of defenders of liberty.[71]

The Greek cause may still have been a noble endeavor for Pushkin, but the Greeks themselves were objects of scorn. Doubts about Greek victory prompted his caustic tone, as did his personal observations of Greek merchants and refugees, many of whom had inadequate means of sustenance and eked out a precarious existence. Sam Driver, in his recent study of the poet's social views, has suggested that aristocratic propriety led Pushkin to rebuke Greek beggars and shopkeepers. He did not care to associate or to rub shoulders with them, although he applauded their goal of Greek liberty.[72] His scathing attack of "these new Leonidases in the streets of Odessa and Kishinev" also reflected the disenchantment that he and many philhellenes felt when Greek factionalism, banditry, and outrages tarnished the Russians' classically inspired perception of the contemporary Hellenes. Based on Greek conduct in the War of Independence, the insurgents bore little resemblance to this heroic but mythical image of their classical ancestors.

Pushkin's letter of June 1824 to Viazemskii conveyed his aristocratic propriety and his indignation with "these poor wretches invested with the sacred office" of defending liberty:

> About the fate of the Greeks one is permitted to reason, just as of the fate of my brothers the Negroes [on his mother's side Pushkin descended from a captive Abyssinian princeling who became the favorite of Peter the Great]. One may wish both groups freedom from unendurable slavery. But it is unforgivable puerility that all enlightened European peoples should be raving about Greece. The Jesuits have talked our heads off about Themistocles and Pericles, and we have come to imagine that a nasty people, made up of bandits and shopkeepers, are their legitimate descendants and heirs of their school-fame. You will say that I have changed my opinion. If you would come

to us in Odessa to look at the fellow countrymen of Miltiades, you would agree with me.[73]

The negative remarks in the Raevskii and the Viazemskii letters circulated among Pushkin's friends, including V. L. Davydov who had received the lengthy 1821 epistle exuding the poet's excitement and enthusiasm about Greek emancipation. Davydov, a relative of the Raevskii family, lived in Kamenka near the Raevskii estate and happened to be in Kiev when Aleksandr Raevskii received Pushkin's letter. According to the research of the Russian scholar Levkovich, Aleksandr Raevskii shared the news with Davydov, who justifiably now considered Pushkin an opponent of Greek liberation. When Raevskii visited the exiled poet in Odessa, he relayed Davydov's surprise and consternation at Pushkin's change of heart toward the Greeks. Pushkin responded to Davydov in a letter of July 1824 in which the poet attempted to clarify his attitude and to moderate his criticism:

> With astonishment I hear that you consider me an enemy of the liberation of Greece and an advocate of Turkish slavery. Apparently my words have been strangely misinterpreted to you. But whatever you may have been told, you ought not to have believed that my heart would ever feel ill-will for the noble efforts of a people in the process of being reborn.[74]

The letter to Davydov, however, did not mention refugee Greeks in Odessa, the targets of derision in the letters to Raevskii and Viazemskii. Pushkin instead reiterated his approval of the ultimate goal of Greek rebirth, noting that "nothing has yet been so much *of a people* [*narodnoe*] as the Greek affair, although many things have been more important for Europe in a political sense."[75] The phrase "of a people," italicized in the original, correctly underscored the revolt's popularity in Western and Russian public opinion and its broad-based support from the Greek nation. Pushkin's more cautious assessment of the uprising's political significance for Europe replaced the idealism and exuberance of the 1821 Davydov letter, which had hinted at the rebellion's potential dramatic consequences "not only for our land but for all Europe."

The three Odessan letters on the Greek affair marked a clear change in the philhellenic attitude of Pushkin. While the poet still favored Greek liberation, he had understandable misgivings about the capacity of "nasty people, made up of bandits and shopkeepers," to achieve liberty and to perpetuate the classical heritage. The "new Leonidases in the streets of Odessa and Kishinev" hardly resembled their storied ancestors, while educated Europeans uttered "unforgivable puerility" in their ravings about the resurrection of classical Hellas. This hardheaded realism was based on Pushkin's observations of refugee Greeks and on his growing awareness that Greek fractiousness complicated the War of Independence. At a deeper level, his disenchantment with the Hellenic cause was prompted by his disappointment with liberalism and by the psychological disquietude of prolonged exile.

Skepticism about Greek emancipation and about the qualities of Greece's would-be liberators found expression in his reaction to the death of Byron. The poet and critic Viazemskii, who had heralded the British poet's passing as an impetus for "an ocean of poetry," hoped that his exiled friend would join the chorus of eulogizers. Pushkin refused Viazemskii in June 1824 saying that "Your idea of glorifying [Byron's] death in a fifth canto of his Hero ["Childe Harold"] is charming. But it is not in my power—Greece has defiled this idea for me."[76] Pushkin did pay tribute to Byron in "To the Sea" ("K moriu," 1824), begun before his departure from Odessa and completed in Mikhailovskoe. The poem bids farewell to the sea, to the charms of Odessan life, and to Pushkin's Byronism of the early 1820s. Unlike the many Russian commemorative lyrics that bound Byron's fate to Greek freedom, Pushkin likened the English poet's poetic genius to the verve, raw power, and free spirit of the sea: "He vanished, mourned by freedom, leaving the world his crown. Sound forth, rise up in storm: He was, O sea, your singer. He was marked by your image, he was created by your spirit. Like you, he was powerful, deep, and gloomy. Like you, he was indomitable."[77]

In correspondence with Viazemskii during 1825, Pushkin spoke more explicitly about Byron. He mentioned the indelible impact of "Giaour," "Bride of Abydos," and Byron's other Eastern tales on his own "Fountain of Bakhchisaray." Pushkin honored the one-year anniversary of Byron's death by asking the priest at the Mikhailovskoe church to hold a special mass "for the repose of God's servant Boyar Georgy."[78] When Viazemskii regretted that some of Byron's literary notes had been lost, Pushkin responded by praising the confessional nature of Byron's works: "Why do you regret the loss of Byron's notes? The devil with them! Thank God they are lost. He made his confession in his verses, in spite of himself, carried away with the rapture of poetry. In cool prose he would have lied and acted crafty, now trying to sparkle with sincerity, now bedaubing his enemies." Pushkin's generation fathomed Byron well enough without explanatory jottings, and the Russian poet offered the following as an epitaph: "We have seen him on the throne of glory; we have seen him in the torments of his great soul; we have seen him in his coffin in the midst of Greece's rising from the dead. Why should you want to see him on a chamber pot?"[79]

Pushkin temporarily escaped the literary and political controls imposed on him in St. Petersburg, not to mention the humiliating patronage of Tsar Nicholas I, by traveling to the Caucasus during the 1828–29 Russo-Turkish War. The sensations he had experienced during his 1820–21 travels in the Russian South were rekindled. Pushkin visited his brother Lev in the Russian army and accompanied the expedition that occupied the Armenian capital of Arzrum (Erzurum). His "Journey to Arzrum" ("Puteshestvie v Arzrum," 1836) presents his observations of this campaign, his impressions of the ethnically and religiously diverse Caucasus, and his meeting with General Ermolov who was confined under house arrest.[80]

The trip also inspired an unfinished poem, "Once Again We Are Crowned with Glory" ("Opiat' uvenchany my slavoi," 1829), celebrating Russia's military victory over the Turks and the ensuing Adrianople Treaty. This agreement recognized the Russian claim to Georgia, granted autonomy to the Principalities under Russian protection, and obliged the sultan to acknowledge an autonomous Greece. Russian arms had extended tsarist influence in the Balkans and had helped to seal the triumph of Greek independence. In composing his laudatory verse, Pushkin perhaps recalled the question about Russian policy that he had raised to Davydov in his March 1821 letter. Although Russia had not seized "Moldavia and Wallachia under the guise of peace-loving mediators," it had certainly crossed "the Danube as allies of the Greeks and as enemies of their enemies."

Pushkin's philhellenic zeal may indeed have dampened after 1823, yet as a Russian nationalist he rejoiced in imperial might and its impact on the success of the Greek revolt. The final three stanzas of "Once Again," devoted exclusively to Greece, contradict the caustic remarks in the Odessan letters and evoke the poet's earlier enthusiasm for the Hellenic cause:

> Arise, O Greece, arise! Not in vain did you exert your strength, not in vain did battle shake Olympus, Pindus, and Thermopylae. Beneath the ancient shade of their peaks and upon the marmoreal graves of glorious Pericles and Athens, youthful freedom has arisen. The land of heroes and gods has broken the fetters of slavery, inspired by singing the ardent verses of Tyrtaeus, Byron, and Rigas.[81]

The poem links Byron to the martial spirit of both the Spartan bard Tyrtaeus and the Greek poet-revolutionary Rigas. Pushkin's strident tone echoes the rousing appeal in Rigas's "War Hymn," translated into Russian and published by the Hellenist Gnedich in 1821. Pushkin's tribute to Russian arms voices the poet's philhellenic thought that the liberated portions of Greece, after centuries of foreign rule, are now worthy of the heritage and legacy of their illustrious forebears.

The attitude of Pushkin toward the Greek revolt, like his versatile poetic talent in general, combined elements of Romanticism and Realism. His Davydov letter and the poems of 1821 capture the excitement and the expectation shared by many champions of Greek independence. His subsequent writings from Odessa strip the Greeks of their romantic aura and debunk the philhellenic myth that the Greeks embodied the revered qualities of the ancient Hellenes. Whether depicting heroes or cowards, fighters or refugees, beautiful women or crafty bandits, however, Pushkin applauded the vision and attainment of Greek liberty. By voicing support for Greek emancipation, Pushkin and fellow writers of the Golden Age served as a faithful barometer of the philhellenic movement in Russia.

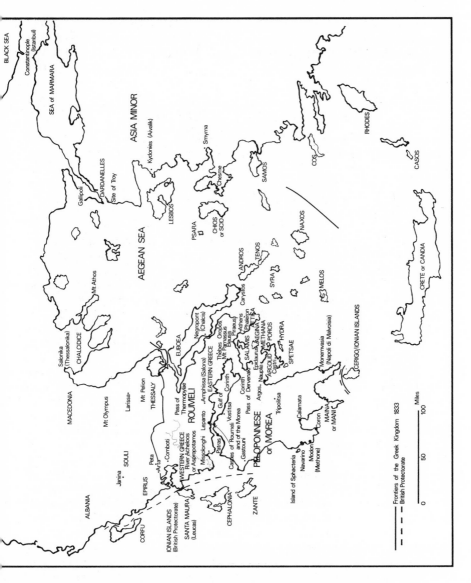

Greece and the Archipelago after the War of Independence:
The Greek Kingdom, Britain's Ionian Protectorate, and Ottoman-ruled Greek
Lands. Reprinted from William St. Clair's *That Greece Might Still Be Free: The
Philhellenes in the War of Independence.*

Expansion of the Modern Greek State, 1821–1829.
Reprinted from Charles and Barbara Jelavich's *The Establishment of the Balkan
National States, 1804–1920,* copyright 1977, University of Washington Press. Map
no. 4, reprinted with permission of the publisher.

Chapter Seven

Legacies of
Russian Philhellenism

THE GREEK WAR OF INDEPENDENCE attracted attention and sympathy
in Russia, and Russian interest in Greek politics and culture remained
strong after the victory of the liberation struggle. The Greek revolt fascinated the Russian imagination because it evoked the Byzantine Orthodox
heritage, the most vital force shaping Russia's religious culture and national identity. The various manifestations of philhellenism shared a common goal of Greek deliverance with Russian help. Popular support for
Greek freedom indicates that Russia's protectorship of Orthodox Christians in the Ottoman Empire appealed to broad sectors of officialdom and
educated society. The philhellenic movement thus suggests the prominence of Orthodoxy in Russian perceptions of the Eastern Question, and
indeed the historical and cultural bond of religion determined tsarist policy in the Near East, along with military, political, and commercial consid-
erations. The regime and public opinion viewed the Eastern Question as a
multifaceted issue with religious, cultural, and strategic implications.

Russian responses to the Greek revolution illumine other specific aspects of the Alexandrine era. The prospect of Greek liberty divided the
government and its enlightened opposition, thus echoing the broader
strains of reaction and reform in Russian political life. Alexander I's condemnation of the Ypsilantis uprising underscored the tension between advocates and opponents of enlightened reform, in particular those opponents, such as Arakcheev and Nessel'rode, who did not condone military

intervention on the Greeks' behalf. Official neutrality intensified Decembrist hostility to the *Arakcheevshchina,* thereby exacerbating the polarization between autocracy and liberal society over military colonies, censorship, and serfdom. Discord over government reaction to the Greek crisis symbolized the two's "parting of ways," to use the phrase of Nicholas Riasanovsky.

Ideological polarization found expression in various forums, including philhellenic verse that implicitly criticizes official policy and alludes to Decembrist reform hopes. Poetic tributes to Greek freedom and valor embody the Russian literary practice of addressing moral, social, and political issues in creative writing. Because of this practice, poets and writers were esteemed by most of their compatriots as spiritual guides, moral teachers, and prophets, and poets of the Golden Age painted vivid word pictures of heroic Greek warriors not only to commemorate the Hellenic rising but to express the ideals of justice and liberty that these writers sought to attain in Russia.

In addition to sharpening the cleavage between regime and liberal society, Russian philhellenism served as a bridge. The Greek cause won support from liberals and conservatives, as well as radicals and reactionaries. The variegated ranks of philhellenes encompassed religious mystic Julie von Krüdener and firebrand poet Ryleev, the political reactionary Sturdza and the republican Pestel', conservative nationalist Sergei Glinka and his Decembrist brother Fedor. Russian friends of Greece included Christian philanthropist Aleksandr Golitsyn and the great patroness of charities, Anna Orlova-Chesmenskaia, who together with Archimandrite Fotii organized the anti-Golitsyn political and religious cabal. Greek relief drives generated wide support across the Empire's diverse regions and social groups, from St. Petersburg to Irkutsk and from landed nobility to peasantry. Greek relief also proved immune to personal, religious, and political antagonisms in the ruling circles. Nicholas I and Golitsyn's successors continued the subscription campaigns until the end of the Greek struggle.

Philhellenism cut across such various movements as Christian pietism, classicism, Decembrism, Romanticism, and nationalism. The support of all these movements imparted to the Greeks multiple identities that strengthened public enthusiasm for their endeavor. The Greeks were both Russia's longtime partners against the Porte and suffering Orthodox Christian coreligionists who needed humanitarian aid. They were symbols of liberty and independence, kindred spirits for Decembrists who sought reform and renewal in Russia. The Greeks were descendants of ancient Hellenes, living reminders of a classical inheritance deeply admired by writers and poets anxious to forge a distinctly Russian national literature. These modern Hellenes were emblematic of an Orthodox-Byzantine heritage that distinguished Russian from Western culture and that inspired Russia's imperial mission to protect Orthodox Christians. These multiple facets of Greek identity explain the appeal of the Greek cause to both proto-Westernizers and proto-Slavophiles.

Despite widespread philhellenism in Russia, Greek liberation was hardly an aim of tsarist Eastern policy in 1821, and formidable constraints prevented Russian military intervention in the crisis. Alexander I adhered to the Concert of Europe and sided with Foreign Minister Nessel'rode who opposed action on the Greeks' behalf because interference threatened to prolong the revolt and to incite liberal unrest against the Metternichean order. Additionally, Russo-Turkish conflict promised to embroil the Great Powers in another fractious round of the Eastern Question, precisely at a time when Russia sought to maintain the status quo with the Porte and the balance of power in Europe. War in the Balkans and Levant also promised to strain the country's financial and economic resources, while tsarist support for Greek liberty posed an ideological threat to autocracy. Finally, any fragmentation of the Ottoman Empire along ethnic or religious lines raised a dangerous precedent for the breakup of Russia's multinational empire.

The Greeks, however, were more than simply rebels. They were fellow Orthodox believers, and Orthodoxy remained a basic component of Russian autocracy, imperial policy, and national self-definition. Ottoman reprisals and violations of treaties escalated the Greek revolt into a Russo-Turkish confrontation. Intervention to protect coreligionists beckoned as an attractive pretext to extend Russian strategic influence in the Danubian Principalities, Black Sea, and Constantinople. Nevertheless, the constraints on Eastern policy were potent enough to reinforce Alexander I's decision to denounce the uprising and to pledge neutrality. Emperor Nicholas I also clung to legitimacy and the Metternichean hierarchy, detesting the Greeks as insurgents. Yet the gendarme-tsar's vigorous stance to uphold Russian treaty rights resulted in the 1828–29 Russo-Turkish War, which together with British and French intervention ensured the triumph of Greek statehood.

Philhellenes thus saw their goal realized, albeit in a roundabout fashion and in a tarnished form. A free Greece had eventually emerged with indirect Russian military help, but the kingdom embraced only a small portion of Greek-inhabited lands: the Peloponnese, part of the mainland, and some of the Aegean islands. Left unredeemed were sizable Greek-populated regions in Thessaly, Epirus, Macedonia, Asia Minor, and the Archipelago. Further, after four centuries of Ottoman rule and after a decade of war and internecine strife, the rump state was a ravaged land marked by social dislocation, economic chaos, and political disorder. The first president, Ioannis Kapodistrias, was assassinated in 1831 by a faction opposed to his social and institutional reforms. Britain, France, and Russia, Greece's three protectors, then searched for a prospective prince among the royal houses of Europe not directly connected to their own, and the kingdom's first monarch was a Catholic prince, Frederick Otto of Wittelsbach, the seventeen-year old son of King Ludwig of Bavaria. King Otto and his German officials aggravated the difficult task of rulership and bruised Greek sensitivities by attempting to impose Western concepts and practices that kindled broad opposition.

The new Greece bore little resemblance to the romanticized vision projected by Russian and Western philhellenes, who were understandably despondent and disappointed when image and reality failed to coincide. Building viable state institutions and implementing economic recovery measures struck the Romantic imagination as less heroic and more mundane than the fight for freedom that had recalled Homeric legend and classical splendor. The gradual divergence between Russian and Greek state interests further dampened philhellenic ardor. Before the War of Independence, defense of Orthodoxy had supported imperial policy and had reinforced Greek hopes in Russian-sponsored deliverance, and indeed Russia had protected Ottoman Greeks, offering them an opportunity in Novorossiia to establish communities that contributed to the Greek revival. After the war, however, friction and strain replaced cooperation in a pattern that would be repeated in Russia's relationship with future autonomous and independent Balkan states. Imperial Russia created favorable conditions for the growth of Balkan national movements, and Russo-Turkish conflict was the crucible for the birth of Greece, Romania, Serbia, and Bulgaria as modern nation-states. Although Balkan Christians were grateful for Russian aid, their fledgling governments resisted tsarist paternalism, tutelage, and guardianship. Greek and other Balkan elites also came to prefer Western models of political, economic, and cultural development. Constitutional rule and economic modernization were two areas that underscored the backwardness of Russian autocracy vis-à-vis the West and thus diminished Russia's attractiveness as an exemplar of nation-state building.[1]

In the case of Greece, this divergence was aggravated by pan-Slavism, the political and cultural movement that asserted Russian leadership of Orthodox Slavic nations under Ottoman and Habsburg control. After the Crimean War, Russia lost sole protectorship over the sultan's Orthodox Christians, and Romania joined Greece as a new national state. These factors, plus the rise of ethnic nationalism in Russia, sharpened the Slavic focus in Russian identification with the East. The Russian pan-Slav movement, particularly the Moscow Slavic Benevolent Society (1858), promoted Slavic Orthodox solidarity through various endeavors, such as financial aid to Serbian and Bulgarian students in Russia; material help to churches and schools in Serbia, Montenegro, and other Orthodox Slavic lands; and publications on Slavic history, culture, and linguistics.[2] The bond of Orthodoxy was now strengthened by the cultivation of ethnic and cultural ties between Russia and Slavdom. Pan-Slavism did not diminish Russia's appreciation of the Byzantine Greek inheritance, nor did it erode educated society's enthusiasm for Greek learning and culture. It did, however, pose obstacles for Russian-Greek official relations. Greek governments realized that they had to rely primarily on their own resources to fulfill the national dream of reclaiming the unredeemed lands. The Greek state also recognized that any attempts to absorb ethnically mixed enclaves, such as Macedonia or Epirus, would be challenged by Russian-assisted Serbs and Bulgarians.

The emergence of pan-Slavism represented one aspect of the broader phenomenon of intensified ethnic nationalism. Nationalistic tension hastened the demise of the Orthodox commonwealth, the association of Slavic, Greek, and Romanian peoples who shared a common faith and religious culture, and ethnicity and loyalty to the nation-state were concepts that gradually displaced religion as the mark of collective identity. Ethnic nationalism in the Balkans provoked border disputes, fractious autocephalous churches, and economic rivalries, all of which fragmented the religious commonwealth into contentious nation-states. The philhellenic movement resonated in Alexandrine Russia precisely because the Greek revolt occurred at a time when cultural and national identity was still largely defined by religious affiliation. As religion competed with ethnicity and language in the makeup of national self-definition, Russian Eastern policy became more attentive to the concerns of Orthodox Slavs than to those of Orthodox Greeks.

Russian responses to the Greek War of Independence created enduring consequences for both state and society. The revolt presented the regime with a fundamental dilemma it had to confront in subsequent Eastern crises, in which pursuit of religious and national objectives ran the risk of provoking the Great Powers, upsetting the balance of power, and undermining Official Philosophy. Indeed, tension between the interests of Orthodoxy and the tsarist commitment to legitimacy was a key factor that sparked the Crimean War. Protection of Balkan Slavs in the Eastern crisis of 1875–78 exacerbated Western russophobia, especially after the San Stefano Treaty created a Greater Bulgaria under Russian auspices. Great Power consternation precipitated the Congress of Berlin (1878) that dismantled San Stefano Bulgaria and thereby reduced the specter of Russia's strategic domination of the Balkan peninsula. World War I was probably the only occasion when Russian Eastern policy fully coincided with the interests of its European allies. Imperial war aims for the Straits and Constantinople were counterbalanced by British and French gains in the post-Ottoman Middle East.

Russian philhellenic zeal suggests the growing voice of public opinion and its potential impact on state policy. The Greek affair was hardly the last Eastern crisis that prompted educated men and women to clamor for a more aggressive stance than that adopted by the regime. In many ways, the philhellenic movement foreshadowed the pan-Slav reaction to the Eastern crisis of 1875–78. The Moscow Slavic Benevolent Committee and its branches in various cities raised funds and relief aid for victims of Turkish reprisals. Pan-Slavists shipped weapons, supplies, and medicine to Slavic insurgents in Bosnia and Bulgaria, while volunteers commanded by General Mikhail G. Cherniaev assisted the Serbian army. The call for Russia's intervention found support among significant sectors of the public and officialdom. Pan-Slav enthusiasm, especially in influential government and diplomatic circles, constituted one of the factors behind Alexander II's declaration of war against Turkey in 1877.[3]

The Near East captivated and held the attention of Russian public opinion more than any other foreign affairs issue in the nineteenth century. For the Decembrists' liberal and radical descendants, the Eastern Question was both a national and an ideological concern. Many liberals and radicals were state patriots who championed imperial prestige, military might, and national self-assertion. As political opponents of autocracy, they also regarded Balkan freedom fighters as kindred souls infused with the common ideals of liberty and justice. Victory for national liberation movements in the Balkans reinforced the Russian liberals' own hopes for political and social transformation in Russia. Also, in line with their Decembrist heirs, liberals and radicals were among the most vociferous in denouncing the regime's reluctance or inability to pursue vigorous action in defense of Russian interests in the Balkans. A case in point is the public outcry when the Congress of Berlin partitioned San Stefano Bulgaria.

For conservative nationalists and religious thinkers, the destiny of Russia was likewise inextricably tied to resolving the Eastern Question. Dostoevskii perhaps spoke for many when he wrote in *Diary of a Writer* in 1877: "Constantinople must be ours, conquered by us, Russians, from the Turks, and remain ours forever. . . . Russia alone is capable of raising in the East the banner of the new idea and of explaining to the whole Eastern world its new mission. For what is the Eastern question? In its essence, it is the solution of the destinies of Orthodoxy which are merged with Russia's mission." According to the messianic philosophy of Dostoevskii, Russian Orthodoxy conserved the image of Christ in all its purity, and by controlling Constantinople, the geographic heart of the Orthodox East, Russia could then fulfill its destiny as the bearer of the Russian idea of Christ. "Such is the mission of the East and this is what the Eastern question means to Russia."[4]

Constantinople symbolized Greek aspirations for a revived Byzantium, but for Russians the City recalled the cradle of their religious culture and national identity. The educated elite in Russia may have turned increasingly to the secular West for cultural inspiration, yet "the Constantinople-centered world view continued its subterranean existence among the half-educated layers of the people well into the nineteenth century."[5] That

Constantinople also conjured up images of the Greek Project and other unfulfilled dreams of imperial expansion may account for the groundswell of patriotism that greeted Russia's entry into the First World War.

Although Russian and Greek state interests diverged after 1830, the Russian-Greek nexus still played an important part in the Eastern Question. Russia and Greece had close commercial and dynastic relations, while Greek churches and monasteries benefited from Russian patronage. Russian policy may have taken on a more Slavic than Hellenic focus, but Russo-Turkish conflict provided an opportunity for Greek governments to pursue the national dream of liberating Greek-populated islands and regions under Ottoman rule.[6] In this sense, the fate of Hellenism was still tethered to Russian military involvement in the Eastern Question, as had been the case before the emergence of the Greek kingdom.

Russia's Greek connection remained alive in other ways. Greek communities were still active in Black Sea trade and provided recruits and money for Russian wars against the Ottoman Empire. Many of Greece's consular officials in Russia were successful Greek merchants who had achieved prominence in St. Petersburg, Moscow, Odessa, or Taganrog. Greeks continued to carve respectable niches in Russian officialdom, philanthropy, learning, and scholarship. Gavriil Destunis exemplified the Greek contribution to Russian higher education and historical scholarship. He taught Greek letters as a member of the Historical-Philological Faculty at St. Petersburg University and published numerous works on Byzantine and post-Byzantine Greek history. Destunis helped lay the groundwork for the tradition of excellence in Russian Byzantine studies. Aleksandr Sturdza combined charitable endeavor with historical research, funding many philanthropic projects in Novorossiia and being instrumental in founding and directing the Odessan Society of History and Antiquities. This latter organization promoted scholarly research on the Black Sea region, and its multivolume *Notes* (1844–1915) remains an excellent source for studying the Greek presence in southern Russia.[7]

As the work of Destunis and Sturdza indicates, cultivating the classical and Byzantine heritage constituted one of the philhellenic legacies. Greek and Roman models inspired Neoclassical architectural landmarks in Moscow, St. Petersburg, Odessa, and other cities. Scholars translated ancient texts, published works on antiquity, and excavated Black Sea artifacts. Devotees of the classical also had a sense of national pride that the ancient world was geographically connected to Russia and that museums in Odessa, Kherson, and St. Petersburg were building valuable collections of antiquities. Byzantine scholarship in Russia was enriched and enhanced by the Russian Archaeological Institute in Constantinople (1894–1922), directed by the leading Byzantinist F. I. Uspenskii (1845–1928). The Institute sponsored historical, ethnographic, and archaeological research on the Byzantine heritage in Greece, Serbia, Bulgaria, Romania, Asia Minor, Palestine, and Mount Athos. Its diverse scholarly and cultural activity served as a reminder of Russia's historical associations with the lands and peoples of the Orthodox East.[8]

The prevalence of Greek themes and motifs in artistic and literary expression represented another legacy of philhellenism. Travelers visited the Near East, increasingly drawn to classical sites yet still sensitive to Orthodox shrines in Jerusalem, Constantinople, Alexandria, and Antioch. Pilgrims, monks, church scholars, and religious publicists focused on Mount Athos, the center of Orthodox spirituality. Travel writing remained a popular genre in Russian letters, and some Eastern travelogues contained rich description of contemporary Greek life. Worthy of note is the album of sketches and watercolors by the well-known painter Karl P. Briullov (1799–1852), who toured the Levant with Vladimir P. Davydov in the 1830s. Briullov's work is a treasure trove not only for classical and Christian monuments but also for local customs and the natural landscape. He sketched scenes from daily life, such as "Captain of a Greek Merchant Ship" and "Coffee House in Smyrna." Briullov commemorated the War of Independence in "Wounded Greek," "Insurgent Greek," and his portrait of military captain Theodoros Kolokotronis.[9] Briullov's and Davydov's writings formed part of the extensive Near Eastern travel literature published during the reign of Nicholas I.[10]

Greek images in Russian art include book illustrations and *lubki,* cheap popular prints that circulated in urban and rural Russia. Grecophile *lubki* depicted prominent personalities in the Hellenic revolt, such as military chieftain Odysseas Androutsos, admirals Konstantinos Kanaris and Andreas Miaoulis, and the legendary heroine Bouboulina.[11] Philhellenic *lubki* were among the stimuli that inspired the early artistic work of renowned maritime painter Ivan I. Aivazovskii (1817–1900). Contacts with Greek sailors in Aivazovskii's native Feodosiia also imparted a sensitivity to Greek subjects, clearly manifested in paintings that commemorated Cretan freedom fighters.[12]

Philhellenic themes in Russian literature are found in the writings of Lermontov, Baratynskii, Fet, Briusov, and others. One of the humorous scenes in *Dead Souls* (1842) by Gogol is Chichikov's visit to the estate of Sobakevich. Everything in that lumbering bear's living room exuded an air of solidity and massiveness, even the illustrations of Greek patriots on the wall, which "all portrayed sturdy fellows, martial Greeks engraved at full length: Mavrokordatos . . . , Kolokotronis, Miaoulis, and Kanaris. All these heroes had such thick thighs and such incredible mustachios that they set the onlooker ashiver." Sobakevich's gallery of warriors includes the elephantine Bouboulina, with "each of her legs thicker than the torsos of the graceful gentlemen who fill contemporary drawing rooms. The host, himself a strong, healthy man, seemed to like having strong, healthy people decorating his living room."[13] Other writers and artists often depicted the

Greeks as exemplars of heroism, courage, and liberty. These images were a reminder of the Greeks' triumphant struggle and suggested the ideals that moved autocracy's political opponents. Furthermore, according to a recent study on Greek motifs in the writings of Aleksandr Kuprin, "Greeks are associated with the south and with the sea, which often are used in Russian literature to symbolize life, vitality, and freedom."[14]

The philhellenic movement left indelible traces in Russian travel writing, letters, art, and scholarship. Grecophilia evoked Russia's sense of mission in the Christian East and reflected the Byzantine heritage that shaped Russian identity and collective memory. Russia's recent rediscovery and renewal of its historical past, evinced in the preservation of Orthodox churches, monasteries, and religious art, signifies the enduring strength of this Byzantine inheritance. Philhellenism was rooted in and inspired by the many links that connect the Greek and Russian worlds and that deepen our understanding of their cultures and societies.

Notes

Abbreviations

BI	*Balkanskie issledovaniia*
BS	*Balkan Studies*
CASS	*Canadian American Slavic Studies*
CMRS	*Cahiers du monde russe et soviétique*
CSS	*Canadian Slavic Studies*
DZh	*Dukh zhurnalov*
EEQ	*East European Quarterly*
ESEE	*Études slaves et est-européennes*
GAOO	Gosudarstvennyi arkhiv Odesskoi oblasti, Odessa
GARF	Gosudarstvennyi arkhiv Rossiiskoi Federatsii, Moscow
HUS	*Harvard Ukrainian Studies*
ISGZh	*Istoricheskii, statisticheskii i geograficheskii zhurnal*
JMGS	*Journal of Modern Greek Studies*
KV	*Kazanskii vestnik*
MERSH	*Modern Encyclopedia of Russian and Soviet History*
MERSL	*Modern Encyclopedia of Russian and Soviet Literature*
MGSY	*Modern Greek Studies Yearbook*
MT	*Moskovskii telegraf*
MV	*Moskovskii vestnik*
NNI	*Novaia i noveishaia istoriia*
OR, GPB	Otdel rukopisei. Gosudarstvennaia publichnaia biblioteka imeni Saltykova-Shchedrina, St. Petersburg
OR, IRLI	Otdel rukopisei. Institut russkoi literatury, St. Petersburg
OZ	*Otechestvennye zapiski*
RBS	*Russkii biograficheskii slovar'*
RESE	*Revue des études sud-est européennes*
RGADA	Rossiiskii gosudarstvennyi arkhiv drevnykh aktov, Moscow
RGIA	Rossiiskii gosudarstvennyi istoricheskii arkhiv, St. Petersburg
RGVIA	Rossiiskii gosudarstvennyi voenno-istoricheskii arkhiv, Moscow
RLT	*Russian Literature Triquarterly*
RV	*Russkii vestnik*
SA	*Severnyi arkhiv*
SEER	*Slavonic and East European Review*
SIRIO	*Sbornik imperatorskogo russkogo istoricheskogo obshchestva*
SO	*Syn otechestva*
SPB	*Sorevnovatel' prosveshcheniia i blagotvoreniia*
SR	*Slavic Review*

UV	*Ukrainskii vestnik*
UZh	*Ukrainskii zhurnal*
VE	*Vestnik Evropy*
VI	*Voprosy istorii*
VPR	*Vneshniaia politika Rossii XIX i nachala XX v.: Dokumenty Rossiiskogo minis-terstva inostrannykh del*
ZhDNP	*Zhurnal departamenta narodnogo prosveshcheniia*
ZOOID	*Zapiski Odesskoi obshchestva istorii i drevnostei*

Archival notation follows the accepted form of abbreviation:

f.	*fond* (collection)
op.	*opis'* (inventory)
d.	*delo, dela* (file, files)
l., ll.	*list, listy* (leaf, leaves)
ch.	*chast'* (part)

Chapter One: Russia and the Greek National Revival

1. This chapter is a revised version of my article, "The Greeks of Russia and the Greek Awakening, 1774–1821," *BS* (1987), 28, no. 2: 259–80.

2. Dimitri Obolensky, *The Byzantine Commonwealth: Eastern Europe, 500–1453* (London, 1971); idem, *Byzantium and the Slavs: Collected Essays* (London, 1971); idem, *Six Byzantine Portraits* (New York, 1988), traces the impact of six Byzantine churchmen in Muscovy. Also see John Meyendorff, *Byzantium and the Rise of Russia: A Study of Byzantino-Russian Relations in the Fourteenth Century* (Cambridge, Eng., 1981); George Majeska, *Russian Travelers to Constantinople in the Fourteenth and Fifteenth Centuries,* (Washington, D.C., 1984); Ihor Ševčenko, *Byzantine Roots of Ukrainian Christianity* (Cambridge, Mass., 1984). G. L. Kurbatov, *Iz istorii vizantii i vizantinovedeniia* (Leningrad, 1991), contains essays by Russian Byzantinists on Byzantine-Russian relations.

3. Nicolae Iorga, *Byzance après Byzance* (Bucharest, 1935).

4. Leandros Vranoussis, "Post-Byzantine Hellenism and Europe: Manuscripts, Books, and Printing Presses," *MGSY* (1986), 2: 1–71; M. I. Manoussacas, "The History of the Greek Confraternity (1498–1953) and the Activity of the Greek Institute of Venice (1966–1982)," *MGSY* (1989), 5: 321–94; Deno Geanakoplos, *Greek Scholars in Venice: Studies in the Dissemination of Greek Learning from Byzantium to Western Europe* (Cambridge, Mass., 1962); idem, *Byzantine East and Latin West: Two Worlds of Christendom in the Middle Ages and Renaissance* (Oxford, 1966); idem, *Interaction of "Sibling" Byzantine and Western Cultures in the Middle Ages and Italian Renaissance (330–1600)* (New Haven, 1976).

5. For a good introduction to post-Byzantine contacts and a description of the available archival and printed sources, see Boris L. Fonkich, "Russia and the Christian East from the Sixteenth to the First Quarter of the Eighteenth Century," *MGSY* (1991), 7: 439–61. Also see the essays in B. N. Floria, ed., *Sviazi Rossii s narodami Balkanskogo poluostrova. Pervaia polovina XVII v.* (Moscow, 1990), and the still useful studies by Nikolai F. Kapterev: *Kharakter otnoshenii Rossii k pravoslavnomu vostoku v XVI i XVII stoletiiakh,* 2d ed. (Sergiev Posad, 1914); *Snosheniia Ierusalimskikh patriarkhov s russkim pravitel'stvom s poloviny XVI do seredny XIX stoletiia,* 2 vols. (St.

Petersburg, 1895–98); "Russkaia blagotvoritel'nost' monastyriam sv. gory afonskoi v XVI, XVII, i XVIII stoletiiakh," *Chtenie v obshchestve liubitelei dukhovnogo prosveshcheniia* (1882), 1: 81–116, 3: 299–324.

6. B. N. Floria, "Greki-emigranty v Russkom gosudarstve vtoroi poloviny XV–nachala XVI v. Politicheskaia i kul'turnaia deiatel'nost'," in *Russko-balkanskie kul'turnye sviazi v epokhu srednevekov'ia* (Sofia, 1982), 123–43; idem, "Vykhodtsy iz balkanskikh stran na russkoi sluzhbe (konets XVI–nachalo XVII v.)," *BI* (1978), 3: 57–63; Robert Croskey, "Byzantine Greeks in Late Fifteenth- and Early Sixteenth-Century Russia," in Lowell Clucas, ed., *The Byzantine Legacy in Eastern Europe* (New York, 1988), 33–56; Gustave Alef, "Diaspora Greeks in Moscow," *Byzantine Studies* (1975), 6: 26–34; M. N. Tikhomirov, "Greki iz Morei v srednevekovoi Rossii," *Srednie veka* (1964), 25: 166–75.

7. E. M. Podgradskaia, *Ekonomicheskie sviazi Moldavskogo kniazhestva i balkanskikh stran s Russkim gosudarstvom v XVII v.* (Kishinev, 1980). Travelers left valuable accounts of the Christian lands and shrines they visited. See the reference guide to this literature compiled by Theofanis G. Stavrou and Peter R. Weisensel, *Russian Travelers to the Christian East from the Twelfth to the Twentieth Century* (Columbus, Ohio, 1986). While travelers were increasingly drawn to classical sites in the nineteenth century, they retained a strong interest in the shrines and landmarks of the Byzantine Orthodox heritage.

8. Boris L. Fonkich, *Grechesko-russkie kul'turnye sviazi v XV–XVII vv.: Grecheskie rukopisi v Rossii* (Moscow, 1977); Hugh M. Olmsted, "A Learned Greek Monk in Muscovite Exile: Maksim Grek and the Old Testament Prophets," *MGSY* (1987), 3: 1–74; idem, "Maxim Grek's 'Letter to Prince Petr Shuiskii': The Greek and Russian Texts," *MGSY* (1989), 5: 267–319; Maria Kotzamanidou, "The Greek Monk Arsenios and His Humanist Activities in Seventeenth-Century Russia," *MGSY* (1986), 2: 73–88; Fonkich's article, "Russia and the Christian East," cites recent and older scholarship on educators, such as the Leichoudis brothers, and on other aspects of Greco-Russian cultural relations.

9. On the Orthodox schools founded by brotherhoods in Kiev, Nezhin, Brest, and Lvov, see Ol'ga B. Strakhov, "Attitudes to Greek Language and Culture in Seventeenth-Century Muscovy," *MGSY* (1990), 6: 123–56; Iaroslav Isaievych, "Greek Culture in the Ukraine: 1550–1650," *MGSY* (1990), 6: 97–122; K. V. Kharlampovich, *Zapadnorusskie pravoslavnye shkoly XVI i nachala XVII v.* (Kazan, 1898).

10. Astérios Argyriou, *Les exégèses grecques de l'Apocalypse à l'époque turque, 1453–1821* (Thessaloniki, 1982), 380–81, 514–19, 557–73; Basil Laourdas, "Greek Religious Texts During the Ottoman Period," in H. Birnbaum and S. Vryonis, eds., *The Balkans: Continuity and Change* (Paris, 1972), 230–42. Richard Clogg, "Elite and Popular Culture in Greece Under Turkish Rule," in John Koumoulides, ed., *Hellenic Perspectives: Essays in the History of Greece* (Lanham, Md., 1980), 28–31, states that "the most truly authentic aspect of Greek popular culture, yet at the same time the least tangible, was the almost universal belief in prophecies and oracles foretelling their eventual liberation." One of the first Greek clerics who cited the oracles as proof of Russia's divinely ordained role in the Greek East was Paisios Ligaridis, whose *Chrismologion* (1656) urged Tsar Aleksis to liberate Orthodox brethren from Ottoman rule. See Harry Hionides, *Paisios Ligaridis* (New York, 1972), 95–98.

11. John Nicolopoulos, "From Agathangelos to the Megale Idea: Russia and the Emergence of Modern Greek Nationalism," *BS* (1985), 26, no. 1: 41–56; Alexis

Politis, "I prosgraphomeni ston Riga proti ekdosi tou *Agathangelou.* To mono gnosto antitypo," *Eranistis* (1962), 7: 173–92. Richard Clogg, "The Greek Mercantile Bourgeoisie: 'progressive' or 'reactionary'?," in Richard Clogg, ed., *Balkan Society in the Age of Greek Independence* (Totowa, N.J., 1981), 87–91, notes that the Amsterdam trader Ioannis Pringos, the epitome of the successful Westernized merchant of the diaspora, still believed in Russia's providential mission in the Greek East.

12. Paul Rycaut, *The History of the Present State of the Ottoman Empire* (London, 1682), 176; Jacob Spon and George Wheler, *Voyage d'Italie, de Dalmatie, de Grèce, et du Levant,* 2 vols. (Paris, 1724), 1: 210–11; Robert Walsh, *A Residence at Constantinople,* 2 vols. (London, 1836), 1: 179–81.

13. M. S. Anderson, *The Eastern Question, 1774–1923* (London, 1966), and V. A. Georgiev et al., *Vostochnyi vopros vo vneshnei politike Rossii konets XVIII–nachalo XX v.* (Moscow, 1978), are good introductions to the political and diplomatic complexities of the Eastern Question.

14. On Catherinian Eastern policy, and in particular the Greek Project, see Hugh Ragsdale, "Evaluating the Traditions of Russian Aggression: Catherine II and the Greek Project," *SEER* (1988), no. 1: 91–117; idem, "Montmarin and Catherine's Greek Project," *CMRS* (1986), 27, no. 1: 27–44; Isabel de Madariaga, *Russia in the Age of Catherine the Great* (London, 1981), 187–238, 377–426; John T. Alexander, *Catherine the Great: Life and Legend* (New York, 1989), 247–53, 260–65.

15. RGADA, f. 18, d. 275, "Proshenie k imperatritse Ekaterine II grecheskogo arkhimandrita Varlaama," ll. 1–4. On Kutchuk-Kainardji, see Roderic Davison, " 'Russian Skill and Turkish Imbecility': The Treaty of Kuchuk-Kainardji Reconsidered," *SR* (1976), 25, no. 3: 463–84, a revisionist view disputing the tsarist interpretation of the vaguely worded religious clause; E. I. Druzhinina, *Kiuchuk-Kainardzhiiskii mir 1774 g.* (Moscow, 1955); and articles by E. I. Druzhinina, I. S. Dostian, and G. L. Arsh in a special issue of *Études balkaniques* (1975, no. 2: 83–113) that commemorates the landmark treaty's two-hundredth anniversary.

16. Western scholarship acknowledges the Russian impact on Greek and Balkan national development but places equal, if not more, emphasis on Western influence. See L. S. Stavrianos, "The Influence of the West on the Balkans," in Barbara and Charles Jelavich, eds., *The Balkans in Transition* (Berkeley, 1963), 184–226; Charles and Barbara Jelavich, *The Establishment of the Balkan National States, 1804–1920* (Seattle, 1977).

17. Irina S. Dostian, ed., *Formirovanie natsional'nykh nezavisimykh gosudarstv na Balkanakh* (Moscow, 1986); idem, *Rossiia i balkanskii vopros* (Moscow, 1972); Grigorii L. Arsh, "Natsional'no-osvoboditel'nye vosstaniia na Balkanakh pervoi treti XIX veka (Opyt sravnitel'noi kharakteristiki)," *BI* (1982), 7: 66–77; E. K. Viazemskaia and S. I. Donchenko, "Russko-grecheskie otnosheniia (posledniaia chetvert' XVIII–nachalo XX v.) v trudakh sovetskikh istorikov," *BI* (1989), 11: 226–41. Arsh has also written about the impact of the French Revolution on Balkan national movements in "Velikaia frantsuzskaia revoliutsiia i Balkany (novye arkhivnye dannye)," *NNI* (1989), no. 5: 40–54. A key source for Russian involvement in the Eastern Question, in particular with Black Sea commerce, with the Danubian Principalities, and with protection of Orthodox Christians, is the documentary collection published by Ministerstvo inostrannykh del SSSR, *Vneshniaia politika Rossii XIX i nachala XX v.: Dokumenty Rossiiskogo ministerstva inostrannykh del,* 14 vols. (Moscow,

1960–85). The first series of *VPR* covers the period 1801–15 in eight volumes, the second series the period 1815–26 in six volumes.

18. An English translation of Korais's *Mémoire* appears in Elie Kedourie, ed., *Nationalism in Asia and Africa* (New York, 1970), 153–88. This passage is quoted from p. 163. An excerpt from the Korais essay was published in the journal *VE* (1803), no. 11: 214–18. A complete Russian translation, *O nyneshnem prosveshchenii Gretsii* (St. Petersburg, 1815), was published by the Greek emigré Alexandros Negris. On Greek military forces during the revolution, see John S. Koliopoulos, *Brigands with a Cause: Brigandage and Irredentism in Modern Greece, 1821–1912* (Oxford, 1987), 20–66; Dennis N. Skiotis, "Greek Mountain Warriors and the Greek Revolution," in V. J. Perry and M. E. Yapp, eds., *War, Technology, and Society in the Middle East* (London, 1975), 308–29.

19. Greek participation in Russo-Turkish wars is treated in Apostolos Vakalopoulos, *Istoria tou neou ellinismou*, 6 vols. (Thessaloniki, 1973–82), 4: 69–75, 375–418, 427–30, 561–68, 710–28. Still useful are the older studies of P. M. Kontogiannis, *Oi Ellines kata ton proton epi Aikaterinis II rossotourkikon polemon, 1768–1774* (Athens, 1903); G. T. Kolias, *Oi Ellines kata ton rossotourkikon polemon, 1787–1792* (Athens, 1940); E. G. Protopsaltis, *I epanastatiki kinisis ton Ellinon kata ton deuteron epi Aikaterinis II rosotourkikon polemon, 1787–1792* (Athens, 1952). Orlov's expedition and the Morean rising are covered by Tasos Gritsopoulos, *Ta Orlophika* (Athens, 1967); idem, "Oi Rossoi eis to Aigaion kata to 1770," *Athina* (1969–70), 71: 85–129; E. V. Tarle, *Chesmenskii boi i pervaia ekspeditsiia v Arkhipelag, 1769–1774* (Moscow, 1945); S. S. Dmitriev, *Chesmenskaia pobeda* (Moscow, 1945); V. I. Sinitsa, "Vosstanie v Moree 1770 i Rossiia," *Voprosy novoi i noveishei istorii* (Minsk, 1974), 12–21; Ariadna Camariano-Cioran, "La guerre russo-turque de 1768–1774 et les Grecs," *RESE* (1965), 3: 513–47.

20. Russian-organized military activity during the Ionian protectorate is documented in Avgusta M. Stanislavskaia, *Rossiia i Gretsiia. Politika Rossii v Ionicheskoi respublike, 1798–1807 gg.* (Moscow, 1976); idem, *Politicheskaia deiatel'nost' F. F. Ushakova v Gretsii v 1798–1800 gg.* (Moscow, 1983); Grigorii L. Arsh, "Materialy k istorii russko-grecheskikh sviazei nachala XIX veka," *BI* (1982), 8: 57–67; Norman Saul, *Russia and the Mediterranean, 1797–1807* (Chicago, 1970), 78–104, 167–74. Reports on the Ionian protectorate appeared in contemporary journals, such as "Respublika Semo-ostrovov," *VE* (1802), no. 14: 145–54; "Opisanie ostrova Korfu," *DZh* (1816), no. 41: 201–14; "Zamechaniia o nyneshnem sostoianii Ionicheskikh ostrovov," *DZh* (1816), no. 45: 237–48, no. 47: 263–73, no. 48: 275–90.

21. On the Greek corps in Moldavia, see Konstantinos Hatzopoulos, "Grecheskii korpus pod komandovaniem N. Pangalosa v 1807 g.," *BI* (1989), 11: 14–23. For more on Greek auxiliaries under tsarist auspices, see Nicholas C. Pappas, "Greeks in Russian Military Service in the Late Eighteenth and Early Nineteenth Centuries," Ph.D. diss., Stanford University, 1982. Pappas's work, with the same title, has been published by the Institute of Balkan Studies, Thessaloniki, 1991.

22. R. W. Seton-Watson's negative view of Phanariot rule in the Principalities, which is found in his *A History of the Rumanians* (Cambridge, Eng., 1934), 126–42, should be countered by the more balanced approach of Denis Deletant, "Romanian Society in the Danubian Principalities in the Early 19th Century," in Clogg, ed., *Balkan Society in the Age of Greek Independence*, 229–48. Also see *Symposium. L'époque phanariote* (Thessaloniki, 1974), essays dedicated to the Greek scholar Cléobule

Tsourkas, and Neagu Djuvara, *Le pays roumain entre orient et occident. Les principautés danubiennes au début du XIX siècle* (Paris, 1989), 47–98. Phanariot intrigue to acquire the lucrative *hospodarships* is described by the British consul in Bucharest, William Wilkinson, in *An Account of the Principalities of Wallachia and Moldavia* (London, 1820).

23. Ariadna Camariano-Cioran, *Les académies princières de Bucarest et de Jassy et leur professeurs* (Thessaloniki, 1974); K. Th. Dimaras, "Peri Phanarioton," *Archeion Thrakis* (1969), 34: 114–40; Athanasios Karathanasis, "La renaissance culturelle hellénique dans les pays roumains, et surtout en Valachie, pendant la période préphanariote (1670–1714)," *BS* (1986), 27, no. 1: 29–59.

24. Cyril Mango, "The Phanariots and the Byzantine Tradition," in Richard Clogg, ed., *The Struggle for Greek Independence* (London, 1973), 41–66.

25. Barbara Jelavich, *Russia and the Formation of the Romanian National State, 1821–1878* (New York, 1984), 1–31; V. N. Vinogradov and L. E. Semenova, "Nekotorye voprosy otnoshenii mezhdu Rossiei i Dunaiskimi kniazhestvami v XVIII–nachale XIX v. v svete materialov sovetskikh arkhivov," *BI* (1982), 8: 6–37; G. S. Grosul, *Dunaiskie kniazhestva v politike Rossii, 1774–1806* (Kishinev, 1975); B. G. Spiridonakis, "L'établissement d'un consulat Russe dans les principalités danubiennes, 1780–1782," *BS* (1963), 4, no. 2: 289–314; D. Dvoichenko-Markov, "Russia and the First Accredited Diplomat in the Danubian Principalities," *ESEE* (1963), 8: 200–29.

26. D. S. Soutzo, "Les familles princières grecques de Valachie et de Moldavie," in *Symposium. L'époque phanariot*, 244–52, makes reference to Phanariot settlement in Russia.

27. Skarlatos Sturdza came from one of the oldest, wealthiest, and most influential *boyar* families in Moldavia, and his wife was the daughter of Prince Konstantinos Mourouzis, a leading Phanariot Greek family in Constantinople. A copy of a geneological tree tracing Sturdza's Moldavian *boyar* roots to the fourteenth century is located in OR, IRLI, f. 288, op. 2, d. 98, ll. 59–63.

28. Information on the state pension and land grants is in GAOO, f. 141, op. 1, d. 3, ll. 1–3; d. 2, ll. 1–2, and in RGIA, f. 733, op. 1, d. 42, ll. 65–67. On Skarlatos Sturdza's tenure as civilian governor, see George Jewsbury, *The Russian Annexation of Bessarabia: A Study of Imperial Expansion* (New York, 1976), 85–89.

29. L. E. Semenova, "Konstantin Ipsilanti i Pervoe serbskoe vosstanie (1804–avgust 1807 g.)," *BI* (1984), 9: 50–63. On the topic of Russia and the Serbian revolt, see Lawrence P. Meriage, *Russia and the First Serbian Revolution, 1804–1813* (New York, 1987); E. P. Naumov, "Zapiski o russkoi pomoshchi serbskim povstantsam v 1804–1813 gg.," *BI* (1982), 8: 38–54; S. A. Nikitin et al., *Pervoe serbskoe vosstanie 1804–1813 gg. i Rossiia* (Moscow, 1980).

30. Grigorii L. Arsh, "Ipsilanti v Rossii," *VI* (1985), no. 3: 88–101, which appears in English in *BS* (1985), no. 1: 73–90. Also useful is the entry on Ypsilantis by James Farsolas in *MERSH* (1987), 45: 35–46.

31. Most of Sturdza's manuscripts are located in GAOO (f. 141) and OR, IRLI (f. 288). These materials, as well as the published literature on Sturdza, are cited in Theophilus C. Prousis, "Aleksandr S. Sturdza: A Russian Conservative Response to the Greek Revolution," *EEQ* (1992), 26, no. 3: 309–44. The entry on Sturdza in *RBS* (1909), 13: 202–06, has a good bibliography of his diverse writings. There is also a five-volume collection of many Sturdza works, *Oeuvres posthumes religieuses, historiques, philosophiques et littéraires d'Alexandre Stourdza* (Paris, 1858–61).

32. Stephen K. Batalden, *Catherine II's Greek Prelate: Eugenios Voulgaris in Russia, 1771–1806* (New York, 1982); Grigorii L. Arsh, "Evgenii Bulgari v Rossii," *VI* (1987), no. 4: 103–13. A key influence in the intellectual development of Aleksandr Sturdza was his personal contact with Voulgaris and Nikiphoros Theotokis, another learned cleric who benefited from Catherine II's patronage. Both churchmen, impressed by the young Sturdza's inquiring mind and devout faith, urged him to use these assets on behalf of the Orthodox church and his Greek compatriots under Ottoman rule. Sturdza heeded their call, especially Voulgaris's, emulating the latter's regimen of reading and writing and defense of Orthodoxy. Sturdza later praised both clerics for their contributions to Greek learning in his "Evgenii Bulgaris i Nikifor Feotokis, predtechi umstvennogo i politicheskogo probuzhdeniia grekov," *Moskvitianin* (1844), no. 2: 337–67.

33. The best account of Kapodistrias's diplomatic career in Russia is Grigorii L. Arsh, *I. Kapodistriia i grecheskoe natsional'no-osvoboditel'noe dvizhenie, 1809–1822 gg.* (Moscow, 1976), based extensively on materials in the Archive of Foreign Policy and in other Russian archival repositories. Also see Patricia Grimsted, *The Foreign Ministers of Alexander I: Political Attitudes and the Conduct of Russian Diplomacy, 1801–1825* (Berkeley, 1969), 226–68; C. M. Woodhouse, *Capodistria: The Founder of Greek Independence* (London, 1973), 47–281; Eleni Koukkou, *Ioannis Kapodistrias. O Anthropos-O Diplomatis (1800–1828)*, 2d ed. (Athens, 1984), 32–158; Zacharias N. Tsirpanlis, "Mémoires et rapports de Jean Capodistrias (1809–1822) (problèmes et recherche)," *BS* (1978), 19: 3–32. Stephen K. Batalden, "John Kapodistrias and the Structure of Greek Society on the Eve of the War of Independence: An Historiographical Essay," *EEQ* (1979), 13, no. 3: 297–314, introduces the scholarship on Kapodistrias and the related issue of pre-emancipation Greek society.

34. Arsh and Grimsted, in their studies of Kapodistrias cited above, make reference to his correspondence with Sturdza, which is housed in OR, IRLI, f. 288, op. 1, d. 185, 186. Some Sturdza reports on Danubian affairs are located among his manuscripts in OR, IRLI, f. 288, op. 1, d. 27, 27b, ll. 1–235; d. 308, ll. 1–6a; op. 2, d. 21a, ll. 1–48; d. 48, ll. 1–38. A more complete collection of Sturdza's diplomatic reports is most likely in the Archive of Russian Foreign Policy.

35. The Destunis family archive has material on Ivan P. Destunis's stint as burgomaster in Odessa: OR, GPB, f. 250, d. 227, l. 1; d. 228, l. 1; d. 229, ll. 1–2. Theophilus Prousis, "The Destunis Collection in the Saltykov-Shchedrin State Public Library in Leningrad," *MGSY* (1989), 5: 395–452, covers Spyridon Destunis's service career and diverse writings. One of Destunis's works was *Military Trumpet (Voennaia truba)* (St. Petersburg, 1807), translated from Korais's *Salpisma polemistirion* (Paris, 1801). While the francophile Korais urged fellow Greeks to seek emancipation from enlightened France, Destunis affirmed that Orthodox Russia was the traditional champion of Greek interests and had a sacred task to deliver Greece from Ottoman rule.

36. Batalden, *Catherine II's Greek Prelate,* 30–31, 94–98, 141. Material in RGADA, f. 20, d. 268, ll. 1–65, describes the Greek Gymnasium's curriculum and lists students who received awards for their studies.

37. As consul general in Smyrna, Destunis sent reports to the embassy in Constantinople. These and other consular records, housed in the Archive of Russian Foreign Policy, are valuable sources on official policy and on internal conditions in the Ottoman Empire. Some of them are published in *VPR.* One Destunis

memorandum proposed ways to broaden diplomatic protection of the sultan's Orthodox Christians, measures that would both enhance their well-being and maintain Russian influence in the region: OR, GPB, f. 250, d. 21, "Zapiska o neobkhodimosti priniatiia mer k rasshireniiu rossiiskoi protektsii nad khristianami-turetskami poddanymi v Turtsii," ll. 1–17.

38. On diaspora communities in western and central Europe, see Vakalopoulos, *Istoria tou neou ellinismou*, 2: 466–82, 4: 157–236, 457–63, 586–90, 736–37; D. A. Zakythinos, *The Making of Modern Greece* (Oxford, 1976), 115–39.

39. Traian Stoianovich, "The Conquering Balkan Orthodox Merchant," *The Journal of Economic History* (1960), 20, no. 2: 234–313. Copies of the charters received by Nezhin's Greek community are in *Akty grecheskogo Nezhinskogo bratstva* (Kiev, 1884); OR, GPB, f. 253, d. 217, ll. 1–124; RGIA, f. 1261, op. 2, d. 115, ll. 1–6; RGADA, f. 18, d. 22, ll. 1–8. Also see the accounts by N. K. Storozhevskii, *Nezhinskie greki* (Kiev, 1863), and by M. M. Plokhinskii, "Inozemtsy v staroi Malorossii," *Trudy XII arkheologicheskogo s'ezda v Khar'kove* (1905), 2: 175–409, which uses regional archives in the Ukraine for details on Greek settlement in Nezhin and other Ukrainian towns.

40. On the economic significance and administrative consolidation of New Russia, see Marc Raeff, "In the Imperial Manner," in Marc Raeff, ed., *Catherine the Great: A Profile* (New York, 1972), 197–246; John LeDonne, *Ruling Russia: Politics and Administration in the Age of Absolutism, 1762–1796* (Princeton, 1984), 297–306. Travelers, often commissioned by the Imperial Academy of Sciences, described the topography, ethnography, climate, and other aspects of the region. See *Puteshestvennye zapiski Vasil'ia Zueva ot Peterburga do Khersona v 1781 i 1782 gg.* (St. Petersburg, 1787); P. S. Pallas, *Travels through the Southern Provinces of the Russian Empire in the Years 1793–1794*, 2 vols. (London, 1802–03).

41. V. M. Kabuzan, *Zaselenie Novorossii (Ekaterinoslavskoi i Khersonskoi gubernii) v XVIII–pervoi polovine XIX v., 1719–1858 gg.* (Moscow, 1976); E. I. Druzhinina, *Severnoe prichernomor'e, 1775–1800* (Moscow, 1959); D. I. Bagalei, *Kolonizatsiia Novorossiiskogo kraia i pervye shagi po puti kul'tury* (Kiev, 1889); A. A. Skal'kovskii, *Khronologicheskoe obozrenie istorii Novorossiiskogo kraia, 1730–1823*, 2 vols. (Odessa, 1825–38); idem, *Opyt statisticheskogo opisaniia Novorossiiskogo kraia*, 2 vols. (Odessa, 1850–53). See V. I. Timofeenko, *Formirovanie gradostroitel'noi kul'tury iuga Ukrainy* (Kiev, 1986) and *Goroda severnogo prichernomor'ia vo vtoroi polovine XVIII v.* (Kiev, 1984), on the development of town life, and Gavriil (archbishop of Kherson), *Istoriko-khronologicheskoe opisanie tserkvei eparkhi Khersonskoi i Tavricheskoi* (Odessa, 1848), on the founding of Orthodox churches from 1752 to 1837. For an introduction to the growth of New Russia, see Roger Bartlett, *Human Capital: The Settlement of Foreigners in Russia, 1762–1804* (Cambridge, Eng., 1979), 109–42.

42. RGIA has many files on the fiscal incentives, land grants, fishing privileges, and other inducements which spurred Greek and Bulgarian settlement: Mariupol (f. 1261, op. 2, d. 17, ll. 1–12; f. 379, op. 1, d. 190, ll. 1–263; d. 191, ll. 1–349; d. 192, ll. 1–196; d. 194, ll.1–38); Bessarabia (f. 1308, op. 1, d. 27, ll. 1–13; f. 378, op. 29, d. 418, ll. 61–97a); Nikolaev, Tiraspol, Taganrog, and Kherson (f. 383, op. 29, d. 178, ll. 1–224; d. 181, ll. 1–32; d. 182, ll. 1–17; d. 184, ll. 1–97; d. 185, ll. 1–33; d. 204, ll. 1–28; d. 216, ll. 1–10). The best published studies on Greek migration are Grigorii L. Arsh, *Eteristskoe dvizhenie v Rossii. Osvoboditel'naia bor'ba grecheskogo naroda v nachale XIX v. i russko-grecheskie sviazi* (Moscow, 1970), 129–66; idem,

"Grecheskaia emigratsiia v Rossiiu v kontse XVIII–nachale XIX v.," *Sovetskaia etnografiia* (1969), no. 3: 85–95; G. M. Piatigorskii, "Grecheskie pereselentsy v Odesse v kontse XVIII–pervoi treti XIX v.," in V. N. Vinogradov, ed., *Iz istorii iazyka i kul'tury stran Tsentral'noi i Iugo-Vostochnoi Evropy* (Moscow, 1985), 33–60. Arsh and Piatigorskii have provided population estimates for specific Greek settlements, such as Mariupol (11,500) and the Crimea (16,500). Their future works will hopefully ascertain the approximate size of the entire Greek population in the Black Sea littoral before 1821.

43. For the Greek role in Black Sea commerce, see Grigorii L. Arsh, "Materialy k istorii russko-grecheskikh sviazei," *BI* (1982), 8: 67–86; V. I. Sheremet, "Russko-turetskaia torgovlia i Balkanskie zemli (konets XVIII–pervaia polovina XIX v.)," *BI* (1984), 9: 76–78; John Nicolopoulos, "Correspondance commerciale d'Odessa: Quelques renseignements sur l'activité des Grecs en Russie méridionale en XIX siècle," *Eranistis* (1981), 17: 224–35, based on French consular records. On the Greek fleet, see George Leon, "The Greek Merchant Marine (1453–1850)," in S. Papadopoulos, ed., *The Greek Merchant Marine* (Athens, 1972), 13–52; Vasilis Kremmydas, *Elliniki nautilia, 1766–1835,* 2 vols. (Athens, 1985–86), 1: 57–92.

44. Patricia Herlihy has examined Greek commercial success in Odessa in "The Ethnic Composition of the City of Odessa in the Nineteenth Century," *HUS* (1977), 1: 53–78; "Greek Merchants in Odessa in the Nineteenth Century," *HUS* (1979–80), 3/4: 399–420; "The Greek Community in Odessa, 1861–1917," *JMGS* (1989), 7: 235–52. Herlihy's research on Odessan Greeks is incorporated in her *Odessa: A History, 1794–1914* (Cambridge, Mass., 1986), which discusses the enlightened administration of Duc de Richelieu (Armand-Emmanuel du Plessis), Aleksandr F. Langeron, and Mikhail S. Vorontsov during the city's formative decades. Also useful is Viron Karidis, "A Greek Mercantile *paroikia*: Odessa, 1774–1829," in Clogg, ed., *Balkan Society in the Age of Greek Independence,* 111–36, which is based partly on British consular reports. The Western traveler Henry Holland in his *Travels in the Ionians, Albania, Thessaly, and Macedonia* (London, 1815), 148–50, notes the family and business networks linking Greek traders in Europe, Russia, and the Mediterranean.

45. The personal archive of Inglezis, located in GAOO, f. 268, op. 1, d. 1–15, provides the basis for Theophilus C. Prousis, "Dēmētrios S. Inglezēs: Greek Merchant and City Leader of Odessa," *SR* (1991), 50, no. 3: 672–79. The Odessan Greek tradition of municipal activism was perhaps best embodied in the public and philanthropic endeavors of Grigorios G. Maraslis, mayor from 1878 to 1894. See Konstantinos Papoulidis, *Grigorios G. Maraslis (1831–1907): I Zoi kai to Ergo tou* (Thessaloniki, 1989).

46. The Greek Enlightenment's Russian context is noted in Grigorii L. Arsh, "Novogrecheskoe Prosveshchenie i Rossiia (k postanovke problemy)," *BI* (1984), 9: 304–13; Athanasios Karathanasis, "Dukhovnaia zhizn' grekov v Rossii v XIX v.," *BI* (1989), 11: 5–13. For general studies of the intellectual awakening, see K. Th. Dimaras, *La Grèce aux temps des lumières* (Geneva, 1969); idem, *Neoellinikos diaphotismos* (Athens, 1977); Catherine Koumarianou, "The Contribution of the Intelligentsia toward the Greek Independence Movement, 1798–1821," in Clogg, ed., *The Struggle for Greek Independence,* 67–86; G. P. Henderson, *The Revival of Greek Thought, 1620–1830* (Albany, N.Y., 1970); Raphael Demos, "The Neohellenic Enlightenment, 1750–1821: A General Survey," *Journal of the History of Ideas* (1958), no. 4: 523–41.

47. *I en Odisso Elliniki Ekklisia tis Agias Triadas, 1808–1908* (Odessa, 1908), provides a good historical sketch.

48. The most thorough account of the Commercial Gymnasium is still Ch. Voulodimos, *Proti pentikontaetiris tis en Odisso Ellinoemporikis scholis (1817–1867)* (Odessa, 1871), with details on the school's merchant patrons, administrators, teachers, and students. Documents in the Ministry of Public Education (RGIA, f. 733, op. 49, d. 291, ll. 1–7; f. 732, op. 2, d. 87, ll. 1–6) deal with the school's founding and organization. These and other archival sources are used in Grigorii L. Arsh, "Grecheskoe kommercheskoe uchilishche Odessy v 1817–1830 gg.: Iz istorii novogrecheskogo Prosveshcheniia," *BI* (1987), 10: 31–62. For more on the school's Greek teachers, see G. Printzipas, "Konstantinos Vardalachos, enas protoporos daskalos tou Genous," *Theologia* (1984), 55: 1144–79; Eleni Koukkou, "Konstantinos Vardalachos, 1775–1830," *Byzantinisch-Neugriechische Jahrbücher* (1966), 19: 123–216; N. Lentz, *Uchebno-vospitatel'nye zavedeniia iz kotorykh obrazovalsia Rishel'evskii litsei (1804–1817)* (Odessa, 1903), 340–82. The Commercial Gymnasium and its significance for Greek learning are briefly introduced in Konstantinos Papoulidis, "I Ellinoemporiki scholi tis Odissou (1817–1917)," *Archeion Pontou* (1982), 37: 142–52; idem, "Prosvetitel'skaia i kul'turnaia deiatel'nost' grekov Odessy v XIX i XX v.," *BI* (1989), 11: 190–99.

49. Koumas's description appears in Voulodimos, *Proti pentikontaetiris tis en Odisso Ellinoemporikis scholis*, 108–10, and in Konstantinos Oikonomos, *Autoschedios diatrivi peri Smyrnis* (London, 1831), 3–8. It is also cited in E. G. Vallianatos, "Constantine Koumas and the Philological Gymnasium of Smyrna, 1810–1819," *EEQ* (1973), 6: 439–40. The Odessan school attracted mention in the Russian press, "O grecheskom uchilishche v Odesse," *VE* (1820), no. 7: 202–8.

50. On the various plays performed at the Greek theater, see Aggeliki Phenerli-Panagiotopoulou, "To theatriko ergo 'Souliotes', 1809–1827," *Eranistis* (1965), 3: 157–69; Dimitris Spathis, "O 'Philoktitis' tou Sophokli diaskeuasmenos apo ton Nikolao Pikkolo," *Eranistis* (1979), 15: 265–320; Anna Tampaki, "To elliniko theatro sti Odisso (1814–1818)," *Eranistis* (1980), 16: 229–38; G. Zoidis, "To theatro tis *Philikis Etaireias*. O rolos tou stin ideologiki proetoimasia tou 1821," in J. Irmscher and M. Mineemi, eds., *O ellinismos eis to exoterikon* (Berlin, 1968), 397–436. Zoidis's essay is an outgrowth of his study on Greco-Russian relations, *Patro-paradoti philia. Ellada-Rossia (oikonomikoi, politikoi, politistikoi desmoi)* (Athens, 1958).

51. Excerpts of *Elliniki nomarchia* are in Richard Clogg, ed., *The Movement for Greek Independence, 1770–1821: A Collection of Documents* (London, 1976), 106–17.

52. P. P. Filevskii, *Ocherk iz proshlogo Taganrogskoi gimnazii* (Taganrog, 1906); S. Lambros, "To ellinikon scholeion Niznis," *Neos Ellinomneimon* (1916), 13: 136–37; OR, GPB, f. 253, d. 215, ll. 1–96; V. V. Latyshev, *K nachal'noi istorii Mariupolia* (Odessa, 1914), 14–24; D. A. Kharadzhev, ed., *Mariupol' i ego okrestnosti* (Mariupol, 1892), 406–37; I. I. Sokolov, "Mariupol'skie greki," *Trudy instituta slavianovedeniia akademii nauk SSSR* (1932), 1: 287–317; F. A. Braun, "Mariupol'skie greki," *Zhivaia starina* (1890), 2: 78–92.

53. RGIA, f. 733, op. 49, d. 826, ll. 1–12; d. 773, ll. 1–9; op. 7, d. 446, ll. 1–4.

54. K. Th. Dimaras, "I scholi tou agiou orous sta 1800," *Ellinika* (1957), 15: 153–58.

55. On Varvakis, see Arsh, *Eteristskoe dvizhenie v Rossii*, 143–44, 231; A. Goudas, *Vioi paralliloi ton epi tis anagenniseos tis Ellados diaprepsanton andron*, 8 vols. (Athens, 1870–76), 3: 155–92; *VE* (1810), no. 1: 73–75. E. Nikolaidou, "Epirskie emigranty v Rossii v XIX v. i ikh vlad v razvitie Epira," *BI* (1989), 11: 123–30, draws upon Greek primary and secondary sources for his introduction to Epirot merchant patronage. Kaplanis's will was published in *Redkii blagodetel'nyi podvig Z. K. Kaplani* (Moscow, 1809), a commemorative text reviewed prior to publication in *RV* (1808), no. 7: 134–40.

56. Phanis Michalopoulos, *Ta Giannina kai i neo elliniki anagennisi, 1648–1820* (Athens, 1930), 12–87; Henderson, *The Revival of Greek Thought, 1620–1830*, 142–58; Stephen G. Chaconas, *Adamantios Korais: A Study in Greek Nationalism* (New York, 1942). The Korais-Zosimas partnership was mentioned in Russian press reports on the Greek Enlightenment: "O sostoianii slovesnosti i nauki u nyneshnykh grekov," *VE* (1809), no. 1: 23–37; *VE* (1811), no. 10: 125–41, along with excerpts from the Korais edition of Aesop's *Fables;* "Ot doktora Korai k grekam, ego sootchicham," *VE* (1820), no. 12: 274–90.

57. Destunis's two translations, published in one volume, were from Russian and French moralistic writings: *Oikonomia tis zois, itoi synopsis tis ithikis* and *Ithiki ton paidon, i synomiliai ithikai dia paidia* (Moscow, 1802). Other educational texts funded with Zosimas support were *Greko-rossiiskaia azbuka* (Moscow, 1818); *Novaia polnaia prakticheskaia grammatika grecheskaia* (Moscow, 1817–19); *Grammatiki rossiko-graiki, itoi methodos dia na spoudasi tis eukolos tin rossikin dialekton* (Moscow, 1816), which was by the Greek language teacher Konstantinos Pappadopoulos and which was dedicated to Kapodistrias; *Vzor na nyneshnee sostoianie Gretsii* (Moscow, 1806), a bilingual pamphlet by Mikhail Dmitrevskii for Greek youths studying Russian.

58. RGADA, f. 1184, op. 2, d. 3472, "O napechatanii Biblii na grecheskom iazyke v chislo piat' tysiacha ekzempliarov," ll. 1–5; I. Evseev, "Bibliograficheskaia zametka. Moskovskoe izdanie grecheskoi Biblii 1821 g.," *Bogoslovskii vestnik* (1902), no. 1: 207–11; *RBS* (1916), 7: 471–72. Zosimas philanthropic work was reported in the press: *VE* (1805), no. 5: 57–59, (1818), no. 19: 181–96; *ZhDNP* (1821), no. 8: 509–10; *MT* (1826), no. 24: 242–46.

59. The will of Nikolaos P. Zosimas appears in *Diathiki tou aoidimou N. P. Zosima, eugenous graikou kai ippotou tou tagmatos tou Sotiros* (Moscow, 1843) and in "I diathiki tou N. Zosima," *Ipeirotiki Estia* (1953), 2: 1123–27.

60. Aleksandr S. Sturdza, *Opyt uchebnogo prednachertaniia dlia prepodavaniia rossiiskomu iunoshestvu grecheskogo iazyka* (St. Petersburg, 1817), 4–8.

61. Spyridon Iu. Destunis, *Plutarkhovy sravnitel'nye zhizneopisaniia slavnykh muzhei*, 13 parts (St. Petersburg, 1814–21), whose publication was announced by journals such as *Vestnik Evropy* and *Syn otechestva*. A brief note in *SO* (1815), no. 3: 97–99, praised Destunis for exposing readers to the classical heritage and for enriching the Russian language with his lively translation.

62. A copy of the *ukaz* (January 1817) is in RGIA, f. 560, op. 38, d. 104, ll. 14–15. The Plutarch translation and the intercession of Sturdza, Kapodistrias, and other benefactors are detailed by Spyridon's son, Gavriil Destunis, in his study, *Iz uchenoi deiatel'nosti Spiridona Iu. Destunisa. Ego perevod sravnitel'nykh zhizneopisanii Plutarkha* (St. Petersburg, 1886).

63. Spyridon's Byzantine translations and the scholarly writings by Gavriil

Destunis are cited in Prousis, "The Destunis Collection," *MGSY* (1989), 5: 400–3, 448–50.

64. Kapodistrias's endeavor to promote Greek learning during his career in the Foreign Service is documented in Arsh, *Kapodistriia,* 125–69, 283–88, 298–302; idem, "Grecheskii uchenyi D. Gobdelas v Rossii," *BI* (1980), 6: 161–72. Russian patronage of the *Philomousos Etaireia* is also covered in Eleni Koukkou, *Kapodistrias kai i Paideia, 1803–1822. I Philomousos Etaireia tis Viennis* (Athens, 1958). Additional Greek historical literature on the educational society is cited in Vakalopoulos, *Istoria tou neou ellinismou,* 5: 52–62.

65. In his official report "Mémoire sur l'état actuel des Grecs" (1811), Kapodistrias described the social groups of Ottoman Greece and recommended church-directed education under Russian auspices as the best means to prepare the Greek nation for statehood. Arsh published the memorandum in *Kapodistriia,* 256–75, and in " 'Zapiski o nyneshnem sostoianii grekov' (1811) I. Kapodistrii," *Slaviano-balkanskie issledovaniia* (Moscow, 1972), 359–86. In an unfinished and undated manuscript, Sturdza also linked Greece's political future to Russian-supported education: GAOO, f. 141, op. 1, d. 19, ll. 13–20.

66. Eleni Koukkou, "La comtesse Roxandra Stourdza-Edling et sa contribution à l'éducation des étudients Hellènes en Europe," in *Symposium. L'époque phanariote,* 175–86; Koula Xiradaki, *Philellinides. Istoriki meleti,* 2d ed. (Athens, 1976), 37–42. News about the *Philomousos Etaireia* appeared in *VE* (1815), no. 20: 299–300, (1816), no. 13: 76–79, including Destunis's notice that announced its educational mission.

67. *Mémoires de la comtesse Edling (née Stourdza)* (Moscow, 1888); "Iz zapisok grafini Edling, urozhdennoi Sturdzy," *Russkii arkhiv* (1887), 25: 194–228, 289–304, 405–38; "Iz bumag grafini R. S. Edling," *Russkii vestnik* (1899), no. 2: 483–88. Roksandra Sturdza-Edling's correspondence with Kapodistrias is published in A. F. Shidlovskii, "Perepiska grafa I. A. Kapodistriia," *Vestnik vsemirnoi istorii* (1900), nos. 2–3, 5, 7.

68. Historians of Russian education invariably mention Sturdza in the context of the conservative shift in educational affairs during the last decade of the Alexandrine era. James T. Flynn, *The University Reform of Tsar Alexander I, 1802–1835* (Washington, D.C., 1988), 82–84, describes the "Instruction" and cites the relevant literature on tsarist educational policy. Sturdza's role on the Academic Committee is documented in RGIA, f. 732, op. 1, d. 11, ll. 1–19; f. 734, op. 1, d. 5, ll. 1–23, and in GAOO, f. 141, op. 1, d. 8, ll. 1–42, along with a draft of the "Instruction" (ll. 11–26).

69. RGIA, f. 734, op. 1, d. 9, ll. 1–11; d. 12, ll. 1–5; d. 7, ll. 1–14, d. 10, ll. 1–22.

70. OR, IRLI, f. 288, op. 1, d. 27, "Proekt instruktsii dlia naznachaemogo v Odesse pri grecheskom tipograficheskom obshchestve tsenzora," ll. 117–38. Arsh, *Kapodistriia,* 148–52, cites another copy of the document in discussing Kapodistrias's role in this project (RGIA, f. 733, op. 118, d. 430).

71. Voulodimos, *Proti pentikontaetiris tis en Odisso Ellinoemporikis scholis,* 94–97; S. Ia. Borovoi, "Kniga v Odesse v pervoi polovine XIX v.," *Kniga* (1967), 14: 155–58. Publications by the Commercial Gymnasium included Konstantinos Vardalachos, *Mathimata ek ton Asiopeidon* (Odessa, 1830); idem, *I kat epitomin grammatiki tis ellinikis glossis* (Odessa, 1834); Michail Palaiologos, *Syllogi ek diaphoron ellinon syggrapheon kai*

poiiton eis chrisis ton Ellinikon Scholeion, 2 vols. (Odessa, 1833); idem, *Nea methodiki geographia* (Odessa, 1834); idem, *Grammatiki tis simerinis ellinikis glossis eis ton mathiton tou Ellinoemporikou Scholeiou* (Odessa, 1845).

72. The catalog in the Section of Rare Books and Manuscripts in Odessa's Gor'kii Public Library contains many entries of Greek works published locally in the late nineteenth and early twentieth centuries.

73. Vakalopoulos's account of the *Philiki Etaireia, Istoria tou neo ellinismou,* 5: 63–111, cites Greek nationalist and Marxist works on the subject. See also E. G. Protopsaltis, ed., *I Philiki Etaireia. Anamnistikon teuchos epi ti 150etiridi* (Athens, 1964). For the Marxist and neo-Marxist perspective, see Gianis Kordatos, *I koinoniki simasia tis Ellinikis Epanastaseos tou 1821* (Athens, 1924); Nikos Svoronos, *Le commerce de Salonique au XVIII siècle* (Paris, 1956); Vasilis Kremmydas, *To emporio tis Peloponnisou sto 18 aiona* (Athens, 1972); idem, *Eisagogi stin istoria tis neoellinikis koinonias, 1700–1821* (Athens, 1976); idem, "En Grèce au début du XIX siècle: conjoncture et commerce (les conséquences sociales et idéologiques d'une activité commerciale)," *Études balkaniques* (1981), no. 1: 130–41.

74. George D. Frangos, "The Philike Etaireia, 1814–1821: A Social and Historical Analysis," Ph.D. diss., Columbia University, 1971; idem, "The *Philiki Etairia:* A Premature National Coalition," in Clogg, ed., *The Struggle for Greek Independence,* 87–103. The founders of the *Philiki Etaireia* were Emmanouil Xanthos of Patmos, a clerk in a firm that was out of business; Nikolaos Skouphas of Epirus, an artisan who lost property due to bankruptcy; and Athanasios Tsakaloff of Ioannina, a minor clerk in a shipping company. Xanthos left a memoir on the secret society, *Apomnimoneumata peri tis Philikis Etaireias* (Athens, 1845), excerpted in Richard Clogg's collection of primary sources, *The Movement for Greek Independence,* 182–200. The documents in the Clogg work shed light on the broader issue of complexity in pre–1821 Greek society.

75. John Petropulos, *Politics and Statecraft in the Kingdom of Greece, 1833–1843* (Princeton, 1968); idem, "Introduction," in Nikiforos P. Diamandouros et al., eds., *Hellenism and the First Greek War of Liberation (1821–1830): Continuity and Change* (Thessaloniki, 1976), 19–41. This collection of essays is appropriately titled because the independence movement was followed by subsequent struggles in the nineteenth and early twentieth centuries that extended the boundaries of liberated Greece. See the useful bibliographical essay by Diamandouros on the War of Independence (pp. 193–230). Diamandouros has also treated Greek social and cultural fissures in his unpublished thesis, "Political Modernization, Social Conflict, and Cultural Cleavage in the Formation of the Modern Greek State, 1821–1828," Ph.D. diss., Columbia University, 1972. For an introduction to the historiographical debate on pre-liberation society, see Batalden, "John Kapodistrias and the Structure of Greek Society on the Eve of the War of Independence," (cf. chap. 1, n. 33).

76. Frangos, "The Philike Etaireia, 1814–1821: A Social and Historical Analysis," 136–39. Arsh, *Eteristskoe dvizhenie v Rossii,* 167–296, documents *etairist* activity in Russia. Arsh and G. M. Piatigorskii, "Nekotorye voprosy istorii Filiki Eterii v svete novykh dannykh sovetskikh arkhivov," *BI* (1989), 11: 24–42, treat the society's founding and its recruiting in Ottoman lands. Also see the illustrated guide to Odessa's *Philiki Etaireia* Museum by A. Malykh, *Muzei Filiki Eteriia. Putevoditel'* (Odessa, 1988).

77. Herlihy, *Odessa,* 97–98.

78. Arsh, *Eteristskoe dvizhenie v Rossii,* 259–61.
79. Ibid., 189–99, 207–10, 224; D. Oikonomidis, "O Philikos Giorgios Levendis," *Peloponnisiaka* (1957), 2: 58–90; Ioannis Philimon, *Dokimion istorikon peri tis Ellinikis Epanastaseos,* 4 vols. (Athens, 1859–61), 1: 388–89, 404–7.
80. S. Papadopoulos, *Giorgios Lassanis, o Kozanitis agonistis kai logios* (Thessaloniki, 1977). On merchant donors, see Arsh, *Eteristskoe dvizhenie v Rossii,* 256–59. Alexander Handjeri, a former Moldavian *hospodar* who emigrated to Russia, described the *Philiki Etaireia*'s origins, activity, and merchant support in an 1825 memorandum requested by the diplomat Dmitrii V. Dashkov (1788–1839), who served in Constantinople. Handjeri's historical sketch contended that eminent traders, such as Zosimas and Maraslis, donated funds to liberate Greece because they expected the *Philiki Etaireia* to use this money for books, schools, and other means to advance education, their preferred approach to national liberation. They did not grasp that, for the *Etaireia*'s leadership, "liberating Greece" meant using donations for arms and supplies to prepare insurrection. This report is located in RGIA, f. 1630, op. 1, d. 168, "Memuary kniazia A. Handjery o revoliutsionnom dvizhenii v Gretsii (geterii) i ego pis'ma Dashkovu, Dmitriiu Vasil'evichu," ll. 1–19. It is also published in *VPR* (1985), series 2, volume 4: 780–83.
81. Arsh, *Kapodistriia,* 189–93; N. Botzaris, *Visions balkaniques dans la préparation de la révolution grecque, 1789–1821* (Paris, 1962), 94–95.
82. Kapodistrias's attitude toward the *Philiki Etaireia,* in particular his rejection of requests to become its leader, is convincingly treated in Arsh, *Kapodistriia,* 170–212; C. M. Woodhouse, "Kapodistrias and the *Philiki Etairia,* 1814–1821," in Clogg, ed., *The Struggle for Greek Independence,* 104–34; Koukkou, *Ioannis Kapodistrias. O Anthropos-O Diplomatis,* 101–10. Another good source on this subject is Kapodistrias's memoir "Aperçu de ma carrière publique, depuis 1798 jusqu'à 1822," in *SIRIO* (St. Petersburg, 1868), 3: 163–292.
83. E. Prevelakis, "I egkyklia epistoli tou Ioanni Kapodistria tis 6/18 apriliou 1819," *Praktika, Triton Panonion Synedrion* (Athens, 1967), 298–328, parts of which are in Clogg, *The Movement for Greek Independence,* 131–36. Also see Woodhouse, *Capodistria: The Founder of Greek Independence,* 198–205, and Koukkou, *Ioannis Kapodistrias. O Anthropos-O Diplomatis,* 89–96.
84. Arsh, *Kapodistriia,* 184–86, 194–98, 288–96. Arsh has published both the French original and the Russian translation of Kapodistrias's letter to Stroganov in April 1819, "I. Kapodistriia o svoem prebyvanii v Gretsii nakanune revoliutsii 1821 g.," in V. A. Diakov, ed., *Istoriografiia i istochnikovedenie stran Tsentral'noi i Iugo-Vostochnoi Evropy* (Moscow, 1986), 244–71. OR, GPB, f. 250, d. 167, ll. 7–15, contains Kapodistrias's letter of April 1819 to Destunis in Smyrna that mentioned the former's letter to Vlasopulos and summarized his memorandum "Observations sur les moyens d'améliorer le sort des Grecs." Arsh provides further evidence of Kapodistrias's nonrevolutionary approach to Greek and Balkan liberation in "Balkanskie proekty I. Kapodistrii nakanune grecheskoi revoliutsii 1821," *BI* (1976), 2: 48–55.
85. Many factors contributed to the outbreak of the 1821 revolution, an issue treated in the Diamandouros collection of essays (cf. chap. 1, n. 75). While conventional historiography has emphasized national patriotism and the conspiratorial *Philiki Etaireia,* Dennis Skiotis reminds us of the important regional perspective in his essay, "The Greek Revolution: Ali Pasha's Last Gamble," 97–109, that links the revolt to events in Epirus. The reformist Sultan Mahmud II launched an expedition

against the powerful Ali Pasha of Ioannina to reassert Ottoman rule in western Greece. Skiotis makes a good case that the struggle between Ali Pasha and the Ottoman central government was a key factor prompting revolt in both the Principalities and the Morea.

86. For an adequate discussion of this controversy, see Woodhouse, "Kapodistrias and the *Philiki Etairia,* 1814–1821," in Clogg, ed., *The Struggle for Greek Independence,* 120–31; Arsh, *Kapodistriia,* 205–10.

87. Insurgent preparations are covered in Arsh, *Eteristskoe dvizhenie v Rossii,* 245–96; Ivan F. Iovva, *Bessarabiia i grecheskoe natsional'no-osvoboditel'noe dvizhenie* (Kishinev, 1974), 1–123.

88. Barbara Jelavich, *History of the Balkans: Eighteenth and Nineteenth Centuries* (New York, 1983), 206–9.

89. On the intrigues of Metternich, see Grimsted, *The Foreign Ministers of Alexander I,* 249–55; Woodhouse, *Capodistria: The Founder of Greek Independence,* 151–59, 178–99, 253–57.

90. Grigorii L. Arsh, "Grecheskii vopros vo vneshnei politike Rossii (1814–1820 gg.)," *Istoriia SSSR* (1978), no. 3: 154; idem, *Kapodistriia,* 212.

91. Konstantinos Hatzopoulos, "Obrashchenie vosstavshikh grekov Peloponnesa k tsariu Aleksandru I ot 16 aprelia 1821," *BI* (1989): 43–52 includes the text of a petition to the tsar initiated by the Maniot leader Petrobey Mavromichalis. No record has been found suggesting that this document was actually sent, but the appeal voiced the general belief of many rebels who anticipated Russian help in 1821.

Chapter Two: The War Party

1. For an introduction to the divergent responses of regime and society, see A. V. Fadeev, "Grecheskoe natsional'no-osvoboditel'noe dvizhenie i russkoe obshchestvo pervykh desiatiletii XIX veka," *NNI* (1964), no. 3: 41–52; A. L. Narochnitskii, "Grecheskoe natsional'no-osvoboditel'noe dvizhenie i Rossiia (1801–1831 gg.)," *BI* (1982), 7: 115–31, originally published in *VI* (1980), no. 12: 57–68. For the historical literature on Western philhellenism, see Loukia Droulia, *Philhellénisme. Ouvrages inspirés par la guerre de l'indépendance grecque (1821–1833)* (Athens, 1974); Apostolos Vakalopoulos, *Istoria tou neo ellinismou,* 6 vols. (Thessaloniki, 1973–82), 5: 568–606; Nikos Svoronos, *Episkopisi tis neoellinikis istorias,* 2d ed. (Athens, 1976), 282–85.

2. Richard Clogg, ed., *The Movement for Greek Independence, 1770–1821: A Collection of Documents* (London, 1976), 200–3. Copies of the proclamation are in RGVIA, f. 14057 *(Moldavskaia armiia),* op. 182, d. 18, ll. 42–48.

3. The letter to Alexander I is located in RGVIA, f. *Voenno-uchenyi arkhiv,* d. 737, "Vozmushchenie kniazia Ipsilanti v Moldavii i Valakhii v 1821 godu," ll. 92–95; f. 14057, op. 182, d. 19, ll. 18–21.

4. Russian official policy toward the Ypsilantis affair and the ensuing War of Independence is covered in Grigorii L. Arsh et al., *Mezhdunarodnye otnosheniia na Balkanakh, 1815–1830 gg.* (Moscow, 1983); Irina S. Dostian, *Rossiia i balkanskii vopros* (Moscow, 1972), 196–331; A. V. Fadeev, *Rossiia i vostochnyi krizis 20–kh godov XIX v.*

(Moscow, 1958); Ol'ga B. Shparo, *Osvobozhdenie Gretsii i Rossiia, 1821–1829* (Moscow, 1965); Alexandre Despotopoulos, "La révolution grecque, Alexandre Ypsilantis et la politique de la Russie," *BS* (1966), 7, no. 2: 395–410. For an introduction, see Barbara Jelavich, "Tsarist Russia and Greek Independence," in John Koumoulides, ed., *Greek Connections: Essays in Culture and Diplomacy* (South Bend, Ind., 1987), 75–101; idem, *Russia and Greece During the Regency of King Othon, 1832–1835* (Thessaloniki, 1962), 15–24. The published documents from the Foreign Ministry for the period 1821 to 1827 (*VPR*, series 2, volumes 4–6) contain material on Balkan and Greek affairs. For a review of the relevant documents in volume 4, covering the years 1821 and 1822, see Konstantinos Papoulidis, "I Rosia kai i Elliniki Epanastasi tou 1821–1822," *Valkanika symmeikta* (1983), no. 2: 187–203.

5. The conflict between Greek and Romanian national hopes in 1821 is treated in Dan Berindei, *L'année révolutionnaire 1821 dans les pays roumains* (Bucharest, 1973); E. D. Tappe, "The 1821 Revolution in the Rumanian Principalities," in Richard Clogg, ed., *The Struggle for Greek Independence* (London, 1973), 135–55. Two good introductions to the broader War of Independence are Douglas Dakin, *The Greek Struggle for Independence, 1821–1833* (London, 1973), and C. M. Woodhouse, *The Greek War of Independence: Its Historical Setting* (London, 1952). Several nineteenth-century Russian works dealt with the Greek struggle: E. Feoktisov, *Bor'ba Gretsii za nezavisimost'* (St. Petersburg, 1863); G. Paleolog and M. Sivinis, *Istoricheskii ocherk narodnoi voiny za nezavisimost' Gretsii i vosstanovleniia korolevstva pri vmeshatel'stve velikikh derzhav* (St. Petersburg, 1867); A. Annenskaia, "Osvobozhdenie Gretsii," *Osvoboditel'nye voiny XIX v.* (St. Petersburg, 1900), 3–54.

6. Patricia Herlihy, *Odessa: A History, 1794–1914* (Cambridge, Mass., 1986), 99–101; G. Nebolsin, *Statisticheskie zapiski o vneshnei torgovle Rossii*, 2 vols. (St. Petersburg, 1835), 2: 14–18. Documents in *VPR*, series 2, volume 5: 88–89, 118–22, 144, 216–17, volume 6: 63–67, 181, 192, 196, 221, 273, 749–50, indicate that traders and government officials expressed grave concern over Odessa's commercial slump in the early 1820s.

7. A copy of the encyclical is in Clogg, ed., *The Movement for Greek Independence*, 203–6. On the reprisals, see Robert Walsh, *A Residence at Constantinople*, 2 vols. (London, 1836), 1: 306–37; Charles Frazee, *The Orthodox Church and Independent Greece, 1821–1852* (Cambridge, Eng., 1969), 22–35; K. A. Vovolinis, *I ekklisia eis ton agona tis eleutherias* (Athens, 1952), 112–22.

8. The ultimatum is published in *VPR*, series 2, volume 4: 203–10.

9. The diplomatic ramifications of the revolt are studied in Paul W. Schroeder, *Metternich's Diplomacy at Its Zenith, 1820–1823* (Austin, 1962); Charles Webster, *The Foreign Policy of Castlereagh, 1815–1822* (London, 1947); C. W. Crawley, *The Question of Greek Independence: A Study of British Policy in the Near East, 1821–1833* (Cambridge, Eng., 1930); Édouard Driault and Michel Lhéritier, *Histoire diplomatique de la Grèce de 1821 à nos jours*, 5 vols. (Paris, 1925), with volume 1 on the years 1821 to 1830.

10. Of the various biographies of Alexander I, the best in English are Allen McConnell, *Tsar Alexander I: Paternalistic Reformer* (New York, 1970), and Alan Palmer, *Alexander I: Tsar of War and Peace* (London, 1974). For the currents of reform and absolutism in Alexandrine political culture, see Richard Pipes, *Karamzin's Memoir on Ancient and Modern Russia* (Cambridge, Mass., 1959); Marc Raeff, *Michael Speransky, Statesman of Imperial Russia* (The Hague, 1957). On the divergent political

views of Nessel'rode and Kapodistrias, see Patricia Grimsted, *The Foreign Ministers of Alexander I: Political Attitudes and the Conduct of Russian Diplomacy, 1801–1825* (Berkeley, 1969), 194–225, 269–86.

11. Dostian, *Rossiia i balkanskii vopros,* 210–21; Fadeev, *Rossiia i vostochnyi krizis,* 56–64; V. G. Sirotkin, "Bor'ba v lagere konservativnogo russkogo dvorianstva po voprosam vneshnei politiki posle voiny 1812 goda i otstavka I. Kapodistrii v 1822 g.," in A. L. Narochnitskii, ed., *Problemy mezhdunarodnykh otnoshenii i osvoboditel'nykh dvizhenii* (Moscow, 1975), 3–47. While the noninterventionists opposed war on the Greeks' behalf, they did not scorn or denounce Greek Christians who were fellow Orthodox believers and traditional allies against the Porte. For this reason, the term "anti-war" or "noninterventionist" is more appropriate than "mishellenic" or "anti-hellenic" to describe this group.

12. On the reports of Western envoys in St. Petersburg, see Grand Duke Nikolai Mikhailovich, *Imperator Aleksandr I. Opyt istoricheskogo issledovaniia,* 2 vols. (St. Petersburg, 1912), 2: 361–412; *VPR,* series 2, volume 4: 197, 286; Grimsted, *The Foreign Ministers of Alexander I,* 262–63. Sample press reports on the Ypsilantis rising and the subsequent revolts in Ottoman Greece are *SO* (1821), no. 15: 49–51; no. 24: 185–87; no. 25: 235–38; no. 26: 276–80; no. 27: 41–46; no. 36: 138–43; *VE* (1821), no. 7/8: 299–300; no. 10: 151–52; no. 11: 238–40.

13. Francis Ley, *Madame Krüdener et son temps, 1764–1824* (Paris, 1961), 573–84; Ernest J. Knapton, *The Lady of the Holy Alliance: The Life of Julie de Krüdener* (New York, 1939), 214–16.

14. The Golitsyn and Miloradovich quotations are from Grigorii L. Arsh, *I. Kapodistriia i grecheskoe natsional'no-osvoboditel'noe dvizhenie, 1809–1822 gg.* (Moscow, 1976), 226.

15. Cited in W. Bruce Lincoln, *Nicholas I, Emperor and Autocrat of All the Russias* (Bloomington, 1978), 115.

16. Arsh, *Kapodistriia,* 216–47; Grimsted, *The Foreign Ministers of Alexander I,* 261–68; C. M. Woodhouse, *Capodistria: The Founder of Greek Independence* (London, 1973), 260–83.

17. The correspondence to Ypsilantis, R. Sturdza-Edling, and A. Sturdza is in *VPR,* series 2, volume 4: 68, 72–73; A. F. Shidlovskii, "Perepiska grafa I. A. Kapodistriia," *Vestnik vsemirnoi istorii* (1900), no. 5: 171–72.

18. *VPR,* series 2, volume 4: 192–94, 242–48, 256–65, 327–30, 371–79, 500–6, 515–16. Konstantinos Svolopoulos, "Pozitsiia Rossii v otnoshenii grecheskoi revoliutsii v period Laibakhskogo kongressa," *BI* (1989), 11: 53–73, also discusses Kapodistrias's emphasis on treaty rights.

19. Ioannis A. Kapodistrias, "Aperçu de ma carrière publique, depuis 1798 jusqu'à 1822," in *SIRIO* (St. Petersburg, 1863), 3: 268–69. Also see *VPR,* series 2, volume 4: 405–6, 686–87, for more on the foreign secretary's failure to alter the tsar's position.

20. *Pis'ma Karamzina k Alekseiu F. Malinovskomu* (Moscow, 1860), 66–67; "Perepiska grafa Kapodistrii s N. M. Karamzinym," *Utro* (Moscow, 1866), no. 2: 195–210; "Pis'ma Karamzina k kniaziu P. A. Viazemskomu (1810–1826)," *Starina i novizina* (St. Petersburg, 1897), no. 1: 114–17, 124, 135, 158; Ia. Grot and P. Pekarskii, *Pis'ma N. M. Karamzina k I. I. Dmitrievu* (St. Petersburg, 1866), 305–13, 390–91.

21. Eleni Koukkou, *Ioannis Kapodistrias. O Anthropos-O Diplomatis (1800–1828),* 2d ed. (Athens, 1984), 159–338; Konstantinos Vakalopoulos, *Scheseis Ellinon*

kai Elveton Philellinon kata tin elliniki epanastasi tou 1821. Symvoli stin istoria tou elveti-kou philellinismou (Thessaloniki, 1975); Michelle Bouvier-Bron, *Jean-Gabriel Eynard (1775–1863) et le philhellénisme genevois* (Geneva, 1963). The appeal to Stroganov (December 1826) is in *VPR*, series 2, volume 6: 697–98.

22. Grigorii L. Arsh, "Capodistria et le gouvernement russe (1826–1827)," in *Les relations Gréco-Russes pendant la domination turque et la guerre d'indépendance grecque* (Thessaloniki, 1983), 119–32; Koukkou, *Ioannis Kapodistrias. O Anthropos-O Diplomatis*, 213–25.

23. OR, IRLI, f. 288, op. 2, d. 6, ll. 1–45; op. 1, d. 21, ll. 1–13; d. 15, ll. 1–14. Grimsted, *The Foreign Ministers of Alexander I*, 57–63, 242. This section on Sturdza is based on my "Aleksandr Sturdza: A Russian Conservative Response to the Greek Revolution," *EEQ* (1992), 26, no. 3: 309–44.

24. Aleksandr S. Sturdza, *Mémoire sur l'état actuel d'Allemagne* (Paris, 1818); "Zapiska Sturdzy o reformakh Germanii, podannaia na Aakhenskii kongress," *Pravoslavnoe obozrenie* (1862), no. 4: 166–70; McConnell, *Tsar Alexander I: Paternalistic Reformer*, 156–59. The Sturdza collection has a separate file on the Aachen Congress: OR, IRLI, f. 288, op. 2, d. 4, ll. 1–110.

25. The following files in OR, IRLI, f. 288 shed light on Sturdza's antipathy to liberal-constitutional government and to secret societies: op. 1, d. 5, ll. 1–152; d. 26, ll. 5–16, 150–73; d. 25, "Proekty raportov k grafu Kapodistriiu," ll. 3–22; d. 309, "Bumagi o zapreshchenii v Rossii masonstva," ll. 1–8; op. 2, d. 8, "Aperçu des relations du Cabinet de Russie avec les cours allies à la suite des ouvertures de l'Autriche sur la révolution des deux Siciles," ll. 31–61a. More information on the views of Sturdza and Kapodistrias toward revolutionary unrest in Europe can be gleaned from *VPR*, series 2, volume 3: 540–47, 567–76, 726–27, 784, 790–91.

26. The draft of Sturdza's letter is in OR, IRLI, f. 288, op. 1, d. 25, ll. 29–34a. Part of the letter is published in *VPR*, series 2, volume 4: 94–96.

27. OR, IRLI, f. 288, op. 1, d. 28, "Proekt depeshi (diplom.) k Nessel'rode, gr. K. V.," ll. 1–8.

28. OR, IRLI, f. 288, op. 1, d. 22, "Kopiia zapiski o grecheskikh delakh," ll. 1–7.

29. Bulgarin's memorandum is in GARF, f. 48, op. 1, d. 12, "Politika. Vzgliady na nyneshnee sostoianie del v Gretsii," ll. 3–7. Nicholas Riasanovsky, *Nicholas I and Official Nationality in Russia, 1825–1855* (Berkeley, 1969), 65–70, discusses Bulgarin's role as a conservative publicist.

30. Sturdza's *La Grèce en 1821 et 1822* appears in *Oeuvres posthumes religieuses, historiques, philosophiques et littéraires d'Alexandre de Stourdza*, 5 vols. (Paris, 1858–61), 5: 219–313.

31. OR, IRLI, f. 288, op. 1, d. 86, "Pis'ma k materi i k sestre Roksandre," ll. 207–16, 221–34, 249–60.

32. RGIA, f. 1686, op. 1, d. 74, ll. 1–2.

33. *VPR*, series 2, volume 4: 113–19, 132–33, 154–59, 162–68, 176–78, 203–10, 224–27, 637–48. Also see Arsh, *Kapodistriia*, 218–19, 223, 227–29, 236–37; Jelavich, "Tsarist Russia and Greek Independence," 84–86.

34. RGADA, f. 15, d. 294, "Pis'mo Barona G. Stroganova k Imperatoru Nikolaiu kasatil'no politike po vostochnym delam," ll. 1–7.

35. Sergei I. Turgenev's account has been published with a commentary by

Glynn R. Barratt, " 'Notice sur l'Insurrection des Grecs contre l'Empire Ottoman': A Russian View of the Greek War of Independence," *BS* (1973), 14, no. 1: 47–115.

36. *VPR*, series 2, volume 4: 47–48, 86–89, 126–29, 627, 632, 638.

37. The Destunis diary is located in OR, GPB, f. 250, d. 57, "Dnevnik o Smirnskikh smutakh," ll. 1–118. For an English translation, see Theophilus Prousis, "Smyrna 1821: A Russian View," *MGSY* (1991), 7: 145–68. The British consul general Francis Werry corroborated Destunis's account of sectarian conflict and civil disorder. See Richard Clogg, "Smyrna in 1821: Documents from the Levant Company Archives in the Public Record Office," *Mikrasiatika Chronika* (1972), 15: 318–41. Destunis's reports to Stroganov (unavailable to me) probably have more information on the unrest in Smyrna. They are in OR, GPB, f. 250, d. 39, ll. 1–332; d. 40, ll. 1–275; d. 54, ll. 1–278.

38. OR, GPB, f. 250, d. 57, ll. 32a–34a.

39. OR, GPB, f. 250, d. 81, "Oborona nyneshnikh grekov. Zapiska," ll. 1–32. Destunis collected documents on military, political, and diplomatic aspects of the Greek war: d. 94, "Kopii materialov, sobrannye S. Iu. Destunisa, po istorii Novoi Gretsii," ll. 15–75.

40. OR, GPB, f. 250, d. 58, ll. 15–20, 35–40, 47–48.

41. OR, GPB, f. 250, d. 60, ll. 1–8. Destunis expressed negative views of Ottoman state and society in other manuscripts, such as d. 55, "Dnevnik, Smirna do smuty," ll. 3–5, 55–57, 101–4, 130–36, 150–53, and d. 89, "Sravnenie grekov s turkami i kharakteristika turok i turetskogo pravitel'stva," ll. 1–23. His anti-Turkish comments were in line with traditional European Christian attitudes that associated the Islamic Turk with oppression and despotism. See Edward Said, *Orientalism* (New York, 1978), and Norman Daniel, *Islam, Europe, and Empire* (Edinburgh, 1966).

42. Arsh, *Kapodistriia*, 233–34; Dostian, *Rossiia i balkanskii vopros*, 218, 226–27.

43. *Russkii arkhiv* (1901), 39, no. 1: 61–64. The Bulgakov correspondence was published in successive issues of this journal from 1900 to 1906.

44. RGVIA, f. 14057, op. 182, d. 19, ll. 8–10; d. 21, ll. 1–20; f. *Voenno-uchenyi arkhiv*, d. 737, ll. 1–127; GAOO, f. 2, op. 1, d. 44a, "O proizshestviiakh v Turetskoi imperii," ch. 1, ll. 1–171; *VPR*, series 2, volume 4: 39–40, 79, 149–52, 630.

45. Sabaneev's and Rudzevich's comments are cited in Ivan F. Iovva, *Bessarabiia i grecheskoe natsional'no-osvoboditel'noe dvizhenie* (Kishinev, 1974), 174–75.

46. Fadeev, *Rossiia i vostochnyi krizis*, 83–86; A. N. Shebunin, *Rossiia na blizhnem vostoke* (Leningrad, 1926), 35–38.

47. Kiselev's letters are in "Bumagi grafa Arseniia A. Zakrevskogo," in *SIRIO* (St. Petersburg, 1891), 78: 63–67.

48. A. P. Zablotskii-Desiatovskii, *Graf P. D. Kiselev i ego vremia*, 4 vols. (St. Petersburg, 1881–82), 1: 142.

49. "Bumagi grafa Arseniia A. Zakrevskogo," 69–105; Zablotskii-Desiatovskii, *Graf P. D. Kiselev*, 1: 148–58, 207–30, 257–313.

50. Langeron was governor-general from 1816 to 1822 and city chief from 1816 to 1820. Inzov was vicegerent from 1818 to 1822 and Langeron's successor as governor-general from 1822 to 1823. On their administrative and economic policies, see Herlihy, *Odessa*, 114–17; N . . . , "I. N. Inzov, Bessarabskii namestnik i popechitel' bulgarskikh poselentsev," *Iug* (1882), 2: 127–37; Aleksandr S. Sturdza, *Vospominaniia ob I. N. Inzove* (Odessa, 1847).

51. *VPR*, series 2, volume 4: 129–32, 639–40.

52. GAOO, f. 1, op. 200, d. 2, "Raport polnomochnogo namestnika Bessara-bskoi oblasti I. N. Inzova Aleksandru I o prebyvanii A. Ipsilanti v Odesse nakanune ego ot'ezda v Moldaviiu i Valakhiiu," ll. 1–13; f. 2, op. 1, d. 44a, ch. 1, ll. 81–82.

53. Grigorii L. Arsh, *Eteristskoe dvizhenie v Rossii. Osvoboditel'naia bor'ba grech-eskogo naroda v nachale XIX v. i russko-grecheskie sviazi* (Moscow, 1970), 261–63; Iovva, *Bessarabiia*, 169–71.

54. Historians have documented the philhellenic reaction of Russian Greeks: Arsh, *Eteristskoe dvizhenie v Rossii*, 297–328; Iovva, *Bessarabiia*, 124–32, 140–52, 173–74; L. N. Oganian, *Obshchestvennoe dvizhenie v Bessarabii*, 2 vols. (Kishinev, 1974), 2: 53–75; S. G. Sakellariou, *Philiki Etaireia* (Odessa, 1909); G. Laïos, *Anekdotes epistoles kai eggrapha tou 1821. Istorika dokoumenta apo ta austriaka archeia* (Athens, 1958), 42–46.

55. GAOO, f. 268, op. 1, d. 1, l. 15.

56. "Bumagi grafa Arseniia A. Zakrevskogo," 63–64; Aleksandr F. Vel'tman, "Vospominaniia v Bessarabii," in L. Maikov, *Istoriko-literaturnye ocherki* (St. Peters-burg, 1895), 110–12. Vel'tman wrote poems, tales, short stories, and novels, many of which were set in Bessarabia and the Balkans. His story "Radoi" (1839) suggests the tension between Greek and Romanian national aspirations. In this story, Ypsil-antis seeks Vladimirescu's help, claiming that "we have common enemies," but the Romanian social rebel retorts: "Your enemies are Turks, ours are Phanariot Greeks." "Radoi" is in Vel'tman's *Povesti i rasskazy* (Moscow, 1979).

57. *VPR*, series 2, volume 4: 68, 639–40; Arsh, *Eteristskoe dvizhenie v Rossii*, 304–5, 312–14; G. M. Piatigorskii, "Vostochnyi krizis 20–kh godov XIX v. i grech-eskaia emigratsiia Odessy," *Sovetskoe slavianovedenie* (1985), no. 1: 51–52.

58. Piatigorskii, "Vostochnyi krizis," 53–54.

59. Arsh, *Eteristskoe dvizhenie v Rossii*, 333–46; Sakellariou, *Philiki Etaireia*, 18–29. The Russian translation of the society's charter and Langeron's letter approving the organization are in GAOO, f. 1, op. 221, d. 4, ch. 4, ll. 16–22.

60. The Nessel'rode-Langeron correspondence is in *VPR*, series 2, volume 4: 400–1, 408–9, 683–84. The Philanthropic Society's aid to three hundred needy families is documented in RGIA, f. 797, op. 2, d. 6395, ll. 142–45a. Arsh, *Eteristskoe dvizhenie v Rossii*, 337, notes that the society helped about five thousand persons, both noncombatants and former insurgents, who sought haven in Odessa and Bes-sarabia.

61. For the relevant historical literature, see W. Bruce Lincoln, "Decem-brists," *MERSH* (1978), 8: 229–37; M. V. Nechkina, "Decembrists' Uprising of 1825," *MERSH* (1978), 8: 237–47; idem, *Dvizhenie dekabristov*, 2 vols. (Moscow, 1955); idem, "Dekabristy vo vsemirno-istoricheskom protsesse," *VI* (1975), no. 12: 3–18; John Gooding, "The Decembrists in the Soviet Union," *Soviet Studies* (1988), 40: 196–209; Marc Raeff, *The Decembrist Movement* (Englewood Cliffs, 1966); Anatole Mazour, *The First Russian Revolution 1825: Its Origins, Development, and Significance* (Berkeley, 1937).

62. Russian and Soviet historiography has treated the Decembrist-Greek con-nection, with Soviet works emphasizing the fraternal relations and revolutionary solidarity between the Russian intelligentsia and Balkan national movements. See Irina S. Dostian, *Russkaia obshchestvennaia mysl' i balkanskie narody: Ot Radishcheva do dekabristov* (Moscow, 1980), 222–89; Ivan F. Iovva, *Iuzhnye dekabristy i grecheskoe*

natsional'no-osvoboditel'noe dvizhenie (Kishinev, 1963); idem, *Dekabristy v Moldavii* (Kishinev, 1975); idem, *Peredovaia Rossiia i obshchestvenno-politicheskoe dvizhenie v Moldavii (pervaia polovina XIX v.)* (Kishinev, 1986), 63–164; Ol'ga V. Orlik, *Dekabristy i evropeiskoe osvoboditel'noe dvizhenie* (Moscow, 1975), 102–25; idem, *Dekabristy i vneshniaia politika Rossii* (Moscow, 1984), 84–100. Pre–1917 Russian works also examined the impact of the Greek revolt on the Decembrists. See V. I. Semevskii, *Politicheskie i obshchestvennye idei dekabristov* (St. Petersburg, 1909), 250–56, and A. N. Pypin, *Obshchestvennoe dvizhenie v Rossii pri Aleksandre I,* 3d ed. (St. Petersburg, 1900), 161–64.

63. A. N. Shebunin, "Dekabristy i voprosy vneshnei politiki," *Russkoe proshloe* (Petrograd, 1923), no. 4: 27–30; Vladimir I. Shteingel', "O vnutrennem sostoianii Rossii pri tsarstvovanii imperatora Nikolaia Pavlovicha," *Russkii arkhiv* (1895), no. 2: 171–72; Aleksandr M. Murav'ev, *Zapiski* (Petrograd, 1922), 12.

64. *Izbrannye sotsial'no-politicheskie i filosofskie proizvedeniia dekabristov,* 3 vols. (Moscow, 1951), 1: 380–81.

65. Mikhail A. Fonvizin, "Zapiski dekabrista 1823 goda," *Golos minuvshego* (1916), no. 10: 145, 148–49; idem, "Obozrenie proiavlenii politicheskoi zhizni v Rossii," in V. I. Semevskii et al., eds., *Obshchestvennye dvizheniia v Rossii v pervuiu polovinu XIX v.,* 2 vols. (St. Petersburg, 1905), 1: 181.

66. *Izbrannye proizvedeniia dekabristov,* 1: 505.

67. *Vosstanie dekabristov. Materialy po istorii vosstaniia dekabristov. Dela verkhovnogo ugolovnogo suda i sledstvennoi komissii,* 17 vols. (Moscow, 1925–80), 1: 343. The Decembrist Ivan D. Iakushkin recalled that "We passionately loved the ancients. Plutarch, Titus, Livy, Cicero, Tacitus, and others were essential reading for each of us" (S. Ia. Shtraikh, ed., *Zapiski, stat'i, i pis'ma dekabrista I. D. Iakushkina* [Moscow, 1951], 20).

68. The views of Pestel' toward Greek and Balkan liberation are discussed in Dostian, *Russkaia obshchestvennaia mysl' i balkanskie narody,* 233–52; Iovva, *Bessarabiia,* 192–209; B. E. Syroechkovskii, "Balkanskaia problema v politicheskikh planakh dekabristov," in B. E. Syroechkovskii, *Iz istorii dvizheniia dekabristov* (Moscow, 1969), 216–303; N. M. Lebedev, *Pestel': Ideolog i rukovoditel' dekabristov* (Moscow, 1972), 115–21.

69. Zablotskii-Desiatovskii, *Graf P. D. Kiselev,* 4: 10–15; *VPR,* series 2, volume 4: 119.

70. Syroechkovskii, "Balkanskaia problema," 231–36.

71. Ibid., 218–21, 249–61; Dostian, *Russkaia obshchestvennaia mysl' i balkanskie narody,* 243–52.

72. Dostian, *Russkaia obshchestvennaia mysl' i balkanskie narody,* 253–68; Iovva, *Bessarabiia,* 209–39; Arsh, *Eteristskoe dvizhenie v Rossii,* 277–83; S. S. Landa, *Dukh revoliutsionnykh preobrazovanii: Iz istorii formirovaniia ideologii i politicheskikh organizatsii dekabristov, 1816–1825* (Moscow, 1975), 160–91; idem, "Zarubezhnye revoliutsionnye sviazi dekabrista M. F. Orlova," *NNI* (1975), no. 6: 42–54.

73. Mikhail F. Orlov, *Kapitulatsiia Parizha. Politicheskie sochineniia i pis'ma* (Moscow, 1963), 232.

74. S. S. Volk, *Istoricheskie vzgliady dekabristov* (Moscow, 1958), 277; Iovva, *Bessarabiia,* 191.

75. *Arkhiv brat'ev Turgenevykh. Tom 3: Dnevnik i pis'ma N. I. Turgeneva za 1816–1824 gg.* (Petrograd, 1921), 279.

76. Ibid., 314, 321–26.

77. Peter Christoff, *An Introduction to Nineteenth-Century Russian Slavophilism: A. S. Xomjakov* (The Hague, 1961), 27–28.

78. Spyros Loukatos, "Pamiatnik russkim filellinam," *BI* (1989), 11: 74–76; N. Todorov, "Quelques renseignements sur les insurgés grecs dans les principautés danubiennes en 1821," in *Essays in Memory of Basil Laourdas* (Thessaloniki, 1975), 471–75; Arsh, *Eteristskoe dvizhenie v Rossii,* 299, 322–24.

79. Loukatos, "Pamiatnik russkim filellinam," 76–88.

80. B. M. Markevich, "N. A. Raiko: Biograficheskii ocherk," *Russkii arkhiv* (1868), no. 6: 297–308; Irina S. Dostian, "Russkii uchastnik grecheskoi revoliutsii," *VI* (1978), no. 4: 210–15.

81. For the shift in Alexandrine policy, see Dostian, *Rossiia i balkanskii vopros,* 230–37; Grimsted, *The Foreign Ministers of Alexander I,* 284–85; McConnell, *Tsar Alexander I: Paternalistic Reformer,* 180–84. Documents in *VPR*, series 2, volumes 5–6, on the years 1823 through 1826, reveal Russian diplomatic efforts to mediate the Greek crisis and to resolve treaty disputes.

82. Lincoln, *Nicholas I, Emperor and Autocrat of All the Russias,* 118, 122–29; Dostian, *Rossiia i balkanskii vopros,* 238–330.

83. C. M. Woodhouse, *The Battle of Navarino* (London, 1965); I. G. Gutkina, "Navarinskoe srazhenie i evropeiskaia diplomatiia," *Uchenye zapiski Leningradskogo gosudarstvennogo pedagogicheskogo instituta. Ocherki vseobshchei istorii* (Leningrad, 1969), 230–53.

84. Russian aid to the Greek government is covered in O. V. Vasilenko, "O pomoshchi Rossii v sozdanii nezavisimogo grecheskogo gosudarstva (1829–1831 gg.)," *NNI* (1959), no. 3: 148–57; Dostian, *Rossiia i balkanskii vopros,* 289–95. V. I. Sheremet, *Turtsiia i Adrianopol'skii mir* (Moscow, 1975), examines the provisions and impact of the Adrianople Treaty. For a Greek Marxist view, based largely on Soviet interpretations, see Dimitris Loules, *O rolos tis Rossias sti diamorphosi tou ellinikou kratous* (Athens, 1981); idem, "Obrazovanie grecheskogo gosudarstva i Rossiia (1821–1832)," *Sovetskoe slavianovedenie* (1980), no. 3: 37–52.

85. "Bumagi grafa Arseniia A. Zakrevskogo," 154, 304.

86. "Graf A. Kh. Benkendorf o Rossii v 1827–1830 gg.," *Krasnyi arkhiv* (1929), 37: 157–60.

87. OR, IRLI, f. 288, op. 1, d. 3, ll. 57–70. Sturdza's reports on the Principalities are in f. 288, op. 2, d. 21b; op. 1, d. 29, 313–15.

88. Piatigorskii, "Vostochnyi krizis," 57–64.

Chapter Three: Greek Relief Aid

1. Theophilus Prousis, "Russian Philorthodox Relief during the Greek War of Independence," *MGSY* (1985), 1: 31–62, which relied heavily on archival documents in the Chancelleries of the Holy Synod and the chief procurator (RGIA, f. 796, 797). It has been recast, based on additional research in RGIA and an opportunity to use relief files in the State Archive of Odessa *Oblast'* (GAOO).

2. Robert Walsh, *A Residence at Constantinople,* 2 vols. (London, 1836), 1: 316–17. The Russian press described outbreaks of violence against Greek Christians in Constantinople, Smyrna, Cyprus, and other areas. See *VE* (1821), no. 12: 326–31;

no. 21: 73–76; no. 23: 236–38; no. 24: 354–56. The monthly issues of *ISGZh* (1821) also reported Ottoman reprisals.

3. GAOO, f. 2, op. 1, d. 44a, "O proizshestviiakh v Turetskoi imperii," ch. 1, ll. 124–24a.

4. The ecumenical patriarch's arrival and funeral in Odessa are covered in S. S., "Grigorii V, patriarkh Konstantinopol'skii postradavshii ot turok v 1821," *Moskvitianin* (1844), no. 10: 441–48; "Sovremennye bumagi o konchine i pogrebenii patriarkha Grigoriia, 1821," *Russkii arkhiv* (1871), no. 11: 1920–39, along with Synodal documents and Governor-General Langeron's account of the funeral; Sviashch. V. Zhmakin, "Pogrebenie Konstantinopol'skogo patriarkha Grigoriia V v Odesse," *Russkaia starina* (1894), no. 12: 198–213; *I en Odisso Elliniki Ekklisia tis Agias Triadas, 1808–1908* (Odessa, 1908), 38–48. An anonymous work, V. A. Ia, "Demonstratsiia protiv evreev v Odesse," *Iug* (1882), 1: 200–5, described the strife between Greek and Jewish communities during the patriarch's funeral. When a group of Odessan Jews refused to remove their hats during the procession, they were assaulted by Greeks and Russians. Violence flared for one day, with seventeen dead and sixty injured.

5. On Oikonomos, see Gavriil S. Destunis, *O zhizni i trudakh K. Ekonomosa* (St. Petersburg, 1860); K. Sathas, *Neoelliniki philologia* (Athens, 1868), 731–36; D. S. Valanos, "Konstantinos Oikonomos o ex Oikonomon," *Ekklisia* (1957), no. 24: 491–98. Oikonomos's biographical sketch of his close friend Sturdza, *Alexandros o Stourdzas. Viographikon schediasma* (Athens, 1855), briefly described Sturdza's prolific writings on religion, philosophy, history, and education.

6. Konstantinos Oikonomos, *Logos epitaphios eis ton aemniston Patriarchin Konstantinoupoleos Grigorion* (St. Petersburg, 1821). Sturdza translated the eulogy into Russian and published a bilingual edition, *Perevod nadgrobnogo slova blazhennomu Konstantinopol'skomu patriarkhu Grigoriiu* (St. Petersburg, 1821). The funeral oration appeared in *VE* (1821), no. 15: 211–38. Sturdza later paid tribute to the patriarch in his "Pamiat' Grigoriia V, patriarkha Konstantinopol'skogo," *Moskvitianin* (1842), no. 6: 380–84. On the eulogy and its translation into Russian, French, and German, see Konstantinos Papoulidis, "Tria anekdota grammata tou Konstantinou Oikonomou tou ex Oikonomon sti Roxandra kai ston Alexandron Stourtza," *Klironomias* (1979), 11, no. 2: 451–75.

7. *VPR*, series 2, volume 4: 39–40, 630; series 2, volume 5: 50–52. Quarantine reports from Bessarabia, from March 1821 to June 1822, are in GAOO, f. 1, op. 214, d. 7, "O pereshedshikh v Bessarabiiu po sluchaiu vosstaniia v Moldavii eteristakh i zagranichnykh semeistvakh. Put' i vsia perepiska ob eteristakh," ch. 1, ll. 1–352; ch. 2, ll. 1–367; ch. 3, ll. 1–97.

8. RGVIA, f. *Voenno-uchenyi arkhiv*, d. 1018, ll. 126–126a, 134–34a.

9. *VPR*, series 2, volume 4: 149–53.

10. For a brief account of the 1821 refugee influx and the initial relief effort, see Ivan F. Iovva, *Peredovaia Rossiia i obshchestvenno-politicheskoe dvizhenie v Moldavii (pervaia polovina XIX v.)* (Kishinev, 1986), 155–64; idem, *Bessarabiia i grecheskoe natsional'no-osvoboditel'noe dvizhenie* (Kishinev, 1974), 152–62.

11. RGIA, f. 797, op. 2, d. 6395, "O posobii grecheskim prishchel'stam v Odessu i Kishinev i ob obezpechenii pribyvshikh v Rossiiu grekov dukhovnogo i svetskogo zvaniia, 1821," ll. 2–2a.

12. Grigorii L. Arsh, *Eteristskoe dvizhenie v Rossii. Osvoboditel'naia bor'ba grech-eskogo naroda v nachale XIX v. i russko-grecheskie sviazi* (Moscow, 1970), 330–31, claims that Sturdza proposed the refugee drive. Sturdza founded a hospice for invalids from the 1812 War and initiated the publication of *Zhurnal imperatorskogo chelovekoliubivogo obshchestva* in order to disseminate news about the Imperial Philanthropic Society. He contributed two articles to the journal in 1818: "Rassuzhdenie o chastnykh i obshchikh zaniatiiakh blagotvoritel'nosti" and "O liubvi k otechestvu." Information on these endeavors can be gleaned from Sturdza's manuscript collections: GAOO, f. 141, op. 1, d. 8, "Mémoire sur la foundation d'asyles pour les invalides et les veterans en Russie," ll. 33–38a; OR, IRLI, f. 288, op. 1, d. 308, "Mnenie o uchrezhdenii literaturnogo komiteta i izdanii onym zhurnala," ll. 13–16.

13. On Golitsyn's government service and philanthropy, see Walter W. Sawatsky, "Prince Alexander N. Golitsyn (1773–1844): Tsarist Minister of Piety," Ph.D. diss., University of Minnesota, 1976, and the relevant sections in James T. Flynn, *The University Reform of Tsar Alexander I, 1802–1835* (Washington, D.C., 1988).

14. Konstantinos Oikonomos, *Slova, govorennye v Odesse na grecheskom iazyke v 1821 i 1822 godakh, pri pogrebenii Konstantinopol'skogo patriarkha Grigoriia i pri drugikh sluchaiakh* (St. Petersburg, 1829), this edition of his sermons being dedicated to Golitsyn for the latter's help to Greek Christians. Aleksandr S. Sturdza, *Dan' pamiati vel'mozhikhristianina kniazia A. N. Golitsyna* (Odessa, 1845), emphasized the importance of Greek relief among the many charitable works of Golitsyn; idem, "Zapiski A. S. Sturdzy: O sud'be pravoslavnoi russkoi tserkvi v tsarstvovanie imperatora Aleksandra I-go," *Russkaia starina* (1876), 15, no. 1: 266–88.

15. Numerous studies cover Alexandrine philanthropy and cite the relevant Russian historical literature: Judith Cohen Zacek, "The Imperial Philanthropic Society in the Reign of Alexander I," *CASS* (1975), 9, no. 4: 427–36; idem, "A Case Study in Russian Philanthropy: The Prison Reform Movement in the Reign of Alexander I," *CSS* (1967), 1, no. 2: 196–211; Barry Hollingsworth, "John Venning and Prison Reform in Russia, 1819–1830," *SEER* (1971), 48: 538–57; Franklin A. Walker, "Christianity, the Service Ethic and Decembrist Thought," in Geoffrey Hosking, ed., *Church, Nation and State in Russia and Ukraine* (New York, 1991), 79–95; Adele Lindenmeyr, "The Ethos of Charity in Imperial Russia," *Journal of Social History* (1990), 23, no. 4: 679–94; idem, "Public Poor Relief and Private Charity in Late Imperial Russia," Ph.D. diss., Princeton University, 1980, especially 107–31.

16. RGIA, f. 797, op. 2, d. 6403, ll. 3–3a.

17. RGIA, f. 797, op. 2, d. 6395, ll. 1–3a.

18. RGIA, f. 797, op. 2, d. 6395, ll. 6–6a, 10–11a. Greek copies of the circular and Golitsyn's correspondence with Inzov on the drive are also in GAOO, f. 1, op. 214, d. 8, ll. 5–10.

19. RGIA, f. 797, op. 2, d. 6395, ll. 4–5a, 13–19a, 23–26.

20. RGIA, f. 797, op. 2, d. 6484, "Ob izdanii otcheta po sboru i upotrebleniiu grecheskikh summ v posobie grekov," ll. 1–19a. The report, "Otchet o vspomoshchestvovanii grecheskim semeistvam," was published in the newspapers of the capitals—*Peterburgskie vedomosti* and *Moskovskie vedomosti*—and in the bulletins of the Foreign Ministry and the Academy of Sciences—*Le Conservateur Impartial* and *Akademicheskie vedomosti*.

21. L. S. Stavrianos, *The Balkans Since 1453* (New York, 1958), 83–85; Halil Inalcik, *The Ottoman Empire: The Classical Age, 1300–1600* (London, 1973), 130–33.

22. On Chios and the massacre, see Apostolos Vakalopoulos, *Istoria tou neou ellinismou,* 6 vols. (Thessaloniki, 1973–82), 6: 65–124; Philip Argenti, ed., *The Massacres of Chios Described in Contemporary Diplomatic Reports* (London, 1932), ix–xxxiv; idem, *Bibliography of Chios from Classical Times to 1936* (Oxford, 1940), 415–34.

23. Walsh, *A Residence at Constantinople,* 2: 72–73. His account of Chios before and during the invasion is in 1: 398–409.

24. Walsh, *A Residence at Constantinople,* 2: 6–10; Argenti, ed., *The Massacres of Chios Described in Contemporary Diplomatic Reports,* 40–41. Russian press reports on the massacre and its aftermath include *VE* (1822), no. 9/10: 152–54; no. 13/14: 156–59; *ISGZh* (1824), no. 11: 93–113; *Galateia* (1829), no. 18: 99–118.

25. The Delacroix painting and other artistic work inspired by the revolt are discussed in Nina M. Athanassoglou-Kallmyer, *French Images from the Greek War of Independence, 1821–1830: Art and Politics under the Restoration* (New Haven, 1989).

26. Greek and French copies of the petition to the tsar are in RGIA, f. 1308, op. 1, d. 85, "O pozvolenii nakhodiashchimsia v Bessarabii grecheskim dukhovnym otkryt' podpisku dlia vykupa plennykh zhitelei ostrova Khio i gorodov Kassandra i Kidonii," ll. 2–3a.

27. RGIA, f. 1308, op. 1, d. 85, ll. 1–1a, 4–11; f. 797, op. 2, d. 6496, "Po otkrytiiu sbora na vykup grekov," ll. 1–4a.

28. RGIA, f. 797, op. 2, d. 6496, ll. 6–8a, 12–16, 26–27, 36–39, along with Oikonomos's French translation of the subscription announcement; f. 796, op. 103, d. 1102, "Po predlozheniiu ministra dukhovnogo del i narodnogo prosveshcheniia ob otkrytii podpiski na iskuplenie plennykh grecheskikh semeistv," ll. 1–21, along with handwritten and printed copies of the circular. The Synodal decree on the ransom project is published in *VPR,* series 2, volume 4: 605–6.

29. RGIA, f. 797, op. 2, d. 6496, ll. 11–11a, 29–41a, 55–62; f. 1308, op. 1, d. 85, ll. 15–15a, 19–23; f. 1284, op. 7, d. 214, "O sodeistvii k rasprostraneniiu podpiski na vykup grecheskikh plennykh," ll. 1–29, along with Kochubei's dispatches to governors. The dispatch to Governor-General Miloradovich of St. Petersburg is published in *VPR,* series 2, volume 4: 613.

30. RGIA, f. 797, op. 3, d. 10099, ll. 1–7a; f. 1287, op. 2, d. 1, ll. 1–2a; f. 565, op. 13, d. 2061, ll. 1–1a. See *VPR,* series 2, volume 6: 486–87, on Nicholas I's continuation of his brother's Greek relief projects. In the early nineteenth century, Russia had a monetary system of two currencies, paper rubles (or assignats) and metal (silver and gold) rubles, with the value of the two currencies based on the fluctuating exchange rate on the St. Petersburg bourse. Prices were generally stated in assignats but payment was accepted in either form of money. In the 1820s, one assignat was worth about one quarter of a silver ruble, and one silver ruble was worth about nine English pence. The Greek relief records I have examined indicate that the vast majority of donations were in assignats, although there are examples of silver and gold ruble donations from the upper nobility, church hierarchs, and monasteries. In recording and tabulating relief aid contributions, I have not distinguished between assignat and metal donations. For a brief discussion of monetary matters and the two currencies, see Walter M. Pintner, *Russian Economic Policy under Nicholas I* (Ithaca, 1967), 184–98.

31. RGIA, f. 797, op. 2, d. 6395, ll. 152–53a; d. 6418, l. 1. D. 6491, ll. 1–21,

mentions Mariia Fedorovna's aid to Greek Cypriot clergy who fled to Marseilles after the 1821 execution of Archbishop Kyprios of Cyprus.

32. A. F. Shidlovskii, "Iz bumag grafini R. S. Edling," *Russkii vestnik* (1899), no. 3: 188–89; idem, "Pis'ma imperatritsy Elizavety Alekseevny k R. S. Sturdze (grafine Edling)," *Russkii arkhiv* (1888), 26: 379–80; RGIA, f. 535, op. 1, d. 33, ll. 57–60a.

33. RGIA, f. 797, op. 2: d. 6546, ll. 1–4a; d. 6523, ll. 1–9; d. 6511, ll. 1–32; d. 6518, ll. 1–113; d. 6515, ll. 1–38; d. 6395, ll. 7–7a; d. 6416, ll. 1–11; d. 6484, ll.16–17; d. 6505, ll. 18–18a; d. 6504, ll. 11–11a; d. 6534, ll. 1–7; d. 6538, ll. 1–4; d. 6520, ll. 7–8. *VPR*, series 2, volume 5: 22–23, cites the January 1823 decision by the Committee of Ministers to supplement relief funds with fifty thousand rubles from the state treasury.

34. With the creation of the Ministry of Public Education in 1802, the Empire was divided into six educational districts: Moscow, St. Petersburg, Kazan, Kharkov, Dorpat, and Vilna. Each was headed by a curator, who also served as the rector of the district university. Relief aid from educational institutions is covered in RGIA, f. 797, op. 2: d. 6418, ll. 2–3a; d. 6414, ll. 1–10a, 21–26a; d. 6419, ll. 1–39; d. 6631, ll. 1–115. Donations from the Commission of Ecclesiastical Schools are cited in d. 6395, ll. 109–11; d. 6449, ll. 28–29, 80, 92; *VPR*, series 2, volume 4: 282.

35. There were six postal regions in the Empire by the early nineteenth century. Records document relief funds from postal officials in Moscow, St. Petersburg, Riazan, Simbirsk, Kazan, Irkutsk, Smolensk, Mogilev, Ekaterinoslav, Iaroslavl, Vladimir, Tver, Tambov, and Kolomenskoe, as well as the Crimean towns of Kherson, Tiraspol, Olviopol, Feodosia, Kerch, and Evpatoria. See RGIA, f. 797, op. 2: d. 6415, ll. 1–129; d. 6430, ll. 1–182a; d. 6513, ll. 1–19; d. 6527, ll. 1–7; d. 6586, ll. 1–2.

36. RGIA, f. 797, op. 2, d. 6395, ll. 95–95a; d. 6516, ll. 1–56; d. 6628, ll. 1–8; d. 6579, ll. 1–101; d. 6423, ll. 1–20; op. 3, d. 9971, ll. 24–27; d. 9979, ll. 1–10.

37. RGIA, f. 797, op. 2, d. 6515, ll. 38–47.

38. The boundaries of administrative provinces *(gubernii)* and dioceses *(eparkhii)* were usually identical. Files in RGIA, f. 797, op. 2, document Greek aid from these provinces and dioceses: Moscow (d. 6412, 6490, 6519, 6522, 6537); St. Petersburg (d. 6422, 6529, 6542); Novgorod and Pskov (d. 6407, 6420, 6462, 6584); Tver (d. 6454, 6470, 6603); Iaroslavl (d. 6436, 6452, 6566, 6580); Kostroma (d. 6478, 6624); Vologda (d. 6512); Vladimir (d. 6597); Tula (d. 6413, 6485, 6606); Riazan (d. 6575, 6589); Kaluga (d. 6403, 6539); Nizhnii Novgorod (d. 6585, 6600); Penza (d. 6440, 6563); Tambov (d. 6570); Kazan (d. 6414, 6432, 6571); Simbirsk (d. 6376, 6448, 6564); Viatka (d. 6383, 6561, 6569); Astrakhan (d. 6568); Kursk (d. 6532, 6562); Voronezh (d. 6408, 6569); Smolensk (d. 6376, 6448, 6564); Minsk (d. 6426, 6595); Chernigov (d. 6566); Mogilev (d. 6612, 6540); Kiev (d. 6434, 6445, 6637); Kharkov (d. 6401, 6528); Poltava (d. 6577); Podolia (d. 6640); Kishinev (d. 6616); Ekaterinoslav (d. 6450, 6651).

39. RGIA, f. 797, op. 2: Olonets (d. 6499, 6581); Arkhangelsk (d. 6468, 6574); Perm and Orenburg (d. 6425, 6548, 6615, 6617, 6623); Tomsk, Tobolsk, and Irkutsk (d. 6417, 6439, 6467, 6583, 6596, 6599).

40. RGIA, f. 797, op. 2, d. 6439, ll. 1–3; d. 6599, ll. 1–7a; op. 3, d. 9974, ll. 16–25a.

41. Pledges from diocesan hierarchs to Golitsyn are located in RGIA, f. 797, op. 2, d. 6395, ll. 30–120; d. 6449, ll. 1–42a, 63–88; f. 796, op. 103, d. 1102, ll.

21–125. On the structure and organization of the Russian church in the prereform era, see Gregory L. Freeze, *The Parish Clergy in Nineteenth-Century Russia: Crisis, Reform, Counter-Reform* (Princeton, 1983), 1–187.

42. GAOO, f. 1, op. 221, d. 4a, "Kniga ucheta denezhnykh summ, poluchennykh Khersonskim voennym gubernatorom ot dukhovnykh, voennykh, grazhdanskikh uchrezhdenii i chastnykh lits dlia okazaniia pomoshchi grekam," ll. 1–29.

43. *VPR*, series 2, volume 6: 72–73, 316–17.

44. RGIA, f. 797, op. 2: d. 6418, ll. 1–142; d. 6484, ll. 13a–18a; d. 6504, ll. 1–26; d. 6506, ll. 1–21; d. 6519, ll. 1–61; d. 6582, ll. 1–2.

45. RGIA, f. 797, op. 2, d. 6418, ll. 31, 35–35a; f. 1088, op. 1, d. 661, "Perepiska D. N. Sheremeteva s kn. A. N. Golitsynym o pozhertvovanii deneg na vykup iz plena zhitelei ostrova Khio, Kassandra, i Kidonii," ll. 1–5.

46. Donations from church hierarchs and monasteries are amply documented in RGIA, f. 797, op. 2, d. 6490, ll. 1–245; d. 6521, ll. 1–22a; d. 6542, ll. 1–4a; op. 3, d. 9975, "O pozhertvovanniiakh na vykup grekov," ll. 1–50; f. 796, op. 103, d. 1102, ll. 126–767.

47. RGIA, f. 797, op. 2, d. 6449, ll. 166, 176–76a, 185–87, 191–92; f. 796, op. 116, d. 300, "Raport Evgeniia, mitropolita Kievskogo, o prodazhke dvukh medalii i odnogo dukata pozhertvovannykh na iskuplenie plennykh grekov," ll. 1–2.

48. RGIA, f. 797, op. 2, d. 6414 (Kazan), ll. 24–24a; d. 6532 (Kursk), ll. 1–185. On the status and material condition of parish clergy in the prereform era, see Freeze, *The Parish Clergy in Nineteenth-Century Russia*, 52–65.

49. RGIA, f. 797, op. 2: d. 6448, ll. 3–15; d. 6422, ll. 1–7a; d. 6407, ll. 1–3; d. 6519, ll. 5–8; d. 6395, ll. 85–85a; d. 6484, ll. 1–13a.

50. RGIA, f. 797, op. 2, d. 6424, ll. 1–10a; d. 6416, ll. 1–6a; f. 796, op. 2, d. 1338, ll. 1–2.

51. RGIA, f. 797, op. 2, d. 6422, ll. 7–7a, 16–48a.

52. RGIA, f. 797, op. 2, d. 6385, ll. 1–91; d. 6400, ll. 1–90; d. 6444, ll. 1–47; d. 6446, ll. 1–4; d. 6576, ll. 1–69; d. 6602, ll. 1–5; op. 3, d. 9971, ll. 32–35; d. 9980, ll. 1–47; *VPR*, series 2, volume 5: 151–52.

53. RGIA, f. 797, op. 2: d. 6474, ll. 1–90; d. 6409, ll. 1–35; d. 6594, ll. 1–43; d. 6477, ll. 1–2; d. 6484, ll. 17a–19.

54. RGIA, f. 797, op. 2, d. 6400, ll. 70–89; d. 6418, ll. 83–83a. M. N. Akopian, "Osvodozhdenie Gretsii i armianskaia obshchestvennaia mysl'," in V. N. Vinogradov, ed., *Tsentral'naia i Iugo-Vostochnaia Evropa v novoe vremia* (Moscow, 1974), 150–57.

55. Theophilus C. Prousis, "Dēmētrios S. Inglezēs: Greek Merchant and City Leader of Odessa," *SR* (1991), 50, no. 3: 672–79.

56. GAOO, f. 268, op. 1, d. 1, ll. 21–27a, 34–35; d. 14, ll. 4–6. RGIA, f. 797, op. 2, d. 6449, ll. 48–53a, 86; d. 6517, ll. 20–21.

57. RGIA, f. 797, op. 2, d. 6418, ll. 130–41. Additional references to Greek patrons are in d. 6395, ll. 81–83, 126–27a, 142–45a; d. 6449, ll. 90–91, 100–106a, 125–25a, 136–40, 160–62; d. 6484, ll. 13a, 19–19a; d. 6496, ll. 65–65a; d. 6517, ll. 1–21.

58. RGIA, f. 797, op. 2, d. 6418, ll. 135–37; d. 6517, ll. 14–18.

59. The manuscript collection of Spyridon Iu. Destunis contains a Greek-language appeal exhorting Odessan Greeks to aid refugees from Constantinople and Moldavia. Names of donors are scrawled on the back of the petition, along

with the amount of their contributions, which totalled 9,025.60 rubles by late August 1822. OR, GPB, f. 250, d. 94, ll. 45–46.

60. RGIA, f. 797, op. 2, d. 6453, "Po otnosheniiu grafa Kapodistriia o vspomoshchenii Greku Antonu Isaii," ll. 1–8; d. 6450, ll. 139–41; d. 6520, ll. 63–68a, 73–74a, 115; d. 6618, ll. 1–15; d. 6433, ll. 2–13a.

61. Roksandra Sturdza-Edling's charitable activities are described in the commemorative tribute by Aleksandr Sturdza, *Dan' pamiati grafini Roksandry S. Edling, urozhdennoi Sturdzy* (Odessa, 1848). Also useful are documents from A. Sturdza's manuscript collections: GAOO, f. 141, op. 1, d. 31, ll. 9–16; OR, IRLI, f. 288, op. 2, d. 99, ll. 3–5.

62. The 1830 subscription is mentioned in OR, IRLI, f. 288, op. 1, d. 308, "Appel à la charité chrétienne des habitants d'Odessa," ll. 19–21. Sturdza served on a municipal committee to combat plague, was vice-president of the Society of Rural Economy in southern Russia, was a founding member of the Odessan Society of History and Antiquities, and established the Odessan Society of Sisters of Mercy. These and other charitable works are covered in *K materialam dlia istorii Odesskogo Arkhangelo-Mikhailovskogo zhenskogo monastyriia i zametki dlia biografii A. S. Sturdzy* (Odessa, 1902).

63. Relief donations after 1824 are documented in RGIA, f. 797, op. 3, d. 10099, "Okonchatel'noe proizvodstvo po sboram summ v posobie i na iskuplenie grekov," ll. 14a–62; f. 796, op. 103, d. 1102, ll. 602–767; op. 105, d. 1310, "Prikhodoraskhodnaia kniga o summe v pol'zu grekov i na drugie predmety," ll. 1–40; d. 1322, "Vedomosti o summakh postupaiushchikh v pol'zu grekov i na drugie predmety," ll. 1–20.

64. RGIA, f. 796, op. 105, d. 1323, "Otpuski ispol'nitel'nykh raportov po predpisaniiam o postupaiushchei v pol'zu grekov i na drugie predmety summe," ll. 12a–16a; op. 103, d. 1102, ll. 751–52a.

65. Judith Cohen Zacek, "The Russian Bible Society and the Russian Orthodox Church," *Church History* (1966), 35, no. 4: 411–37, which is based on her thesis "The Russian Bible Society," Ph.D. diss., Columbia University, 1964; A. N. Pypin, *Religioznye dvizheniia pri Aleksandre I* (Petrograd, 1916), 155–222; Stephen K. Batalden, "Printing the Bible in the Reign of Alexander I: Toward a Reinterpretation of the Imperial Russian Bible Society," in Hosking, ed., *Church, Nation and State in Russia and Ukraine*, 65–78; Joseph L. Wieczynski, "Apostle of Obscurantism: the Archimandrite Photius of Russia (1792–1838)," *Journal of Ecclesiastical History* (1971), 22, no. 4: 319–31; Georges Florovsky, *Ways of Russian Theology. Part One*, tr. Robert Nichols (Belmont, Mass., 1979), 162–201.

66. N. Elagin, *Zhizn' grafini Anny Alekseevny Orlovoi-Chesmenskoi* (St. Petersburg, 1853), discussed Orlova-Chesmenskaia's relationship with Fotii. From their correspondence with Golitsyn, it is clear that Arakcheev and Minister of Finance Gur'ev, both of whom opposed intervention in the Greek crisis, were active in organizing relief aid: RGIA, f. 797, op. 2, d. 6398, "Perepiska s ministrom finansov ob otpravlenii summ v posobie grekam," ll. 1–186; d. 6533, "O prinosheniiakh v pol'zu grekov po otnosheniiu Arakcheeva," ll. 1–5.

67. E. P. Karnovich, *Zamechatel'nye i zagadochnye lichnosti XVII i XIX stoletii*, 2d ed. (St. Petersburg, 1893), 358–59, which is part of the section on Fotii and Golitsyn (pp. 339–469). Golitsyn's correspondence with Fotii and Anna Orlova indicates

that he deeply admired their religious zeal and their renovation of Iurevskii Monastery: "Pis'ma kniazia Aleksandra Nikolaevicha Golitsyna k grafine Anne Alekseevne Orlovoi-Chesmenskoi v 1822 i 1823 godakh," *Russkii arkhiv* (1869): 943–58; "Kniaz' A. N. Golitsyn i Arkhimandrit Fotii v 1822–1825 godakh," *Russkaia starina* (1882), 33: 765–81; 34: 205–22, 427–42, 683–700; 35: 275–96. Karnovich and Wieczynski suggest that Golitsyn's friendship with Fotii was partially motivated by the desire to gain Orlova's financial support for the ransom drive. That may well be, but his letters to Fotii contain no mention of the relief projects.

68. RGIA, f. 797, op. 3, d. 9971, ll. 39–44; d. 9972, ll. 1–22; d. 9980, ll. 1–52; f. 1673, op. 1, d. 91, ll. 1–2a. Alexander M. Martin, "Conservative Thought and the Construction of National Identity in the Reign of Alexander I," unpublished paper, American Association for the Advancement of Slavic Studies Convention, Phoenix, Arizona, 1992, discusses the political and cultural conservatism of Shishkov in the context of the several strains of Alexandrine conservative thought.

69. GAOO, f. 1, op. 221, d. 4, "Ob uchrezhdennii vremennogo komiteta dlia vspomoshchestvovaniia pribyvshim v Odessu Konstantinopol'skim grekam i Odesskoi grecheskoi vspomogatel'noi komissii," ch. 1, ll. 1–169; op. 214, d. 8, "Ob uchrezhdennii v Kishineve grecheskoi vspomogatel'noi komissii i ob organizatsii sbora pozhertvovanii v pol'zu grecheskikh bezhentsev," ll. 1–542.

70. RGIA, f. 797, op. 2, d. 6446, ll. 1–7. Governor-General Vorontsov's contributions to New Russia's development are treated in Anthony L. H. Rhinelander, *Prince Michael Vorontsov: Viceroy to the Tsar* (Montreal, 1990), 57–120; Patricia Herlihy, *Odessa: A History, 1794–1914* (Cambridge, Mass., 1986), 76–82, 116–37.

71. G. M. Piatigorskii, "Deiatel'nost' Odesskoi grecheskoi vspomogatel'noi komissii v 1821–1831 gg. (Po materialam Gosudarstvennogo arkhiva Odesskoi obl.)," *BI* (1982), 8: 135–52, examines the ORC based almost exclusively on materials in GAOO. In addition to some of these files, I have relied on Synodal holdings to describe the relief aid committees.

72. *Otchety* prepared by the ORC and KRC are in RGIA, f. 797, op. 2: d. 6395, ll. 125–31a, 146–52; d. 6450, ll. 4–12, 29–35, 44–52, 69–79a, 91–96, 118–26, 157–99; d. 6520, ll. 2–5, 22–48a, 83–96, 118–44. GAOO, f. 1: op. 200, d. 72, "O deistviiakh Odesskoi grecheskoi vspomogatel'noi komissii," ll. 8–9, 106–9, 315–25; d. 71, "O deistviiakh Kishinevskoi grecheskoi vspomogatel'noi komissii," ll. 100, 108, 118, 134–38, 142–45, 155–71; op. 214, d. 22, "O deiatel'nosti Kishinevskoi grecheskoi vspomogatel'noi komissii," ll. 19–26, 249–52, 289–92, 308–11, 377–80, 486–92. Several *otchety* appear in *VPR*, series 2, volume 6: 18, 217–18, 333, 711–12, 718–22, 741–43, 774–76.

73. GAOO, f. 268, op. 1, d. 14, ll. 1–2a, 8.

74. On the distribution process, see RGIA, f. 797, op. 2, d. 6395, ll. 131–45a; d. 6520, ll. 10–21. GAOO, f. 1, op. 221, d. 4, ch. 3, ll. 1–58; ch. 4, ll. 118–20, 124–25, 132–33, 293–94. Piatigorskii, "Deiatel'nost' Odesskoi grecheskoi vspomogatel'noi komissii," 138–41.

75. Petitions for aid are located in GAOO, f. 1: op. 221, d. 4, ch. 3, ll. 59–62a, 70–77; ch. 4, ll. 1–614; ch. 5, ll. 1–533; op. 214, d. 8, ll. 125–28, 176–88, 202–3, 279–84, 303–8, 359–61, 461–64a, 491–92, 531–38; d. 22, ll. 151–56, 171–72; op. 200, d. 71, ll. 13–14, 30, 45–45a, 52.

76. RGIA, f. 797, op. 2, d. 6489, "Po pis'mu grafa Bulgari o posobii Greku

Spiro Panaioti," ll. 1–7. Additional appeals to Golitsyn are in d. 6573, ll. 1–10; d. 6607, ll. 1–9; d. 6638, ll. 1–7; d. 6643, ll. 1–5a; d. 6649, ll. 1–7.

77. RGIA, f. 797, op. 2, d. 6460, "Po prosheniiu Greka doktora Gobdelasa o posobii," ll. 1–6.

78. RGIA, f. 797, op. 2, d. 6493, ll. 1–11; d. 6475, ll. 1–14; d. 6481, ll. 1–12; d. 6572, ll. 1–20; d. 6613, ll. 1–4.

79. Aid to refugee clergy is cited in RGIA, f. 797, op. 2: d. 6450, ll. 14–16, 53–57, 63–74, 90–98, 101–15, 129–81, 216–51; d. 6491, ll. 1–21; d. 6618, ll. 1–15; d. 6632, ll. 4–9, 27–28.

80. Noble pensions are documented in RGIA, f. 565, op. 13, d. 2061, "O proizvodstve i posobii grecheskim emigrantam nakhodiashchimsia v iuzhnom kraia Rossii," ll. 2–54, and in GAOO, f. 1, op. 221, d. 4, "O vydache ezhemesiachnykh pansionov dlia blagotrodnykh grecheskikh semeistv," ll. 1–125; op. 200, d. 72, ll. 9–16, 246–73, 306–14, 326–43, 391–412a; d. 71, ll. 84–86a, 99–99a, 169–70, 178–84. The published *otchet* in VPR, series 2, volume 5: 675–76, indicates generous support for aristocratic emigrants in Bessarabia from November 1821 to October 1822.

81. Piatigorskii, "Deiatel'nost' Odesskoi grecheskoi vspomogatel'noi komissii," 144–46; GAOO, f. 1, op. 200, d. 72, ll. 343–90.

82. RGIA, f. 733, op. 78, d. 52, ll. 1–31; GAOO, f. 1, op. 200, d. 72, ll. 287–88, 338–39, 420; VPR, series 2, volume 5: 243–48.

83. RGIA, f. 565, op. 13, d. 2061, ll. 106–91; f. 797, op. 2, d. 6471, ll. 1–20.

84. RGIA, f. 797, op. 2, d. 6450, ll. 84–100a; f. 1286, op. 3, d. 291, "O razmeshchenii nizhnikh sostoianii grecheskikh vykhodtsev nakhodiashchikhsia v Odesse," ll. 1–10.

85. RGIA, f. 797, op. 2, d. 6450, ll. 101–9a, 204–15a, 249–50a.

86. VPR, series 2, volume 5: 22–23.

87. RGIA, f. 797, op. 2, d. 6450, ll. 202–3a; d. 6402, "Po predlozheniiu grafa Orlova-Denisova v pol'zu grecheskikh semeistv," ll. 1–17.

88. GAOO, f. 1, op. 214, d. 7, "Po pros'bam o priniatii v rossiiskoe poddanstvo," ll. 1–137; d. 5, ll. 1–16.

89. GAOO, f. 1, op. 200, d. 72, ll. 23–24, 58–62a, 115–16, 123–24a, 152–53, 169–72, 180–85, 203–11, 220–22, 453–58, 470–72, 483–87; d. 71, ll. 34–37, 70–77; VPR, series 2, volume 5: 111–12, 139, 280.

90. GAOO, f. 1, op. 200, d. 6, ll. 1–3; RGIA, f. 1409, op. 5, d. 63, ll. 1–7.

91. RGIA, f. 797, op. 3, d. 10099, ll. 7a–14a; op. 2, d. 6449, "Po otkrytiiu sbora na vykup grekov i sredstvakh proizvodit' vykup," ll. 43–44, 48–53a.

92. Sample petitions for ransom help are in RGIA, f. 797, op. 2, d. 6635, ll. 1–3; d. 6645, ll. 1–6; d. 6648, ll. 1–5.

93. RGIA, f. 797, op. 2, d. 6498, "Po prosheniiu Greka Dimitriia Kostandulaki o posobii na vykup rodstvennikov ego," ll. 1–43.

94. These various proposals are discussed in RGIA, f. 797, op. 2, d. 6496, ll. 21–22; d. 6449, ll. 72–75a, 98–99, 103–4a, 119–24a, 141–56a; f. 1308, op. 1, d. 85, ll. 25–32.

95. VPR, series 2, volume 6: 35, 82, 718–22, 725.

96. Kapodistrias's request is mentioned in Grigorii L. Arsh, "Capodistria et

le gouvernement russe (1826–1827)," in *Les relations Gréco-Russes pendant la domination turque et la guerre d'indépendance grecque* (Thessaloniki, 1983), 130; Eleni Koukkou, *Ioannis Kapodistrias. O Anthropos-O Diplomatis (1800–1828)*, 2d ed. (Athens, 1984), 222–25, 350.

97. RGIA, f. 797, op. 3, d. 10099, ll. 28–29, 31–43, 55–56; f. 796, op. 103, d. 1102, ll. 757–65a; op. 111, d. 979, ll. 13–19; GAOO, f. 1, op. 200, d. 72, l. 126, 130.

98. Argenti, ed., *The Massacres of Chios Described in Contemporary Diplomatic Reports*, 39–43, 96.

99. *VPR*, series 2, volume 6: 519.

100. "Zapiska o trekh maloletnikh grekakh privezennykh v Odessu iz Konstantinopolia," *KV* (1823), no. 10: 108–13; RGIA, f. 797, op. 3, d. 9971, l. 49; GAOO, f. 1, op. 200, d. 72, l. 384a. The ORC and Governor-General Langeron funded the education of six refugees in Nezhin, as noted in N. A. Lavrovskii, *Gimnaziia vysshikh nauk kn. Bezborodko v Nezhine, 1820–1832* (Kiev, 1879), 36–37. On Magnitskii's reactionary educational policy, see Flynn, *The University Reform of Tsar Alexander I, 1802–1835*, 90–105, 162–67.

101. Dmitrii N. Bukharov, *Rossiia i Turtsiia: Ot vozniknoveniia politicheskikh mezhdu nimi otnoshenii do Londonskogo traktata marta 1871 g.* (St. Petersburg, 1878), 65.

Chapter Four: Russia's Classical Awakening

1. For the impact of classical Greece on eighteenth-century European thought, see Elizabeth Rawson, *The Spartan Tradition in European Thought* (Oxford, 1969); M. I. Finley, ed., *The Legacy of Greece: A New Appraisal* (New York, 1984); Harold Parker, *The Cult of Antiquity and the French Revolutionaries* (Chicago, 1937).

2. Winckelmann's writings, *Gedanken über die Nachahmung der griechischen Werken* (1754) and *Geschichte der Kunst des Altertums* (1764), and their influence are discussed in David Irwin, ed., *Winckelmann: Writings on Art* (London, 1972); Wolfgang Leppmann, *Winckelmann* (New York, 1970); Henry C. Hatfield, *Winckelmann and His German Critics, 1775–1781: A Prelude to the Classical Age* (New York, 1943).

3. Hugh Honour, *Neo-classicism* (Hammondsworth, 1968); Gilbert Highet, *The Classical Tradition: Greek and Roman Influences on Western Literature* (Oxford, 1949), 335–453; G. W. Clarke, ed., *Rediscovering Hellenism: The Hellenic Inheritance and the English Imagination* (New York, 1989); E. T. Webb, *English Romantic Hellenism, 1700–1824* (Manchester, 1982); Joseph M. Crook, *The Greek Revival: Neo-classical Attitudes in British Architecture, 1760–1870* (London, 1972).

4. *Medieval Russia's Epics, Chronicles, and Tales*, ed. and tr. Serge A. Zenkovsky, 2d ed. (New York, 1974), 4.

5. Harold B. Segel, "Classicism and Classical Antiquity in Eighteenth- and Early Nineteenth-Century Russian Literature," in John G. Garrard, ed., *The Eighteenth Century in Russia* (Oxford, 1973), 48–71; Harold B. Segel, *The Literature of Eighteenth-Century Russia: A History and Anthology*, 2 vols. (New York, 1967), 1: 15–116; William E. Brown, *A History of Eighteenth-Century Russian Literature* (Ann Arbor, 1980), 31–155; Evelyn Bristol, *A History of Russian Poetry* (New York, 1991), 45–89; G. V. Moskvicheva, *Russkii klassitsizm* (Moscow, 1978); I. Z. Serman, *Russkii klassitsizm: Poeziia-Drama-Satira* (Leningrad, 1973).

6. See Antony Lentin, ed., *Voltaire and Catherine II: Selected Correspondence*

(London, 1974); B. Knös, "Voltaire et la Grèce," *L'Hellénisme Contemporain* (1955): 1–28, on Voltaire's enthusiasm for ancient Greece and his advocacy of Catherine II's Greek Project. For an introduction to eighteenth-century Russia's interest in classical antiquity, see the two studies by P. N. Cherniaev: *Sledy znakomstva drevne-klassicheskoi literatury v veke Ekateriny II* (Voronezh, 1906), and *Puti proniknoveniia v Rossiiu svedenii ob antichnom mire* (Voronezh, 1911).

7. On the grecophile aspects of Catherinian policy, see Hugh Ragsdale, "Evaluating the Traditions of Russian Aggression: Catherine II and the Greek Project," *SEER* (1988), no. 1: 91–117; David M. Griffiths, "The Greek Project," *MERSH* (1979), 13: 128–32; idem, "Russian Court Politics and the Question of an Expansionist Foreign Policy under Catherine II, 1762–1783," Ph.D. diss., Cornell University, 1967; Stephen K. Batalden, *Catherine II's Greek Prelate: Eugenios Voulgaris in Russia, 1771–1806* (New York, 1982), 24–31, 74–77.

8. N. N. Kovalenskaia, *Russkii klassitsizm: Zhivopis', skulptura, grafika* (Moscow, 1964); E. V. Nikolaev, *Klassicheskaia Moskva* (Moscow, 1975); Albert Schmidt, *The Architecture and Planning of Classical Moscow: A Cultural History* (Philadelphia, 1989); idem, "Architecture in Nineteenth-Century Russia: The Enduring Classic," in Theofanis G. Stavrou, ed., *Art and Culture in Nineteenth-Century Russia* (Bloomington, 1983), 172–93; Janet Kennedy, "The Neoclassical Ideal in Russian Sculpture," in Stavrou, ed., *Art and Culture*, 194–210; James Cracraft, *The Petrine Revolution in Russian Architecture* (Chicago, 1989), 232–66.

9. Pavel I. Sumarokov, *Puteshestvie po vsemu Krymu i Bessarabii v 1799 g.* (Moscow, 1800). His two-volume *Dosugi krymskogo sud'i, ili vtoroe puteshestvie v Tavridu* (St. Petersburg, 1803–05) illustrated ancient monuments and inscriptions and described the customs of Crimean Christian and Muslim communities.

10. Ivan M. Murav'ev-Apostol, *Puteshestvie po Tavride v 1820* (St. Petersburg, 1823), is reviewed in *SA* (1824), no. 20: 113–26. Murav'ev-Apostol also published a brief study on the ancient site of Olbia, *Ol'via. Otryvok iz puteshestviia v Tavridu v 1820 g.* (St. Petersburg, 1821).

11. Pushkin's letters to Viazemskii and Del'vig are in *The Letters of Alexander Pushkin: Three Volumes in One*, tr. J. Thomas Shaw (Madison, 1967), 141, 268–70, 297–98. The letter to Del'vig appeared in *Severnye tsvety* (1826): 101–6.

12. On Russian and Western archaeological findings in the Black Sea area, see P. M. Leont'ev, "Obzor issledovanii o klassicheskikh drevnostiakh severnogo berega Chernogo moria," *Propilei* (1852), 1: 67–101; E. D. Frolov, *Russkaia istorio-grafiia antichnosti (do serediny XIX v.)* (Leningrad, 1967), 100–15; D. B. Shelov, "Greek Cities in the Northern Black Sea Region," *MERSH* (1988), 48: 183–87.

13. V. Iurgevich, *Istoricheskii ocherk piatidesiatiletiia imperatorskogo Odesskogo ob-shchestva istorii i drevnostei, 1839–1889* (Odessa, 1889), and M. G. Popruzhenko, *Uka-zatel' statei pomeshchennykh v I–XXX tt. Zapisok Odesskogo obshchestva istorii i drevnostei* (Odessa, 1914), are good introductions to the scholarly activity and publications of the Odessan Society.

14. V. P. Semennikov, *Sobranie staraiushcheesia o perevode inostrannykh knig uch-rezhdennoe Ekaterinoi II, 1768–1783 gg.* (St. Petersburg, 1913). Publications with a moral and didactic message often drew upon the classics, such as *Protsvetaiushchaia Gretsiia, ili kratkoe opisanie zhizni shestidesiati znamenitykh muzhei* (Tambov, 1792), with its brief accounts of sixty prominent figures from antiquity.

15. For an excellent guide to publications on Greek antiquity, including

translations of Greek classics, see P. A. Prozorov, *Sistematicheskii ukazatel' knig i statei po grecheskoi filologii, napechatannykh v Rossii s XVII stoletiia po 1892 na russkom s inostrannykh iazykakh* (St. Petersburg, 1898).

16. On the immediate and widespread success of *Anacharsis* in Europe, see Maurice Badolle, *L'Abbé Jean-Jacques Barthélemy et l'hellénisme en France dans la second moitié du XVIIIme siècle* (Paris, 1926); Olga Augustinos, "From Hellenism to Philhellenism: The Emergence of Modern Greece in French Literature, 1770–1820," Ph.D. diss., Indiana University, 1976. The complete Russian translation, *Puteshestvie mladshego Anakharsisa po Gretsii,* appeared in two multivolume editions. The first was published in Moscow (1803–19), the second in St. Petersburg (1804–09).

17. Karamzin reviewed and excerpted *Anacharsis* in *Moskovskii zhurnal* (1791), no. 7: 97–113; no. 8: 201–17; no. 9: 333–41; in *Panteon inostrannoi slovesnosti* (1798), 2: 93–199; and in *VE* (1803), no. 13: 57–58. The War of Independence recalled the bravery of ancient warriors and thus rekindled interest in *Anacharsis.* Barthélemy's description of Leonidas's stand at Thermopylae was published in the journal *Blagonamerennyi* (1821), no. 13: 33–38. See A. G. Cross, *N. M. Karamzin: A Study of His Literary Career, 1783–1803* (Carbondale, 1971), 116–18; idem, "N. M. Karamzin and Barthélemy's *Voyage du jeune Anacharsis,*" *Modern Language Review* (1966), no. 3: 467–72.

18. Mikhail M. Kheraskov, *Izbrannye proizvedeniia* (Leningrad, 1961), 143–76. Narezhnyi's play is in V. A. Bochkarev, *Stikhotvornaia tragediia kontsa XVIII–nachala XIX v.* (Moscow, 1964), 131–207. Bochkarev's *Russkaia istoricheskaia dramaturgiia nachala XIX v.* (Kuibyshev, 1959) discusses numerous examples of historical dramas based on Greek myth and legend, including the dramas of Ozerov. Also see Simon Karlinsky, *Russian Drama from Its Beginnings to the Age of Pushkin* (Berkeley, 1985), 193–217; William E. Brown, *A History of Russian Literature of the Romantic Period* (hereafter cited as *Russian Literature—Romantic Period*), 4 vols. (Ann Arbor, 1986), 1: 33–47.

19. On Herder's *Volksgeist,* see Robert Ergang, *Herder and the Foundations of German Nationalism* (New York, 1931), 82–112, 239–66, and F. M. Barnard, *Herder's Social and Political Thought: From Enlightenment to Nationalism* (Oxford, 1965). The growth of Romantic nationalism in Russia is treated in Hans Rogger, *National Consciousness in Eighteenth-Century Russia* (Cambridge, Mass., 1960), 126–85, 253–84, and in Edward Thaden, *Conservative Nationalism in Nineteenth-Century Russia* (Seattle, 1964), 25–37.

20. There are no sharp demarcations between literary and artistic movements, especially in late-eighteenth- and early-nineteenth-century Russia when so many Western ideas appeared in the country within a short time. On the relationship between Neoclassicism and Romanticism in Russian literature and on Russian culture's quest for *narodnost'* and *samobytnost',* see Ivan I. Zamotin, *Romantizm dvadtsatykh godov XIX v.,* 3d ed. (Petrograd, 1919); N. L. Brodskii, *Literaturnye salony i kruzhki* (Moscow, 1930), 3–172; M. K. Azadovskii, *Istoriia russkoi fol'kloristiki,* 2 vols. (Moscow, 1958), 1: 112–368; N. I. Mordovchenko, *Russkaia kritika pervoi chetverti XIX v.* (Moscow, 1959); Lauren G. Leighton, *Russian Romanticism: Two Essays* (The Hague, 1975); Rudolf Neuhauser, *Towards the Romantic Age: Essays on Sentimental and Preromantic Literature* (The Hague, 1974); Peter Christoff, *The Third Heart: Some Intellectual-Ideological Currents and Cross-Currents in Russia, 1800–1830* (The Hague,

1970); D. S. Mirsky, *A History of Russian Literature from Its Beginnings to 1900,* 4th ed. (New York, 1958), 73–126.

21. Mary Stuart, *Aristocrat-Librarian in Service to the Tsar. Aleksei Nikolaevich Olenin and the Imperial Public Library* (New York, 1986). Her work draws from the standard Russian accounts of Nikolai Stoianovskii, *Ocherk zhizni A. N. Olenina* (St. Petersburg, 1881), and L. V. Timofeev, *V krugu druzei i muz. Dom A. N. Olenina* (Leningrad, 1983). Still useful is the biographical entry by Ivan Kubasov in *RBS* (1905), 12: 215–24.

22. *Arkheologicheskie trudy A. N. Olenina,* 2 vols. (St. Petersburg, 1877–82). His *Riazanskie russkie drevnosti* (St. Petersburg, 1831) contributed to the scientific study of Russian antiquities.

23. Stuart, *Aristocrat-Librarian in Service to the Tsar,* 97–115. Examples of the diverse material published in *Zhurnal iziashchnykh iskusstv* are "O proiskhozhdenii khudozhestv" (1823), no. 1: 18–24; "Sushchnost', tsel' i pol'za iziashchnykh iskus-stv" (1823), no. 3: 177–93; "O vliianii klimata, odnoi iz glavneishikh prichin razlich-iia v khudozhestvakh" (1823), no. 3: 194–209; "Vzgliad na Parfenon afinskii" (1823), no. 4: 314–34. For more on this periodical, see S. Ernst, "*Zhurnal iziashch-nykh iskusstv* 1823–1825 gg.," *Russkii bibliofil* (1914), no. 3: 5–26.

24. OR, GPB, f. 250, d. 244, ll. 117–24, for Olenin's letter of 9 August 1818 instructing Destunis on which artifacts to purchase and noting their significance for the study of ancient art and architecture. Aleksandr S. Sturdza, vice-president of the Odessan Society of History and Antiquities, was grateful to Destunis for the marble bas-reliefs, burial inscriptions, and pottery donated to the society's collec-tion of antiquities, which later formed part of Odessa's Archaeological Museum. Sturdza's letter of December 1840 is in OR, GPB, f. 250, d. 40, l. 10.

25. V. V. Latyshev, *K istorii arkheologicheskikh issledovanii v iuzhnoi Rossii. Iz pere-piski A. N. Olenina* (Odessa, 1888), also appearing in *ZOOID* (1889), 15: 61–149.

26. Stuart, *Aristocrat-Librarian in Service to the Tsar,* 46–49; Irina N. Medvedeva, "Vladislav Ozerov," in *V. A. Ozerov: Tragediia, stikhotvoreniia* (Leningrad, 1970), 5–72.

27. Nikolay Stepanov, *Ivan Krylov* (New York, 1973); Brown, *Russian Litera-ture—Romantic Period,* 1: 124–35.

28. Konstantin N. Batiushkov, *Opyty v stikhakh i proze* (Moscow, 1977), 71–94; idem, *Polnoe sobranie stikhotvorenii* (Moscow, 1964), 189–90, 205–8, 236–39. For bio-graphical information, see I. Z. Serman, *Konstantin Batyushkov* (New York, 1974), and Brown, *Russian Literature—Romantic Period,* 1: 227–55.

29. Leonid N. Maikov, *Batiushkov: Ego zhizn' i sochineniia,* 2d ed. (St. Peters-burg, 1896), 200–3.

30. Sergei S. Uvarov: *Essai sur les Mystères d'Éleusis* (St. Petersburg, 1812), *Exa-men critique de la fable d'Hercule* (St. Petersburg, 1817), *Nonnos von Panopolis, der Dichter* (St. Petersburg, 1818), *Mémoire sur les tragiques grecs* (St. Petersburg, 1824).

31. Cynthia H. Whittaker, *The Origins of Modern Russian Education: An Intellec-tual Biography of Count Sergei Uvarov, 1786–1855* (Dekalb, 1984), 25–29. See also chapters four and six on Uvarov's establishment of a classical curriculum in Russian gymnasia.

32. Batiushkov, *Polnoe sobranie stikhotvorenii,* 229–33. *O grecheskoi antologii* was favorably reviewed in *SO* (1820), no. 12: 269–75; no. 23: 145–51; and in *SPB* (1821),

no. 11: 205–6. See Whittaker, *The Origins of Modern Russian Education,* 26–27, and Serman, *Konstantin Batyushkov,* 142–43.

33. *O grecheskoi antologii* (St. Petersburg, 1820), 2–14.

34. John Mersereau, Jr., *Baron Delvig's "Northern Flowers" (1825–1832): Literary Almanac of the Pushkin Pleiad* (Carbondale, 1967).

35. Mirsky, *A History of Russian Literature,* 81; Anton A. Del'vig, *Polnoe sobranie stikhotvorenii* (Leningrad, 1959), 180–85; *Severnye tsvety* (1825): 46–57. For a discussion of Del'vig's works, see Ludmilla Koehler, *Anton A. Del'vig: A Classicist in the Time of Romanticism* (The Hague, 1970), and Brown, *Russian Literature—Romantic Period,* 3: 275–88.

36. *VE* (1808), no. 2: 174–79.

37. "Novaia Sparta," *VE* (1803), no. 5: 24–33; (1808), no. 22: 143–47. Lev N. Nevakhovich, *Sul'ety, ili spartansy os'mnadtsatogo stoletiia. Istoricheskoe i dramaticheskoe predstavlenie v piati deistviiakh* (St. Petersburg, 1810), suggested that classical and modern Greeks were closely related in their customs, valor, and patriotism. The play is discussed in V. A. Bochkarev, *Russkaia istoricheskaia dramaturgiia nachala XIX v.* (Kuibyshev, 1959), 294–306. *Sul'ety* was performed in St. Petersburg in 1824, one of numerous plays with Greek motifs and themes staged in Russia during the Greek revolt. On this aspect of the philhellenic movement, see Pimen Arapov, *Letopis' russkogo teatra* (St. Petersburg, 1861), 303–83.

38. Pavel N. Svin'in, *Vospominaniia na flote,* 2 vols. (St. Petersburg, 1818–19), 2: 216–18. Vladimir B. Bronevskii, *Zapiski morskogo ofitsera,* 3 vols. (St. Petersburg, 1818–19). Both works were excerpted and reviewed in *Blagonamerennyi, SO, VE,* and other journals. Western travel writings on Ottoman Greece, such as Savary's *Lettres sur la Grèce* (Paris, 1798) and Chateaubriand's *Itinéraire de Paris à Jérusalem* (Paris, 1811), were also excerpted in the press: *VE* (1806), no. 18: 81–90; (1810), no. 17: 18–47; no. 22: 138–44; *SPB* (1819), no. 3: 319–52.

39. On Martynov, see "Avtobiograficheskie zapiski I. I. Martynova," *Zaria* (1871), no. 6: 73–110; E. Ia. Kolbasin, *Literaturnye deiateli prezhnego vremeni* (St. Petersburg, 1859), 7–168; idem, "I. I. Martynov, perevodchik grecheskikh klassikov," *Sovremennik* (1856), no. 3: 1–46; no. 4: 75–126; A. Zaldkin, *I. I. Martynov, 1771–1833. Deiatel' prosveshcheniia v nachale XIX v.* (Tiflis, 1902). Batalden, *Catherine II's Greek Prelate,* 79–83, discusses the impact of Voulgaris on Martynov and on Russian classical studies in general. On the censorship edict of 1804, see Charles Ruud, *Fighting Words: Imperial Censorship and the Russian Press, 1804–1906* (Toronto, 1982), 26–27.

40. Ivan I. Martynov, *Filosoficheskaia i politicheskaia perepiska imperatritsy Ekateriny II s Vol'terom s 1763 po 1778* (St. Petersburg, 1802). For Martynov's translations of classical authors, see in particular the four volumes of *Litsei* published in 1806. "Izvestie o arkhiepiskope Evgenii Bulgare," *Litsei* (1806), 3, no. 1: 34–53.

41. On Martynov's high regard for the classics, especially their important role in Russian education and literature, see "Avtobiograficheskie zapiski Martynova," passim; Zaldkin, *I. I. Martynov,* passim. Along with Uvarov and Martynov, another proponent of classical learning in Russian schools was Friedrich Schmidt, professor of philosophy and Greek. At the opening of the Demidov School of Higher Learning in Iaroslavl, Schmidt stated that the Athenian ideal of humanistic education should be emulated because it imbued youth with civic spirit, love of

learning, patriotism, and other virtues necessary for citizenship. See "Slovo o drevnem vospitanii grekov, govorennoe v torzhestvennyi den' Iaroslavskogo Demidovskogo vsshikh nauk uchilitshcha 29 aprelia 1806, doktorom i professorom filosofii i grecheskogo iazyka Fridrikhom Shmidom," *Periodicheskoe sochinenie o uspekhakh narodnogo prosveshcheniia* (St. Petersburg, 1806), 436–48.

42. Ivan I. Martynov, *Grecheskie klassiki,* 26 vols. (St. Petersburg, 1823–29). *Basni Ezopovy* (1823), i-vi. Martynov's announcements in Russian periodicals ranged from two to seven pages: *SA* (1822), no. 20: 173–77; *SPB* (1822), no. 7: 95–98; no. 12: 329–34; *Blagonamerennyi* (1822), no. 43: 109–13; (1823), no. 13: 72–73; no. 23: 396–98; (1824), no. 7: 70–72; (1825), no. 32: 177–82; *ZhDNP* (1822), no. 6: 252–56; no. 10: 219–26; (1823), no. 7: 298–99.

43. Metropolitan Evgenii's letters to Martynov are cited in Kolbasin, *Literaturnye deiateli prezhnego vremeni,* 90–91, 121–26. As a noted historian and bibliographer, Evgenii Bolkhovitinov readily appreciated the historical and cultural importance of Martynov's endeavor to translate the classics.

44. Ivan I. Martynov, *Sovet rossiiskomu iunoshestvu o proiznoshenii nekotorykh grecheskikh bukv* (St. Petersburg, 1822), 3. This essay originally appeared in *ZhDNP* (1822), no. 1: 52–77.

45. Dimitrios Pappadopoulos, *Novye razgovory rossiiskie i grecheskie, razdelennye na sto urokov, dlia iunoshestva i vsekh nachinaiushchikh uchit'sia sim iazykam* (St. Petersburg, 1826), a handbook for beginning students reviewed in *MT* (1826), no. 24: 265–68. Because of its sizable Greek community, numerous Russian-language manuals for Greek language instruction were published in Odessa. For example, Michail Palaiologos, *Kratkaia grammatika novogrecheskogo iazyka* (Odessa, 1843; 2d ed., 1895), and idem, *Razgovory russko-frantsuzsko-grecheskie* (Odessa, 1844).

46. Konstantinos Oikonomos, *Opyt o blizhaishem srodstve iazyka slaviano-rossiiskogo s grecheskim,* 3 vols. (St. Petersburg, 1828), which is discussed in S. Smirnov, *K. Ekonomos i sochinenie ego o srodstve slaviano-russkogo iazyka s ellinskim* (Moscow, 1873), 18–27. Ivan I. Martynov, *Nastavlenie ob istinnom proiznoshenii nekotorykh grecheskikh bukv, izvlechennoe iz knigi o sem zhe predmete grecheskogo sviashchennika Ekonomosa* (St.Petersburg, 1831).

47. On Gnedich, see N. P. Izvolenskii, *Gnedich kak orator, filolog i patriot* (Poltava, 1883); P. Tikhonov, *N. I. Gnedich. Neskol'ko dannykh dlia ego biografii po neizdannym istochnikam* (St. Petersburg, 1884); the entry by G. Georgievskii in *RBS* (1915), 5: 410–27; Brown, *Russian Literature—Romantic Period,* 1: 257–76; the introduction by Irina N. Medvedeva, *N. I. Gnedich. Stikhotvoreniia* (Moscow, 1963), 5–68.

48. Nikolai I. Gnedich, "Rassuzhdenie o prichinakh zamedliaiushchikh uspekhi nashei slovesnosti," *Opisanie torzhestvennogo otkrytiia publichnoi biblioteki* (St. Petersburg, 1814), 82–83. Gnedich expressed similar views in "O vkuse i ego vliianii na slovesnost' i nravy," *SPB* (1819), no. 3: 275–89.

49. Nikolai I. Gnedich, *Rech' iz XV chasti trudov vysochaishe utverzhdennogo vol'nogo obshchestva liubitelei rossiiskoi slovesnosti* (St. Petersburg, 1821), 1–19.

50. On Kostrov's translation from the *Iliad,* see Brown, *A History of Eighteenth-Century Russian Literature,* 475–83.

51. Uvarov's letter is published in "Pis'mo k N. I. Gnedichu o grecheskom ekzametre," *Chtenie v besede liubitelei russkogo slova* (1813), 13: 56–68. This English translation is taken from Brown, *Russian Literature—Romantic Period,* 1:272. Zhukovskii's letter of 1814 to Gnedich is in OR, GPB, f. 286, op. 2, d. 94, l. 1.

52. Gnedich was not the first Russian writer to adopt the classical hexameter. Trediakovskii used a modified form of this meter in his 1766 verse adaptation of Fénélon's prose novel *Les Aventures de Télémaque*, while Mikhail N. Murav'ev (1757–1807) used the hexameter in his rendition of Homeric verses (1778). On Gnedich's experimentation with the classical hexameter and the debate it generated in Russian literary circles, see A. N. Egunov, *Gomer v russkikh perevodakh XVIII–XIX vv.* (Moscow, 1964), 174–94, and Richard Burgi, *A History of the Russian Hexameter* (Hamden, Conn., 1954), 98–103.

53. The Gnedich *fond* (197) contains drafts and revisions of the *Iliad* translation from its inception to the final version of 1829. See the *Iliad* files in OR, GPB, f. 197: d. 19, ll. 1–63; d. 34, ll. 1–9; d. 20, ll. 1–4; d. 18, ll. 1–22; d. 23, ll. 1–13; d. 22, ll. 1–157. Two manuscript copies of the entire epic are in d. 21, ll. 1–316 and in d. 24, ll. 1–358. The same *fond* has a file from the 1820s, d. 29, ll. 1–2, with Gnedich's translation of passages from the *Odyssey*, including its opening lines and parts of book eleven.

54. See the correspondence between Olenin and Gnedich in *Arkheologicheskie pis'ma A. N. Olenina k N. I. Gnedichu* (St. Petersburg, 1872); *Perepiska Olenina s raznymi litsami po povodu predpriniatogo Gnedichem perevoda Gomerovoi Iliady*, in volume 1 of *Arkheologicheskie trudy Olenina* (St. Petersburg, 1877); G. P. Georgievskii, "A. N. Olenin i N. I. Gnedich; novye materialy iz Oleninskogo arkhiva," *Sbornik otdeleniia russkogo iazyka i slovesnosti imperatorskoi akademii nauk* (1914), 91, no. 1: 1–137. For more on the close relationship between Olenin and Gnedich, see Stuart, *Aristocrat-Librarian in Service to the Tsar*, 8–10, 46–58; Timofeev, *V krugu druzei i muz*, 34–36, 52–60, 83–91, 97–108, 157–61, 252–59.

55. Nikolai I. Gnedich, *Iliad Gomera*, 2 vols. (St. Petersburg, 1829), iii–iv, xv. Subsequent editions were published in 1839, 1862, 1884, 1935, and 1978. Excerpts from the *Iliad* are in *N. I. Gnedich. Stikhotvoreniia*, 226–399.

56. On the 1821 recitation, see *SPB* (1821), no. 2: 304–11; (1822), no. 6: 333–41. Reviews praising the Gnedich *Iliad* include *VE* (1830), no. 3: 233–35; *MT* (1830), no. 1: 87–90; *MV* (1830), no. 4: 372–408; *Galateia* (1830), no. 18: 79–90. *Severnye tsvety* (1831): 35–36, called the translation "the most remarkable poetic work of the year." Marc Slonim, *The Epic of Russian Literature from Its Origins through Tolstoy* (New York, 1964), 61, describes the Russian *Iliad* as one of the finest translations of Homer in the world.

57. *The Letters of Alexander Pushkin*, 83–84.

58. Aleksandr S. Pushkin, *Polnoe sobranie sochinenii*, 10 vols. (Moscow, 1962–66), 3: 183, 203, 238. This translation is from Babette Deutsch, cited in *The Poems, Prose, and Plays of Alexander Pushkin*, ed., Avrahm Yarmolinsky (New York, 1936), 75.

59. *Pushkin on Literature*, tr. and ed. Tatiana Wolff, rev. ed. (London, 1986), 232–33.

60. Vissarion G. Belinskii, *Polnoe sobranie sochinenii*, 13 vols. (Moscow, 1954), 5: 553–54.

61. Brown, *Russian Literature—Romantic Period*, 1: 209–12

62. *N. I. Gnedich. Stikhotvoreniia*, 111–20, 171–226. OR, GPB, f. 197, d. 4, ll. 1–13, contains a printed copy of "Birth of Homer" with corrections by Gnedich and with penciled comments by Zhukovskii. Brown, *Russian Literature—Romantic Period*, 1: 268–71.

63. Gnedich's attitude toward the Decembrist movement and his contact with

Decembrist writers, many of whom dedicated poems to him for his *Iliad,* are discussed in Irina N. Medvedeva, "N. I. Gnedich i dekabristy," in M. P. Alekseev and B. S. Meilakh, eds., *Dekabristy i ikh vremia: Materialy i soobshcheniia* (Moscow, 1951), 101–54.

64. *VE* (1821), no. 20: 258–60; also in *N. I. Gnedich. Stikhotvoreniia,* 140–41. Another Russian translation of Rigas's "War Hymn," by P. P. Shkliarevskii and entitled "Ancient Greek Song" ("Drevniaia grecheskaia pesn'," 1821), is published in Lidiia Ia. Ginzburg, ed., *Poety 1820–1830-kh gg.,* 2 vols. (Leningrad, 1972), 1: 484–85.

65. Medvedeva, "N. I. Gnedich i dekabristy," *Dekabristy i ikh vremia,* 135–41.

66. Nikolai I. Gnedich, *Prostonarodnye pesni nyneshnikh grekov* (St. Petersburg, 1825), which is also included in his collected poems, *N. I. Gnedich. Stikhotvoreniia,* 403–30. On Fauriel's publication and its significance for the study of Greek folk poetry, see Miodrag Ibrovac, *Claude Fauriel et la fortune européenne des poésies populaires grecque et serbe* (Paris, 1966), along with a brief account of the Gnedich publication on pp. 221–25.

67. On the historical and the literary importance of the *klephtic* ballads, see Linos Politis, *A History of Modern Greek Literature* (Oxford, 1973), 83–97; Roderick Beaton, *Folk Poetry of Modern Greece* (Cambridge, Eng., 1980), 102–11; Alexis Politis, *Ta dimotika tragoudia. Klephtika* (Athens, 1973).

68. Azadovskii, *Istoriia russkoi fol'kloristiki,* 1: 200–9; Hugh Honour, *Romanticism* (New York, 1979), 240–44.

69. Gnedich, *Prostonarodnye pesni nyneshnikh grekov,* v–xl. More accurate from an historical and literary point of view is the study by N. L. Ruchkina on the Byzantine roots of the *klephtic* ballads, in particular the impact of the twelfth-century epic *Digenis Akritas* and the Akritic cycle of heroic poems, "Geneticheskie sviazi akritskogo eposa i kleftskikh pesen," *Slavianskii i balkanskii fol'klor* (Moscow, 1981), 189–223.

70. Excerpts from and reviews of Gnedich's *Folk Songs* were published in numerous journals, such as *MT* (1825), no. 6: 125–37; *UZh* (1825), no. 3: 188–201; *Severnye tsvety* (1825): 266–69.

71. *The Letters of Alexander Pushkin,* 204.

72. *VE* (1824), no. 23: 229–32. *VE* (1825), no. 15/16: 309–18; no. 20: 321. *MV* (1827), no. 14: 85–103; no. 15: 284–304, for Kireevskii's review. Another work by Rizos-Neroulos, *Histoire de la Grèce depuis la chute de l'empire d'orient* (Geneva, 1828), was excerpted in *VE* (1829), no. 1: 43–50; *KV* (1829), no. 5/6: 83–96; no. 7: 206–16.

73. Russian collections and studies of Greek poetry are mentioned in N. L. Ruchkina, "Izuchenie novogrecheskogo pesennogo fol'klora v nashei strane," *BI* (1979), 5: 260–68. Of special note are G. Evlampios, *Amarantos, ili rozy vozrozhdennoi Ellady* (St. Petersburg, 1843), with parallel modern Greek/Russian text; I. P. Sozonovich, *Izucheniia novogrecheskoi narodnoi poezii* (Warsaw, 1880); and the several works on Greek poetry by the Neohellenist Gavriil S. Destunis that are cited in Theophilus Prousis, "The Destunis Collection in the Manuscript Section of the Saltykov-Shchedrin State Public Library in Leningrad," *MGSY* (1989), 5: 403, 450–51.

Chapter Five: Russian Writers

1. For an introduction to the intellectual transition between the Decembrist generation and the Romantic nationalism of the Marvelous Decade, see Nicholas Riasanovsky, *A Parting of Ways: Government and the Educated Public in Russia, 1801–1855* (Oxford, 1976), and Peter Christoff, *The Third Heart: Some Intellectual-Ideological Currents and Cross-Currents in Russia, 1800–1830* (The Hague, 1970).

2. V. G. Bazanov, *Ocherki dekabristskoi literatury: Publitsistika, proza, kritika* (Moscow, 1953); idem, *Ocherki dekabristskoi literatury: Poeziia* (Moscow, 1961). Soviet anthologies invariably include philhellenic poetry as a manifestation of Decembrist civicism. See Vladimir N. Orlov, ed., *Dekabristy: Poeziia, dramaturgiia, proza, publitsistika, literaturnaia kritika* (Leningrad, 1951); idem, *Poety Pushkinskoi pory*, 3d ed. (Moscow, 1972); Lidiia Ia. Ginzburg, ed., *Poety 1820–1830-kh gg.*, 2 vols. (Leningrad, 1972). The prominent scholar Grigorii A. Gukovskii, in his *Pushkin i russkie romantiki*, 2d ed. (Moscow, 1965), 186–223, describes philhellenic verse as an example of liberal and civic heroic literature that embodied the ideals of liberty, patriotism, and valor.

3. William E. Brown, *A History of Russian Literature of the Romantic Period* (hereafter cited as *Russian Literature—Romantic Period*), 4 vols. (Ann Arbor, 1986), especially 1: 162, 289; 2: 13, 99; 3: 354–56. Lauren G. Leighton, *Russian Romanticism: Two Essays* (The Hague, 1975); idem, "Decembrism" and "Romanticism," in Victor Terras, ed., *Handbook of Russian Literature* (New Haven, 1985), 94–96, 372–76. Also useful is Walter Vickery, "Decembrist Poetry," *MERSL* (1981), 5: 99–106.

4. S. S. Volk, *Istoricheskie vzgliady dekabristov* (Moscow, 1958), 155–207; Iulian G. Oksman, "Iz istorii agitatsionno-propagandistskoi literatury dvadtsatykh godov XIX v.," *Ocherki iz istorii dvizheniia dekabristov* (Moscow, 1954), 451–515.

5. Articles on the revival of Greek learning often compared the modern Greeks to their illustrious classical heirs. See "Novaia Ellada," *VE* (1811), no. 13: 73–77; "O grecheskom iazyke i ego narechiiakh," *VE* (1813), no. 5/6: 56–66; "Vzgliad na nyneshnee sostoianie uchilishch grecheskikh," *VE* (1815), no. 10: 147–56; "Zaria prosveshcheniia novykh grekov," *DZh* (1816), no. 48: 291–96; "O slovesnosti nyneshnikh grekov," *DZh* (1819), no. 21: 185–92.

6. Reports on the Greek war regularly appeared in the news section of *VE, SO, SA, MT,* and *ISGZh.* For a brief sketch of Russian press coverage, see Irina S. Dostian, *Russkaia obshchestvennaia mysl' i balkanskie narody: Ot Radishcheva do dekabristov* (Moscow, 1980), 160–73. On the Western philhellenic press, see the works by J. Dimakis, A. Dimopoulos, and C. Zimmerman cited in the bibliography.

7. On Western philhellenic poetry, see Terence Spencer, *Fair Greece Sad Relic: Literary Philhellenism from Shakespeare to Byron* (London, 1954); Marios Byron Raizis and Alexander Papas, *American Poets and the Greek Revolution, 1821–1828: A Study in Byronic Philhellenism* (Thessaloniki, 1972); idem, *The Greek Revolution and the American Muse: A Collection of Philhellenic Poetry, 1821–1828* (Thessaloniki, 1972). For an introduction to Russian philhellenic verse, see S. Ia. Kolmykov, "Deiateli russkoi kul'tury o natsional'no-osvoboditel'noi bor'be grecheskogo naroda," *BI* (1989), 11: 242–50, and N. N. Balandina, "Grecheskoe vosstanie 20-kh godov XIX v. i russkaia literatura," *Vzaimosviaz' russkoi i sovetskoi literatury s literaturoi stran Azii, Afriki i Latinskoi Ameriki* (Moscow, 1980), 75–97.

8. Fedor N. Glinka, *Izbrannye proizvedeniia* (Leningrad, 1957), 204–5, 462.

Glinka's "Fate of Napoleon" first appeared in *SO* (1821), no. 41: 35. In addition to their publication in contemporary journals, poems on classical and modern Greek themes were published in the anthology *Sobranie novykh russkikh sochinenii i perevodov v stikhakh s 1823 po 1825 gg.* (St. Petersburg, 1824). For information on the life and work of Glinka, see Brown, *Russian Literature—Romantic Period*, 1: 284–96.

9. Glinka, *Izbrannye proizvedeniia*, 226–27. Glinka's brother, the publicist Sergei N. Glinka (1776–1847), was a tribune of conservative nationalism, who authored numerous works that upheld autocracy and serfdom, criticized French cultural influence, and defended Russian tradition. That the Greek cause appealed across the lines of political division in Alexandrine Russia is seen in Sergei Glinka's translation of Plutarch's *Lives* and his account of the Greek revolt: *Plutarkh v pol'zu vospitaniia*, 6 parts (Moscow, 1822–23), and *Kartina istoricheskaia i politicheskaia novoi Gretsii* (Moscow, 1829), a description of the war from 1821 until the presidency of Kapodistrias. Despite divergent political beliefs, the Glinkas esteemed the classical legacy and the Russian national heritage, which explains their philhellenism. See Franklin A. Walker, "Reaction and Radicalism in the Russia of Tsar Alexander I: The Case of the Brothers Glinka," *Canadian Slavonic Papers* (1979), 21, no. 4: 489–502.

10. Vladimir F. Raevskii, *Polnoe sobranie stikhotvorenii* (Moscow, 1967), 151–55, 240–41. For biographical material, see Brown, *Russian Literature—Romantic Period*, 2: 99–111.

11. Kondratii F. Ryleev, *Polnoe sobranie stikhotvorenii* (Leningrad, 1971), 91–93, 97, 105–82, 269–71. On Ryleev's political and literary activity, see Patrick O'Meara, *K. F. Ryleev: A Political Biography of the Decembrist Poet* (Princeton, 1984); Franklin A. Walker, "Ryleev: A Self-Sacrifice for Revolution," *SEER* (1969), 47, no. 109: 436–46.

12. Ryleev, *Polnoe sobranie stikhotvorenii*, 69. On Ermolov, see Mikhail P. Pogodin, *Aleksei P. Ermolov: Materialy dlia ego biografii* (Moscow, 1864).

13. Ryleev, *Polnoe sobranie stikhotvorenii*, 78, 353–55. Ryleev's philhellenic poems are discussed in V. I. Maslov, *Literaturnaia deiatel'nost' Ryleeva* (Kiev, 1912), 277–94.

14. On the life and work of Kiukhel'beker, see Brown, *Russian Literature—Romantic Period*, 2: 11–57, 154–56, 171–74. For a brief account of *Mnemosyne* and the Wisdom Lovers, see Riasanovsky, *A Parting of Ways*, 155–59; Christoff, *The Third Heart;* the relevant entries in Terras, ed., *Handbook of Russian Literature*, 241–42, 284, 314, 518–19.

15. Vil'gel'm K. Kiukhel'beker, *Izbrannye proizvedeniia*, 2 vols. (Moscow, 1967), 1: 329–46. Poems and translations inspired by the classical tradition also include "Socratism" ("Sokratism," 1817), "Hymn to Bacchus" ("Gimn Bakkusu," 1817), "Hymn to Apollo" ("Gimn Apollonu," 1817), "Hymn to Earth" ("Gimn zemle," 1817), "Hercules Avenged" ("Otomshchennyi Gerkules," 1818), "To Prometheus" ("K Promefeiu," 1820), and "Olympic Games" ("Olimpiiskie igry," 1822), in *Izbrannye proizvedeniia*, 1: 81–92, 156–58.

16. Kiukhel'beker, *Izbrannye proizvedeniia*, 2: 175–274, 677–729. Only the prologue of *Argives* was published during Kiukhel'beker's lifetime, appearing in *Mnemozina* (1824), 2: 1–28. For a brief account of the play, see Simon Karlinsky, *Russian Drama from Its Beginnings to the Age of Pushkin* (Berkeley, 1985), 221–22. The literary

scholar Iurii N. Tynianov in *Arkhaisty i novatory* (Leningrad, 1929), 292–329, discusses *Argives* in the context of the linguistic controversy between Shishkovite archaists and Karamzinist modernists. Kiukhel'beker belonged to the former, espousing a language and style grounded in Old Church Slavonic as opposed to the modernized language used by the Karamzinists. That linguistic labels had very little bearing on political views is evinced in the ardent liberalism of the archaist Kiukhel'beker and the political conservatism of such modernists as Karamzin and Zhukovskii.

17. Kiukhel'beker relied on the recent Russian translation of Plutarch's *Lives of Great Men* by Spyridon Iu. Destunis, *Plutarkhovy sravnitel'nye zhizneopisaniia slavnykh muzhei*, 13 parts (St. Petersburg, 1814–21). Soviet literary criticism has highlighted the political message of *Argives*, describing the play as a good example of republican-spirited tragedy that appealed to the Decembrists. See V. A. Bochkarev, *Russkaia istoricheskaia dramaturgiia perioda podgotovki vosstaniia dekabristov (1816–1825)* (Kuibyshev, 1968), 189–228; A. V. Arkhipova, "O tragedii V. K. Kiukhel'bekera *Argiviane*," *Uchenye zapiski Leningradskogo gosudarstvennogo pedagogicheskogo instituta A. I. Gertsena* (1958), no. 1: 59–90.

18. Bochkarev, *Russkaia istoricheskaia dramaturgiia perioda podgotovki vosstaniia dekabristov*, 102–20; Karlinsky, *Russian Drama*, 220–21.

19. Pavel A. Katenin, *Izbrannye proizvedeniia* (Moscow, 1965), 207–15.

20. Kiukhel'beker, *Izbrannye proizvedeniia*, 1: 144.

21. Ibid., 1: 144–46.

22. Ibid., 1: 150–51.

23. Ibid., 1: 186–87.

24. Next to Homer, Tyrtaeus was the most popular ancient Greek writer among the Decembrists. The classical scholar and poet Aleksei F. Merzliakov (1778–1830), a professor of Russian literature at Moscow University, published his translations of Tyrtaeus's odes and elegies on Spartan valor in *VE* (1805), no. 21: 28–40. These translations are also in A. F. Merzliakov, *Stikhotvoreniia* (Leningrad, 1958), 148–56. Merzliakov translated additional excerpts from Aeschylus, Sophocles, Euripides, Homer, Theocritus, Sappho, Horace, and Ovid. See Brown, *Russian Literature—Romantic Period*, 1: 168–79.

25. Kiukhel'beker, *Izbrannye proizvedeniia*, 1: 158–61.

26. Ibid., 2: 275–443. Brown, *Russian Literature—Romantic Period*, 2: 49–52; Karlinsky, *Russian Drama*, 223–25.

27. Leighton, *Russian Romanticism*, 52–54; John Mersereau, Jr., "Orest Somov: An Introduction," *SEER* (1965), no. 101: 357–70; idem, "Yes, Virginia, There was a Russian Romantic Movement," *RLT* (1972), no. 3: 128–46; idem, *Baron Delvig's "Northern Flowers" (1825–1832): Literary Almanac of the Pushkin Pleiad* (Carbondale, 1967), 20–25, 30–38, 48–69, 177–93.

28. Somov's "Greece" is in Ginzburg, ed., *Poety 1820–1830-kh gg.*, 1: 220–222, and was originally published in *SPB* (1822), no. 2: 195–98.

29. Orest M. Somov, *Zapiski polkovnika Vut'e o nyneshnei voine grekov*, 2 vols. (St. Petersburg, 1824). The preface to volume 1 (i-xi) was drawn from Somov's "O nyneshnem sostoianii nauk i prosveshcheniia v Gretsii," *SO* (1822), no. 36: 119–32; no. 37: 145–60; no. 38: 215–17. *Zapiski* was reviewed and excerpted in the periodical press: *MT* (1825), no. 12: 247–49; *UZh* (1825), no. 18: 344–64; *SPB* (1825), no. 3: 257–70; *Blagonamerennyi* (1825), no. 6: 204–8. *Padenie Khiosa* was published as a separate text in addition to being serialized in *SO* (1824).

30. Pouqueville's multivolume works, *Voyage en Morée, à Constantinople, en Albanie et dans plusieurs autres parties de l'Empire ottoman* (Paris, 1805), *Voyage dans la Grèce comprenant la description ancienne et moderne* (Paris, 1820), and *Histoire de la régeneration de la Grèce* (Paris, 1826–27), were excerpted in *VE* (1805), no. 16: 283–90; (1824), no. 13: 57–67; (1827), no. 5: 51–68; *ISGZh* (1821), no. 11: 92–103; *SA* (1822), no. 13: 130–52.

31. On Kapnist's literary work, see William E. Brown, *A History of Eighteenth-Century Russian Literature* (Ann Arbor, 1980), 455–71; Karlinsky, *Russian Drama*, 172–76. See OR, GPB, f. 122, d. 49, 50, 52, for his Russian translations from the *Iliad* and *Odyssey*.

32. Vasilii V. Kapnist, *Izbrannye proizvedeniia* (Leningrad, 1973), 318–22. I came across two manuscript copies of Kapnist's "Appeal to Aid Greece," one in OR, GPB, f. 859, d. 13, ll. 113–17, the other in RGVIA, f. *Voenno-uchenyi arkhiv*, d. 18199, ll. 2–5. The collection in RGVIA contains reports from the Russian Second Army on the Greek revolt. Kapnist's unpublished poem may very well have circulated among philhellenic officers stationed in Bessarabia, such as Pavel Pestel' and Mikhail Orlov. This would explain why a copy of the poem is in the archival collection of the Second Army.

33. David Saunders, *The Ukrainian Impact on Russian Culture, 1750–1850* (Edmonton, 1985), 145–230.

34. On Kachenovskii, see G. V. Makarova, "M. T. Kachenovskii i stanovlenie slavianovedeniia v Rossii," in Vladimir A. Diakov, ed., *Istoriograficheskie issledovaniia po slavianovedeniiu i balkanistike* (Moscow, 1984), 63–96; *Bibliograficheskie zapiski* (1892), no. 4: 259–69, no. 5: 329–37; *RBS* (1897), 8: 577–80; J. L. Black, *Nicholas Karamzin and Russian Society in the Nineteenth Century: A Study in Russian Political and Historical Thought* (Toronto, 1975), 137–46. Kachenovskii's publications include a student handbook on ancient Greek and excerpts from Byron's Eastern tales, *Uchebnaia knizhka drevnego grecheskogo iazyka* (Moscow, 1807–09), which appeared in several editions; *Vybor iz sochinenii Lorda Beirona* (Moscow, 1821), containing passages from "Siege of Corinth," "Giaour," and "Bride of Abydos."

35. S. Ia. Borovoi, "Puteshestvie Onegina i Odesskaia tema v russkoi literature pervoi treti XIX v.," *Pushkin na iuge* (Kishinev, 1961), 2: 265–88, examines the treatment of Odessa in works by Pushkin, Tumanskii, and other contemporaries. For more on Tumanskii, see the biographical sketch by S. N. Brailovskii in Vasilii I. Tumanskii, *Stikhotvoreniia i pis'ma* (St. Petersburg, 1912); Brown, *Russian Literature—Romantic Period*, 4: 107–11.

36. Tumanskii, *Stikhotvoreniia i pis'ma*, 127–28.

37. Ibid., 156–57. Tumanskii's "Greece" originally appeared in *SPB* (1825), no. 2: 217–18.

38. OR, GPB, f. 794, d. 5, ll. 1–2. The manuscript copy of the poem is entitled "Pesn' v chest' Marka Botsarisa, Lorda Bairona i Karaiskaki, geroev umershikh za svobodu Gretsii" and is signed by Tumanskii.

39. Ivan I. Kozlov, *Polnoe sobranie stikhotvorenii* (Leningrad, 1960), 71–72. A manuscript copy of Kozlov's "Captive Greek in Prison" is in OR, GPB, f. 357, d. 8, ll. 51–51a. On the life and work of Kozlov, see Brown, *Russian Literature—Romantic Period*, 3: 241–65; Glynn R. Barratt, *Ivan Kozlov: A Study and a Setting* (Toronto, 1972).

40. Grigor'ev's "Greek Girl" is in Ginzburg, ed., *Poety 1820–1830-kh gg.*, 1:

382–83, and was first published in *SPB* (1825), no. 2: 157–59. Press reports on Psara include *VE* (1824), no. 14: 154–55; no. 16: 316–18; *KV* (1824), no. 8: 262–65.

41. Leighton, *Russian Romanticism*, 79–84; Brown, *Russian Literature—Romantic Period*, 3: 340–63; Larry Andrews, "D. V. Venevitinov: A Sketch of His Life and Work," *RLT* (1974), no. 8: 373–84.

42. Dmitrii V. Venevitinov, *Polnoe sobranie stikhotvorenii* (Leningrad, 1960), 77–78; idem, "Complete Poetry," tr. Donald Boucher and Larry Andrews, *RLT* (1974), no. 8: 125–27. "Song of the Greek" first appeared in *Severnye tsvety* (1827): 292–94.

43. Obodovskii's letter to President Kapodistrias is published in I. Kubasov, "Platon G. Obodovskii," *Russkaia starina* (1903), no. 11: 359–60. Also see B. M. Gorodetskii, *Platon G. Obodovskii: Biobibliograficheskii ocherk* (St. Petersburg, 1904).

44. Platon G. Obodovskii, *Khiosskii sirota* (St. Petersburg, 1828), 49. A hand-written manuscript copy of the verse narrative is located in OR, IRLI, f. 1000, op. 2, d. 969, "Khiosskii sirota. Poema," ll. 1–24.

45. Obodovskii, *Khiosskii sirota*, 51–70. Reviews heralded the work's "color-ful, vivid imagery" and "sincere feeling," as well as the author's charitable intent. See *SO* (1828), no. 17: 96–98; *MT* (1828), no. 17: 111–14; *MV* (1828), no. 20: 358–59.

46. On Byron and Byronism, see M. Byron Raizis, ed., *Lord Byron: Byronism-Liberalism-Philhellenism: Proceedings of the 14th International Byron Symposium, Athens, 6–8 July 1987* (Athens, 1988); Paul Trueblood, ed., *Byron's Political and Cultural Influence in Nineteenth-Century Europe: A Symposium* (Atlantic Highlands, N.J., 1981); Leslie A. Marchand, *Byron: A Portrait* (New York, 1970).

47. Byron's activity in Greece and his legacy to the philhellenic movement are covered in the standard accounts of European philhellenism: David Howarth, *Lord Byron and Other Eccentrics in the War of Independence* (New York, 1976); William St. Clair, *That Greece Might Still Be Free: The Philhellenes in the War of Independence* (London, 1972); C. M. Woodhouse, *The Philhellenes* (London, 1969); Douglas Dakin, *British and American Philhellenes during the War of Greek Independence, 1821–1833* (London, 1955). Also useful are the older studies by Harold Spender, *Byron and Greece* (London, 1924), and by Harold Nicolson, *Byron: The Last Journey, April 1823–April 1824* (Boston, 1924).

48. For an index to the many reviews, translations, and adaptations of By-ron's works published in Russian journals of the early nineteenth century, see V. I. Maslov, *Nachal'nyi period baironizma v Rossii* (Kiev, 1915), 1–89. Byron's activity in Greece was covered in many journals, such as *VE* (1824), no. 12: 296–98; no. 15: 211–17.

49. The Byronic impact on Russian Romantic literature has been treated by several scholars: Sandra G. Stahl, "Byron's Influence on the Lives and Works of Representative Russian Poets of the Romantic Period, 1815–1825," Ph.D. diss., Northwestern University, 1978; M. P. Alekseev, *Russko-angliiskie literaturnye sviazi XVIII v.–pervaia polovina XIX v.* (Moscow, 1982), 410–68; Nina Diakonova and Vadim Vacuro, "Byron and Russia," in Trueblood, ed., *Byron's Political and Cultural Influence in Nineteenth-Century Europe*, 143–59; E. J. Simmons, *English Literature and Culture in Russia (1553–1840)* (Cambridge, Mass., 1935), 269–307. Byron's influ-ence on Pushkin is discussed in the next chapter.

50. Aleksandr Turgenev had various state appointments, including directorship of the Dual Ministry's Department for the Religious Affairs of Foreign Confes-
sions, which he held until the ouster of his patron, Golitsyn, in 1824. Turgenev's
official position and his active philanthropy also made him an important organizer
of the Greek relief drives. As a founding member of the Karamzinist literary society
Arzamas, Turgenev had close ties to such writers as Zhukovskii, Viazemskii, and
Pushkin. Additionally, he contributed to Russian historical research by collecting
resource materials in Russian and European archives. For an introduction to this
key figure in Alexandrine Russia, see Richard Tempest, "Turgenev, Aleksandr Iva-
novich," *MERSH* (1990), 54: 97–104. Turgenev's signature is on many of the Greek
relief documents in the Synodal collection cited in chapter three. For his support
of the relief drive, see Petr A. Viazemskii, *Ostaf'evskii arkhiv*, 5 vols. (St. Petersburg,
1899–1913), 2: 181–83, 200–1.

51. Viazemskii, *Ostaf'evskii arkhiv*, 3: 48–49.

52. *Literaturnoe nasledstvo* (1956), 60, no. 1: 219. The impact of Byron on the
literary work of Bestuzhev-Marlinskii is discussed in Lauren G. Leighton, *Alexander
Bestuzhev-Marlinsky* (Boston, 1975), 82–88.

53. Most of these commemorative poems are in Maslov, *Nachal'nyi period baironizma v Rossii*, 90–126.

54. Stahl, "Byron's Influence," 88–130. The Decembrist image of Byron as
the champion of the politically oppressed became the standard Soviet interpretation. See L. V. Sidorchenko, *Bairon i natsional'no-osvoboditel'noe dvizhenie na Balkanakh* (Leningrad, 1977).

55. Leighton, *Russian Romanticism*, 66–68; Brown, *Russian Literature—
Romantic Period*, 2: 19–23. For an English translation of Kiukhel'beker's essay on
lyric poetry, see Christine Rydel, ed., *The Ardis Anthology of Russian Romanticism*
(Ann Arbor, 1984), 407–11.

56. Kiukhel'beker, *Izbrannye proizvedeniia*, 1: 200–6. The poem appeared in
the almanac *Mnemozina* (1824), 3: 189–99, and as a separate publication, *Smert'
Bairona. Stikhotvorenie* (Moscow, 1824).

57. Excerpts from Bestuzhev-Riumin's "Byron on His Deathbed" are in Maslov, *Nachal'nyi period baironizma v Rossii*, 106–14. They first appeared in the anthology *Sobranie sochinenii i perevodov v stikhakh i proze* (1826), 1: 90–100, 131–33.

58. Ryleev, *Polnoe sobranie stikhotvorenii*, 95–97. His ode to Byron was first published in *Al'bom severnykh muz* (1828): 244–47.

59. Stahl, "Byron's Influence," 6–16; Brown, *Russian Literature—Romantic Period*, 1: 185–226; Abbott Gleason, "Zhukovsky," in Terras, ed., *Handbook of Russian
Literature*, 531–32.

60. Stahl, "Byron's Influence," 16–26; Glynn R. Barratt, *I. I. Kozlov: The
Translations from Byron* (Berne, 1972); idem, "Somov, Kozlov, and Byron's Russian
Triumph," *Canadian Review of Comparative Literature* (1974), 1: 104–22. A manuscript of Kozlov's "Bride of Abydos" translation is located in OR, GPB, f. 357, d. 9,
ll. 1–52.

61. Kozlov, *Polnoe sobranie stikhotvorenii*, 88–91. "Byron" was first published
in *Novosti literatury* (1824), no. 10: 85–90.

62. Venevitinov, *Polnoe sobranie stikhotvorenii*, 73–76; idem, "Complete Poetry," tr. Donald Boucher and Larry Andrews, *RLT* (1974), no. 8: 117–19.

63. Petr A. Viazemskii, *Stikhotvoreniia* (Leningrad, 1958), 195–97. His

"Byron" first appeared in *MT* (1827), no. 2: 41–44, but was most likely written in 1824 shortly after Byron's death.

64. Leslie A. Marchand, ed., *Byron's Letters and Journals,* 12 vols. (Cambridge, Mass., 1973–82), 11: 86–154.

65. Ibid., 11: 126.

Chapter Six: Pushkin and Greece

1. Pushkin's response to the revolution has been treated in articles by Russian, Greek, and Western scholars: O. R. Airapetov, "Vzgliady A. S. Pushkina na vostochnuiu politiku Rossii XVIII–nachala XIX v.," *Vestnik Moskovskogo universiteta. Istoriia* (1988), no. 2: 64–88; N. Svirin, "Pushkin i grecheskoe vosstanie," *Znamia* (1935), no. 11: 204–40; V. I. Selinov, "Pushkin i grecheskoe vosstanie," *Pushkin. Stat'i i materialy* (Odessa, 1926), no. 2: 5–31; M. Laskaris, "O Pouskin kai i elliniki epanastasis," *Nea Estia* (1937), no. 7: 485–92; Demetrios J. Farsolas, "The Greek Revolution in the Principalities as seen by Pushkin," *Neo-Hellenika* (1975), 2: 98–119; idem, "Alexander Pushkin: His Attitude toward the Greek Revolution, 1821–1829," *BS* (1971), no. 1: 57–80. This chapter, while based to some extent on these previous studies, examines Pushkin in the context of the wider philhellenic movement and incorporates recent scholarship by Sam Driver and Stephanie Sandler.

2. A. Efros, *Risunki poeta* (Moscow, 1933), 65, 206–8, 218–20; T. G. Tsiavlovskaia, *Risunki Pushkina,* 4th ed. (Moscow, 1986), 60, 138, 360–61. Pushkin's sketches of *klephts* are on display in the Pushkin Museum in Moscow.

3. Pushkin's knowledge of classical antiquity and its influence on his writings are examined in A. A. Formozov, *Pushkin i drevnosti. Nabliudeniia arkheologa* (Moscow, 1979); D. P. Iakubovich, "Antichnost' v tvorchestve Pushkina," *Pushkin. Vremennik Pushkinskoi komissii* (1941), 6: 92–159; M. M. Pokrovskii, "Pushkin i antichnost'," *Pushkin. Vremennik Pushkinskoi komissii* (1939), 4/5: 27–56; S. S. Liubomudrov, *Antichnyi mir v poezii Pushkina* (Moscow, 1899); idem, *Antichnye motivy v poezii Pushkina,* 2d ed. (St. Petersburg, 1901); P. N. Cherniaev, *A. S. Pushkin kak liubitel' antichnogo mira i perevodchik drevne-klassicheskikh poetov* (Kazan, 1899). Also see William E. Brown, *A History of Russian Literature of the Romantic Period* (hereafter cited as *Russian Literature—Romantic Period*), 4 vols. (Ann Arbor, 1986), 3: 141–88; Roberta Reeder, "The Greek Anthology and Its Influence on Pushkin's Poetic Style," *CASS* (1976), 10, no. 2: 205–27.

4. *The Letters of Alexander Pushkin: Three Volumes in One,* tr. J. Thomas Shaw (Madison, 1967), 84, 204. I have used Shaw's translations in all subsequent quotations from Pushkin's letters.

5. Ibid., 99.

6. Pushkin's social and political views are covered in Sam Driver, *Pushkin: Literature and Social Ideas* (New York, 1989), and in Walter Vickery, "Pushkin: Russia and Europe," *Review of National Literatures* (1972), 3, no. 1: 15–39. His ties to the Decembrists are studied by N. Ia. Eidel'man, *Pushkin i dekabristy* (Moscow, 1979); Iu. G. Oksman, "Pushkin i dekabristy," *Osvoboditel'noe dvizhenie v Rossii* (Saratov, 1971), 2: 70–88; George Vernadsky, "Pushkin and the Decembrists," in S. H. Cross and E. J. Simmons, eds., *Centennial Essays for Pushkin* (Cambridge, Mass., 1937), 45–76.

7. Vickery, "Pushkin: Russia and Europe," 19.

8. Victor Terras, *A History of Russian Literature* (New Haven, 1991), 211.

9. Driver, *Pushkin: Literature and Social Ideas,* 32–37; *The Letters of Alexander Pushkin,* 302. The illustrated works of Ivan N. Khalippa, *Gorod Kishinev vremen zhizni v nem A. S. Pushkina (1820–1823)* (Kishinev, 1899), and V. Tymchishin, *Pushkin v Moldavii* (Kishinev, 1979), are useful for their portrayal of Kishinev's ethnic diversity and literary milieu during Pushkin's exile.

10. *Pushkin on Literature,* tr. and ed. Tatiana Wolff, rev. ed. (London, 1986), 39, 47.

11. This translation is from *Pushkin Threefold: Narrative, Lyric, Polemic, and Ribald Verse,* tr. Walter Arndt (New York, 1972), 176–79.

12. *Pushkin on Literature,* 44–47.

13. Stephanie Sandler, *Alexander Pushkin and the Writing of Exile* (Palo Alto, 1989). Also good on his literary development in the South are Iurii M. Lotman, *Aleksandr S. Pushkin. Biografiia pisatelia* (Leningrad, 1983), 52–110, and Petr I. Bartenev, *Pushkin v iuzhnoi Rossii. Materialy dlia ego biografii* (Moscow, 1862).

14. *The Letters of Alexander Pushkin,* 75–76, 141, 268–70.

15. The most thorough study of Byron's influence on Pushkin is V. M. Zhirmunskii, *Bairon i Pushkin* (Leningrad, 1924). For an introduction, see Walter Vickery, *Alexander Pushkin* (New York, 1970), 35–48; John Bayley, *Pushkin: A Comparative Commentary* (Cambridge, Eng., 1971), 71–106; Sandra G. Stahl, "Byron's Influence on the Lives and Works of Representative Russian Poets of the Romantic Period, 1815–1825," Ph. D. diss., Northwestern University, 1978, 30–80; Brown, *Russian Literature—Romantic Period,* 3: 27–64.

16. Vickery, *Alexander Pushkin,* 202; *The Letters of Alexander Pushkin,* 139.

17. William Mills Todd, *The Familiar Letter as a Literary Genre in the Age of Pushkin* (Princeton, 1976), 70–75. See also the useful introduction by J. Thomas Shaw in *The Letters of Alexander Pushkin,* 25–56.

18. Pushkin's contacts with the Russian, Moldavian, and Greek communities of Kishinev and his knowledge of the *Philiki Etaireia* are treated in E. M. Dvoichenko-Markova, *Pushkin v Moldavii i Valakhii* (Moscow, 1979); Boris A. Trubetskoi, *Pushkin v Moldavii,* 5th ed. (Kishinev, 1983); Ivan F. Iovva, *Peredovaia Rossiia i obshchestvenno-politicheskoe dvizhenie v Moldavii (pervaia polovina XIX v.)* (Kishinev, 1986), 109–22.

19. *The Letters of Alexander Pushkin,* 79–81. The Russian version is in Aleksandr S. Pushkin, *Polnoe sobranie sochinenii,* 10 vols. (Moscow, 1962–66), 10: 22–24.

20. *Pushkin on Literature,* 44; Vickery, "Pushkin: Russia and Europe," 20.

21. *The Letters of Alexander Pushkin,* 75–76.

22. Ibid., 567, 589.

23. Pushkin, *Polnoe sobranie sochinenii,* 8: 17; *Pushkin on Literature,* 39.

24. Pushkin, *Polnoe sobranie sochinenii,* 2: 41–42, 402.

25. *The Letters of Alexander Pushkin,* 83, which mentions Ovid in a letter of March 1821 to Gnedich. The fate of Pushkin resembled Ovid's, except that Ovid "mean-spiritedly devoted his elegiac lyre to his deaf idol. . . . I do not sing paeans of flattery, in blind hope, to Octavian." Pushkin's letters often referred to Tsar Alexander I as Augustus or Octavian.

26. Pushkin, *Polnoe sobranie sochinenii,* 2: 67–70, 405. Translated by Sandler, *Alexander Pushkin and the Writing of Exile,* 53, along with an insightful discussion of the poem (pp. 39–56).

27. *Eugene Onegin,* tr. Vladimir Nabokov, 4 vols., rev. ed. (Princeton, 1975), 3: 316.

28. Richard Clogg, *A Short History of Modern Greece,* 2d ed. (Cambridge, Eng., 1986), 52.

29. *The Letters of Alexander Pushkin,* 204.

30. Pushkin, *Polnoe sobranie sochinenii,* 2: 32–33, 401.

31. *The Letters of Alexander Pushkin,* 107.

32. Pushkin, *Polnoe sobranie sochinenii,* 2: 66, 405.

33. Ibid., 2: 92, 403.

34. Ibid., 2: 115–16, 411. David Magarshack, *Pushkin: A Biography* (New York, 1968), 114–15, provides a brief account of Calypso Polychroni.

35. Pushkin, *Polnoe sobranie sochinenii,* 2: 126. Translated by Arndt, *Pushkin Threefold,* 181.

36. Tsiavlovskaia, *Risunki Pushkina,* 138.

37. *The Letters of Alexander Pushkin,* 111.

38. Vasilii I. Tumanskii, *Stikhotvoreniia i pis'ma* (St. Petersburg, 1912), 169–71. His "To a Greek Girl" was first published in *MV* (1827), no. 8: 309.

39. *Eugene Onegin,* "Fragments of *Onegin's Journey,*" 1: 330–34. Also see Pushkin's correspondence with Tumanskii, *The Letters of Alexander Pushkin,* 241–42, 339.

40. Pushkin, *Polnoe sobranie sochinenii,* 4: 401, 573–74; 8: 123–24, 551–53. Penda-Deka (Pendedekas) was another *etairist* who fought with Ypsilantis in Moldavia. The unfinished poem includes sketches of a Greek warrior and a turbaned Turk with a *yataghan.*

41. Trubetskoi, *Pushkin v Moldavii,* 317–30; L. N. Oganian, "Novye arkhivnye materialy o geroe povesti A. S. Pushkina 'Kirdzhali,' " *Pushkin na iuge* (Kishinev, 1958), 1: 37–58. Paul Debreczeny, *The Other Pushkin: A Study of Alexander Pushkin's Prose Fiction* (Palo Alto, 1983), 278–80, includes "Kirdjali" in his excellent analysis of Pushkin's prose. The tale's multiple narrative perspectives—historical, eyewitness, and legendary—are the subject of Andrej Kodjak and Lorraine Wynne's, "Pushkin's 'Kirdzhali': An Informational Model," *Russian Literature* (1979), 7: 45–63.

42. Hugh Honour, *Romanticism* (New York, 1979), 240–44. For Pushkin's interest in the theme of brigandage, see Ju. M. Lotman, "Gogol's 'Tale of Captain Kopejkin': Reconstruction of the Plan and Ideo-Compositional Function," in Ju. M. Lotman and B. A. Uspenskij; Ann Shukman, ed., *The Semiotics of Russian Culture* (Ann Arbor, 1984), 215–20.

43. *The Letters of Alexander Pushkin,* 142.

44. Peter Sugar, *Southeastern Europe under Ottoman Rule, 1354–1804* (Seattle, 1977), 242–44; Barbara Jelavich, *History of the Balkans: Eighteenth and Nineteenth Centuries* (New York, 1983), 61–62, 75–76, 97, 175, 193.

45. *The Complete Prose Tales of Alexander S. Pushkin,* tr. Gillon R. Aitken (New York, 1966), 309, 313. Subsequent passages quoted in the text are from Aitken's translation.

46. *The Complete Prose Tales of Pushkin,* 309.

47. See Jelavich, *History of the Balkans,* 208–14, and Clogg, *A Short History of Modern Greece,* 50–52, for a concise view of the Moldavian campaign.

48. *The Complete Prose Tales of Pushkin,* 309.

49. N. V. Izmailov, "Poema Pushkina o geteristakh," *Pushkin: Vremennik Push-kinskoi komissii* (1937), 3: 339–48; Dvoichenko-Markova, *Pushkin v Moldavii i Vala-khii,* 75–78. On Olympios, see Douglas Dakin, *The Greek Struggle for Independence, 1821–1833* (London, 1973), 43–44, 53–55, 61–62; Nestor Camariano, "L'activité de Georges Olympios dans les principautés roumaines avant la révolution de 1821," *RESE* (1964), no. 2: 433–46.

50. *The Complete Prose Tales of Pushkin,* 309–11.

51. Ibid., 311–12.

52. *The Letters of Alexander Pushkin,* 182, 271.

53. Ibid., 190.

54. *The Complete Prose Tales of Pushkin,* 82.

55. J. Thomas Shaw, "Pushkin's 'The Shot,' " *Indiana Slavic Studies* (1963), 3: 122–24. Debreczeny, *The Other Pushkin,* 102–19, highlights Pushkin's use of irony and parody and suggests comparisons between Silvio, Rudin, and Dostoevskii's un-derground man.

56. See Clogg, *A Short History of Modern Greece,* 56–61, for a brief account of disunity and internecine strife during the War of Independence. Russian press re-ports often mentioned Greek factionalism in military and political affairs: *SO* (1821), no. 39: 283–87; *VE* (1822), no. 16: 312–15; (1823), no. 10: 148–58; (1824), no. 14: 138–43; *MT* (1826), no. 3: 293–300.

57. *The Letters of Alexander Pushkin,* 135–38, 140–43, 157–60. For Pushkin and indeed for many visitors and residents in nineteenth-century Odessa, the charms of Odessan life were offset by the port's dusty and muddy roads, shortage of drinking water, and chronic bouts of plague. See Patricia Herlihy, *Odessa: A History, 1794–1915* (Cambridge, Mass., 1986), 45–46, 130–35, 234–38, 268–71.

58. Ibid., 141–42, 145.

59. Ibid., 141, 155, 163–65.

60. Ibid., 135–36, 168.

61. Ibid., 149–50, 153, 160, 162.

62. Ibid., 165, 182. The verse "To Vorontsov" also appears in Arndt's *Pushkin Threefold,* 184–85.

63. Anthony L. H. Rhinelander, *Prince Michael Vorontsov: Viceroy to the Tsar* (Montreal, 1990), 75–76, 233.

64. *The Letters of Alexander Pushkin,* 156.

65. Vickery, "Pushkin: Russia and Europe," 22–24.

66. Translated by Vickery, *Alexander Pushkin,* 165–66. Another translation by Arndt is in *Pushkin Threefold,* 182–83.

67. *The Letters of Alexander Pushkin,* 296.

68. There is an English translation of this poem by Max Eastman in D. S. Mirsky, *Pushkin* (New York, 1963), 272.

69. *Pushkin Threefold,* 216–17, Arndt's translation. The Greek poet Arion (seventh century B.C.), thrown overboard by pirates who stole his recently won gold prize for poetry, was saved by a dolphin charmed by his music. In "Childe Harold," Canto II, Byron alludes to the story of Arion in his depiction of the ship-mate whose music entertains the voyagers. On Pushkin's "Arion," see G. S. Glebov, "Ob 'Arion,' " *Pushkin. Vremennik Pushkinskoi komissii* (1941), 6: 296–304.

70. Vickery, *Alexander Pushkin,* 203.

71. Ia. L. Levkovich, "Tri pis'ma Pushkina o Grecheskoi revoliutsii 1821 g.,"

Vremennik Pushkinskoi komissii (1987), 21: 16–23, demonstrates that this particular letter was addressed to A. N. Raevskii rather than to V. L. Davydov as suggested by Shaw in *The Letters of Alexander Pushkin*, 167. The Russian version is in Pushkin, *Polnoe sobranie sochinenii*, 10: 99.

72. Driver, *Pushkin: Literature and Social Ideas*, 35–36.

73. *The Letters of Alexander Pushkin*, 161. Pushkin, *Polnoe sobranie sochinenii*, 10: 92–93.

74. *The Letters of Alexander Pushkin*, 166. Levkovich, "Tri pis'ma Pushkina o Grecheskoi revoliutsii 1821 g.," 19–21.

75. *The Letters of Alexander Pushkin*, 166. Pushkin, *Polnoe sobranie sochinenii*, 10: 98.

76. *The Letters of Alexander Pushkin*, 161.

77. Translated by Sandler, *Alexander Pushkin and the Writing of Exile*, 69–70, along with a lucid analysis of the poem (pp. 57–76). "To the Sea" was first published in the literary almanac *Mnemozina* (1825), 4: 103–4. Pushkin, *Polnoe sobranie sochinenii*, 2: 198–200.

78. *The Letters of Alexander Pushkin*, 213.

79. Ibid., 263–64.

80. *A Journey to Arzrum*, tr. Birgitta Ingemanson (Ann Arbor, 1974); Brown, *Russian Literature-Romantic Period*, 3: 196–200; Monika Frenkel Greenleaf, "Pushkin's 'Journey to Arzrum': The Poet at the Border," *SR* (1991), 50, no. 4: 940–53.

81. Pushkin, *Polnoe sobranie sochinenii*, 3: 148, 504–5. Other publications, in the same spirit as Pushkin's poem, hailed Russia's military victory for its impact on Greece. *Spasaemaia Gretsiia, ili kartina voennykh deistvii rossiiskikh protiv turok v 1827 i 1828 gg.* (St. Petersburg, 1829) was an anonymous work that suggested the close connection between the Russo-Turkish War and Greece's salvation. An anonymous poem inspired by the Adrianople Treaty, *Na mir s Ottomanskoiu Portoiu* (St. Petersburg, 1829), alludes to classical Greece and its Russian-assisted revival.

Chapter Seven: Legacies of Russian Philhellenism

1. Barbara Jelavich, *Russia's Balkan Entanglements, 1806–1914* (New York, 1991); Charles Jelavich, *Tsarist Russia and Balkan Nationalism* (Berkeley, 1958).

2. Michael Petrovich, *The Emergence of Russian Panslavism, 1856–1870* (New York, 1956).

3. David MacKenzie, *The Serbs and Russian Panslavism, 1875–1878* (Ithaca, 1967); B. H. Sumner, *Russia and the Balkans, 1870–1880* (Oxford, 1937); S. A. Nikitin, *Slavianskie komitety v Rossii v 1858–1876 godakh* (Moscow, 1960). Pan-Slav public enthusiasm is vividly depicted, and criticized, by Tolstoi in the last chapters of *Anna Karenina*.

4. F. M. Dostoevskii, *Diary of a Writer*, tr. Boris Brasol (Santa Barbara, 1979), 904–8. On the broader issue of Orthodoxy and the Byzantine tradition in Russian conservative thought, see Edward Thaden, *Conservative Nationalism in Nineteenth-Century Russia* (Seattle, 1964).

5. Ihor Ševčenko, "Byzantine Cultural Influences," in Cyril Black, ed., *Rewriting Russian History: Soviet Interpretations of Russia's Past* (New York, 1956), 148. For another perspective on the importance of Constantinople and Mount Athos in Russian perceptions of the Near East, see Theofanis Stavrou, "Russian Policy in

Constantinople and Mount Athos in the Nineteenth Century," in Lowell Clucas, ed., *The Byzantine Legacy in Eastern Europe* (New York, 1988), 225–49.

6. V. N. Vinogradov et al., *Mezhdunarodnye otnosheniia na Balkanakh, 1856–1878 gg.* (Moscow, 1986); Evangelos Kofos, *Greece and the Eastern Crisis, 1875–1878* (Thessaloniki, 1975); idem, "Rossiia i ellinism v period vostochnogo krizisa, 1875–1878 gg.," *BI* (1989), 11: 144–54; G. L. Arsh, "Gretsiia i vostochnyi krizis 70–kh godov XIX v.," *BI* (1978), 4: 168–90; S. Papadopoulos, "Otnoshenie grekov k Rossii v period Krymskoi voiny (1853–1856 gg.)," *BI* (1989), 11: 87–94; Maria Todorova, "The Greek Volunteers in the Crimean War," *BS* (1984), 25: 539–63; Domna Dontas, *Greece and the Great Powers, 1863–1875* (Thessaloniki, 1966).

7. The Destunis and Sturdza families are case studies of the Greek contribution to Russian life in the nineteenth century. Biographical sketches of other prominent Greeks and descriptions of their manuscript collections will continue to shed light on Russia's Greek communities. G. L. Kurbatov, "Iz istorii vozniknoveniia otechestvennoi shkoly nauchnogo vizantinovedeniia (G. S. Destunis)," *Palestinskii sbornik* (1971), 23: 179–91, assesses Gavriil Destunis's place in Russian Byzantine studies. For an index to the first thirty volumes of *Zapiski Odesskogo obshchestva istorii i drevnostei,* see M. G. Popruzhenko, *Ukazatel' statei* (Odessa, 1914). Works by Patricia Herlihy and Konstantinos Papoulidis, which are cited in the bibliography, provide specific leads on Russia's Greek presence in the late nineteenth and early twentieth centuries.

8. K. Papoulidis, *To Rosiko archaiologiko institouto Konstantinoupoleos, 1894–1914* (Thessaloniki, 1987); S. A. Zhebelev, "F. I. Uspenskii i russkii arkheologicheskii institut v Konstantinopole," in *Pamiati akademika Fedora Ivanovicha Uspenskogo, 1845–1928* (Leningrad, 1929), 53–66. Key sources on the Institute's founding, membership, and scholarly work are its archive (RGIA, f. 757) and its sixteen volumes of *Izvestiia russkogo arkheologicheskogo instituta v Konstantinopole* (1896–1911), which include annual *otchety.*

9. Karl P. Briullov, *Atlas k putevym zapiskam Davydova po Ionicheskim ostrovam, Gretsii, Maloi Azii i Turtsii* (St. Petersburg, 1840), a companion volume to Vladimir P. Davydov's *Putevye zapiski vedennye vo vremia prebyvaniia na Ionicheskikh ostrovakh, v Gretsii, Maloi Azii i Turtsii v 1835 g.* (St. Petersburg, 1839–40). E. Smirnova, *Briullov-puteshestvennik* (Moscow, 1969), discusses Briullov's paintings inspired by travel to Italy, Greece, Turkey, and Spain. Briullov's works commemorating the Greek revolt are located in St. Petersburg's Russian Museum and in Moscow's Tretyakov Gallery and Pushkin Fine Arts Museum.

10. Andrei N. Murav'ev, *Puteshestvie k sviatym mestam v 1830 g.,* 2 vols. (St. Petersburg, 1832); idem, *Pis'ma s vostoka v 1849–50 gg.* (St. Petersburg, 1851); Konstantin M. Bazili, *Arkhipelag i Gretsiia v 1830–31 gg.,* 2 vols. (St. Petersburg, 1834); idem, *Ocherki Konstantinopolia,* 2 vols. (St. Petersburg, 1835); idem, *Bosfor i novye ocherki Konstantinopolia,* 2 vols. (St. Petersburg, 1836). See Boris L. Fonkich, "The Greek Manuscripts of A. N. Murav'ev," *MGSY* (1988), 4: 235–54, on Murav'ev's interest in the Greek church. Bazili, a Greek refugee from Istanbul whose family settled in Odessa in 1821, served as Russian consul in Beirut from 1839 to 1853. The travelogues of Murav'ev and Bazili are still useful sources on the Greek East.

11. Philhellenic images in book illustrations and *lubki* are discussed in the valuable works of Russian scholar Ol'ga A. Belobrova, "O grecheskoi teme v russkom iskusstve pervoi treti XIX v.," *BI* (1980), 6: 140–61; "Grecheskaia tema v

russkoi knizhnoi illiustratsii pervoi poloviny XIX v.," *BI* (1989), 11: 95–122. See also V. M. Polevoi, *Iskusstvo Gretsii,* 2 vols., 2d ed. (Moscow, 1984), 1: 424–28. Belobrova and Polevoi include illustrations of philhellenic themes in Russian art.

12. N. Barsamov, *Ivan K. Aivazovskii* (Moscow, 1967), 12; I. G. Senkevich, *Rossiia i kritskoe vosstanie 1866–1869 gg.* (Moscow, 1970), 88.

13. Nikolai Gogol', *Dead Souls,* tr. Andrew MacAndrew (New York, 1961), 109.

14. Irina H. Corten, "Reality or Ideal: Images of Greeks in the Works of Aleksandr Kuprin," *MGSY* (1990), 6: 288, describes the writer's literary sketches of Greek fishermen in Balaklava.

Selected Bibliography

Archival Collections

Gosudarstvennyi arkhiv Odesskoi oblasti, Odessa (GAOO). F. 1, 2, 141, 268.
Gosudarstvennyi arkhiv Rossiiskoi Federatsii, Moscow (GARF). F. 48, 109.
Otdel rukopisei. Gosudarstvennaia publichnaia biblioteka imeni Saltykova-Shchedrina, St. Petersburg (OR, GPB). F. 122, 197, 250, 253, 286, 357, 794, 859.
Otdel rukopisei. Institut russkoi literatury, St. Petersburg (OR, IRLI). F. 288, 1000.
Rossiiskii gosudarstvennyi arkhiv drevnykh aktov, Moscow (RGADA). F. 15, 18, 20, 379, 1184, 1409.
Rossiiskii gosudarstvennyi istoricheskii arkhiv, St. Petersburg (RGIA). F. 13, 378, 379, 383, 535, 560, 565, 732, 733, 734, 757, 796, 797, 1088, 1261, 1287, 1308, 1409, 1630, 1673, 1686.
Rossiiskii gosudarstvennyi voenno-istoricheskii arkhiv, Moscow (RGVIA). F. 36, 14057, *Voenno-uchenyi arkhiv.*

Contemporary Journals and Almanacs

Amfion, 1815
Atenei, 1828–30
Avrora, 1805–6
Blagonamerennyi, 1818–26
Drug prosveshcheniia, 1804–6
Dukh zhurnalov, 1815–20
Galateia, 1829–30
Genii vremen, 1807–9
Ippokrena, 1799–1801
Istoricheskii, statisticheskii i geograficheskii zhurnal, 1821–25
Journal d'Odessa/ Odesskii vestnik, 1827–28
Kazanskii vestnik, 1821–33
Korifei, ili kliuch literatury, 1802–7
Litsei, 1806
Minerva, 1806–7
Mnemozina, 1824–25
Moskovskii telegraf, 1825–30
Moskovskii vestnik, 1827–30
Moskovskii zhurnal, 1791–92
Moskovskii zritel', 1804
Muza, 1796

Novosti literatury, 1822–26
Novosti russkoi literatury, 1802–5
Otechestvennye zapiski, 1820–30
Panteon inostrannoi slovesnosti, 1798
Poliarnaia zvezda, 1823–25
Russkii vestnik, 1808–20
Severnye tsvety, 1825–32
Severnyi arkhiv, 1822–28
Severnyi vestnik, 1804–5
Sorevnovatel' prosveshcheniia i blagotvoreniia, 1818–25
Syn otechestva, 1812–44
Ukrainskii vestnik, 1816–19
Ukrainskii zhurnal, 1824–25
Ulei, 1811–12
Vestnik Evropy, 1802–30
Zhurnal drevnei i novoi slovesnosti, 1818–19
Zhurnal iziashchnykh iskusstv, 1823–25

Printed Materials
Primary Sources

Akty grecheskogo Nezhinskogo bratstva. Kiev, 1884.

Argenti, Philip, ed. *The Massacres of Chios Described in Contemporary Diplomatic Reports.* London, 1932.

Arkhiv brat'ev Turgenevykh. Tom 3: Dnevnik i pis'ma Nikolaia I. Turgeneva za 1816–1824 gg. Petrograd, 1921.

Arsen'ev, K. *Istoriia narodov i respublik drevnei Gretsii.* 2 vols. St. Petersburg, 1825–26.

Arsh, G. L. "I. Kapodistriia o svoem prebyvanii v Gretsii nakanune revoliutsii 1821 g." V. A. Diakov, ed., *Istoriografiia i istochnikovedenie stran Tsentral'noi i Iugo-Vostochnoi Evropy* (Moscow, 1986), 244–71.

———. " 'Zapiski o nyneshnem sostoianii grekov' (1811) I. Kapodistrii." *Slaviano-balkanskie issledovaniia* (Moscow, 1972), 359–86.

Barratt, Glynn R. " 'Notice sur l'insurrection des Grecs contre l'Empire Ottoman': A Russian View of the Greek War of Independence." *BS* (1973), 14, no. 1: 47–115.

Batiushkov, K. N. *O grecheskoi antologii.* St. Petersburg, 1820.

———. *Opyty v stikhakh i proze.* Moscow, 1964.

———. *Polnoe sobranie stikhotvorenii.* Moscow, 1964.

Bazili, K. M. *Arkhipelag i Gretsiia v 1830–31 gg.* 2 vols. St. Petersburg, 1834.

———. *Bosfor i novye ocherki Konstantinopolia.* 2 vols. St. Petersburg, 1836.

———. *Ocherki Konstantinopolia.* 2 vols. St. Petersburg, 1835.

Bolkhovitinov, E. (Metropolitan of Kiev, 1822–37). *Slovar' istoricheskii o byvshikh v Rossii pisateliakh dukhovnogo china greko-rossiiskoi tserkvi.* 2 vols. St. Petersburg, 1818–27.

Briullov, K. P. *Atlas k putevym zapiskam Davydova po Ionicheskim ostrovam, Gretsii, Maloi Azii i Turtsii.* St. Petersburg, 1840.

Bronevskii, V. B. *Zapiski morskogo ofitsera.* 3 vols. St. Petersburg, 1818–19.

Bronnikov, K. I. *Puteshestvie k sviatym mestam.* Moscow, 1824.

Bulgarin, F. V. *Kartina voiny Rossii s Turtsieiu v tsarstvovanie imperatora Nikolaia I.* St. Petersburg, 1830.

"Bumagi grafa Arseniia A. Zakrevskogo." *SIRIO* (1891), 78.

Buturlin, D. P. *Kartina voiny Rossii s Turtsieiu v tsarstvovaniia imperatritsy Ekateriny II i imperatora Aleksandra I.* St. Petersburg, 1829.

Clogg, Richard, ed. *The Movement for Greek Independence, 1770–1821: A Collection of Documents.* London, 1976.

———. "Smyrna in 1821: Documents from the Levant Company Archives in the Public Record Office." *Mikrasiatika Chronika* (1972), 15: 313–71.

Correspondance du Comte Jean Capodistrias, Président de la Grèce, 1827–1831. Geneva, 1839.

Davydov, V. P. *Putevye zapiski vedennye vo vremia prebyvaniia na Ionicheskikh ostrovakh, v Gretsii, Maloi Azii i Turtsii v 1835 g.* St. Petersburg, 1839–40.

Del'vig, A. A. *Polnoe sobranie stikhotvorenii.* Leningrad, 1959.

Destunis, S. Iu. *Ekstrateia tou Frantsezon eis tin Rossian kata to 1812 etos.* St. Petersburg, 1813.

———. *Plutarkhovy sravnitel'nye zhizneopisaniia slavnykh muzhei.* 13 parts. St. Petersburg, 1814–21.

———. *Voennaia truba.* Translated from A. Korais, *Salpisma polemistirion.* St. Petersburg, 1807.

Diathiki tou aoidimou Nikolaou P. Zosima, eugenous graikou kai ippotou tou tagmatos tou Sotiros. Moscow, 1843. Also published in "I diathiki tou N. Zosima," *Ipeirotiki Estia* (1953), 2: 1123–27.

Dmitrevskii, M. *Vzor na nyneshnee sostoianie Gretsii.* Moscow, 1806.

Evlampios, G. *Amarantos, ili rozy vozrozhdennoi Ellady.* St. Petersburg, 1843.

Fonvizin, M. A. "Obozrenie proiavlenii politicheskoi zhizni v Rossii." V. I. Semevskii et al., eds., *Obshchestvennye dvizheniia v Rossii v pervuiu polovinu XIX v.* 2 vols. (St. Petersburg, 1905), 1: 93–203.

———. "Zapiski dekabrista 1823 g." *Golos minuvshego* (1916), 10: 139–49.

Gerakov, G. V. *Prodolzhenie putevykh zapisok 1820–nachala 1821.* St. Petersburg, 1830.

———. *Putevye zapiski po mnogim Rossiiskim guberniiam v 1820 g.* St. Petersburg, 1828.

Ginzburg, L. Ia., ed. *Poety 1820–1830-kh gg.* 2 vols. Leningrad, 1972.

Glinka, F. N. *Izbrannye proizvedeniia.* Leningrad, 1957.

Glinka, S. N. *Kartina istoricheskaia i politicheskaia novoi Gretsii.* Moscow, 1829.

———. *Kartina istoricheskaia i politicheskaia Porty Ottomanskoi.* Moscow, 1830.

———. *Obozrenie vnutrennosti Turtsii Evropeiskoi.* Moscow, 1829.

———. *Plutarkh v pol'zu vospitaniia.* 6 parts. Moscow, 1822–23.

———. *Turetskaia imperiia v drevnem i nyneshnem ee sostoianii.* Moscow, 1829.

Gnedich, N. I. *Iliad Gomera.* 2 vols. St. Petersburg, 1829.

———. *N. I. Gnedich. Stikhotvoreniia.* Moscow, 1963.

———. *Prostonarodnye pesni nyneshnikh grekov.* St. Petersburg, 1825.

———. "Rassuzhdenie o prichinakh zamedliaiushchikh uspekhi nashei slovesnosti." *Opisanie torzhestvennogo otkrytiia publichnoi biblioteki.* St. Petersburg, 1814.

———. *Rech' iz XV chasti trudov vysochaishe utverzhdennogo vol'nogo obshchestva liubitelei rossiiskoi slovesnosti.* St. Petersburg, 1821.

"Graf A. Kh. Benkendorf o Rossii v 1827–1830 gg." *Krasnyi arkhiv* (1927), 37: 138–74.

Grot, Ia., and P. Pekarskii. *Pis'ma N. M. Karamzina k I. I. Dmitrievu.* St. Petersburg, 1866.

Holland, Henry. *Travels in the Ionians, Albania, Thessaly, and Macedonia.* London, 1815.

Izbrannye sotsial'no-politicheskie i filosofskie proizvedeniia dekabristov. 3 vols. Moscow, 1951.

Izmailov, V. *Puteshestvie v poludennuiu Rossiiu.* 2 vols. Moscow, 1805.

Kachenovskii, M. T. *Uchebnaia knizhka drevnego grecheskogo iazyka.* Moscow, 1807–9.

————. *Vybor iz sochinenii Lorda Beirona.* Moscow, 1821.

Kanones ton dioikiton tou ellinikou emporikou scholeiou ton en Odisso graikon. Vilna, 1819.

Kapnist, V. V. *Izbrannye proizvedeniia.* Leningrad, 1973.

Kapodistrias, I. A. "Aperçu de ma carrière publique, depuis 1798 jusqu'à 1822." *SIRIO* (1868), 3: 163–292.

Katenin, P. A. *Izbrannye proizvedeniia.* Moscow, 1965.

Kheraskov, M. M. *Izbrannye proizvedeniia.* Leningrad, 1961.

Kiukhel'beker, V. K. *Izbrannye proizvedeniia.* 2 vols. Moscow, 1967.

————. *Smert' Bairona. Stikhotvorenie.* Moscow, 1824.

"Kniaz' A. N. Golitsyn i Arkhimandrit Fotii v 1822–1825 godakh." *Russkaia starina* (1882), 33: 765–81; 34: 205–22, 427–42, 683–700; 35: 275–96.

Korais, A. "Report on the Present State of Civilization in Greece." Elie Kedourie, ed., *Nationalism in Asia and Africa* (New York, 1970), 153–88.

Kozlov, I. I. *Polnoe sobranie stikhotvorenii.* Leningrad, 1960.

Laïos, G. *Anekdotes epistoles kai eggrapha tou 1821. Istorika dokoumenta apo ta austriaka archeia.* Athens, 1958.

Laskaris, M. *Autobiographia tou Ioannou Kapodistria.* Athens, 1940.

Latyshev, V. V. *K istorii arkheologicheskikh issledovanii v iuzhnoi Rossii. Iz perepiski A. N. Olenina.* Odessa, 1888.

Lentin, Antony, ed. *Voltaire and Catherine II: Selected Correspondence.* London, 1974.

Lorer, N. I. *Zapiski dekabrista.* Moscow, 1931.

Lunin, M. S. *Sochineniia i pis'ma.* Petrograd, 1923.

Marchand, Leslie A. *Byron's Letters and Journals.* 12 vols. Cambridge, Mass., 1973–82.

Martsella, S. Ia. *Opravdanie grekov, v pol'zu sirot i vdov grekov, pozhertvovavshikh zhizniu za veru i otechestvo.* St. Petersburg, 1826.

Martynov, I. I. "Avtobiograficheskie zapiski." *Zaria* (1871), 3, no. 6: 73–110.

————. *Filosofichicheskaia i politicheskaia perepiska imperatritsy Ekateriny II s Vol'terom s 1763 po 1778.* St. Petersburg, 1802.

————. *Grecheskie klassiki.* 26 vols. St. Petersburg, 1823–29.

————. *Nastavlenie ob istinnom proiznoshenii nekotorykh grecheskikh bukv, izvlechennoe iz knigi o sem zhe predmete grecheskogo sviashchennika Ekonomosa.* St. Petersburg, 1831.

————. *Sovet rossiiskomu iunoshestvu o proiznoshenii nekotorykh grecheskikh bukv.* St. Petersburg, 1822.

Mavriki, A. *Panegiricheskie ody Aleksandromu Pervomu.* Odessa, 1804.

Mémoires de la comtesse Edling (née Stourdza). Moscow, 1888.

Merzliakov, A. F. *Stikhotvoreniia.* Leningrad, 1958.

Metaxas, N. *Istoriia grecheskikh proisshestvii obstoiatel'no i podrobno opissanykh ot pervona-chal'nogo deistviia grekov.* 2 vols. Moscow, 1824.

Ministerstva inostrannykh del SSSR. *Vneshniaia politika Rossii XIX i nachala XX v.: Dokumenty Rossiiskogo ministerstva inostrannykh del.* 14 vols. Moscow, 1960–85.

Murav'ev, A. M. *Zapiski.* Petrograd, 1922.

Murav'ev, A. N. *Pis'ma s vostoka v 1849–50 gg.* St. Petersburg, 1851.

————. *Puteshestvie k sviatym mestam v 1830 g.* 2 vols. St. Petersburg, 1832.

Murav'ev-Apostol, I. M. *Ol'via. Otryvok iz puteshestviia v Tavridu v 1820 g.* St. Petersburg, 1821.

————. *Puteshestvie po Tavride v 1820.* St. Petersburg, 1823.

Na mir s Ottomanskoiu Portoiu. St. Petersburg, 1829.

Negris, A. *O nyneshnem prosveshchenii Gretsii.* Translated from A. Korais, *Mémoire sur l'état actuel de la civilisation dans la Grèce.* St. Petersburg, 1815.

Nevakhovich, L. N. *Sul'ety, ili spartansy os'mnadtsatogo stoletiia. Istoricheskoe i dramaticheskoe predstavlenie v piati deistviiakh.* St. Petersburg, 1810.

Obodovskii, P. G. *Khioskii sirota.* St. Petersburg, 1828.

Oikonomos, K. *Autoschedios diatrivi peri Smyrnis.* London, 1831.

————. *Logos epitaphios eis ton aeimniston Patriarchin Konstantinoupoleos Grigorion.* St. Petersburg, 1821.

————. *Opyt o blizhaishem srodstve iazyka slaviano-rossiiskogo s grecheskim.* 3 vols. St. Petersburg, 1828.

————. *Slova, govorennye v Odesse na grecheskom iazyke v 1821 i 1822 godakh, pri pogrebenii Konstantinopol'skogo patriarkha Grigoriia i pri drugikh sluchaiakh.* St. Petersburg, 1829.

Olenin, A. N. *Arkheologicheskie pis'ma A. N. Olenina k N. I. Gnedichu.* St. Petersburg, 1872.

————. *Arkheologicheskie trudy.* 2 vols. St. Petersburg, 1877–82.

————. *Riazanskie russkie drevnosti.* St. Petersburg, 1831.

Orlov, M. F. *Kapitulatsiia Parizha. Politicheskie sochineniia i pis'ma.* Moscow, 1963.

Orlov, V. N., ed. *Dekabristy: Poeziia, dramaturgiia, proza, publitsistika, literaturnaia kritika.* Leningrad, 1951.

————. *Poety Pushkinskoi pory.* 3d ed. Moscow, 1972.

Ozerov, V. A. *V. A. Ozerov: Tragediia, stikhotvoreniia.* Leningrad, 1970.

Palaiologos, M. *Grammatiki tis simerinis ellinikis glossis eis ton mathiton tou Ellinoemporikou Scholeiou.* Odessa, 1845.

————. *Kratkaia grammatika novogrecheskogo iazyka.* Odessa, 1843; 2d ed., 1895.

————. *Nea methodiki geographia.* Odessa, 1834.

————. *Razgovory russko-frantsuzsko-grecheskie.* Odessa, 1844.

————. *Syllogi ek diaphoron ellinon syggrapheon kai poiiton eis chrisi ton Ellinikon Scholeion.* 2 vols. Odessa, 1833.

Pallas, P. S. *Travels through the Southern Provinces of the Russian Empire in the Years 1793–1794.* 2 vols. London, 1802–3.

Papoulidis, K. "Tria anekdota grammata tou Konstantinou Oikonomou tou ex Oikonomon sti Roxandra kai ston Alexandros Stourtza." *Klironomias* (1979), 11, no. 2: 451–75.

Pappadopoulos, D. *Novye razgovory rossiiskie i grecheskie, razdelennye na sto urokov, dlia iunoshestva i vsekh nachinaiushchikh uchit'sia sim iazykam.* St. Petersburg, 1826.

Pappadopoulos, K. *Grammatiki rossiko-graiki, itoi methodos dia na spoudasi tis eukolos tin rossikin dialekton.* Moscow, 1816.

"Perepiska grafa Kapodistrii s N. M. Karamzinym." *Utro* (Moscow, 1866), no. 2: 195–210.

Pis'ma Karamzina k Alekseiu F. Malinovskomu. Moscow, 1860.

"Pis'ma Karamzina k kniaziu P. A. Viazemskomu (1810–1826)." *Starina i novizina* (St. Petersburg, 1897), no. 1: 114–58.

"Pis'ma kniazia Aleksandra Nikolaevicha Golitsyna k grafine Anne Alekseevne Orlovoi-Chesmenskoi v 1822 i 1823 godakh." *Russkii arkhiv* (1869): 943–58.

Prevelakis, E. "I egkyklia epistoli tou Ioanni Kapodistria tis 6/18 apriliou 1819." *Praktika, Triton Panonion Synedrion* (Athens, 1967), 293–328.

Prousis, Theophilus. "Smyrna 1821: A Russian View." *MGSY* (1991), 7: 145–68.

Pushkin, A. S. *The Complete Prose Tales of Pushkin.* Tr. Gillon R. Aitken. London, 1966.

———. *Eugene Onegin.* Tr. Vladimir Nabokov. 4 vols. Rev. ed. Princeton, 1975.

———. *A Journey to Arzrum.* Tr. Birgitta Ingemanson. Ann Arbor, 1974.

———. *The Letters of Alexander Pushkin: Three Volumes in One.* Tr. J. Thomas Shaw. Madison, 1967.

———. *The Poems, Prose, and Plays of Alexander Pushkin.* Ed. Avrahm Yarmolinsky. New York, 1936.

———. *Polnoe sobranie sochinenii.* 10 vols. Moscow, 1962–66.

———. *Pushkin on Literature.* Ed. and tr. Tatiana Wolffe. Rev. ed. London, 1986.

———. *Pushkin Threefold: Narrative, Lyric, Polemic, and Ribald Verse.* Tr. Walter Arndt. New York, 1972.

Puteshestvennye zapiski Vasil'ia Zueva ot Peterburga do Khersona v 1781 i 1782 gg. St. Petersburg, 1787.

Raevskii, V. F. *Polnoe sobranie stikhotvorenii.* Moscow, 1967.

Redkii blagodetel'nyi podvig Z. K. Kaplani. Moscow, 1809.

Rydel, Christine, ed. *The Ardis Anthology of Russian Romanticism.* Ann Arbor, 1984.

Ryleev, K. F. *Polnoe sobranie stikhotvorenii.* Leningrad, 1971.

Shidlovskii, A. F. "Iz bumag grafini R. S. Edling." *Russkii vestnik* (1899), no. 3.

———. "Perepiska grafa I. A. Kapodistriia." *Vestnik vsemirnoi istorii* (1900), nos. 2, 3, 5, 7.

Shteingel', V. I. "O vnutrennem sostoianii Rossii pri tsarstvovanii imperatora Nikolaia Pavlovicha." *Russkii arkhiv* (1895), no. 2: 161–75.

Shtraikh, S. Ia. *Zapiski, stat'i, i pis'ma dekabrista I. D. Iakushkina.* Moscow, 1951.

Sobranie novykh russkikh sochinenii i perevodov v stikhakh s 1823 po 1825 gg. St. Petersburg, 1824.

Somov, O. M. *Padenie Khiosa.* St. Petersburg, 1824.

———. *Zapiski polkovnika Vut'e o nyneshnei voine grekov.* 2 vols. St. Petersburg, 1824.

"Sovremennye bumagi o konchine i pogrebenii patriarkha Grigoriia, 1821." *Russkii arkhiv* (1871), no. 9: 1920–39.

Spasaemaia Gretsiia, ili kartina voennykh deistvii rossiiskikh protiv turok v 1827 i 1828 gg. St. Petersburg, 1829.

Sturdza, A. S. *Dan' pamiati grafini R. S. Edling, urozhdennoi Sturdzy.* Odessa, 1848.

———. *Dan' pamiati vel'mozhikhristianina kniazia A. N. Golitsyna.* Odessa, 1845.

———. *Egcheiridion tou orthodoxou Christianou.* St. Petersburg, 1830. The Russian version, *Ruchnaia kniga pravoslavnogo khristianina,* translated by Spyridon Destunis, was published in St. Petersburg (1830) and in Odessa (1849).

———. "Evgenii Bulgaris i Nikifor Feotokis, predtechi umstvennogo i politicheskogo probuzhdeniia grekov." *Moskvitianin* (1844), no. 2: 337–67.

————. *La Grèce en 1821 et 1822.* Leipzig, 1822.

————. *Logos epitaphios eis ton kyvernitin tis Ellados Ioannin Antoniou komita Kapodistrian.* Odessa, 1831.

————. *Mémoire sur l'état actuel d'Allemagne.* Paris, 1818.

————. *Oeuvres posthumes religieuses, historiques, philosophiques et littéraires d'Alexandre Stourdza.* 5 vols. Paris, 1858–61.

————. *Opyt uchebnogo prednachertaniia dlia prepodavaniia rossiiskomu iunoshestvu grecheskogo iazyka.* St. Petersburg, 1817.

————. *Oraison funèbre de Comte Capodistrias.* Odessa, 1831.

————. "Pamiat' Grigoriia V, patriarkha Konstantinopol'skogo." *Moskvitianin* (1842), no. 6: 380–84.

————. *Perevod nadgrobnogo slova blazhennomu Konstantinopol'skomu patriarkhu Grigoriiu.* St. Petersburg, 1821.

————. *Vospominaniia moi o Karamzine.* Odessa, 1847.

————. *Vospominaniia ob I. N. Inzove.* Odessa, 1847.

————. *Vospominaniia o zhizni i deianiiakh grafa Kapodistrii, pravitelia Gretsii.* Moscow, 1864.

————. "Zapiski A. S. Sturdzy: O sud'be pravoslavnoi russkoi tserkvi v tsarstvovanie imperatora Aleksandra I-go." *Russkaia starina* (1876), 15, no. 1: 266–88.

Sumarokov, P. I. *Dosugi krymskogo sud'i, ili vtoroe puteshestvie v Tavridu.* 2 vols. St. Petersburg, 1803–5.

————. *Puteshestvie po vsemu Krymu i Bessarabii v 1799 g.* Moscow, 1800.

Svin'in, P. P. *Vospominaniia na flote.* 2 vols. St. Petersburg, 1818–19.

Tumanskii, V. I. *Stikhotvoreniia.* St. Petersburg, 1881.

————. *Stikhotvoreniia i pis'ma.* St. Petersburg, 1912.

Uvarov, S. S. *Essai sur les Mystères d'Éleusis.* Paris, 1816.

————. *Examen critique de la fable d'Hercule.* St. Petersburg, 1817.

————. *Mémoire sur les tragiques grecs.* St. Petersburg, 1824.

————. "Pis'mo k N. I. Gnedichu o grecheskom ekzametre." *Chtenie v besede liubitelei russkogo slova* (1813), 13: 56–68.

Vardalachos, K. *I kat epitomin grammatiki tis ellinikis glossis.* Odessa, 1834.

————. *Mathimata ek ton Asiopeidon.* Odessa, 1830.

Vel'tman, A. F. *Povesti i rasskazy.* Moscow, 1979.

————. "Vospominaniia o Bessarabii." L. Maikov, *Istoriko-literaturnye ocherki* (St. Petersburg, 1895), 110–12.

Venevitinov, D. V. "Complete Poetry." Tr. Donald Boucher and Larry Andrews. *RLT* (1974), no. 8: 117–27.

————. *Polnoe sobranie stikhotvorenii.* Leningrad, 1960.

Veshniakov, I. I. *Putevye zapiski vo sviatyi grad Ierusalem i v okrestnosti.* Moscow, 1813.

Viazemskii, P. A. *Ostaf'evskii arkhiv.* 5 vols. St. Petersburg, 1899–1913.

————. *Stikhotvoreniia.* Leningrad, 1958.

Walsh, Robert. *A Residence at Constantinople.* 2 vols. London, 1836.

Wilkinson, William. *An Account of the Principalities of Wallachia and Moldavia.* London, 1820.

Xanthos, E. *Apomnimoneumata peri tis Philikis Etaireias.* Athens, 1845.

Zhizn' Ali-pashi Ianninskogo so vremeni ego detstva do 1821 g. 3 vols. St. Petersburg, 1822–24.

Secondary Sources

Airapetov, O. R. "Vzgliady A. S. Pushkina na vostochnuiu politiku Rossii XVIII–nachala XIX v." *Vestnik Moskovskogo universiteta. Istoriia* (1988), no. 2: 64–88.

Alef, Gustave. "Diaspora Greeks in Moscow." *Byzantine Studies* (1975), 6: 26–34.

Alekseev, M. P. *Russko-angliiskie literaturnye sviazi XVIII v.–pervaia polovina XIX v.* Moscow, 1982.

Alexander, John T. *Catherine the Great: Life and Legend.* New York, 1989.

Anderson, M. S. *The Eastern Question, 1774–1923.* London, 1966.

Andrews, Larry. "D. V. Venevitinov: A Sketch of His Life and Work." *RLT* (1974), no. 8: 373–84.

Angelomatis-Tsougarakis, Helen. *The Eve of the Greek Revival: British Travellers' Perceptions of Early Nineteenth-Century Greece.* London, 1990.

Annenskaia, A. "Osvobozhdenie Gretsii." *Osvoboditel'nye voiny XIX v.* (St. Petersburg, 1900), 3–54.

Arapov, P. *Letopis' russkogo teatra.* St. Petersburg, 1861.

Argenti, Philip. *Bibliography of Chios from Classical Times to 1936.* Oxford, 1940.

Argyriou, A. *Les exégèses grecques de l'Apocalypse à l'époque turque, 1453–1821.* Thessaloniki, 1982.

Arkhipova, A. V. "O tragedii V. K. Kiukhel'bekera *Argiviane.*" *Uchenye zapiski Leningradskogo gosudarstvennogo pedagogicheskogo instituta A. I. Gertsena* (1958), no. 1: 59–90.

Arsh, G. L. *Albaniia i Epir v kontse-XVIII–nachale XIX v.* Moscow, 1963.

———. "Balkanskie proekty I. Kapodistrii nakanune grecheskoi revoliutsii 1821." *BI* (1976), 2: 48–55.

———. *Eteristskoe dvizhenie v Rossii. Osvoboditel'naia bor'ba grecheskogo naroda v nachale XIX v. i russko-grecheskie sviazi.* Moscow, 1970.

———. "Grecheskaia emigratsiia v Rossiiu v kontse XVIII–nachale XIX v." *Sovetskaia etnografiia* (1969), no. 3: 85–95.

———. "Grecheskaia revoliutsiia 1821–1829 gg." *NNI* (1971), no. 3: 18–35.

———. "Grecheskii uchenyi D. Gobdelas v Rossii." *BI* (1980), 6: 161–72.

———. "Grecheskii vopros vo vneshnei politike Rossii (1814–1820 gg.)." *Istoriia SSSR* (1978), no. 3: 139–54.

———. "Grecheskoe kommercheskoe uchilishche Odessy v 1817–1830 gg.: Iz istorii novogrecheskogo Prosveshcheniia." *BI* (1987), 10: 31–62.

———. "Gretsiia i vostochnyi krizis 70–kh godov XIX v." *BI* (1978), 4: 168–90.

———. *I. Kapodistriia i grecheskoe natsional'no-osvoboditel'noe dvizhenie, 1809–1822 gg.* Moscow, 1976.

———. "Ipsilanti v Rossii." *VI* (1985), no. 3: 88–101. In English translation in *BS* (1985), no. 1: 73–90.

———. "Materialy k istorii russko-grecheskikh sviazei nachala XIX v." *BI* (1982), 8: 54–86.

———. "Natsional'no-osvoboditel'nye vosstaniia na Balkanakh pervoi treti XIX v. (Opyt sravnitel'noi kharakteristiki)." *BI* (1982), 7: 66–77.

———. "Novogrecheskoe Prosveshchenie i Rossiia (k postanovke problemy)." *BI* (1984), 9: 304–13.

———. *Taino obshchestvo Filiki Eteriia.* Moscow, 1965.

———. "Velikaia frantsuzskaia revoliutsiia i Balkany (novye arkhivnye dannye)." *NNI* (1989), no. 5: 40–54.

Arsh, G. L., and G. M. Piatigorskii. "Nekotorye voprosy istorii Filiki Eterii v svete novykh dannykh sovetskikh arkhivov." *BI* (1989), 11: 24–42.

Arsh, G. L., et al. "Balkany v mezhdunarodnoi zhizni Evropy (XV–nachalo XX v.)." *BI* (1982), 7: 42–66. Originally appeared in *VI* (1981), no. 4: 30–42.

Arsh, G. L., et al. *Mezhdunarodnye otnosheniia na Balkanakh, 1815–1830 gg.* Moscow, 1983.

Athanassoglou-Kallmyer, Nina M. *French Images from the Greek War of Independence, 1821–1830: Art and Politics under the Restoration.* New Haven, 1989.

Augustinos, Olga. "From Hellenism to Philhellenism: The Emergence of Modern Greece in French Literature, 1770–1820." Ph.D. diss., Indiana University, 1976.

Avgitidis, K. G. *Progressivnaia grecheskaia emigratsiia v Odesse (pervaia tret' XIX v.).* Kiev, 1987.

Azadovskii, M. K. *Istoriia russkoi fol'kloristiki.* 2 vols. Moscow, 1958.

Badolle, M. *L'Abbè Jean-Jacques Barthélemy et l'hellénisme en France dans la second moitié du XVIIIme siècle.* Paris, 1926.

Bagalei, D. I. *Kolonizatsiia Novorossiiskogo kraia i pervye shagi po puti kul'tury.* Kiev, 1889.

Balandina, N. N. "Grecheskoe vosstanie 20–kh gg. XIX v. i russkaia literatura." *Vzaimosviaz' russkoi i sovetskoi literatury s literaturoi stran Azii, Afriki i Latinskoi Ameriki* (Moscow, 1980), 75–97.

Bangerter, Kathryn J. "Three Philhellenes in the Struggle for Greek Independence (Romas, Napier, Xanthos)." Ph.D. diss., University of California-Santa Barbara, 1982.

Barnard, F. M. *Herder's Social and Political Thought: From Enlightenment to Nationalism.* Oxford, 1965.

Barratt, Glynn R. *I. I. Kozlov: The Translations from Byron.* Berne, 1972.

———. *Ivan Kozlov: A Study and a Setting.* Toronto, 1972.

———. "Somov, Kozlov, and Byron's Russian Triumph." *Canadian Review of Comparative Literature* (1974), 1: 104–22.

Bartenev, P. I. *Pushkin v iuzhnoi Rossii. Materialy dlia ego biografii.* Moscow, 1862.

Bartlett, Roger. *Human Capital: The Settlement of Foreigners in Russia, 1762–1804.* Cambridge, Eng., 1979.

Batalden, Stephen K. *Catherine II's Greek Prelate: Eugenios Voulgaris in Russia, 1771–1806.* New York, 1982.

———. "John Kapodistrias and the Structure of Greek Society on the Eve of the War of Independence: An Historiographical Essay." *EEQ* (1979), 13, no. 3: 297–314.

———. "Metropolitan Gavriil (Banulesko-Bodoni) and Greek-Russian Conflict over Dedicated Monastic Estates, 1782–1812." *Church History* (1983), no. 4: 468–78.

———. "Printing the Bible in the Reign of Alexander I: Toward a Reinterpretation of the Imperial Russian Bible Society." Geoffrey Hosking, ed., *Church, Nation and State in Russia and Ukraine* (New York, 1991), 65–78.

Bayley, John. *Pushkin: A Comparative Commentary.* Cambridge, Eng., 1971.

Bazanov, V. G. *Dekabristy v Kishineve: (M. F. Orlov i V. F. Raevskii).* Kishinev, 1951.

———. *Ocherki dekabristskoi literatury: Poeziia.* Moscow, 1961.

———. *Ocherki dekabristskoi literatury: Publitsistika, proza, kritika.* Moscow, 1953.

————. *Poety-dekabristy: K. F. Ryleev, V. K. Kiukhel'beker, A. I. Odoevskii.* Moscow, 1950.

Beaton, Roderick. *Folk Poetry of Modern Greece.* Cambridge, Eng., 1980.

Belobrova, O. A. "Grecheskaia tema v russkoi knizhnoi illiustratsii pervoi poloviny XIX v." *BI* (1989), 11: 95–122.

————. "Kipr v drevnerusskoi literature." *Russkaia literatura* (1965), no. 3: 163–71.

————. "O grecheskoi teme v russkom iskusstve pervoi treti XIX v." *BI* (1980), 6: 140–61.

Berindei, D. *L'année révolutionnaire 1821 dans les pays roumains.* Bucharest, 1973.

Birnbaum, H., and S. Vryonis, eds. *The Balkans: Continuity and Change.* Paris, 1972.

Black, J. L. *Nicholas Karamzin and Russian Society in the Nineteenth Century: A Study in Political and Historical Thought.* Toronto, 1975.

Bochkarev, V. A. *Russkaia istoricheskaia dramaturgiia nachala XIX v.* Kuibyshev, 1959.

————. *Russkaia istoricheskaia dramaturgiia perioda podgotovki vosstaniia dekabristov (1816–1825).* Kuibyshev, 1968.

————. *Stikhotvornaia tragediia kontsa XVIII–nachala XIX v.* Moscow, 1964.

Bochkareva, S. I., and E. K. Viazemskaia. "Rossiia i Balkany v XVIII–nachale XX vv." *BI* (1979), 5: 41–79.

Bogdanovich, M. I. *Istoriia tsarstvovaniia Aleksandra I i Rossii v ego vremia.* 6 vols. St. Petersburg, 1869–71.

Borovoi, S. Ia. "Kniga v Odesse v pervoi polovine XIX v." *Kniga* (1967), 14: 145–59.

————. "*Puteshestvie Onegina* i Odesskaia tema v russkoi literature pervoi treti XIX v." *Pushkin na iuge* (Kishinev, 1961), 2: 265–88.

Botzaris, N. *Visions balkaniques dans la préparation de la révolution grecque, 1789–1821.* Geneva, 1962.

Bouvier-Bron, M. *Jean-Gabriel Eynard (1775–1863) et le philhellénisme genevois.* Geneva, 1963.

Braun, F. A. "Mariupol'skie greki." *Zhivaia starina* (1890), 1: 78–92.

Bristol, Evelyn. *A History of Russian Poetry.* New York, 1991.

Brodskii, N. L. *Literaturnye salony i kruzhki.* Moscow, 1930.

Brown, William E. *A History of Eighteenth-Century Russian Literature.* Ann Arbor, 1980.

————. *A History of Russian Literature of the Romantic Period.* 4 vols. Ann Arbor, 1986.

Bukharov, D. N. *Rossiia i Turtsiia ot vozniknoveniia politicheskikh mezhdu nimi otnoshenii do Londonskogo trakta marta 1871 g.* St. Petersburg, 1878.

Burgi, Richard. *A History of the Russian Hexameter.* Hamden, Conn., 1954.

Camariano, N. "L'activité de Georges Olympios dans les principautés roumaines avant la révolution de 1821." *RESE* (1964), 2: 433–46.

Camariano-Cioran, A. *Les académies princières de Bucarest et de Jassy et leurs professeurs.* Thessaloniki, 1974.

————. "La guerre russo-turque de 1768–1774 et les Grecs." *RESE* (1965), 3: 513–47.

Chaconas, Stephen G. *Adamantios Korais: A Study in Greek Nationalism.* New York, 1942.

Cherniaev, P. N. *A. S. Pushkin kak liubitel' antichnogo mira i perevodchik drevne-klassicheskikh poetov.* Kazan, 1899.

————. *Puti proniknoveniia v Rossiiu svedenii ob antichnom mire.* Voronezh, 1911.

————. *Sledy znakomstva drevne-klassicheskoi literatury v veke Ekateriny II.* Voronezh, 1906.

Christoff, Peter. *An Introduction to Nineteenth-Century Russian Slavophilism: A. S. Xomjakov.* The Hague, 1961.

———. *The Third Heart: Some Intellectual-Ideological Currents and Cross-Currents in Russia, 1800–1830.* The Hague, 1970.

Čiževskij, Dmitrij. *History of Nineteenth-Century Russian Literature.* Vol. 1, *The Romantic Period.* Nashville, 1974.

Clarke, G. W., ed. *Rediscovering Hellenism: The Hellenic Inheritance and the English Imagination.* New York, 1989.

Cline, M. A. *American Attitude toward the Greek War of Independence.* Atlanta, 1930.

Clogg, Richard. *A Short History of Modern Greece.* 2d ed. Cambridge, Eng., 1986.

Clogg, Richard, ed. *Balkan Society in the Age of Greek Independence.* Totowa, N.J., 1981.

———. *The Struggle for Greek Independence.* London, 1973.

Clucas, Lowell, ed. *The Byzantine Legacy in Eastern Europe.* New York, 1988.

Corten, Irina H. "Reality or Ideal: Images of Greeks in the Works of Aleksandr Kuprin." *MGSY* (1990), 6: 265–92.

Cracraft, James. *The Petrine Revolution in Russian Architecture.* Chicago, 1989.

Crawley, C. W. *The Question of Greek Independence: A Study of British Policy in the Near East, 1821–1833.* Cambridge, Eng., 1930.

Crook, Joseph M. *The Greek Revival: Neo-classical Attitudes in British Architecture, 1760–1870.* London, 1972.

Cross, A. G. *N. M. Karamzin: A Study of His Literary Career, 1783–1803.* Carbondale, 1971.

———. "N. M. Karamzin and Barthélemy's *Voyage du jeune Anacharsis.*" *Modern Language Review* (1966), no. 3: 467–72.

———. "N. M. Karamzin's *Messenger of Europe (Vestnik Evropy), 1802–1803.*" *Forum for Modern Language Studies* (1969), no. 1: 1–25.

Cross, S. H., and E. J. Simmons, eds. *Centennial Essays for Pushkin.* Cambridge, Mass., 1937.

Dakin, Douglas. *British and American Philhellenes during the War of Greek Independence, 1821–1833.* Thessaloniki, 1955.

———. *The Greek Struggle for Independence, 1821–1833.* London, 1973.

Daniel, Norman. *Islam, Europe, and Empire.* Edinburgh, 1966.

Dantsig, B. M. *Russkie puteshestvenniki na blizhnem vostoke.* Moscow, 1965.

Davison, Roderic. " 'Russian Skill and Turkish Imbecility': The Treaty of Kuchuk-Kainardji Reconsidered." *SR* (1976), 25, no. 3: 463–84.

de Madariaga, Isabel. *Russia in the Age of Catherine the Great.* London, 1981.

Debreczeny, Paul. *The Other Pushkin: A Study of Alexander Pushkin's Prose Fiction.* Palo Alto, 1983.

Demos, Raphael. "The Neo-Hellenic Enlightenment, 1750–1821: A General Survey." *Journal of the History of Ideas* (1958), no. 4: 523–41.

Despotopoulos, A. "La révolution grecque, Alexandre Ypsilantis et la politique de la Russie." *BS* (1966), 7, no. 2: 395–410.

Destunis, G. S. *Iz uchenoi deiatel'nosti Spiridona Iu. Destunisa. Ego perevod sravnitel'nykh zhizneopisanii Plutarkha* (St. Petersburg, 1886).

———. *O Ksanfine. Grecheskaia trapezuntskaia bylina vizantiiskoi epokhi.* St. Petersburg, 1881.

———. *O zhizni i trudakh K. Ekonomosa.* St. Petersburg, 1860.

———. *Ob Armure. Grecheskaia bylina vizantiiskoi epokhi.* St. Petersburg, 1877.

————. *Ocherk kleftskogo byta.* St. Petersburg, 1885.

————. *Ocherki vozrozhdaiushcheisia Gretsii.* St. Petersburg, 1858.

————. *Razyskaniia o grecheskikh bogatyrskikh bylinakh srednevekogo perioda. Opyt perevodnogo i ob'iasnitel'nogo sbornika.* St. Petersburg, 1883.

Diamandouros, Nikiforos P. "Political Modernization, Social Conflict, and Cultural Cleavage in the Formation of the Modern Greek State, 1821–1828." Ph.D. diss., Columbia University, 1972.

Diamandouros, Nikiforos P., et al., eds. *Hellenism and the First Greek War of Liberation (1821–1830): Continuity and Change.* Thessaloniki, 1976.

Diktiadis, *Kratkoe svedenie o zhizni i trudakh A. S. Sturdzy.* Odessa, 1854.

Dimakis, J. *La guerre de l'indépendance grecque vue par la presse française (période de 1821 à 1824).* Thessaloniki, 1968.

————. "Le mouvement philhéllenique et la presse allemande, 1821–1827." *ESEE* (1971), 16: 71–80.

————. "Le philhéllenisme en Europe pendant l'insurrection grecque et la rôle de la press." *ESEE* (1968), 13: 46–53.

————. *La presse française face à la chute de Missolonghi et à la bataille navale de Navarin.* Thessaloniki, 1976.

————. "Les réactions en Occident face à l'insurrection grecque en tant qu'expression des idées politiques du temps." *ESEE* (1974), 19: 109–14.

————. "La 'Societé de la Morale Chrétienne' de Paris et son action en faveur des Grecs lors de l'insurrection de 1821." *BS* (1966), 7, no. 1: 27–48.

Dimaras, K. Th. *La Grèce au temps des lumières.* Geneva, 1969.

————. "I scholi tou agiou orous sta 1800." *Ellinika* (1957), 15: 153–58.

————. *Istoria tis neoellinikis logotechnias.* 4th ed. Athens, 1968.

————. *Korais kai i epochi tou.* Athens, 1958.

————. *Neoellinikos diaphotismos.* Athens, 1977.

————. "Peri Phanarioton." *Archeion Thrakis* (1969), 34: 114–40.

Dimopoulos, A. *L'opinion publique française et la révolution grecque.* Nancy, 1962.

Djuvara, N. *Le pays roumain entre orient et occident. Les principautés danubiennes au début du XIX siècle.* Paris, 1989.

Dmitriev, S. S. *Chesmenskaia pobeda.* Moscow, 1945.

Dontas, Domna. *Greece and the Great Powers, 1863–1875.* Thessaloniki, 1966.

————. *The Last Phase of the Greek War of Independence in Western Greece, 1827–1829.* Thessaloniki, 1966.

Dostian, I. S. "Osnovnye etapy i osobennosti politiki Rossii na Balkanakh s poslednei treti XVIII v. do 1830 g." *Mezhdunarodnye otnosheniia na Balkanakh* (1974), no. 1: 5–38.

————. *Rossiia i balkanskii vopros.* Moscow, 1972.

————. "Rossiia i problema gosudarstvennogo ustroistva balkanskikh narodov v pervoi treti XIX v." *Études balkaniques* (1976), no. 3: 61–70.

————. *Russkaia obshchestvennaia mysl' i balkanskie narody: Ot Radishcheva do dekabristov.* Moscow, 1980.

————. "Russkii uchastnik grecheskoi revoliutsii." *VI* (1978), no. 4: 210–15.

Dostian, I. S., ed. *Formirovanie natsional'nykh nezavisimykh gosudarstv na Balkanakh.* Moscow, 1986.

Driault, É., and M. Lhéritier. *Histoire diplomatique de la Grèce.* 5 vols. Paris, 1925. Volume 1 on the War of Independence.

Driver, Sam. *Pushkin: Literature and Social Ideas.* New York, 1989.

Droulia, L. *Philhellénisme. Ouvrages inspirés par la guerre de l'indépendance grecque (1821–1833).* Athens, 1974.

Druzhinina, E. I. *Iuzhnaia Ukraina v 1800–1825 gg.* Moscow, 1970.

———. *Kiuchuk-Kainardzhiiskii mir 1774 g.* Moscow, 1955.

———. *Severnoe prichernomor'e v 1775–1800 gg.* Moscow, 1959.

Dvoichenko-Markov, D. "Russia and the First Accredited Diplomat in the Danubian Principalities." *ESEE* (1963), 8: 200–29.

Dvoichenko-Markova, E. M. *Pushkin v Moldavii i Valakhii.* Moscow, 1979.

Efros, A. *Risunki poeta.* Moscow, 1933.

Egunov, A. N. *Gomer v russkikh perevodakh XVIII–XIX v.* Moscow, 1964.

Eidel'man, N. Ia. *Pushkin i dekabristy.* Moscow, 1979.

Elagin, N. *Zhizn' grafini Anny Alekseevny Orlovoi-Chesmenskoi.* St. Petersburg, 1853.

Ergang, Robert. *Herder and the Foundations of German Nationalism.* New York, 1931.

Ernst, S. "*Zhurnal iziashchnykh iskusstv* 1823–1825 gg." *Russkii bibliofil* (1914), no. 3: 5–26.

Essays in Memory of Basil Laourdas. Thessaloniki, 1975.

Études balkaniques (1975), no. 2. Commemorative issue on the two-hundredth anniversary of the Kutchuk-Kainardji Treaty.

Evseev, I. "Bibliograficheskaia zametka. Moskovskoe izdanie grecheskoi Biblii 1821 g." *Bogoslovskii vestnik* (1902), no. 1: 207–11.

Fadeev, A. V. "Grecheskoe natsional'no-osvoboditel'noe dvizhenie i russkoe obshchestvo pervykh desiatiletii XIX v." *NNI* (1964), no. 3: 41–52.

———. *Rossiia i vostochnyi krizis 20–kh gg. XIX v.* Moscow, 1958.

Farsolas, Demetrios J. "Alexander Pushkin: His Attitude toward the Greek Revolution, 1821–1829." *BS* (1971), no. 1: 57–80.

———. "The Greek Revolution in the Principalities as seen by Alexander Pushkin." *Neo-Hellenika* (1975), 2: 98–119.

Feoktisov, E. *Bor'ba Gretsii za nezavisimost'.* St. Petersburg, 1863.

Filevskii, P. P. *Istoriia goroda Taganroga. V pamiat' dvukhstoletnego iubileia goroda, 1698–1898.* Moscow, 1898.

———. *Ocherk iz proshlogo Taganrogskoi gimnazii.* Taganrog, 1906.

Finlay, M. I., ed. *The Legacy of Greece: A New Appraisal.* New York, 1984.

Fischer, Alan W. *The Russian Annexation of the Crimea, 1772–1783.* Cambridge, Eng., 1970.

Floria, B. N. "Greki-emigranty v Russkom gosudarstve vtoroi poloviny XV–nachala XVI v. Politicheskaia i kul'turnaia deiatel'nost'." *Russko-balkanskie kul'turnye sviazi v epokhu srednevekov'ia* (Sofia, 1982), 123–43.

———. "Vykhodtsy iz balkanskikh stran na russkoi sluzhbe (konets XVI–nachalo XVII v.)." *BI* (1978), 3: 57–63.

Floria, B. N., ed. *Sviazi Rossii s narodami Balkanskogo poluostrova (pervaia polovina XVII v.).* Moscow, 1990.

Flynn, James T. "Magnitskii's Purge of Kazan University: A Case Study in the Uses of Reaction in Nineteenth-Century Russia." *Journal of Modern History* (1971), 43: 598–614.

———. *The University Reform of Tsar Alexander I, 1802–1835.* Washington, D.C., 1988.

Fonkich, B. L. *Grechesko-russkie kul'turnye sviazi v XV–XVII vv.: Grecheskie rukopisi v Rossii.* Moscow, 1977.

———. "The Greek Manuscripts of A. N. Murav'ev." *MGSY* (1988), 4: 235–54.

———. "Russia and the Christian East from the Sixteenth to the First Quarter of the Eighteenth Century." *MGSY* (1991), 7: 439–61.

Formozov, A. A. *Pushkin i drevnosti. Nabliudeniia arkheologa.* Moscow, 1979.

Frangos, George D. "The Philike Etaireia, 1814–1821: A Social and Historical Analysis." Ph.D. diss., Columbia University, 1971.

Frazee, Charles. *The Orthodox Church and Independent Greece, 1821–1852.* Cambridge, Eng., 1969.

Freeze, Gregory L. *The Parish Clergy in Nineteenth-Century Russia: Crisis, Reform, and Counter-Reform.* Princeton, 1983.

Fridman, N. V. *Poeziia Batiushkova.* Moscow, 1971.

Frolov, E. D. *Russkaia istoriografiia antichnosti (do serediny XIX v.).* Leningrad, 1967.

Gavriil (Archbishop of Kherson and Tavrida). *Istoriko-khronologicheskoe opisanie tserkvei eparkhi Khersonskoi i Tavricheskoi.* Odessa, 1848.

Geanokoplos, Deno. *Byzantine East and Latin West: Two Worlds of Christendom in the Middle Ages and Renaissance.* Oxford, 1966.

———. *Greek Scholars in Venice: Studies in the Dissemination of Greek Learning from Byzantium to Western Europe.* Cambridge, Mass., 1962.

———. *Interaction of "Sibling" Byzantine and Western Cultures in the Middle Ages and Italian Renaissance (330–1600).* New Haven, 1976.

Georgescu, Vlad. *Political Ideas and the Enlightenment in the Romanian Principalities, 1750–1831.* New York, 1971.

Georgiev, V. A., et al. *Vostochnyi vopros vo vneshnei politike Rossii konets XVIII–nachalo XX v.* Moscow, 1978.

Georgievskii, G. P. "A. N. Olenin i N. I. Gnedich; novye materialy iz Oleninskoi arkhiva." *Sbornik otdeleniia russkogo iazyka i slovesnosti imperatorskogo akademii nauk* (1914), 91, no. 1: 1–137.

Georgiou, I. P. *O Thalassomachos Lampros Katsonis.* Athens, 1971.

Glebov, G. S. "Ob 'Arion.' " *Pushkin. Vremennik Pushkinskoi komissii* (1941), 6: 296–304.

Gooding, John. "The Decembrists in the Soviet Union." *Soviet Studies* (1988), 40: 196–209.

Gorodetskii, B. M. *Platon G. Obodovskii. Biobibliograficheskii ocherk.* St. Petersburg, 1904.

Goudas, A. *Vioi paralliloi ton epi tis anagenniseos tis Ellados diaprepsanton andron.* 8 vols. Athens, 1870–76.

Greenleaf, Monika Frenkel. "Pushkin's 'Journey to Arzrum': The Poet at the Border." *SR* (1991), 50, 4: 940–53.

Griffiths, David. "Russian Court Politics and the Question of an Expansionist Foreign Policy under Catherine II, 1762–1783." Ph.D. diss., Cornell University, 1967.

Grimsted, Patricia. *The Foreign Ministers of Alexander I: Political Attitudes and the Conduct of Russian Diplomacy, 1801–1825.* Berkeley, 1969.

Gritsopoulos, T. "Oi Rossoi eis to Aigaion kata to 1770." *Athina* (1969–70), 71: 85–129.

———. *Ta Orlophika.* Athens, 1967.

Grosul, G. S. *Dunaiskie kniazhestva v politike Rossii, 1774–1806.* Kishinev, 1975.

Grosul, V. Ia. *Reformy v Dunaiskikh kniazhestvakh i Rossiia (20–30–e gg. XIX v.)*. Moscow, 1966.

Gukovskii, G. A. *Pushkin i russkie romantiki*. 2d ed. Moscow, 1965.

Gutkina, I. G. "Navarinskoe srazhenie i evropeiskaia diplomatiia." *Uchenye zapiski Leningradskogo gosudarstvennogo pedagogicheskogo instituta. Ocherk vseobshchei istorii* (Leningrad, 1969), 230–53.

——. "Voina grekov za natsional'nuiu nezavisimost' i russkaia obshchestvennost' v 1821–1825 gg." *Uchenye zapiski Leningradskogo gosudarstvennogo pedagogicheskogo instituta imeni Gertsena* (1957), 140: 30–31.

Harvey, Moses. "The Development of Russian Commerce in the Black Sea and Its Significance." Ph.D. diss., University of California-Berkeley, 1938.

Hatfield, Henry C. *Winckelmann and His German Critics, 1775–1781: A Prelude to the Classical Age*. New York, 1943.

Hatzopoulos, K. "Grecheskii korpus pod komandovaniem N. Pangalosa v 1807 g." *BI* (1989), 11: 14–23.

——. "Obrashchenie vosstavshikh grekov Peloponnesa k tsariu Aleksandru I ot 16 aprelia 1821." *BI* (1989), 11: 43–52.

——. "Was Alexander Ypsilantis struck off the list of Officers of the Russian Army?" *BS* (1987), 28, no. 2: 281–95.

Henderson, G. P. *The Revival of Greek Thought, 1620–1830*. Albany, N. Y., 1970.

Herlihy, Patricia. "The Ethnic Composition of the City of Odessa in the Nineteenth Century." *HUS* (1977), 1: 53–78.

——. "The Greek Community in Odessa, 1861–1917." *JMGS* (1989), 7: 235–52.

——. "Greek Merchants in Odessa in the Nineteenth Century." *HUS* (1979–80), 3/4: 399–420.

——. *Odessa: A History, 1794–1914*. Cambridge, Mass., 1986.

Highet, Gilbert. *The Classical Tradition: Greek and Roman Influences on Western Literature*. Oxford, 1949.

Hionides, H. *Paisios Ligaridis*. New York, 1972.

Hollingsworth, Barry. "John Venning and Prison Reform in Russia, 1819–1830." *SEER* (1971), 48: 538–57.

Honour, Hugh. *Neo-classicism*. Hammondsworth, 1968.

——. *Romanticism*. New York, 1979.

Howarth, David. *The Greek Adventure: Lord Byron and Other Eccentrics in the War of Independence*. New York, 1976.

I en Odisso Elliniki Ekklisia tis Agias Triadas, 1808–1908. Odessa, 1908.

Ia, V. A. "Demonstratsiia protiv evreev v Odesse." *Iug* (1882), 1: 200–19.

Iakubovich, D. P. "Antichnost' v tvorchestve Pushkina." *Pushkin. Vremennik Pushkinskoi komissii* (1941), 6: 92–159.

Iastrebov, V. N. "Greki v Elizavetgrade, 1754–1777." *Kievskaia starina* (1884), no. 8: 673–84.

Ibrovac, M. *Claude Fauriel et la fortune européenne des poésies populaires grecque et serbe*. Paris, 1966.

Ikonnikov, V. S. *Opyt issledovaniia o kul'turnom znachenii Vizantii v russkoi istorii*. Kiev, 1869.

Inalcik, Halil. *The Ottoman Empire: The Classical Age, 1300–1600*. London, 1973.

Iorga, N. *Byzance après Byzance*. Bucharest, 1935.

——. *La révolution française et le sud-est de l'Europe*. Bucharest, 1934.

Iovva, I. F. *Bessarabiia i grecheskoe natsional'no-osvoboditel'noe dvizhenie.* Kishinev, 1974.

———. *Dekabristy v Moldavii.* Kishinev, 1975.

———. *Iuzhnye dekabristy i grecheskoe natsional'no-osvoboditel'noe dvizhenie.* Kishinev, 1963.

———. *Peredovaia Rossiia i obshchestvenno-politicheskoe dvizhenie v Moldavii (pervaia polovina XIX v.).* Kishinev, 1986.

Irmscher, J., and M. Mineemi. *O ellinismos eis to exoterikon.* Berlin, 1968.

Irwin, David, ed. *Winckelmann: Writings on Art.* London, 1972.

Isaievych, Iaroslav. "Greek Culture in the Ukraine: 1550–1650." *MGSY* (1990), 6: 97–122.

Iurgevich, V. *Istoricheskii ocherk piatidesiatiletiia Odesskogo obshchestva istorii i drevnostei, 1839–1889.* Odessa, 1889.

Izmailov, N. V. "Poema Pushkina o geteristakh." *Pushkin. Vremennik Pushkinskoi komissii* (1937), 3: 339–48.

Izvolenskii, N. P. *Gnedich kak orator, filolog i patriot.* Poltava, 1883.

Jelavich, Barbara. *History of the Balkans: Eighteenth and Nineteenth Centuries.* New York, 1983.

———. *Russia and the Formation of the Romanian National State, 1821–1878.* New York, 1984.

———. *Russia and Greece During the Regency of King Othon, 1832–1835.* Thessaloniki, 1962.

———. *Russia's Balkan Entanglements, 1806–1914.* New York, 1991.

———. "Tsarist Russia and Greek Independence." John Koumoulides, ed., *Greek Connections: Essays in Culture and Diplomacy* (South Bend, Ind., 1987), 75–101.

Jelavich, Barbara, and Charles Jelavich, eds. *The Balkans in Transition.* Berkeley, 1963.

———. *The Establishment of the Balkan National States, 1804–1920.* Seattle, 1977.

Jelavich, Charles. *Tsarist Russia and Balkan Nationalism.* Berkeley, 1958.

Jewsbury, George. *The Russian Annexation of Bessarabia: A Study of Imperial Expansion.* New York, 1976.

K materialam dlia istorii Odesskogo Arkhangelo-Mikhailovskogo zhenskogo monastyriia i zametki dlia biografii A. S. Sturdzy. Odessa, 1902.

Kabuzan, V. M. *Zaselenie Novorossii (Ekaterinoslavskoi i Khersonskoi gubernii) v XVIII–pervoi polovine XIX v., 1719–1858 gg.* Moscow, 1976.

Kapterev, N. F. *Kharakter otnoshenii Rossii k pravoslavnomu vostoku v XVI i XVIII stoletiiakh.* 2nd ed. Sergiev Posad, 1914.

———. "Russkaia blagotvoritel'nost' monastyriam sv. gory afonskoi v XVI, XVII, i XVIII stoletiiakh." *Chtenie v obshchestve liubitelei dukhovnogo prosveshcheniia* (1882), 1: 81–116, 3: 299–324.

———. *Snosheniia Ierusalimskikh patriarkhov s russkim pravitel'stvom s poloviny XVI do serediny XIX stoletiia.* 2 vols. St. Petersburg, 1895–98.

Karathanasis, A. "Contribution à la connaissance de la vie et de l'oeuvre de deux grecs de la diaspora: A. Kondoidis et A. Skiadas." *BS* (1978), 19, no. 1: 159–87.

———. "Dukhovnaia zhizn' grekov v Rossii v XIX v." *BI* (1989), 11: 5–13.

———. "La renaissance culturelle hellénique dans les pays roumains, et surtout en Valachie, pendant la période préphanariote (1670–1714)." *BS* (1986), 27, no. 1: 29–59.

Karidis, V. "The Greek Communities in Southern Russia: Aspects of Their Formation and Commercial Enterprise, 1774–1829." M.A. thesis, University of Birmingham, 1976.

———. "A Greek Mercantile *paroikia:* Odessa, 1774–1829." Richard Clogg, ed., *Balkan Society in the Age of Greek Independence* (Totowa, N. J., 1981), 111–36.

———. "The Mariupol Greeks: Tsarist Treatment of an Ethnic Minority ca. 1778–1859." *Journal of Modern Hellenism* (1986), no 3: 57–74.

Karlinsky, Simon. *Russian Drama from Its Beginnings to the Age of Pushkin.* Berkeley, 1985.

Karnovich, E. P. *Zamechatel'nye i zagadochnye lichnosti XVIII i XIX stoletii.* 2d ed. St. Petersburg, 1893

Khalippa, I. N. *Gorod Kishinev vremen zhizni v nem A. S. Pushkina (1820–1823).* Kishinev, 1899.

Kharadzhev, D. A., ed. *Mariupol' i ego okrestnosti.* Mariupol, 1892.

Kharlampovich, K. V. *Zapadnorusskie pravoslavnye shkoly XVI i nachala XVII v.* Kazan, 1898.

Knapton, Ernest J. *The Lady of the Holy Alliance: The Life of Julie de Krüdener.* New York, 1939.

Knös, B. *Histoire de la littérature neo-grecque.* Uppsala, 1962.

———. "Voltaire et la Grèce." *L'Hellénisme contemporain* (1955), 1–28.

Kodjak, Andrej, and Lorraine Wynne. "Pushkin's 'Kirdzhali': An Informational Model." *Russian Literature* (1979), 7: 45–63.

Koehler, Ludmilla. *Anton A. Del'vig: A Classicist in the Time of Romanticism.* The Hague, 1970.

Kofos, Evangelos. *Greece and the Eastern Crisis, 1875–1878.* Thessaloniki, 1975.

———. "Rossiia i ellinism v period vostochnogo krizisa, 1875–1878 gg." *BI* (1989), 11: 144–54.

Kolbasin, E. Ia. "I. I. Martynov, perevodchik grecheskikh klassikov." *Sovremennik* (1856), no. 3: 1–46, no. 4: 75–126.

———. *Literaturnye deiateli prezhnego vremeni.* St. Petersburg, 1859.

Kolias, G. T. *Oi Ellines kata ton rossotourkikon polemon, 1787–1792.* Athens, 1940.

Koliopoulos, John S. *Brigands with a Cause: Brigandage and Irredentism in Modern Greece, 1821–1912.* Oxford, 1987.

Kolmykov, S. Ia. "Deiateli russkoi kul'tury o natsional'no-osvoboditel'noi bor'be grecheskogo naroda." *BI* (1989), 11: 242–50.

Kontogiannis, P. M. *Oi Ellines kata ton proton epi Aiketerinis B' rossotourkikon polemon, 1768–1774.* Athens, 1903.

Kordatos, G. *I koinoniki simasia tis Ellinikis Epanastaseos tou 1821.* Athens, 1924.

———. *Istoria tis neoteris Elladas.* 2 vols. Athens, 1957.

Kotzamanidou, Maria. "The Greek Monk Arsenios and His Humanist Activities in Seventeenth-Century Russia." *MGSY* (1986), 2: 73–88.

Koukkou, E. *Ioannis Kapodistrias. O Anthropos-O Diplomatis (1800–1828).* 2d ed. Athens, 1984.

———. *Ioannis-Gavriil Eunardos, o Philos ton Ellinon, 1775–1863.* Athens, 1963.

———. *Kapodistrias kai i Paideia, 1803–1822. I Philomousos Etaireia tis Viennis.* Athens, 1958.

———. "Konstantinos Vardalachos, 1775–1830." *Byzantinisch-Neugriechische Jahrbücher* (1966), 19: 123–216.

Koumoulides, John, ed. *Hellenic Perspectives: Essays in the History of Greece.* Lanham, Md., 1980.

Kovalenskaia, N. N. *Russkii klassitsizm: Zhivopis', skulptura, grafika.* Moscow, 1964.

Kremmydas, V. *Eisagogi stin istoria tis neoellinikis koinonias, 1700–1821.* Athens, 1976.

——. *Elliniki nautilia, 1766–1835.* 2 vols. Athens, 1985–86.

——. "En Grèce au début du XIX siècle: conjoncture et commerce (les conséquences sociales et idéologiques d'une activité commerciale)." *Études balkaniques* (1981), no. 1: 130–41.

——. *To emporio tis Peloponnisou sto 18 aiona.* Athens, 1972.

Kubasov, I. "Platon G. Obodovskii." *Russkaia starina* (1903), no. 11: 353–65.

Kurbatov, G. L. *Iz istorii vizantii i vizantinovedeniia.* Leningrad, 1991.

——. "Iz istorii vozniknoveniia otechestvennoi shkoly nauchnogo vizantinovedeniia (G. S. Destunis)." *Palestinskii sbornik* (1971), 23: 179–91.

Lambros, S. "To ellinikon scholeion Niznis." *Neos Ellinomneimon* (1916), 13: 136–37.

Landa, S. S. *Dukh revoliutsionnykh preobrazovanii: Iz istorii formirovaniia ideologii i politicheskikh organizatsii dekabristov, 1816–1825.* Moscow, 1975.

——. "Zarubezhnye revoliutsionnye sviazi dekabrista M. F. Orlova." *NNI* (1975), no. 6: 42–54.

Larrabee, Stephen A. *Hellas Observed: The American Experience in Greece, 1775–1863.* New York, 1957.

Laskaris, M. "Pouskin kai i elliniki epanastasis." *Nea Estia* (1937), no. 7: 485–92.

Latyshev, V. V. *K nachal'noi istorii Mariupolia.* Odessa, 1914.

Lavrovskii, N. A. *Gimnaziia vysshikh nauk kn. Bezborodko v Nezhine, 1820–1832.* Kiev, 1879.

Lebedev, N. M. *Pestel': Ideolog i rukovoditel' dekabristov.* Moscow, 1972.

LeDonne, John. *Ruling Russia: Politics and Administration in the Age of Absolutism, 1762–1796.* Princeton, 1984.

Leighton, Lauren G. *Alexander Bestuzhev-Marlinsky.* Boston, 1975.

——. *Russian Romanticism: Two Essays.* The Hague, 1975.

Lentz, N. *Uchebno-vospitatel'nye zavedeniia iz kotorykh obrazovalsia Rishel'evskii litsei (1804–1817).* Odessa, 1903.

Leon, George. "The Greek Merchant Marine (1453–1850)." S. Papadopoulos, ed., *The Greek Merchant Marine* (Athens, 1972), 13–52.

Leon'tev, P. M. "Obzor issledovanii o klassicheskikh drevnostiakh severnogo berega Chernogo moria." *Propilei* (1852), 1: 67–101.

Leppman, Wolfgang. *Winckelmann.* New York, 1970.

Levchenko, M. V. *Ocherki po istorii russko-vizantiiskikh otnoshenii.* Moscow, 1956.

Levin, Harry. *The Broken Column: A Study in Romantic Hellenism.* Cambridge, Mass., 1931.

Levkovich, Ia. L. "Tri pis'ma Pushkina o Grecheskoi revoliutsii 1821 g." *Vremennik Pushkinskoi komissii* (1987), 21: 16–23.

Ley, Francis. *Madame de Krüdener et son temps, 1764–1824.* Paris, 1961.

Lincoln, W. Bruce. *Nicholas I, Emperor and Autocrat of All the Russias.* Bloomington, 1978.

Lindenmeyr, Adele. "The Ethos of Charity in Imperial Russia." *Journal of Social History* (1990), 23, no. 4: 679–94.

———. "Public Poor Relief and Private Charity in Late Imperial Russia." Ph.D. diss., Princeton University, 1980.

Liubomudrov, S. S. *Antichnye motivy v poezii Pushkina.* 2d ed. St. Petersburg, 1901.

———. *Antichnyi mir v poezii Pushkina.* Moscow, 1899.

Logachev, K. I. "Grecheskoe prosvetitel'stvo XVIII–nachala XIX v. i problema pis'-mennogo iazyka." *Formirovanie natsional'nykh kul'tur v strankh Tsentral'noi i Iugo-Vostochnoi Evropy* (Moscow, 1977), 281–89.

Lotman, Iu. M. *Aleksandr S. Pushkin. Biografiia pisatelia.* Leningrad, 1983.

———. "Gogol's 'Tale of Captain Kopejkin': Reconstruction of the Plan and Ideo-Compositional Function." Ju. M. Lotman and B. A. Uspenskij; Ann Shukman, ed., *The Semiotics of Russian Culture* (Ann Arbor, 1984), 213–30.

Loukatos, S. "Les Arabes et les Turcs philhéllenes pendant l'insurrection pour l'indépendance de la Grèce." *BS* (1980), 21, no. 2: 233–73.

———. "Pamiatnik russkim filellinam." *BI* (1989), 11: 74–86.

———. "Le philhéllenisme balkanique pendant la lutte pour l'indépendance hellénique." *BS* (1978), 19, no. 2: 249–83.

———. *Scheseis Ellinon meta Servon kai Mauvrovounion kata tin ellinikin epanastasin, 1823–1826.* Thessaloniki, 1970.

Loukos, Ch. *I antipoliteusi kata tou kyverniti Ioannou Kapodistria 1828–1831.* Athens, 1988.

Loules, Dimitris. *The Financial and Economic Policies of President Ioannis Capodistrias, 1823–1831.* Ioannina, 1985.

———. *O rolos tis Rossias sti diamorphosi tou ellinikou kratous.* Athens, 1981.

———. "Obrazovanie grecheskogo gosudarstva i Rossiia (1821–1832)." *Sovetskoe slavianovedenie* (1980), no. 3: 37–52.

McConnell, Allen. *Tsar Alexander I: Paternalistic Reformer.* New York, 1970.

MacKenzie, David. *The Serbs and Russian Panslavism, 1875–1878.* Ithaca, 1967.

Magarshack, David. *Pushkin: A Biography.* New York, 1968.

Maikov, L. N. *Batiushkov: Ego zhizn' i sochineniia.* 2d ed. St. Petersburg, 1896.

Majeska, George P. *Russian Travelers to Constantinople in the Fourteenth and Fifteenth Centuries.* Washington, D.C., 1984.

Makarova, G. V. "M. T. Kachenovskii i stanovlenie slavianovedeniia v Rossii." V. A. Diakov, ed., *Istoriograficheskie issledovaniia po slavianovedeniiu i balkanistike* (Moscow, 1984), 63–96.

Malakis, Emile. *French Travellers in Greece, 1770–1820: An Early Phase of French Philhellenism.* Philadelphia, 1925.

Malykh, A. *Muzei Filiki Eteriia. Putevoditel'.* Odessa, 1988.

Manoussacas, M. I. "The History of the Greek Confraternity (1498–1953) and the Activity of the Greek Institute of Venice (1966–1982)." *MGSY* (1989), 5: 321–94.

Marchand, Leslie A. *Byron: A Portrait.* New York, 1970.

Markevich, A. I. *Iuzhnaia Rus' pri Ekaterine II.* Odessa, 1893.

Markevich, B. M. "N. A. Raiko: Biograficheskii ocherk." *Russkii arkhiv* (1868), no. 6: 297–308.

Markova, O. P. "O proiskhozhdenii tak nazyvaemogo grecheskogo proekta (80–e gg. XVIII v.)." *Istoriia SSSR* (1958), no. 4: 52–78.

Martin, Alexander M. "Conservative Thought and the Construction of National

Identity in the Reign of Alexander I." Unpublished paper, American Association for the Advancement of Slavic Studies Convention. Phoenix, Arizona, 1992.

Maslov, V. I. *Literaturnaia deiatel'nost' Ryleeva.* Kiev, 1912.

———. *Nachal'nyi period baironizma v Rossii.* Kiev, 1915.

Mazour, Anatole. *The First Russian Revolution 1825: Its Origins, Development, and Significance.* Berkeley, 1937.

Medlin, William, and Christos Patrinelis. *Renaissance Influences and Religious Reforms in Russia: Western and Post-Byzantine Impacts on Culture and Education.* Geneva, 1971.

Medvedeva, I. N. "N. I. Gnedich i dekabristy." M. P. Alekseev and B. S. Meilakh, eds., *Dekabristy i ikh vremia: Materialy i soobshcheniia* (Moscow, 1951), 101–54.

Meriage, Lawrence P. *Russia and the First Serbian Revolution, 1804–1813.* New York, 1987.

Mersereau, John, Jr. *Baron Delvig's "Northern Flowers" (1825–1832): Literary Almanac of the Pushkin Pleiad.* Carbondale, 1967.

———. "Orest Somov: An Introduction." *SEER* (1965), no. 101: 357–70.

———. "Yes, Virginia, There was a Russian Romantic Movement." *RLT* (1972), no. 3: 128–46.

Meyendorff, John. *Byzantium and the Rise of Russia: A Study of Byzantino-Russian Relations in the Fourteenth Century.* Cambridge, Eng., 1981.

Michalopoulos, Ph. *Ta Giannina kai i neo elliniki anagennisi, 1648–1820.* Athens, 1930.

Mirsky, D. S. *A History of Russian Literature from Its Beginnings to 1900.* 4th ed. New York, 1958.

———. *Pushkin.* New York, 1963.

Mordovchenko, N. I. *Russkaia kritika pervoi chetverti XIX v.* Moscow, 1959.

Moser, Charles, ed. *The Cambridge History of Russian Literature.* Cambridge, Eng., 1989.

Moskvicheva, G. V. *Russkii klassitsizm.* Moscow, 1978.

Narochnitskii, A. L. "Grecheskoe natsional'no-osvoboditel'noe dvizhenie i Rossiia (1801–1831 gg.)." *BI* (1982), 7: 115–31. Originally published in *VI* (1980), no. 12: 57–68.

———. *Politika Rossii na Balkanakh v 1801–1812 v svete novoi dokumental'noi publikatsii.* Moscow, 1966.

Naumov, E. P. "Zapiski o russkoi pomoshchi serbskim povstantsam v 1804–1813 gg." *BI* (1982), 8: 38–54.

Nebolsin, G. *Statisticheskie zapiski o vneshnei torgovle Rossii.* 2 vols. St. Petersburg, 1835.

Nechkina, M. V. "Dekabristy vo vsemirno-istoricheskom protsesse." *VI* (1975), no. 2: 3–18.

———. *Dvizhenie dekabristov.* 2 vols. Moscow, 1955.

Neuhauser, Rudolf. *Towards the Romantic Age: Essays on Sentimental and Preromantic Literature.* The Hague, 1974.

Nichols, Robert L., and Theofanis G. Stavrou, eds. *Russian Orthodoxy under the Old Regime.* Minneapolis, 1978.

Nicolopoulos, John. "From Agathangelos to the Megale Idea: Russia and the Emergence of Modern Greek Nationalism." *BS* (1985), 26, no. 1: 41–56.

———. "Correspondance commerciale d'Odessa: Quelques renseignements sur l'activité des Grecs en Russie méridionale en XIX siècle." *Eranistis* (1981), 17: 224–35.

Nicolson, Harold. *Byron: The Last Journey, April 1823–April 1824.* Boston, 1924.

Nikitin, S. A. *Slavianskie komitety v Rossii v 1858–1876 godakh.* Moscow, 1960.

Nikolaev, E. V. *Klassicheskaia Moskva.* Moscow, 1975.

Nikolai Mikhailovich, Grand Duke. *Imperator' Aleksandr I. Opyt istoricheskogo issledovaniia.* 2 vols. St. Petersburg, 1912.

Nikolaidou, E. "Epirskie emigranty v Rossii v XIX v. i ikh vlad v razvitie Epira." *BI* (1989), 11: 123–30.

Obolensky, Dimitri. *The Byzantine Commonwealth: Eastern Europe, 500–1453.* London, 1971.

———. *Byzantium and the Slavs: Collected Essays.* London, 1971.

———. *Six Byzantine Portraits.* New York, 1988.

Oganian, L. N. "Novye arkhivnye materialy o geroe povesti A. S. Pushkina 'Kirdzhali.' " *Pushkin na iuge* (Kishinev, 1958), 1: 37–58.

———. *Obshchestvennoe dvizhenie v Bessarabii.* 2 vols. Kishinev, 1974.

Oikonomidis, D. "O Philikos Giorgios Levendis." *Peloponnisiaka* (1957), 2: 58–90.

Oikonomos, K. *Alexandros o Stourdzas. Viographikon schediasma.* Athens, 1855.

Oksman, Iu. G. "Iz istorii agitatsionno-propagandistskoi literatury dvadtsatykh godov XIX v." *Ocherki iz istorii dvizheniia dekabristov* (Moscow, 1954), 451–515.

———. "Pushkin i dekabristy." *Osvoboditel'noe dvizhenie v Rossii* (Saratov, 1971), 2: 70–88.

Olmsted, Hugh M. "A Learned Greek Monk in Muscovite Exile: Maksim Grek and the Old Testament Prophets." *MGSY* (1987), 3: 1–74.

———. "Maxim Grek's 'Letter to Prince Shuiskii': The Greek and Russian Texts." *MGSY* (1989), 5: 267–319.

O'Meara, Patrick. *K. F. Ryleev: A Political Biography of the Decembrist Poet.* Princeton, 1984.

Orlik, O. V. *Dekabristy i evropeiskoe osvoboditel'noe dvizhenie.* Moscow, 1975.

———. *Dekabristy i vneshniaia politika Rossii.* Moscow, 1984.

———. *Peredovaia Rossiia i revoliutsionnaia Frantsiia. Pervaia polovina XIX v.* Moscow, 1973.

———. "Zapadnoevropeiskie revoliutsii 20–kh gg. XIX v." *VI* (1975), no. 11: 140–53.

Orlov, A. *Istoricheskii ocherk Odessy s 1794 po 1803 g.* Odessa, 1885.

Otetea, A. "Les grandes puissances et le mouvement hétairiste dans les principautés roumaines." *BS* (1966), 7: 379–94.

———. "L'Hétaire d'il y a cent cinquante ans." *BS* (1965), 6: 249–64.

Palaiologos, K. A. "O en ti notio Rosia ellinismos apo tou archaiotaton chronon mechri ton kath'imas." *Parnassos* (1880–81), 4–5.

Paleolog, G., and M. Sivinis. *Istoricheskii ocherk narodnoi voiny za nezavisimost' Gretsii i vosstanovleniia korolevstva pri vmeshatel'stve velikikh derzhav.* St. Petersburg, 1867.

Palmer, Alan. *Alexander I: Tsar of War and Peace.* London, 1974.

Papadopoullos, Th. *Studies and Documents Relating to the History of the Greek Church and People Under Turkish Domination.* Brussels, 1952.

Papadopoulos, S. *Giorgios Lassanis, o Kozanitis agonistis kai logios.* Thessaloniki, 1977.

———. "Otnoshenie grekov k Rossii v period Krymskoi voiny (1853–1856 gg.)." *BI* (1989), 11: 87–94.

Papoulidis, K. *Grigorios G. Maraslis (1831–1907): I Zoi kai to Ergo tou.* Thessaloniki, 1989.

———. "Gyro apo tin oikonomiki drastiriotita orismenon Ellinon sti Rosia kata ta teli tou 19ou ai." *Valkaniki vivliographia. Paratima, tom. 7, 1979.* (1982): 99–116.

———. "I Ellinoemporiki scholi tis Odissou (1817–1917)." *Archeion Pontou* (1982), 37: 142–52.

———. "I Rosia kai i Elliniki Epanastasi tou 1821–1822." *Valkanika symmeikta* (1983), no. 2: 187–203.

———. "Prosvetitel'skaia i kul'turnaia deiatel'nost' grekov Odessy v XIX i XX v." *BI* (1989), 11: 190–99.

———. "Themes of Modern Greek History in Recent Soviet Publications on Balkan Studies." *MGSY* (1987), 3: 273–81.

———. *To Rosiko archaiologiko institouto Konstantinoupoleos, 1894–1914.* Thessaloniki, 1987.

Pappas, Nicholas C. "Greeks in Russian Military Service in the Late Eighteenth and Early Nineteenth Centuries." Ph.D. diss., Stanford University, 1982. Published, with the same title, by the Institute of Balkan Studies, Thessaloniki, 1991.

Pappas, Paul C. *The United States and the Greek War of Independence, 1821–1828.* New York, 1985.

Parker, Harold T. *The Cult of Antiquity and the French Revolutionaries.* Chicago, 1937.

Penn, Virginia. "Philhellenism in England (1821–1827)." *Slavonic Review* (1935–36), 14: 363–71, 647–60.

———. "Philhellenism in Europe, 1821–1828." *Slavonic Review* (1937–38), 16: 638–53.

Petropulos, John. *Politics and Statecraft in the Kingdom of Greece, 1833–1843.* Princeton, 1968.

Petrovich, Michael. *The Emergence of Russian Panslavism, 1856–1870.* New York, 1956.

Phenerli-Panagiotopoulou, A. "To theatriko ergo 'Souliotes,' 1809–1827." *Eranistis* (1965), 3: 157–69.

Philimon, I. *Dokimion istorikon peri tis Ellinikis Epanastaseos.* 4 vols. Athens, 1859–61.

———. *Dokimion istorikon peri tis Philikis Etaireias.* Nafplion, 1834.

Piatigorskii, G. M. "Deiatel'nost' Odesskoi grecheskoi vspomogatel'noi komissii v 1821–1831 gg. (Po materialam Gosudarstvennogo arkhiva Odesskoi obl.)." *BI* (1982), 8: 135–52.

———. "Grecheskie pereselentsy v Odesse v kontse XVIII–pervoi treti XIX v." V. N. Vinogradov, ed., *Iz istorii iazyka i kul'tury stran Tsentral'noi i Iugo-Vostochnoi Evropy* (Moscow, 1985), 33–60.

———. "Vostochnyi krizis 20–kh gg. XIX v. i grecheskaia emigratsiia Odessy." *Sovetskoe slavianovedenie* (1985), no. 1: 50–64.

Pinter, Walter M. *Russian Economic Policy under Nicholas I.* Ithaca, 1967.

Pipes, Richard. *Karamzin's Memoir on Ancient and Modern Russia.* Cambridge, Mass., 1959.

Plokhinskii, M. M. "Inozemsty v staroi Malorossii." *Trudy XII arkheologicheskogo s'ezda v Khar'kove* (1905), 2: 175–409.

Podgradskaia, E. M. *Ekonomicheskie sviazi Moldavskogo kniazhestva i balkanskikh stran s Russkim gosudarstvom v XVII v.* Kishinev, 1980.

Pogodin, M. P. *Aleksei P. Ermolov: Materialy dlia ego biografii.* Moscow, 1864.

Pokrovskii, M. M. "Pushkin i antichnost'." *Pushkin. Vremennik Pushkinskoi komissii* (1939), 4/5: 27–56.

Polevoi, V. M. *Iskusstvo Gretsii.* 2 vols. 2d ed. Moscow, 1984.

Politis, A. "I prosgraphomeni ston Riga proti ekdosi tou *Agathangelou.*" *Eranistis* (1962), 7: 173–92.

———. *Ta dimotika tragoudia. Klephtika.* Athens, 1973.

Politis, Linos. *A History of Modern Greek Literature.* Oxford, 1973.

Pomar, Mark. "Russian Historical Drama of the Early Nineteenth-Century." Ph.D. diss., Columbia University, 1978.

Popruzhenko, M. G. *Ukazatel' statei, pomeshchennykh v I–XXX tt. Zapisok Odesskogo obshchestva istorii i drevnostei.* Odessa, 1914.

Printzipas, G. "K. Vardalachos, enas protoporos daskalos tou Genous." *Theologia* (1984), 55: 1144–79.

Protopsaltis, E. G. *I epanastatiki kinisis ton Ellinon kata ton deuteron epi Aiketerinis roso-tourkikon polemon, 1787–1792.* Athens, 1952.

Protopsaltis, E. G., ed. *I Philiki Etaireia. Anamnistikon teuchos epi ti 150etiridi.* Athens, 1964.

Prousis, Theophilus C. "Aleksandr S. Sturdza: A Russian Conservative Response to the Greek Revolution." *EEQ* (1992), 26, no. 3: 309–44.

———. "Dēmētrios S. Inglezēs: Greek Merchant and City Leader of Odessa." *SR* (1991), 50, no. 3: 672–79.

———. "The Destunis Collection in the Manuscript Section of the Saltykov-Shchedrin State Public Library in Leningrad." *MGSY* (1989), 5: 395–452

———. "The Greeks of Russia and the Greek Awakening, 1774–1821." *BS* (1987), 28, no. 2: 259–80.

———. "Oi neoellinikes spoudes sti Rosia (1821–1830)." Translated into Greek by Costas M. Proussis. *Nea Estia* (1987), 121, no. 1435: 546–51.

———. "Russian Philorthodox Relief during the Greek War of Independence." *MGSY* (1985), 1: 31–62.

Prozorov, P. A. *Sistematicheskii ukazatel' knig i statei po grecheskoi filologii napechatnnykh v Rossii s XVII stoletiia po 1892 na russkom i inostrannykh iazykakh.* St. Petersburg, 1898.

Pypin, A. N. *Issledovaniia i stat'i po epokhe Aleksandra I: Ocherki literatury i obshchestvennosti.* Petrograd, 1917.

———. *Obshchestvennoe dvizhenie v Rossii pri Aleksandre I.* 3d ed. St. Petersburg, 1900.

———. *Religioznye dvizheniia pri Aleksandre I.* Petrograd, 1916.

Raeff, Marc. *The Decembrist Movement.* Englewood Cliffs, N. J., 1966.

———. "In the Imperial Manner." Marc Raeff, ed. *Catherine the Great: A Profile* (New York, 1972), 197–246.

———. *Michael Speransky, Statesman of Imperial Russia.* The Hague, 1957.

Ragsdale, Hugh. "Evaluating the Traditions of Russian Aggression: Catherine II and the Greek Project." *SEER* (1988), no. 1: 91–117.

———. "Montmarin and Catherine's Greek Project." *CMRS* (1986), 27, no. 1: 27–44.

Raizis, Marios Byron, ed. *Lord Byron: Byronism-Liberalism-Philhellenism: Proceedings of the 14th International Byron Symposium, Athens, 6–8 July 1987.* Athens, 1988.

Raizis, Marios Byron, and Alexander Papas. *American Poets and the Greek Revolution, 1821–1828: A Study in Byronic Philhellenism.* Thessaloniki, 1972.
————. *The Greek Revolution and the American Muse: A Collection of Philhellenic Poetry, 1821–1828.* Thessaloniki, 1972.
Rawson, Elizabeth. *The Spartan Tradition in European Thought.* Oxford, 1969.
Reeder, Roberta. "The Greek Anthology and Its Influence on Pushkin's Poetic Style." *CASS* (1976), 10, no. 2: 205–27.
Les relations Gréco-Russes pendant la domination turque et la guerre d'indépendance grecque. Thessaloniki, 1983.
Rhinelander, Anthony L. H. *Prince Michael Vorontsov: Viceroy to the Tsar.* Montreal, 1990.
Riasanovsky, Nicholas. *Nicholas I and Official Nationality in Russia, 1825–1855.* Berkeley, 1969.
————. *A Parting of Ways: Government and the Educated Public in Russia, 1801–1855.* Oxford, 1976.
Rogger, Hans. *National Consciousness in Eighteenth-Century Russia.* Cambridge, Mass., 1960.
Ruchkina, N. L. "Geneticheskie sviazi akritskogo eposa i kleftskikh pesen." *Slavianskii i balkanskii fol'klor* (Moscow, 1981), 189–223.
————. "Izuchenie novogrecheskogo pesennogo fol'klora v nashei strane." *BI* (1979), 5: 260–68.
Runciman, Steven. *The Great Church in Captivity.* Cambridge, Eng., 1969.
Ruud, Charles. *Fighting Words: Imperial Censorship and the Russian Press, 1804–1906.* Toronto, 1982.
S. S. "Grigorii V, patriarkh Konstantinopol'skii postradavshii ot turok v 1821." *Moskvitianin* (1844), no. 10: 441–48.
Safonov, S. "Ostatki grecheskikh legionov v Rossii, ili nyneshnee naselenie Balaklavy." *ZOOID* (1844), 1: 205–38.
Said, Edward. *Orientalism.* New York, 1978.
St. Clair, William. *That Greece Might Still Be Free: The Philhellenes in the War of Independence.* London, 1972.
Sakellariou, M. *I Peloponnisos kata tin deuteran tourkokratian, 1715–1821.* Athens, 1939.
Sakellariou, S. G. *Philiki Etaireia.* Odessa, 1909.
Sandler, Stephanie. *Alexander Pushkin and the Writing of Exile.* Palo Alto, 1989.
Sathas, K. *Neoelliniki philologia.* Athens, 1868.
————. *Tourkokratoumeni Ellas.* Athens, 1870.
Saul, Norman. *Russia and the Mediterranean, 1797–1807.* Chicago, 1970.
Saunders, David. *The Ukrainian Impact on Russian Culture, 1750–1850.* Edmonton, 1985.
Sawatsky, Walter W. "Prince Alexander N. Golitsyn (1773–1844): Tsarist Minister of Piety." Ph.D. diss., University of Minnesota, 1976.
Schmidt, Albert. *The Architecture and Planning of Classical Moscow: A Cultural History.* Philadelphia, 1989.
————. "The Restoration of Moscow after 1812." *SR* (1981), 40, no. 1: 37–48.
Schroeder, Paul W. *Metternich's Diplomacy at Its Zenith, 1820–1823.* Austin, Tex., 1962.

Segel, Harold B. "Classicism and Classical Antiquity in Eighteenth- and Early Nineteenth-Century Russian Literature." John G. Garrard, ed., *The Eighteenth Century in Russia* (Oxford, 1973), 48–71.

———. *The Literature of Eighteenth-Century Russia: A History and Anthology.* 2 vols. New York, 1967.

Selinov, V. I. "Pushkin i grecheskoe vosstanie." *Pushkin. Stat'i i materialy* (Odessa, 1926), no. 2: 5–31.

Semennikov, V. P. *Sobranie staraiushcheesia o perevode inostrannykh knig uchrezhdennoe Ekaterinoi II, 1768–1783 gg.* St. Petersburg, 1913.

Semenova, L. E. "Konstantin Ipsilanti i Pervoe serbskoe vosstanie (1804–avgust 1807 g.)." *BI* (1984): 50–63.

Semevskii, V. I. *Politicheskie i obshchestvennye idei dekabristov.* St. Petersburg, 1909.

Senkevich, I. G. *Rossiia i kritskoe vosstanie 1866–1869 gg.* Moscow, 1970.

Serman, I. Z. *Konstantin Batyushkov.* New York, 1974.

———. *Russkii klassitsizm: Poeziia-Drama-Satira.* Leningrad, 1973.

Seton-Watson, R. W. *A History of the Rumanians.* Cambridge, Eng., 1934.

Ševčenko, Ihor. "Byzantine Cultural Influences." Cyril Black, ed., *Rewriting Russian History: Soviet Interpretations of Russia's Past* (New York, 1956), 141–91.

———. *Byzantine Roots of Ukrainian Christianity.* Cambridge, Mass., 1984.

Shaw, J. Thomas. "Pushkin's 'The Shot.' " *Indiana Slavic Studies* (1963), 3: 113–29.

Shaw, Stanford J. *Between Old and New: The Ottoman Empire under Selim III (1789–1807).* Cambridge, Mass., 1971.

Shebunin, A. N. "Dekabristy i voprosy vneshnei politiki." *Russkoe proshloe* (Petrograd, 1923), no. 4.

———. *Rossiia na blizhnem vostoke.* Leningrad, 1926.

Sheremet, V. I. "Russko-turetskaia torgovlia i balkanskie zemli (konets XVIII–pervaia polovina XIX v.)" *BI* (1984), 9: 74–86.

———. *Turtsiia i Adrianopol'skii mir.* Moscow, 1975.

Shil'der, N. K. *Imperator Aleksandr I: Ego zhizn' i tsarstvovanie.* 4 vols. St. Petersburg, 1904.

Shparo, O. B. *Osvobozhdenie Gretsii i Rossiia, 1821–1829.* Moscow, 1965.

Sidorchenko, L. V. *Bairon i natsional'no-osvoboditel'noe dvizhenie na Balkanakh.* Leningrad, 1977.

Simmons, E. J. *English Literature and Culture in Russia (1553–1840).* Cambridge, Mass., 1935.

Simopoulos, K. *Xenoi taxidiotes stin Ellada.* 3 vols. Athens, 1972–73.

Sinitsa, V. I. "Vosstanie v Moree 1770 i Rossiia." *Voprosy novoi i noveishei istorii* (Minsk, 1974), 12–21.

Sirotkin, V. G. "Bor'ba v lagere konservativnogo russkogo dvorianstva po voprosam vneshnei politiki posle voiny 1812 i otstavka I. Kapodistrii v 1822 g." A. L. Narochnitskii, ed., *Problemy mezhdunarodnykh otnoshenii i osvoboditel'nykh dvizhenii* (Moscow, 1975), 3–47.

Skal'kovskii, A. A. *Khronologicheskoe obozrenie istorii Novorossiskogo kraia, 1730–1823.* 2 vols. Odessa, 1825–38.

———. *Opyt statisticheskogo opisaniia Novorossiiskogo kraia.* 2 vols. Odessa, 1850–53.

———. *Pervoe tridtsatiletie istorii goroda Odessy, 1793–1823.* Odessa, 1838.

Skinner, Frederick. "City Planning in Russia: The Development of Odessa, 1795–1892." Ph.D. diss., Princeton University, 1973.

Skiotis, Dennis N. "Greek Mountain Warriors and the Greek Revolution." V. J. Perry and M. E. Yapp, eds., *War, Technology, and Society in the Middle East* (London, 1975), 308–29.

Slonim, Marc. *The Epic of Russian Literature from Its Origins through Tolstoy.* New York, 1964.

Smirnov, S. K. *Ekonomos i sochinenie ego o srodstve slaviano-russkogo iazyka s ellinskim.* Moscow, 1873.

Smirnova, E. *Briullov-puteshestvennik.* Moscow, 1969.

Sokolov, I. I. "Mariupol'skie greki." *Trudy instituta slavianovedeniia akademii nauk SSSR* (1932), 1: 287–317.

Sozonovich, I. P. *Izucheniia novogrecheskoi narodnoi poezii.* Warsaw, 1880.

Spathis, D. "O 'Philoktitis' tou Sophokli diaskeuasmenos apo ton Nikolao Pikkolo." *Eranistis* (1979), 15: 265–320.

Spencer, Terence. *Fair Greece Sad Relic: Literary Philhellenism from Shakespeare to Byron.* London, 1954.

Spender, Harold. *Byron and Greece.* London, 1924.

Spiridonakis, B. G. "L'établissement d'un consulat Russe dans les principalités danubiennes, 1780–1782." *BS* (1963), 4, no. 2: 289–314.

———. *On the Historical Geography of the Greek World in the Balkans During the Turkokratia.* Thessaloniki, 1977.

Stahl, Sandra G. "Byron's Influence on the Lives and Works of Representative Russian Poets of the Romantic Period, 1815–1825." Ph.D. diss., Northwestern University, 1978.

Stanislavskaia, A. M. *Politicheskaia deiatel'nost' F. F. Ushakova v Gretsii, 1798–1800 gg.* Moscow, 1983.

———. *Rossiia i Gretsiia. Politika Rossii v Ionicheskoi respublike, 1798–1807 gg.* Moscow, 1976.

———. *Russko-angliiskie otnosheniia i problemy Sredizemnomor'ia (1798–1807).* Moscow, 1962.

Stavrianos, L. S. "Antecedents to the Balkan Revolutions of the Nineteenth Century." *Journal of Modern History* (1957), 29: 335–48.

———. *The Balkans Since 1453.* New York, 1958.

Stavrou, Theofanis G. "Russian Policy in Constantinople and Mount Athos in the Nineteenth Century." Lowell Clucas, ed., *The Byzantine Legacy in Eastern Europe* (New York, 1988), 225–49.

Stavrou, Theofanis G., ed. *Art and Culture in Nineteenth-Century Russia.* Bloomington, 1983.

Stavrou, Theofanis G., and Peter R. Weisensel. *Russian Travelers to the Christian East from the Twelfth to the Twentieth Century.* Columbus, Oh., 1986.

Stepanov, Nikolay. *Ivan Krylov.* New York, 1973.

Stoianovich, Traian. "The Conquering Balkan Orthodox Merchant." *Journal of Economic History* (1960), 20, no. 2: 234–313.

Stoianovskii, N. *Ocherk zhizni A. N. Olenina.* St. Petersburg, 1881.

Stoneman, Richard. *Land of Lost Gods: The Search for Classical Greece.* Norman, Ok., 1987.

Storozhevskii, N. K. *Nezhinskie greki.* Kiev, 1863.

Strakhov, Ol'ga B. "Attitudes to Greek Language and Culture in Seventeenth-Century Muscovy." *MGSY* (1990), 6: 123–56.

Strasburger, J. "Le philhellénisme en Pologne aux années de l'insurrection grecque 1821–1828." *BS* (1971), 12, no. 1: 103–16.

Strukova, K. L. "Problema natsional'no-osvoboditel'nogo dvizheniia balkanskikh narodov." *BI* (1979), 5: 21–41.

Stuart, Mary. *Aristocrat-Librarian in Service to the Tsar. Aleksei Nikolaevich Olenin and the Imperial Public Library.* New York, 1986.

Sugar, Peter F. *Southeastern Europe under Ottoman Rule, 1354–1804.* Seattle, 1977.

Sumner, B. H. *Russia and the Balkans, 1870–1880.* Oxford, 1937.

Sussex, Roland, ed. *Culture and Nationalism in Nineteenth-Century Europe.* Columbus, Oh., 1985

Svirin, N. "Pushkin i grecheskoe vosstanie." *Znamia* (1935), no. 11: 204–40.

Svolopoulos, K. "Pozitsiia Rossii v otnoshenii grecheskoi revoliutsii v period Laibakhskogo kongressa." *BI* (1989), 11: 53–73.

Svoronos, N. *Le commerce de Salonique au XVIII siècle.* Paris, 1956.

———. *Episkopisi tis neoellinikis istorias.* 2d ed. Athens, 1976.

Symposium. L'époque phanariote. À la mémoire de Cléobule Tsourkas. Thessaloniki, 1974.

Syroechkovskii, B. E. "Balkanskaia problema v politicheskikh planakh dekabristov." B. E. Syroechkouskii, *Iz istorii dvizheniia dekabristov* (Moscow, 1969), 216–303.

Tampaki, A. "To elliniko theatro sti Odisso (1814–1818)." *Eranistis* (1980), 16: 229–38.

Tarle, E. V. *Chesmenskii boi i pervaia ekspeditsiia v Arkhipelag, 1769–1774.* Moscow, 1945.

Terras, Victor, ed. *Handbook of Russian Literature.* New Haven, 1985.

———. *A History of Russian Literature.* New Haven, 1991.

Thaden, Edward. *Conservative Nationalism in Nineteenth-Century Russia.* Seattle, 1964.

Tikhomirov, M. N. "Greki iz Morei v srednevekovoi Rossii." *Srednie veka* (1964), 25: 166–75.

Tikhonov, P. N. *I. Gnedich. Neskol'ko dannykh dlia ego biografii po neizdannym istochnikam.* St. Petersburg, 1884.

Timofeenko, V. I. *Formirovanie gradostroitel'noi kul'tury iuga Ukrainy.* Kiev, 1986.

———. *Goroda severnogo prichernomor'ia vo vtoroi polovine XVIII v.* Kiev, 1984.

Timofeev, L. V. *V krugu druzei i muz. Dom A. N. Olenina.* Leningrad, 1983.

Todd, William Mills. *The Familiar Letter as a Literary Genre in the Age of Pushkin.* Princeton, 1976.

Todorov, N. "L'insurrection grecque de 1821–1829 et les Bulgares." *Études balkaniques* (1971), no. 1: 5–26.

———. "La participation des Bulgares à l'insurrection hétairiste dans les principautés danubiennes." *Études balkaniques* (1964), no. 1: 69–96.

Todorova, Maria. "The Greek Volunteers in the Crimean War." *BS* (1984), 25: 539–63.

Trubetskoi, B. A. *Pushkin v Moldavii.* 5th ed. Kishinev, 1983.

Trueblood, Paul G., ed. *Byron's Political and Cultural Influence in Nineteenth-Century Europe: A Symposium.* Atlantic Highlands, N.J., 1981.

Tsiavlovskaia, T. G. *Risunki Pushkina.* 4th ed. Moscow, 1986.

Tsigakou, Fani-Maria. *The Rediscovery of Greece: Travelers and Painters of the Romantic Era.* London, 1981.

Tsirplanis, Z. N. "Mémoires et rapports de Jean Capodistrias (1809–1822) (problèmes et recherche)." *BS* (1978), 19: 3–32.

Tymchishin, V. *Pushkin v Moldavii.* Kishinev, 1979.

Tynianov, Iu. N. *Arkhaisty i novatory.* Leningrad, 1929.

Udal'tsova, Z. V. "Kul'turnye sviazi Drevnei Rusi i Vizantii." *VI* (1987), no. 4: 56–69.

———. *Osnovnye problemy vizantinovedeniia v sovetskoi istoricheskoi nauke.* Moscow, 1955.

———. *Sovetskoe vizantinovedenie za 50 let.* Moscow, 1969.

Vakalopoulos, A. *Istoria tou neou ellinismou.* 6 vols. Thessaloniki, 1973–82.

Vakalopoulos, K. *Scheseis Ellinon kai Elveton Philellinon kata tin elliniki epanastasi tou 1821. Symvoli stin istoria tou elvetikou philellinismou.* Thessaloniki, 1975.

Valanos, D. S. "Konstantinos Oikonomos o ex Oikonomon." *Ekklisia* (1957), no. 24: 491–98.

Vallianatos, E. G. "Adamantios Korais and the Modernization of Greek Education, 1782–1821." Ph. D. diss., University of Wisconsin-Madison, 1972.

———. "Constantine Koumas and the Philological Gymnasium of Smyrna, 1810–1819." *EEQ* (1973), 6, no. 4: 419–43.

Vasilenko, O. V. "O pomoshchi Rossii v sozdanii nezavisimogo grecheskogo gosudarstva (1829–1831 gg.)." *NNI* (1959), no. 3: 148–57.

Veselovskii, A. N. *Bairon. Biograficheskii ocherk.* Moscow, 1914.

Viazemskaia, E. K., and S. I. Danchenko. "Russko-grecheskie otnosheniia (posledniaia chetvert' XVIII–nachalo XX v.)" *BI* (1989), 11: 226–41.

Vickery, Walter. *Alexander Pushkin.* New York, 1970.

———. "Pushkin: Russia and Europe." *Review of National Literatures* (1972), 3, no. 1: 15–39.

Vinogradov, V. N. "Dzhordzh Kanning, Rossiia i osvobozhdenie Gretsii." *NNI* (1981), no. 6: 112–31. Also published in English in *BS* (1981), 22: 3–32.

Vinogradov, V. N., ed. *Tsentral'naia i Iugo-Vostochnaia Evropa v novoe vremia.* Moscow, 1974.

Vinogradov, V. N., and L. E. Semenova. "Nekotorye voprosy otnoshenii mezhdu Rossiei i Dunaiskimi kniazhestvami v XVIII–nachale XIX v svete materialov sovetskikh arkhivov." *BI* (1982), 8: 6–37.

Volk, S. S. *Istoricheskie vzgliady dekabristov.* Moscow, 1958.

Voulodimos, Ch. *Proti pentikontaetiris tis en Odisso Ellinoemporikis scholis (1817–1867).* Odessa, 1871.

Vovolinis, K. A. *I ekklisia eis ton agona tis eleutherias.* Athens, 1952.

Vranoussis, Leandros. "Post-Byzantine Hellenism and Europe: Manuscripts, Books, and Printing Presses." *MGSY* (1986), 2: 1–71.

Walker, Franklin A. "Christianity, the Service Ethic and Decembrist Thought." Geoffrey Hosking, ed., *Church, Nation and State in Russia and Ukraine* (New York, 1991), 79–95.

———. "Reaction and Radicalism in the Russia of Tsar Alexander I: The Case of the Brothers Glinka." *Canadian Slavonic Papers* (1979), 21, no. 4: 489–502.

———. "Ryleev: A Self-Sacrifice for Revolution." *SEER* (1969), 47, no. 109: 436–46.

Ware, Timothy. *Eustratios Argenti: A Study of the Greek Church under Turkish Rule.* Oxford, 1964.

Webb, E. T. *English Romantic Hellenism, 1700–1824.* Manchester, 1982.

Webster, Charles. *The Foreign Policy of Castlereagh, 1815–1822.* London, 1947.

Whittaker, Cynthia H. *The Origins of Modern Russian Education: An Intellectual Biography of Count Sergei Uvarov, 1786–1855.* Dekalb, 1984.

Wieczynski, Joseph L. "Apostle of Obscurantism: the Archimandrite Photius of Russia (1792–1838)." *Journal of Ecclesiastical History* (1971), 22, no. 4: 319–31.

Woodhouse, C. M. *The Battle of Navarino.* London, 1965.

——. *Capodistria: Founder of Greek Independence.* London, 1973.

——. *The Greek War of Independence: Its Historical Setting.* London, 1952.

——. *The Philhellenes.* London, 1969.

Xiradaki, K. *Philellinides. Istoriki meleti.* 2d ed. Athens, 1976.

Zabelin, Iu. E. "Russkie posol'stva v Turtsiiu v XVII st. Istoricheskii ocherk." *Russkaia starina* (1877), no. 9: 1–33.

Zablotskii-Desiatovskii, A. P. *Graf P. D. Kiselev i ego vremia.* 4 vols. St. Petersburg, 1881–82.

Zacek, Judith Cohen. "A Case Study in Russian Philanthropy: The Prison Reform Movement in the Reign of Alexander I." *CSS* (1967), 1, no. 2: 196–211.

——. "The Imperial Philanthropic Society in the Reign of Alexander I." *CASS* (1975), 9, no. 4: 427–36.

——. "The Russian Bible Society." Ph.D. diss., Columbia University, 1964.

——. "The Russian Bible Society and the Russian Orthodox Church." *Church History* (1966), 36, no. 4: 411–37.

Zagorovskii, E. A. *Ekonomicheskaia politika Potemkina v Novorossii, 1774–1791.* Odessa, 1926.

——. *Organizatsiia upravleniia Novorossii pri Potemkine.* Odessa, 1913.

——. *Voennaia kolonizatsiia Novorossii pri Potemkine.* Odessa, 1913.

Zakythinos, D. A. *The Making of Modern Greece.* Oxford, 1976.

Zaldkin, A. I. I. *Martynov, 1771–1833. Deiatel' prosveshcheniia v nachale XIX v.* Tiflis, 1902.

Zamotin, I. I. *Romantizm dvadtsatykh gg. XIX v.* 3d ed. Petrograd, 1919.

Zenkovsky, Serge A., ed. *Medieval Russia's Epics, Chronicles, and Tales.* 2d ed. New York, 1974.

Zhebelev, S. A. "F. I. Uspenskii i russkii arkheologicheskii institut v Konstantinople." *Pamiati akademika Fedora Ivanovicha Uspenskogo, 1845–1928* (Leningrad, 1929), 53–66.

Zhigarev, S. *Russkaia politika v vostochnom voprose.* Moscow, 1896.

Zhirmunskii, V. V. *Bairon i Pushkin.* Leningrad, 1924.

Zhmakin, S. V. "Pogrebenie Konstantinopol'skogo patriarkha Grigoriia V v Odesse." *Russkaia starina* (1894), no. 12: 198–213.

Zimmerman, Carl R. "Philhellenism in the American Press During the Greek Revolution." *Neo-Hellenika* (1975), 2: 181–211.

Zoidis, G. *Patro-paradoti philia. Ellada-Rossia (oikonomikoi, politikoi, politistikoi desmoi).* Athens, 1958.

Zolotov, V. A. *Vneshniaia torgovlia iuzhnoi Rossii v pervoi polovine XIX v.* Rostov-on-the-Don, 1963.

Index